Pieter Bruegel

(c. 1525-1569)

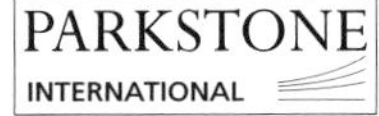

Authors: Émile Michel and Victoria Charles
Translation: Chris Murray

Page 4:
Joannes and **Lucas van Doetecum** (after **Pieter Bruegel the Elder**)
Magdalena Poenitens
c. 1553-1556
Etching for the series *Large Landscapes*, 32.3 x 43 cm
British Museum, London

Layout:
Baseline Co. Ltd
61A-63A Vo Van Tan Street
4th Floor
District 3, Ho Chi Minh City
Vietnam

ISBN: 978-1-906981-42-6

Printed in Italy

A second Hieronymus Bosch,
Who retraced the vivid images of his master,
Whose masterful brush rendered his style with fidelity,
And in doing so, perhaps surpassed him?
You elevate yourself, Pieter, when through your fecund art,
In the style of your old master you draw pleasant things
Made to amuse; with him, you merit
The praise of the greatest artists.

- Dominicus Lampsonius

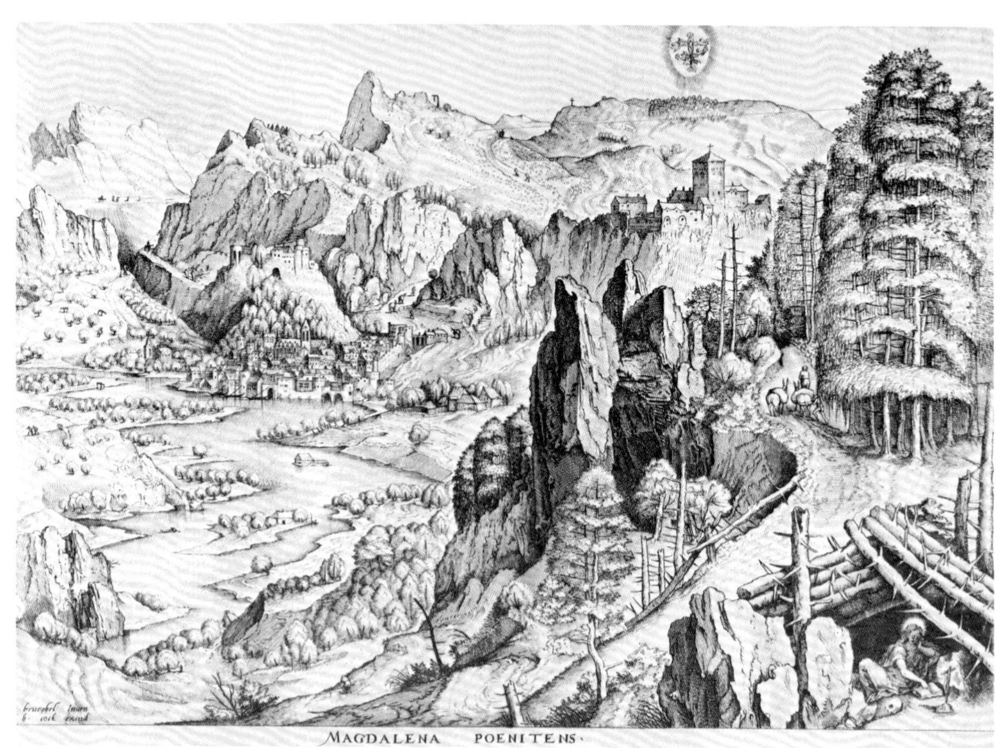
brueghel inuen
h. cock excud
MAGDALENA POENITENS.

Biography

1525	The exact year of Pieter Bruegel the Elder's birth is unknown; it is likely to have been between 1525 and 1530. The whereabouts of his birthplace are just as uncertain, although it was probably Breda, in the province of North Brabant.
1545-1550	Until 1550, Bruegel is thought to have been an apprentice under Pieter Coecke van Aelst in Antwerp.
1550	Bruegel assists with a triptych (whereabouts unknown) commissioned by the Mechlin Glovemakers Guild.
1551	"Peeter Brueghels" is registered as a master with the Antwerp artists' guild, the Guild of Saint Luke.
1552	He travels to Italy, passing through Lyon on the way and returning across the Swiss Alps. In Rome, he is believed to have worked with the miniaturist Ginlio Clovio.
1556	He works at the workshop of Hieronymus Cock in Antwerp, making designs for engravings. *Big Fish Eat Little Fish* and *The Ass in the School* are two of his prints copied as engravings in this year.
1557	Series of seven engravings entitled *The Seven Deadly Sins.*
1559	He follows this with a series of seven engravings with the Virtues. Bruegel paints *The Fight between Carnival and Lent.*
1562	He paints, amongst other works, *The Fall of Rebel Angels* and *The Suicide of Saul.* He probably travels to Amsterdam before settling in Brussels.
1563	He marries Mayken Coecke, the daughter of his old master Pieter Coecke.
1564	Birth of his first son, Pieter Brueghel the Younger, (later known as "Hell" Brueghel).
1565	Completion of a series of paintings depicting the months or seasons.
1568	Birth of his second son, Jan Brueghel the Elder (later known as "Velvet" Brueghel). In this year, Bruegel paints *The Magpie on the Gibbet, The Beggars,* and *The Tempest.*
1569	He probably died on 5 September; he is buried in the Church of Notre-Dame-de-la-Chapelle in Brussels.

BRVEGEL

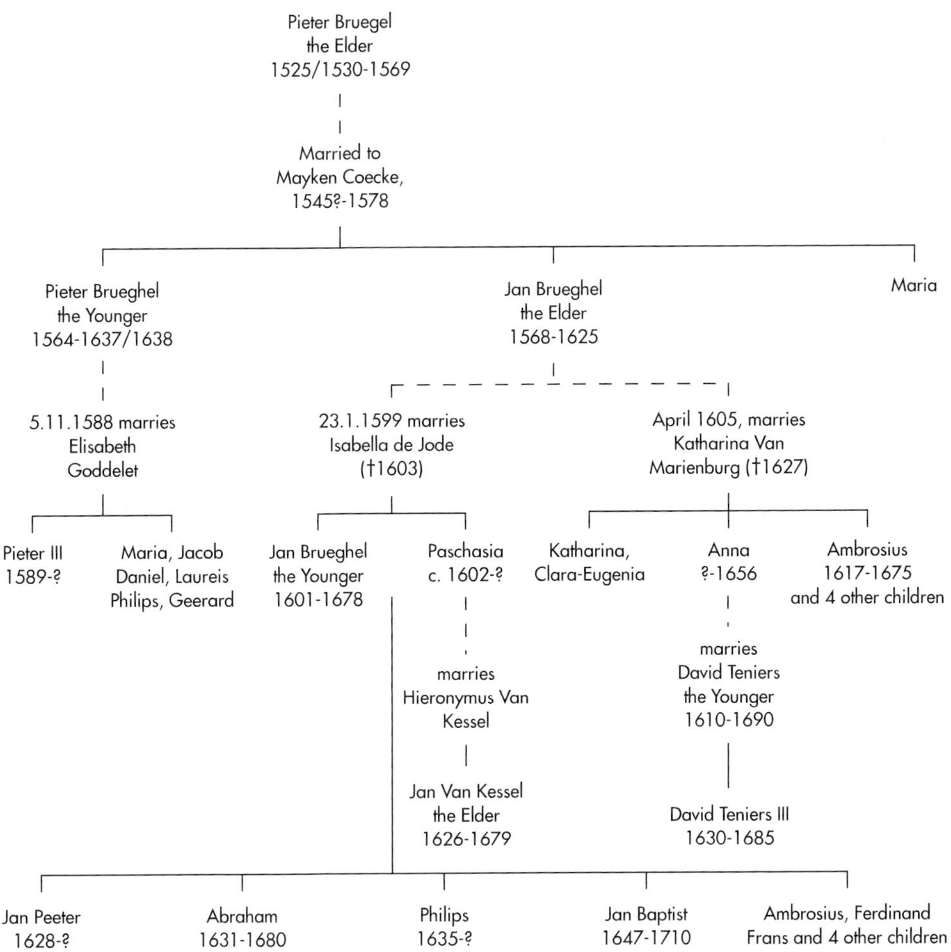
Pieter Bruegel
the Elder
1525/1530-1569
Married to
Mayken Coecke,
1545?-1578
Pieter Brueghel
the Younger
1564-1637/1638
Jan Brueghel
the Elder
1568-1625
Maria
5.11.1588 marries
Elisabeth
Goddelet
23.1.1599 marries
Isabella de Jode
(†1603)
April 1605, marries
Katharina Van
Marienburg (†1627)
Pieter III
1589-?
Maria, Jacob
Daniel, Laureis
Philips, Geerard
Jan Brueghel
the Younger
1601-1678
Paschasia
c. 1602-?
Katharina,
Clara-Eugenia
Anna
?-1656
Ambrosius
1617-1675
and 4 other children
marries
Hieronymus Van
Kessel
marries
David Teniers
the Younger
1610-1690
Jan Van Kessel
the Elder
1626-1679
David Teniers III
1630-1685
Jan Peeter
1628-?
Abraham
1631-1680
Philips
1635-?
Jan Baptist
1647-1710
Ambrosius, Ferdinand
Frans and 4 other children

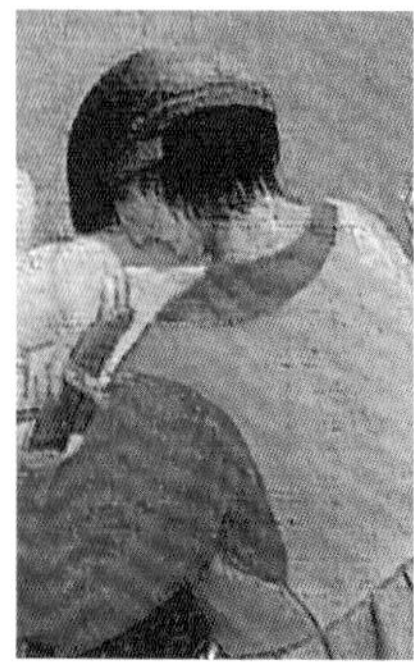

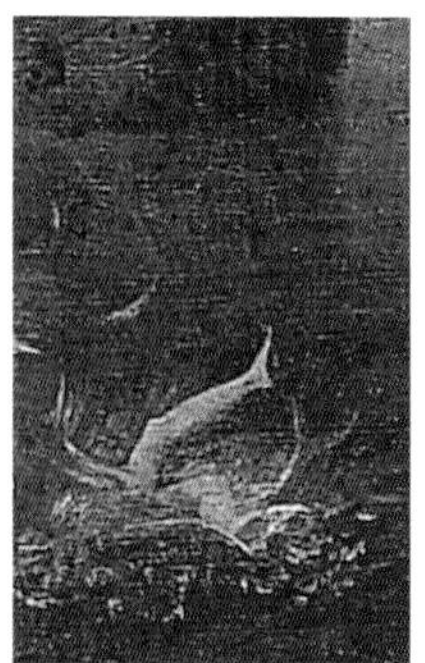

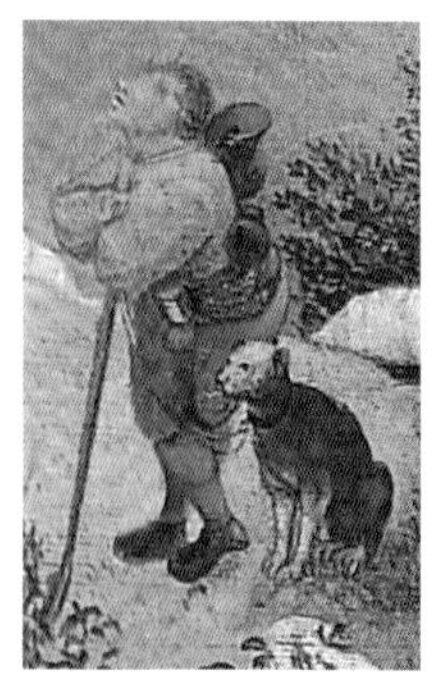

Introduction

There is hardly a master whose works and life are more interesting than those of Pieter Bruegel. The first in a long line of painters, he was the founder of one of many Flemish families in which artistic talent seems to have been hereditary, for instance, the Van Eycks, the Matsys, the Van Orleys,

The Fall of Icarus

c. 1555-1560
Oil on canvas, 73.5 x 112 cm
Königliche Museen der Schönen Künste, Brussels

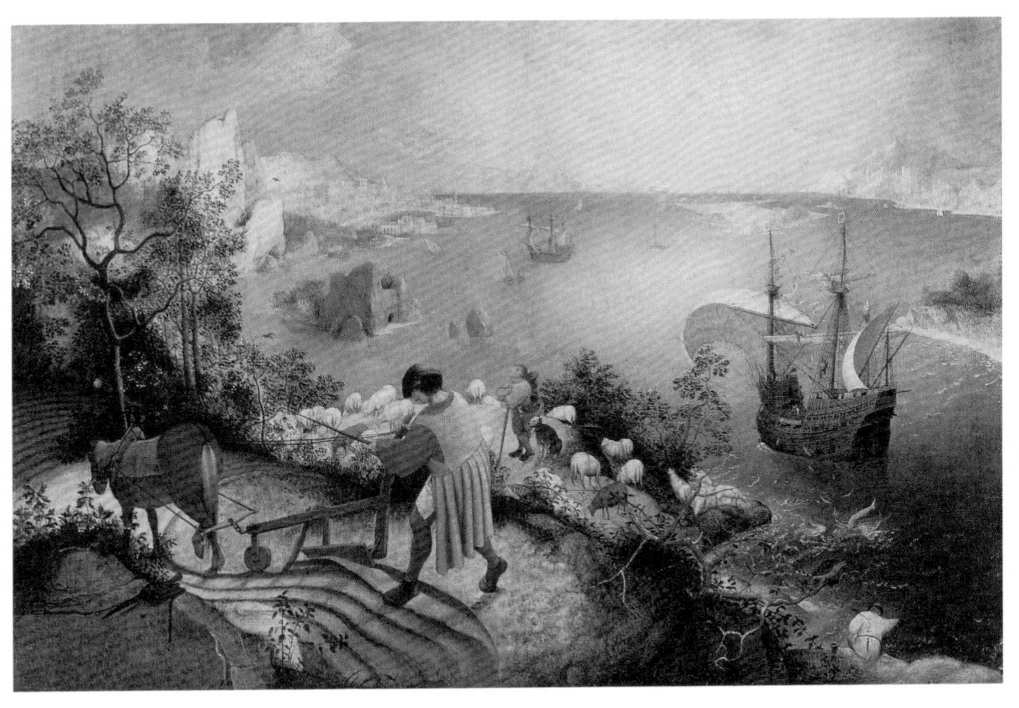

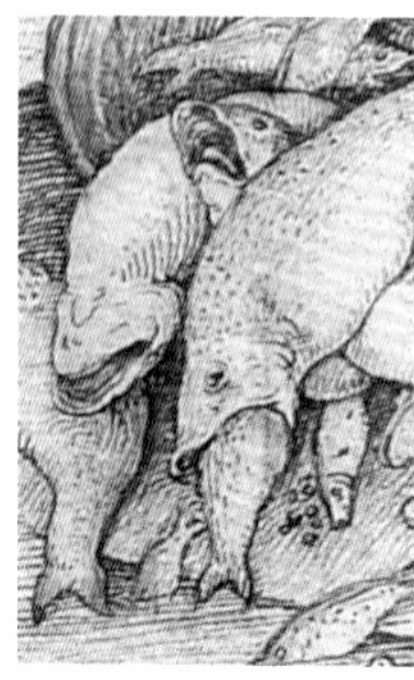

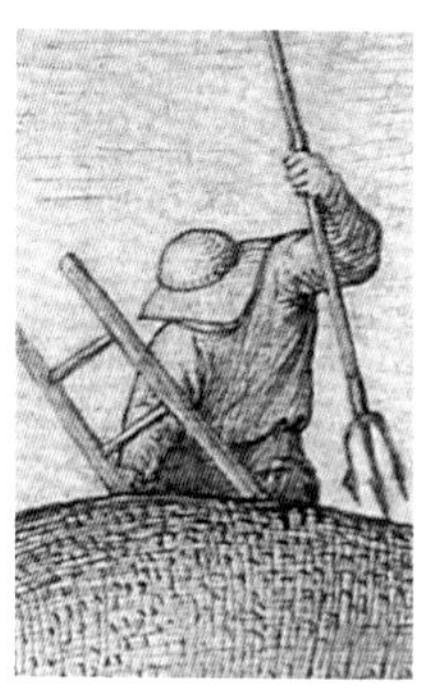

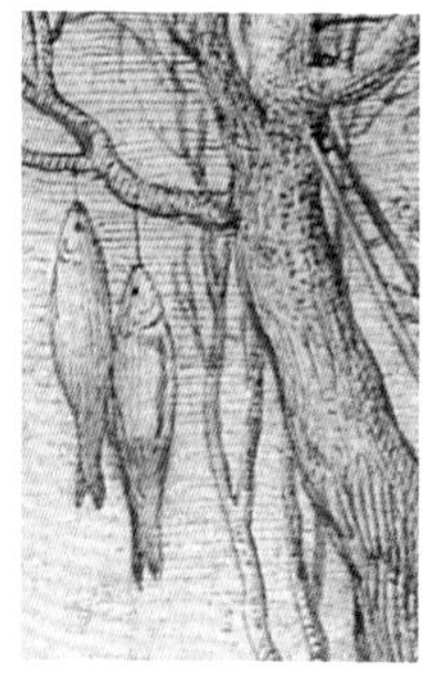

the Pourbus, the Van Cleves, the Coxies, the Keys, the De Vos, and, later, the Teniers.

Having his roots in a line of old Flemish stock, this singular and original artist and thinker drew all of his energy from his native soil and produced a vigorous family tree that sprouted in many directions. One example was his equally renowned son Jan, who is well

Big Fish Eat Little Fish

1556

Pen and ink drawing in grey and black ink, 21.6 x 30.7 cm

Graphische Sammlung, Albertina, Vienna

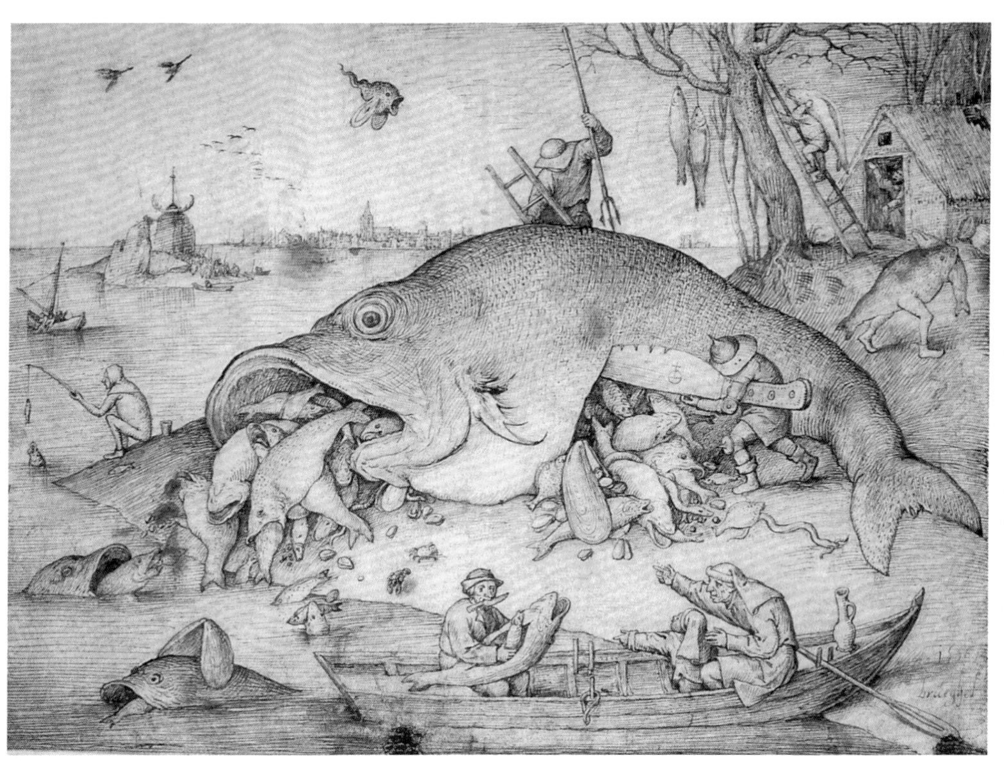

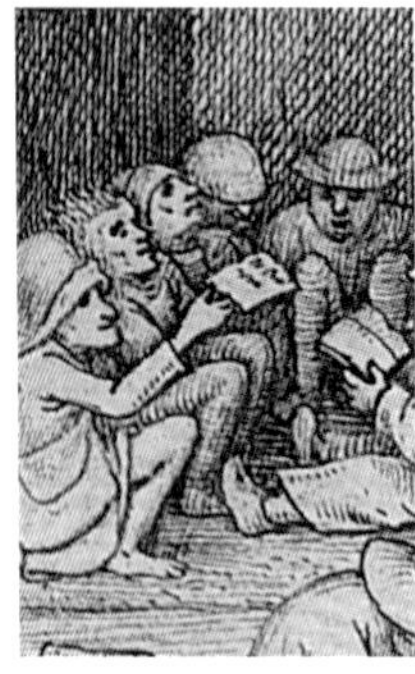

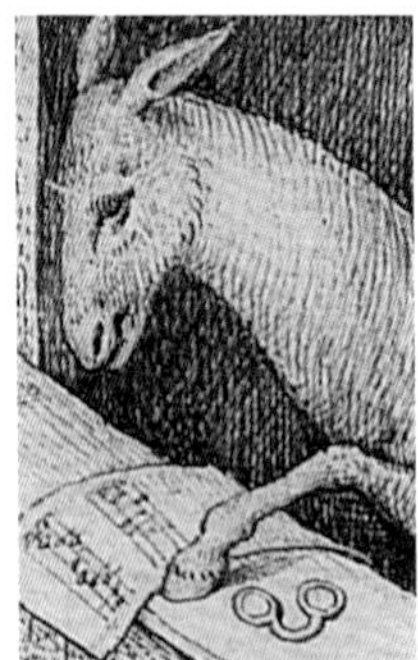

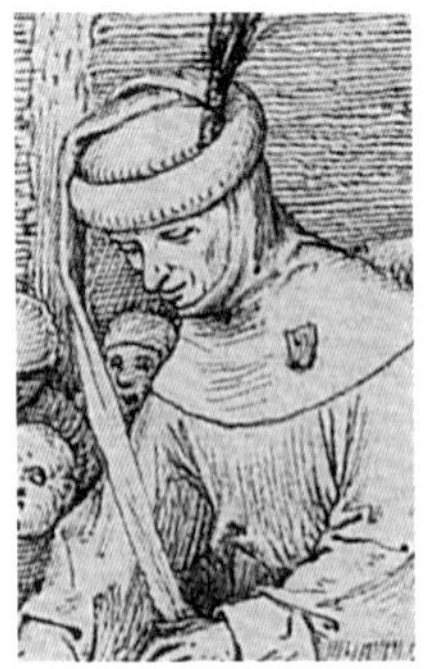

known by his epithet 'Velvet Brueghel', a painter whose exceptional talent contrasted strikingly with that of his father. Through the work of these two markedly different masters, we have the opportunity to follow the different phases of Flemish art during a period when its constitution and aims were undergoing profound change.

The Ass in the School

1556
Pen and Indian ink, 23.2 x 30.2 cm
Staatliche Museen, Kupferstichkabinett, Berlin

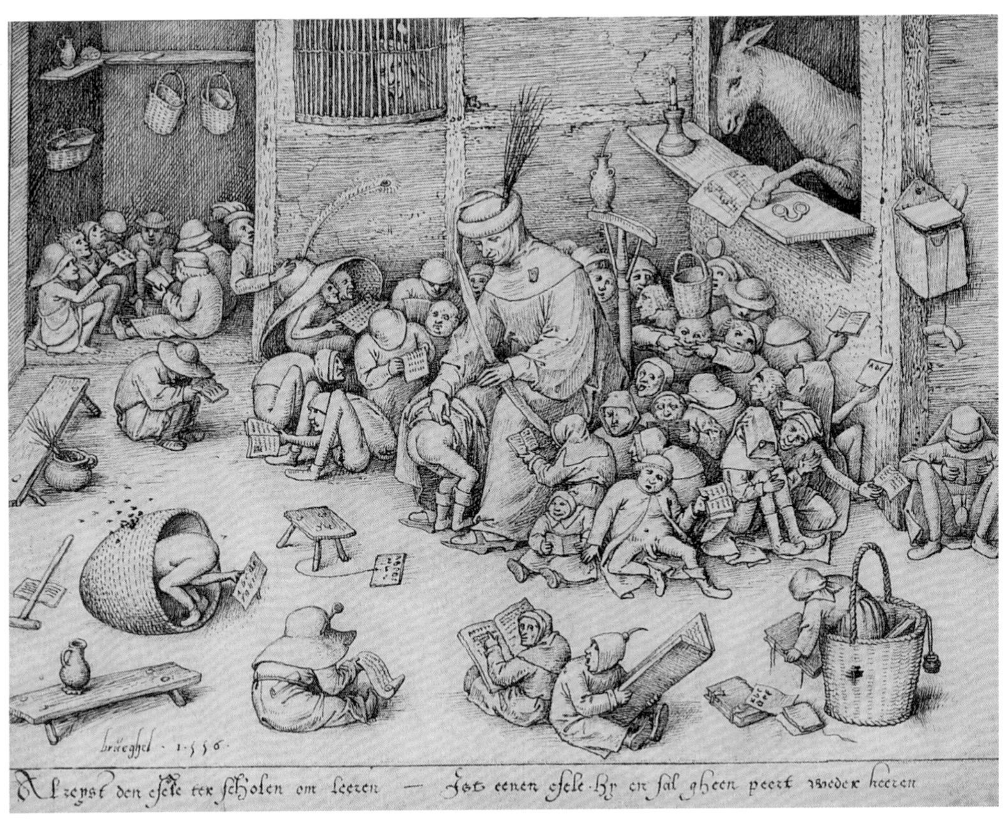
brueghel · 1556
Al reyst den esele ter scholen om leeren — Ist eenen esele hy en sal gheen peert weder keeren

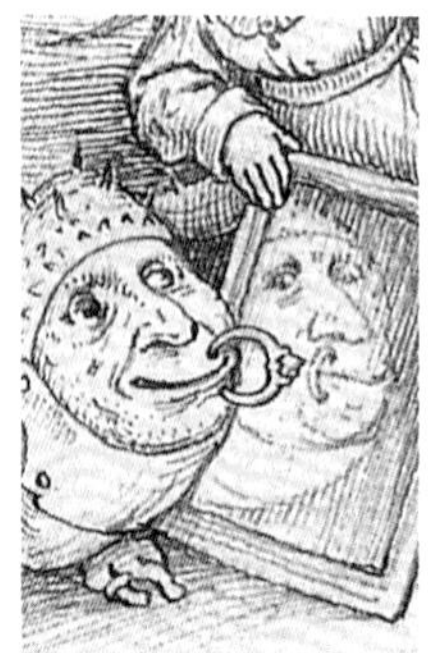

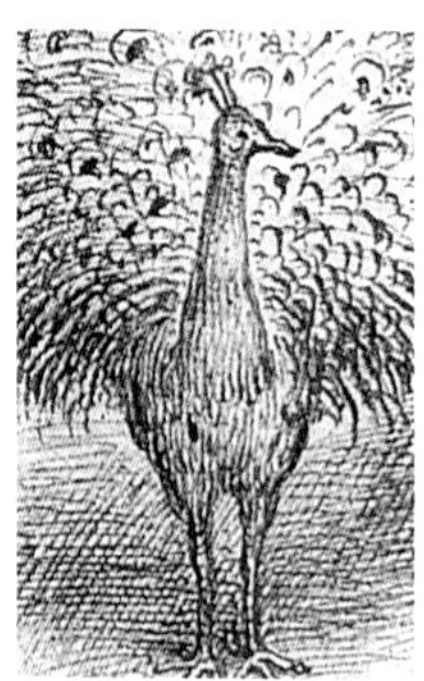

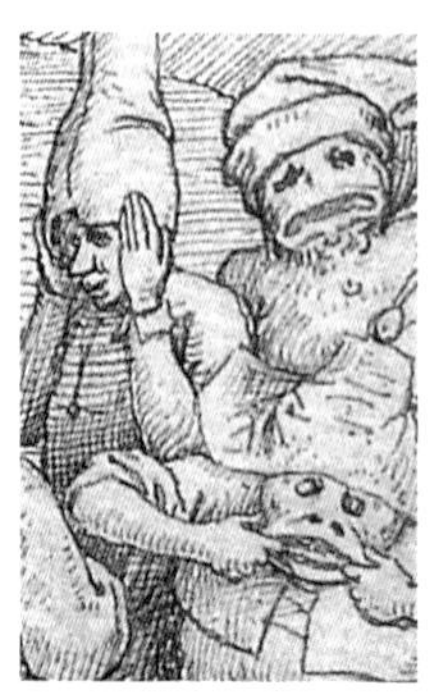

The Century of Pieter Bruegel the Elder

Bruegel's work constitutes a definitive illustration for the most scholarly of historical treatises of this period. He succeeded in capturing the souls of his models in his figure of a dancing peasant or at a delicious feast with a few figures seated around a table. Even in their paintings of gentle fire-lit interiors, the old

Pride from the series Seven Deadly Sins

1557
Pen and brown ink, 22.9 x 30 cm
Institut néerlandais, Fondation Custodia,
F. Lugt Collection, Paris

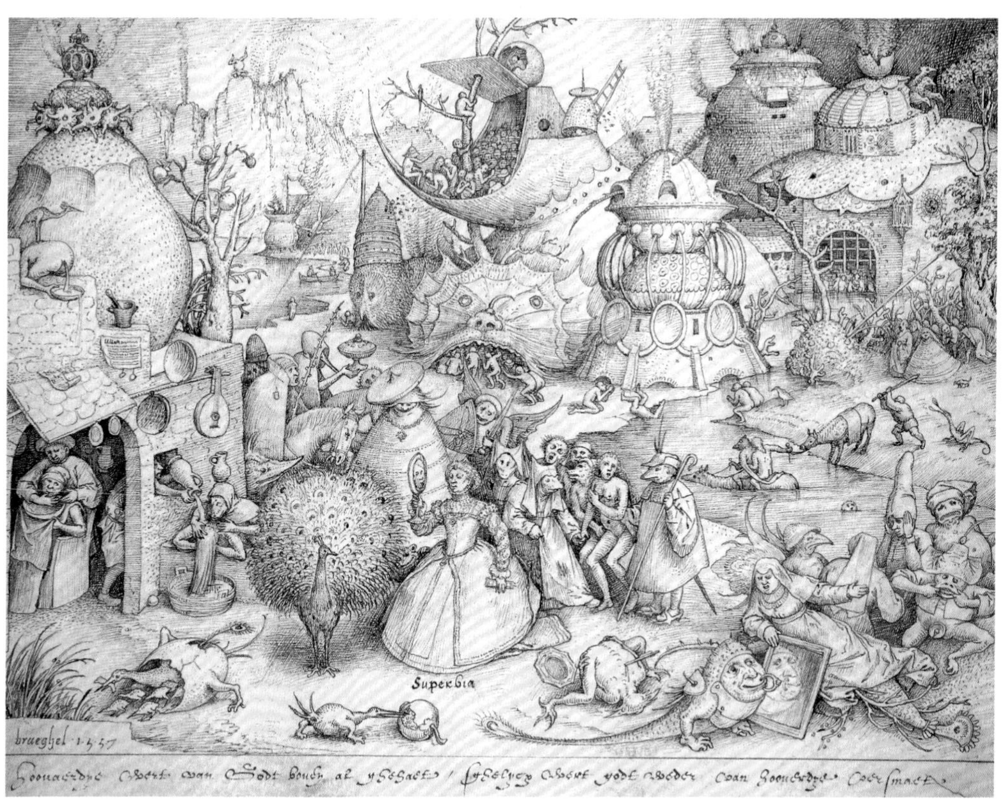
Superbia
brueghel ·1·5·5·7

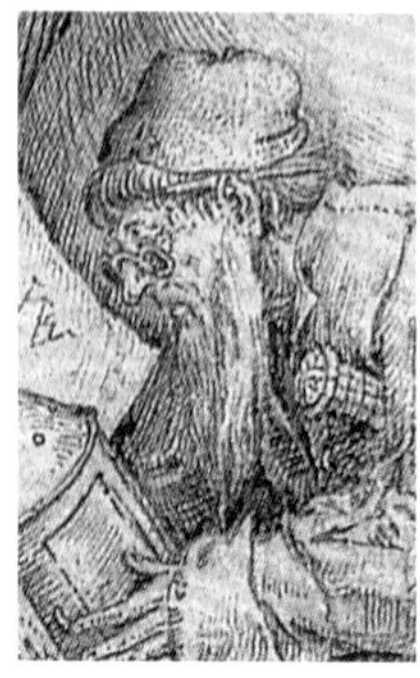

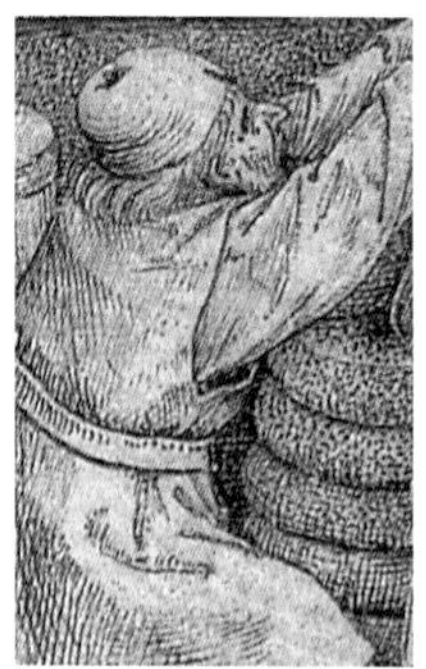

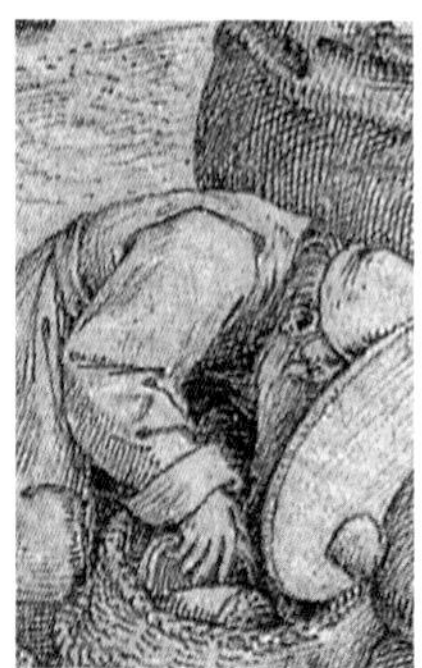

masters always included a window that opened onto the landscape that showed details of contemporary daily life. Pieter Bruegel brought these tiny realist compositions to the foreground, designing them to bring the viewer's sentiment closer to the already poignant scenes of Christ's Passion. This became the subject upon which Bruegel, with his jolly and satirical Flemish verve, exerted his keen sense of observation,

Elck or Everyman

1558
Pen and brown ink, 21 x 29.3 cm
British Museum, London

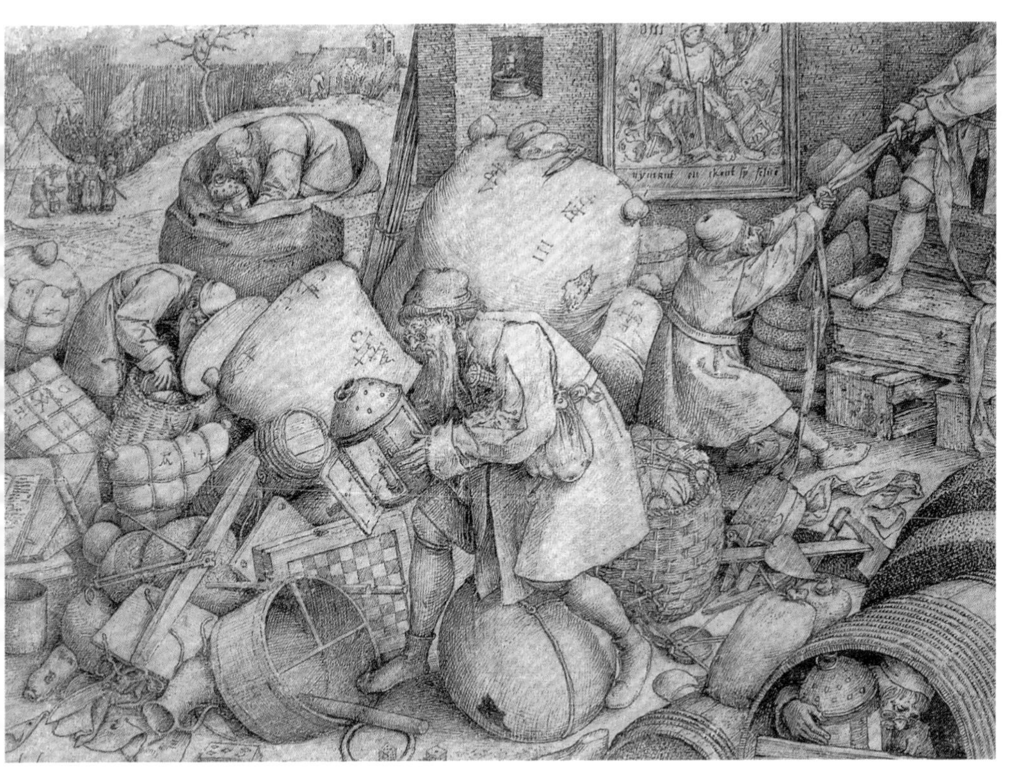

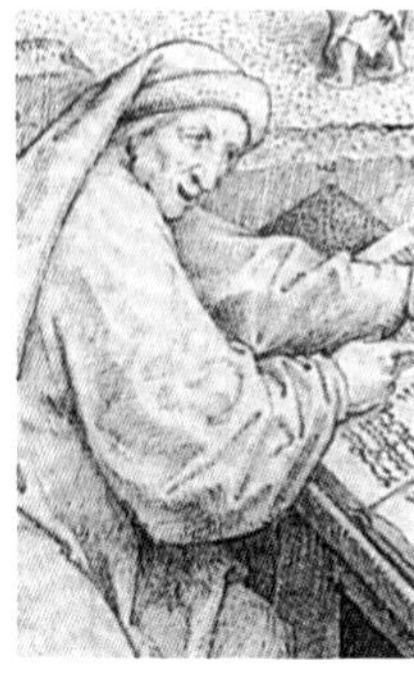

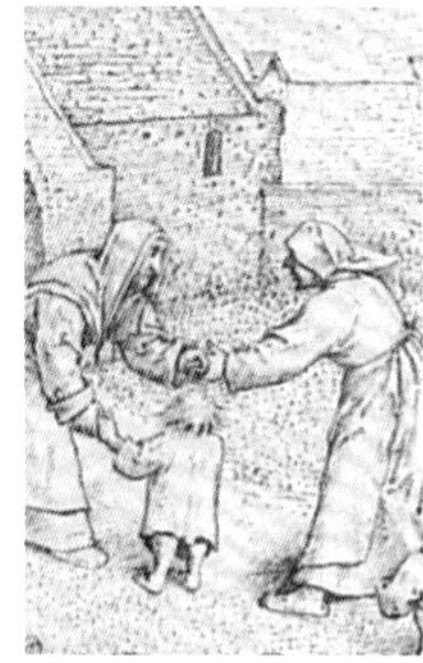

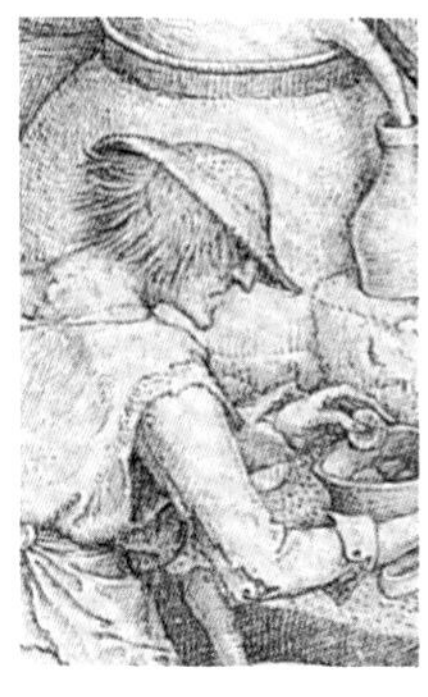

and his marvellous gift for capturing the burlesque or tragic nature of the masses.

When considered from another point of view, it is tempting to define Bruegel, as Van Mander does, as a painter of the peasantry, for it is true that he produced a great number of pastoral scenes. In particular, Bruegel studied the morals of rural life and seems to have been attracted to his subjects through a secret

The Alchemist

1558
Pen and brown ink, 30.8 x 45.3 cm
Staatliche Museen, Kupferstichkabinett, Berlin

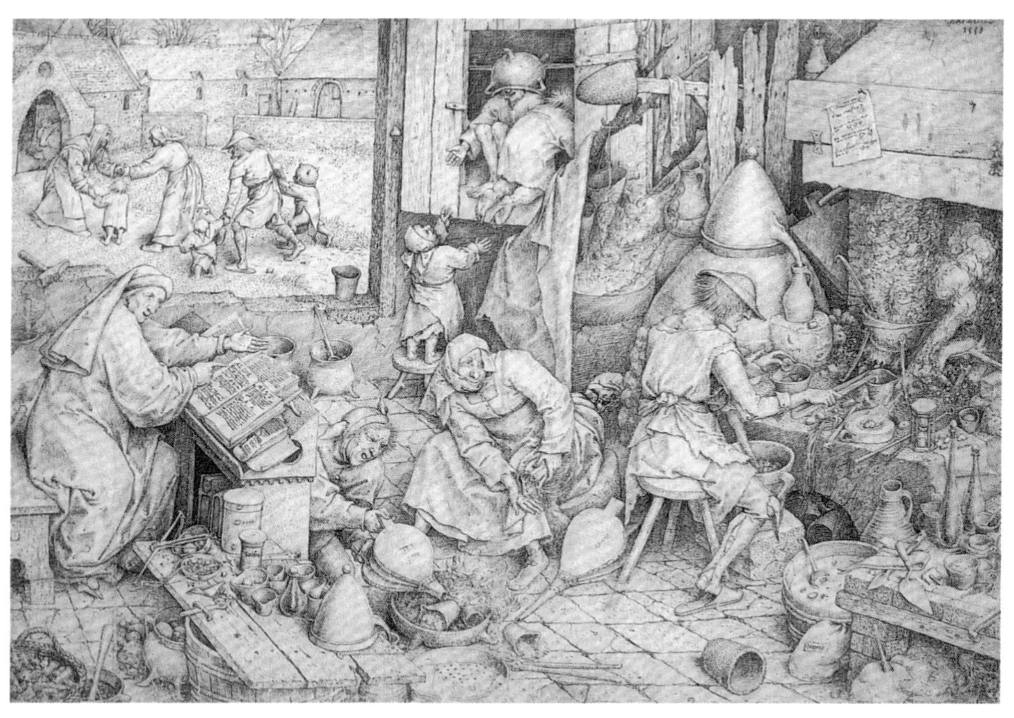

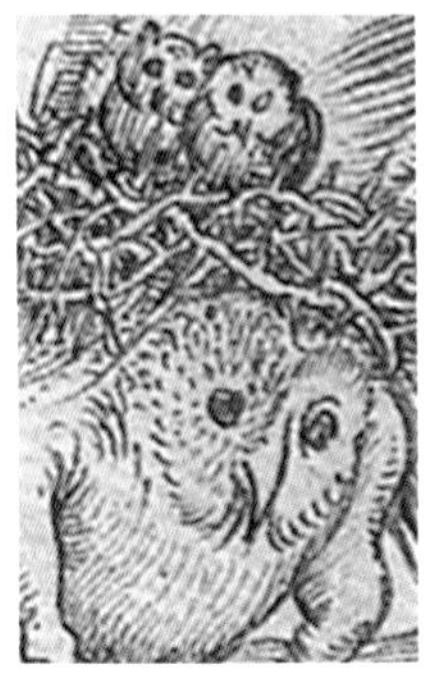

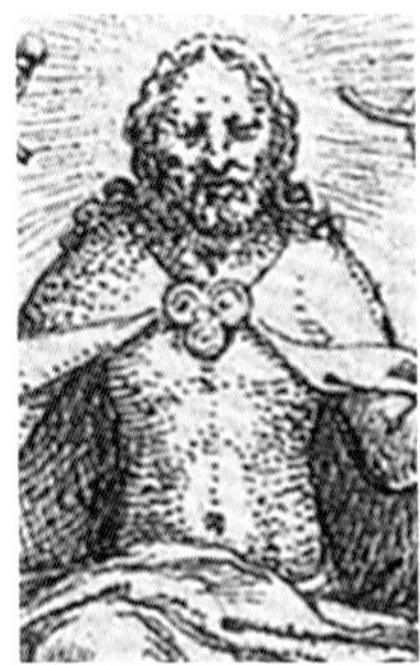

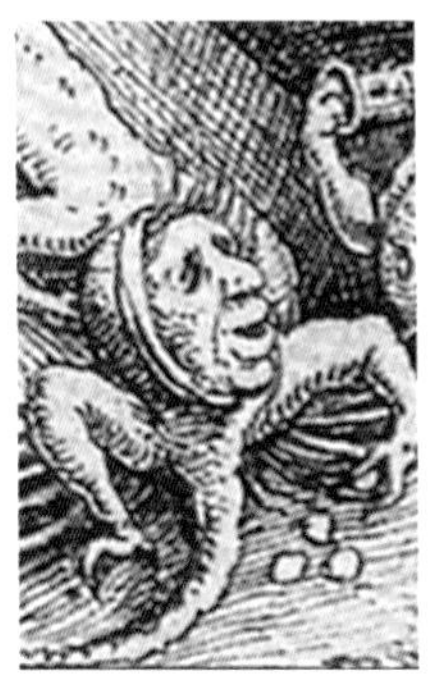

sympathy and certain affinity for their thinking and sentiments which were born out of his own common origins. This connection withstood his stays in large cities, his contact with elite circles of scholars and artists, and his encounters with Italian landscapes and masterpieces. None of this would come to change Bruegel's powerful originality, as it resisted influence like a diamond resists the marks of other stones.

The Last Judgement

1558
Pen and brown ink, 23 x 30 cm
Graphische Sammlung, Albertina, Vienna

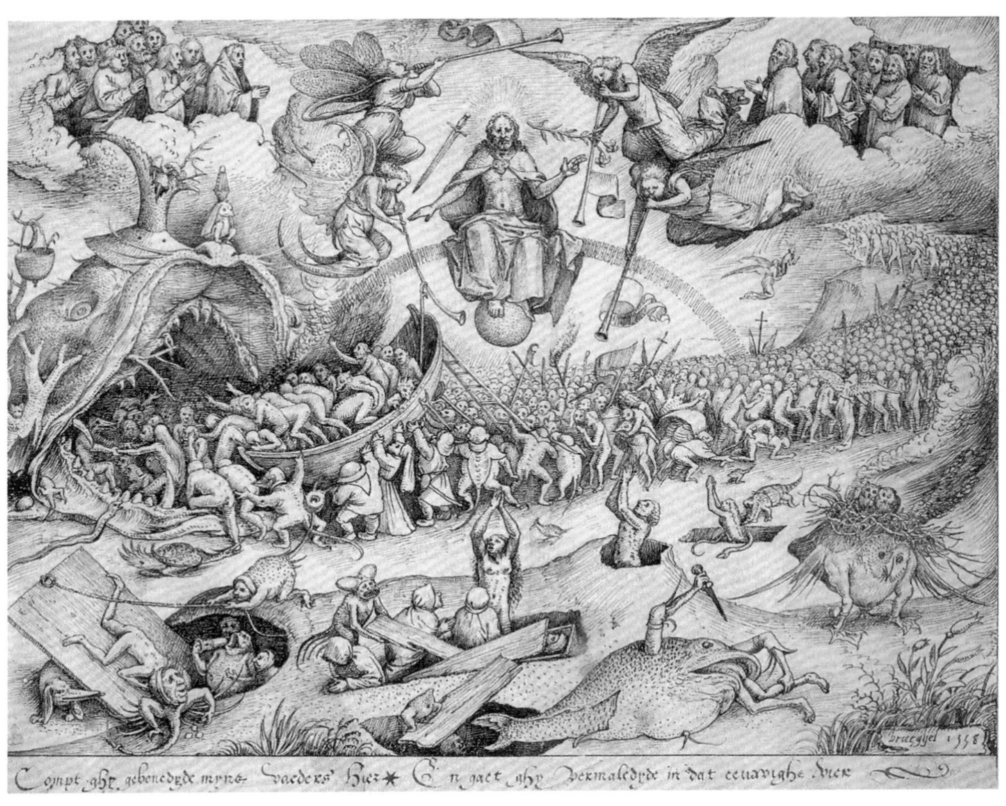
brueghel 1558
Compt ghy gebenedyde myns vaders hier * En gaet ghy vermaledyde in dat eeuwighe vier

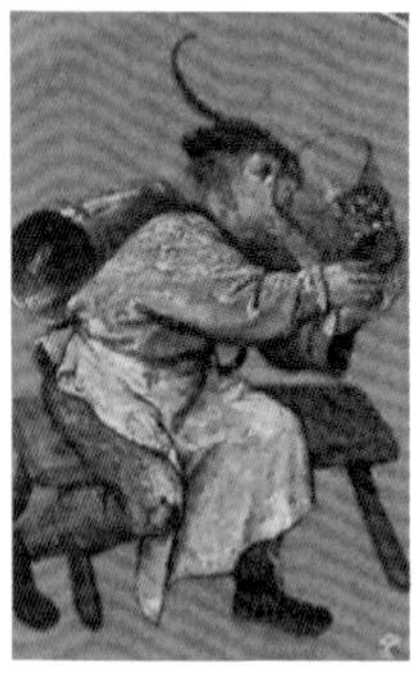

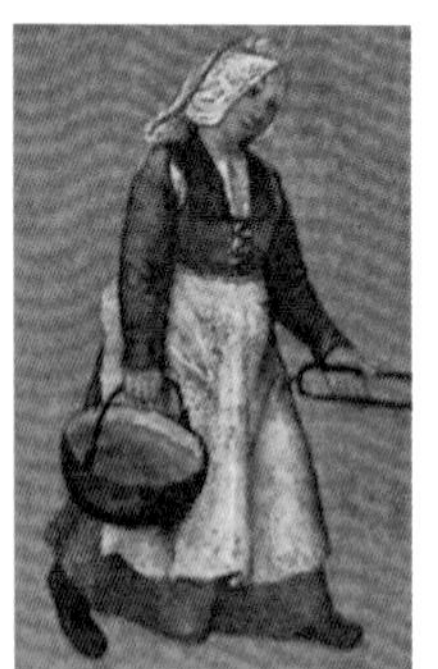

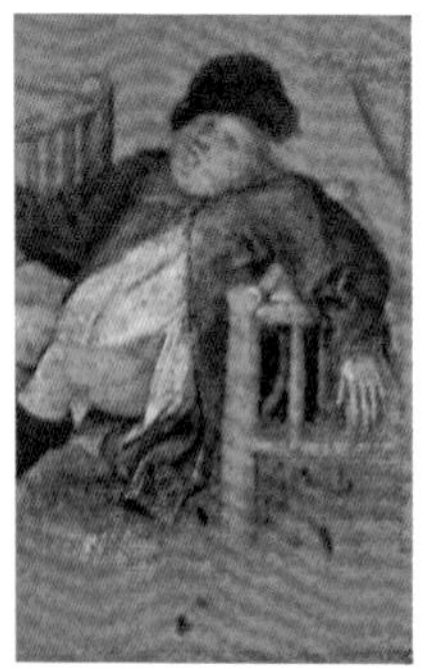

Although Bruegel found lasting pleasure in the portrayal of the lives of the peasantry, it is not a sufficient reason to reduce this illustrator of life to the specialised label of genre painter. His characters, be they rustic or bourgeois, must be seen in the light of the appetites, ulterior motives, material needs, and moral aspirations that were reflections of their time. With a sudden glow, each face, by the hundreds in

Twelve Flemish Proverbs

1558

Tempera on oak, 74.5 x 98.4 cm

Museum Mayer van den Bergh, Antwerp

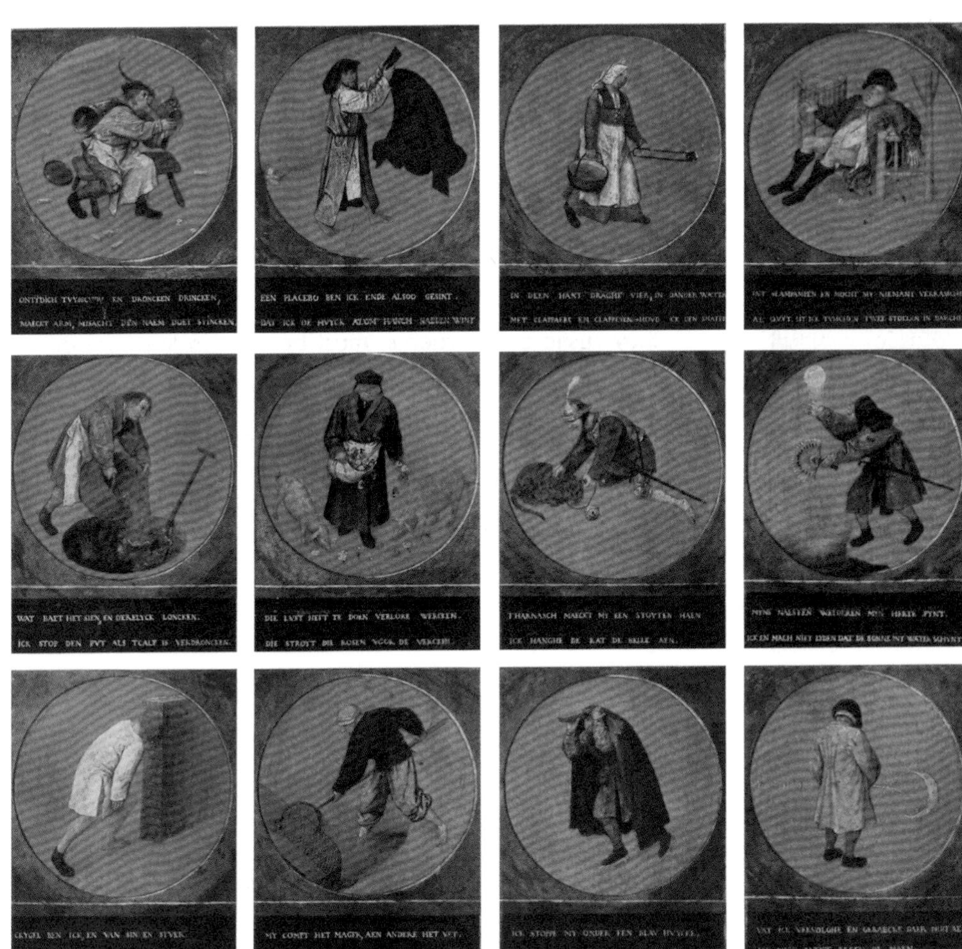

EEN PLACEBO BEN ICK ENDE ALSOO GESINT.
WAT BAET HET SIEN, EN DERAELYCK LONCKEN.
ICK STOP DEN PVT ALS TCALF IS VERDRONCKEN.
DIE LAST HEFT TE DOEN VERLORE WERCKEN.
ICK HANGHE DE KAT DE BELLE AEN.
MY COMPT HET MAGER, AEN ANDERE HET VET.
ICK VISCHE ALTYT ACHTER HET NET.

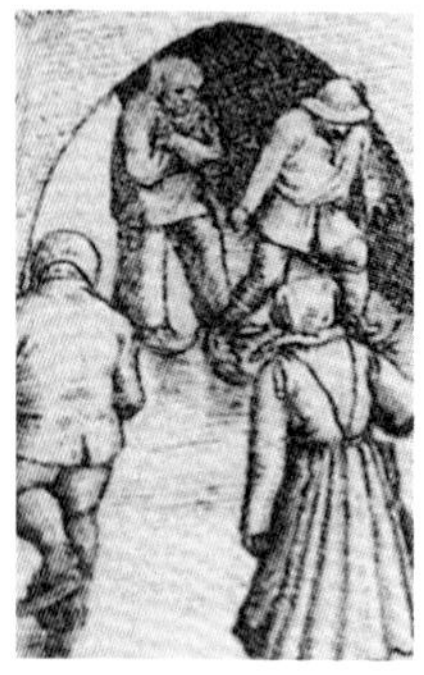

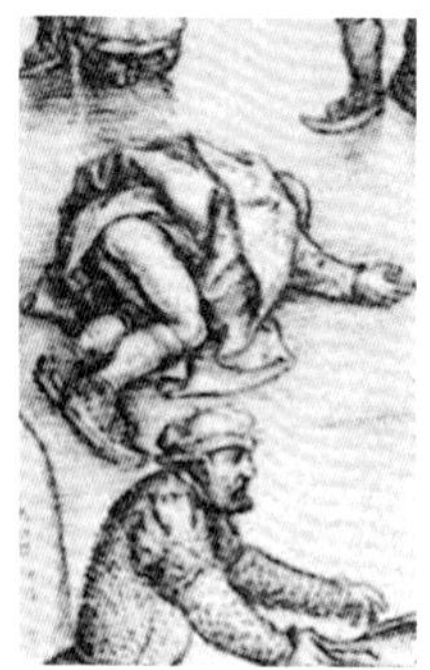

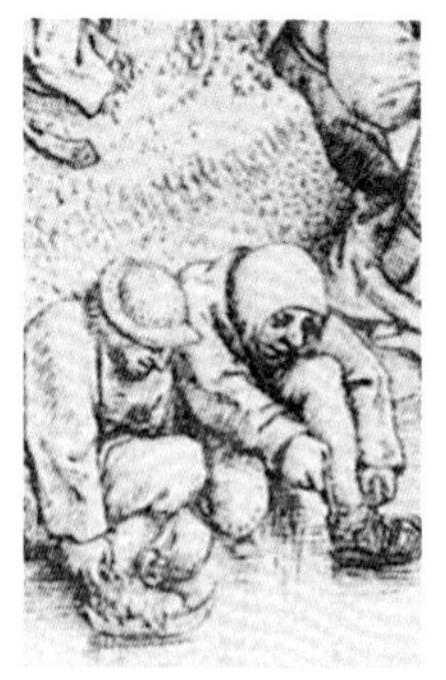

certain canvasses, illuminates anecdotes from Van Vaernewyck's memoirs: blinking eyes in a face creased with malice, others with angular, hastily composed features possessing a carved marionette's strange wooden steadiness, or a particular flat-browed profile with a lipless gash of a mouth. The group compositions reveal the depth of Bruegel's genius even more than their individual faces.

Skaters before the Gate of Saint George

1558-1559
Pen and brown ink, 21.3 x 29.8 cm
Private collection, United States

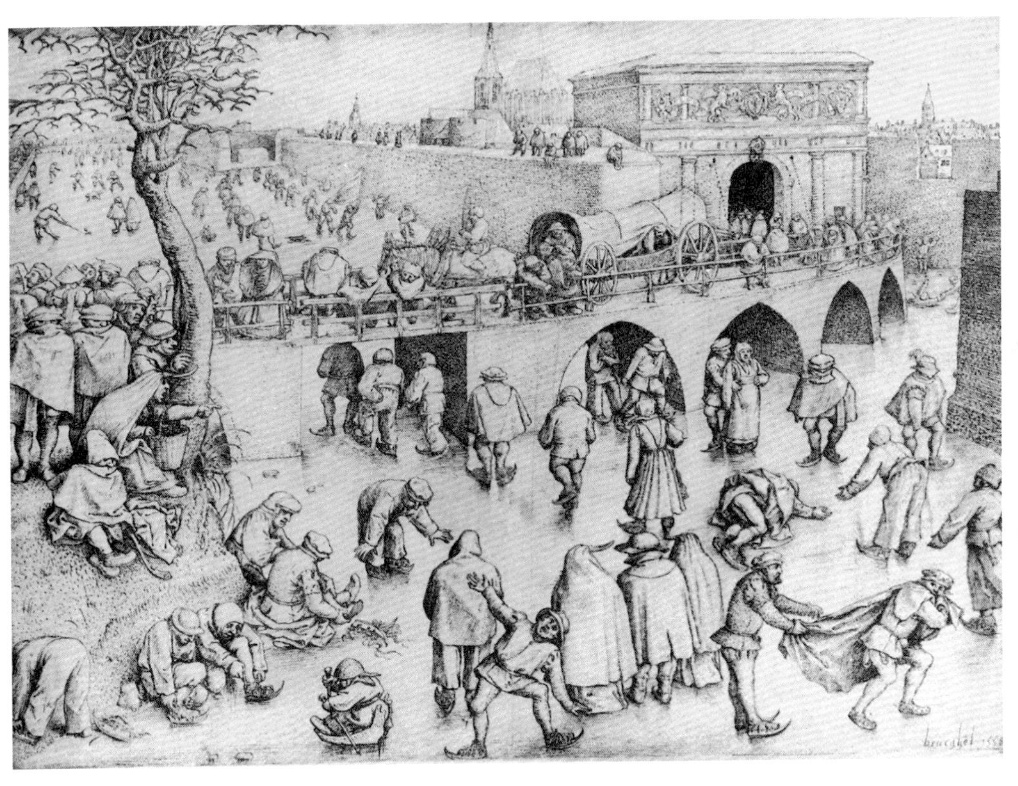
brueghel

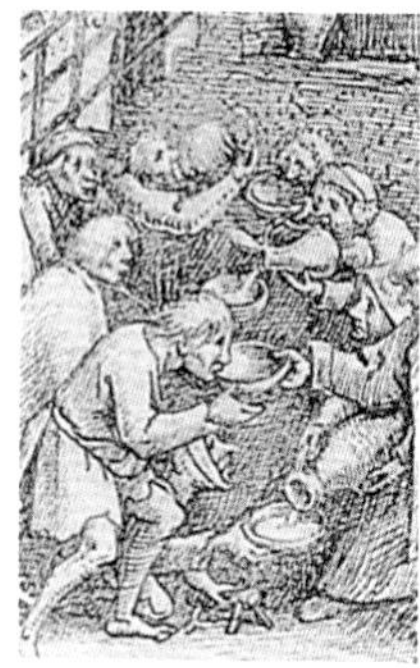

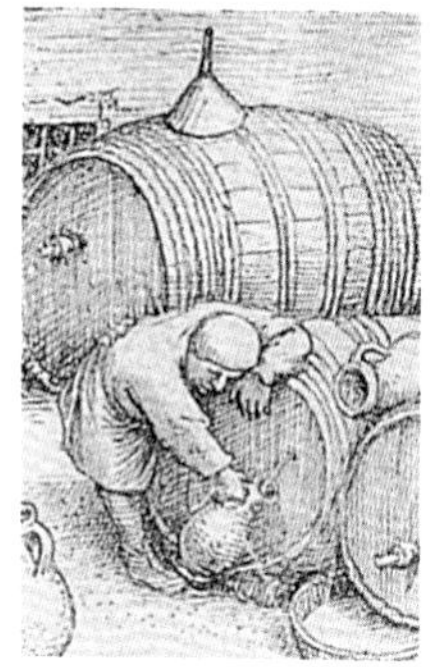

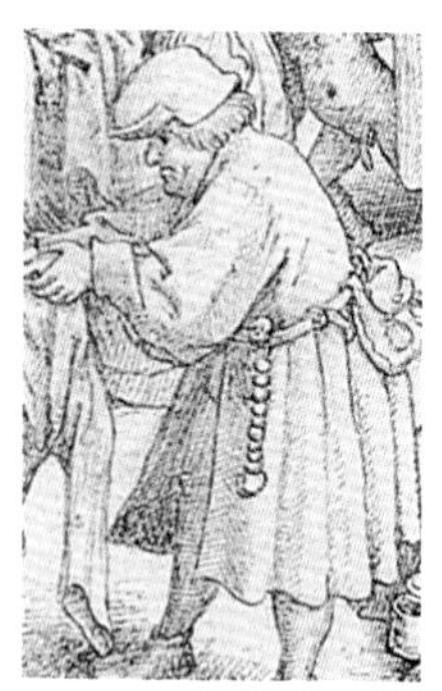

The Massacre of the Innocents represents all of the arrogance, insolence, and the unbearable burden of foreign domination at the hands of these mercenaries, clustered together like a block of steel, contemptuous and invulnerable, pushing before the chests of their horses, the hounded flock of unfortunates. These mothers, these peasants clasping their hands, these women collapsed in suffering, are those that Bruegel

Charity, from the series Seven Virtues

1559
Pen and brown ink, 22.4 x 29.9 cm
Museum Boijmans Van Beuningen, Rotterdam

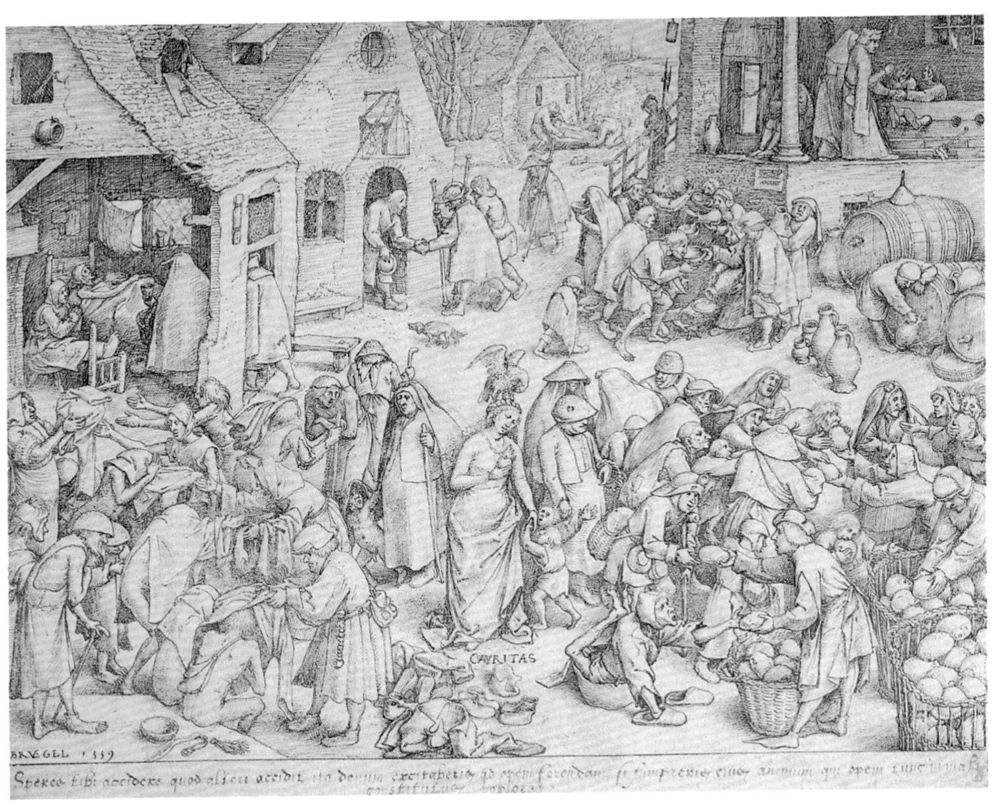
CHARITAS
BRVEGEL 1559

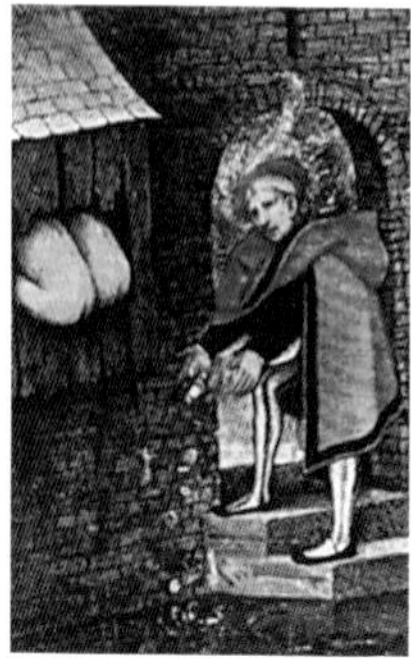

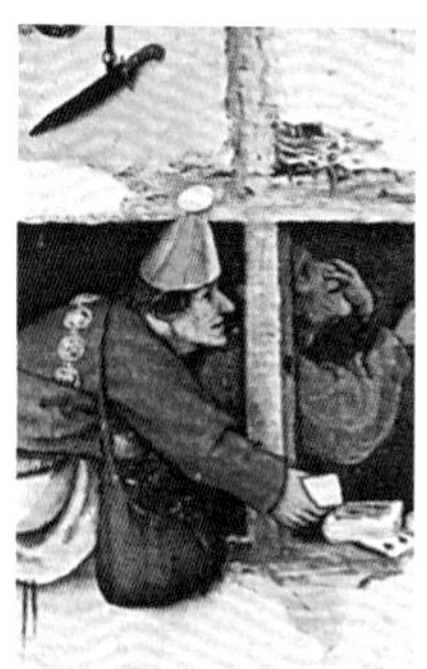

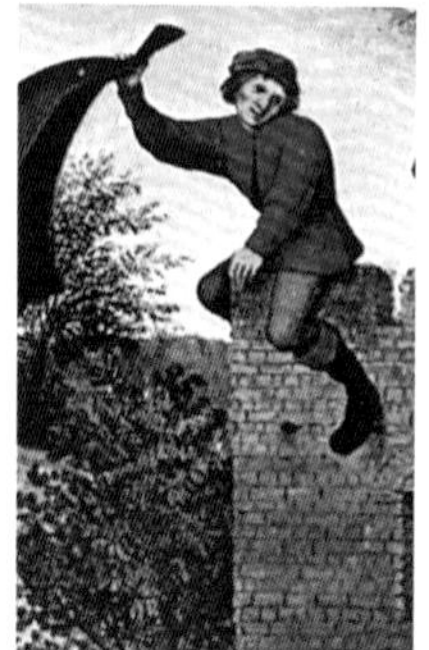

saw begging for their husbands, themselves, or even for their children to be spared. These are the unfortunate women he found weeping alongside the road, under the same December sky and in the same atmosphere of inexpressible sadness that envelops *The Massacre of the Innocents.* Yet the whole of Bruegel's work is far more vast, boldly executed, and teeming with movement than these examples.

Netherlandish Proverbs

1559
Oil on wood panel, 117 x 163.5 cm
Staatliche Museen, Gemäldegalerie, Berlin

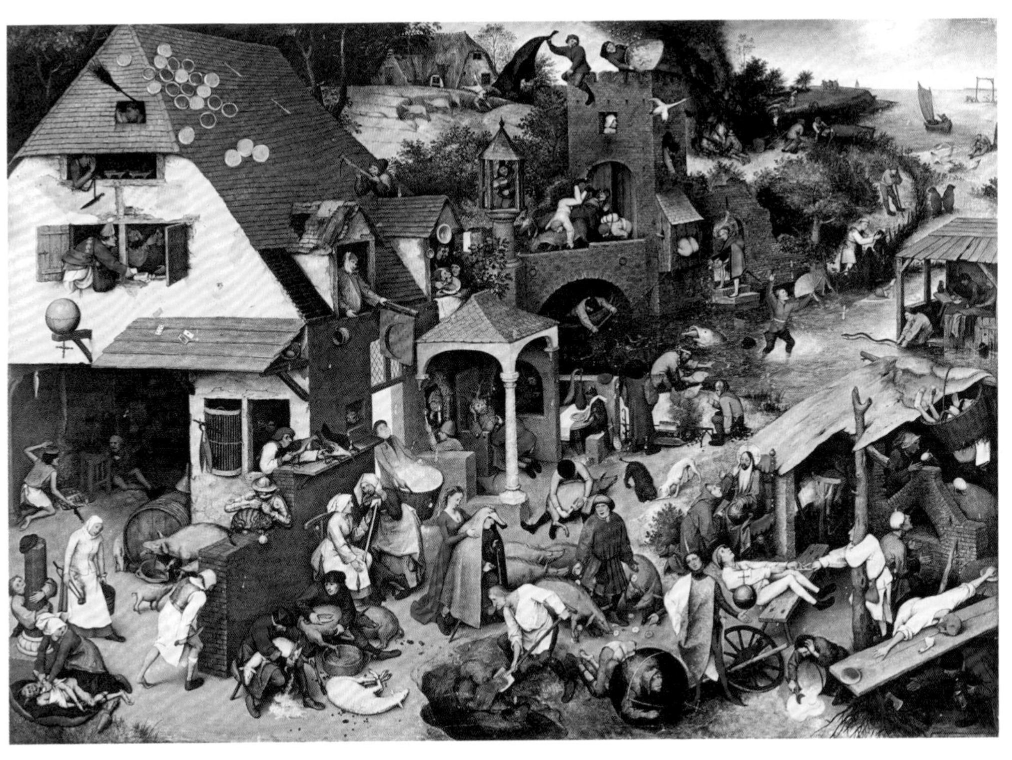

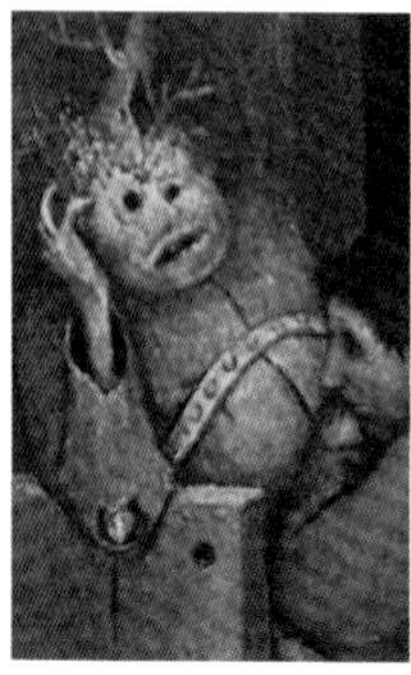

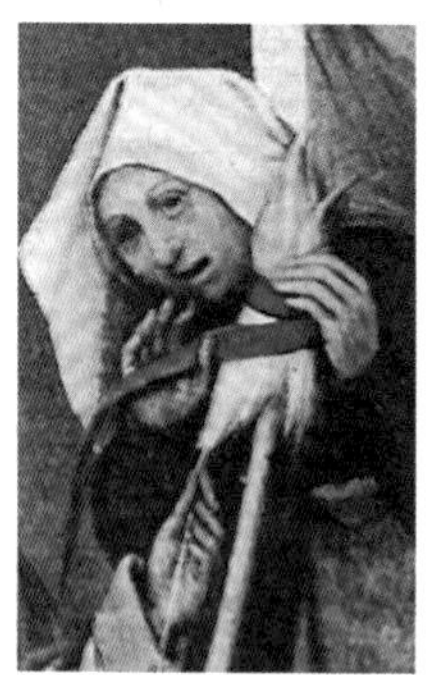

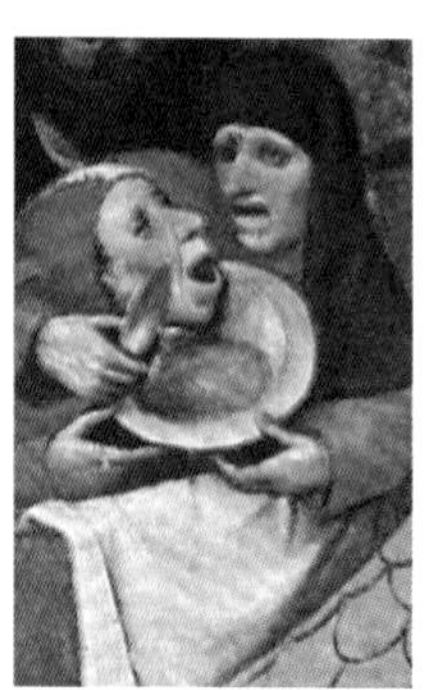

What was Bruegel's position in relation to the other painters of his time? In 1525, a few years before the probable date of Bruegel's birth, Jan Gossaert, known as Mabuse or Maubeuge, returned from his stay in Italy. He was the first Flemish painter to admire the masterpieces accumulated for over two centuries in the churches and palaces of Rome and Florence. This was

Netherlandish Proverbs (detail)

1559
Oil on wood panel, 117 x 163.5 cm
Staatliche Museen, Gemäldegalerie, Berlin

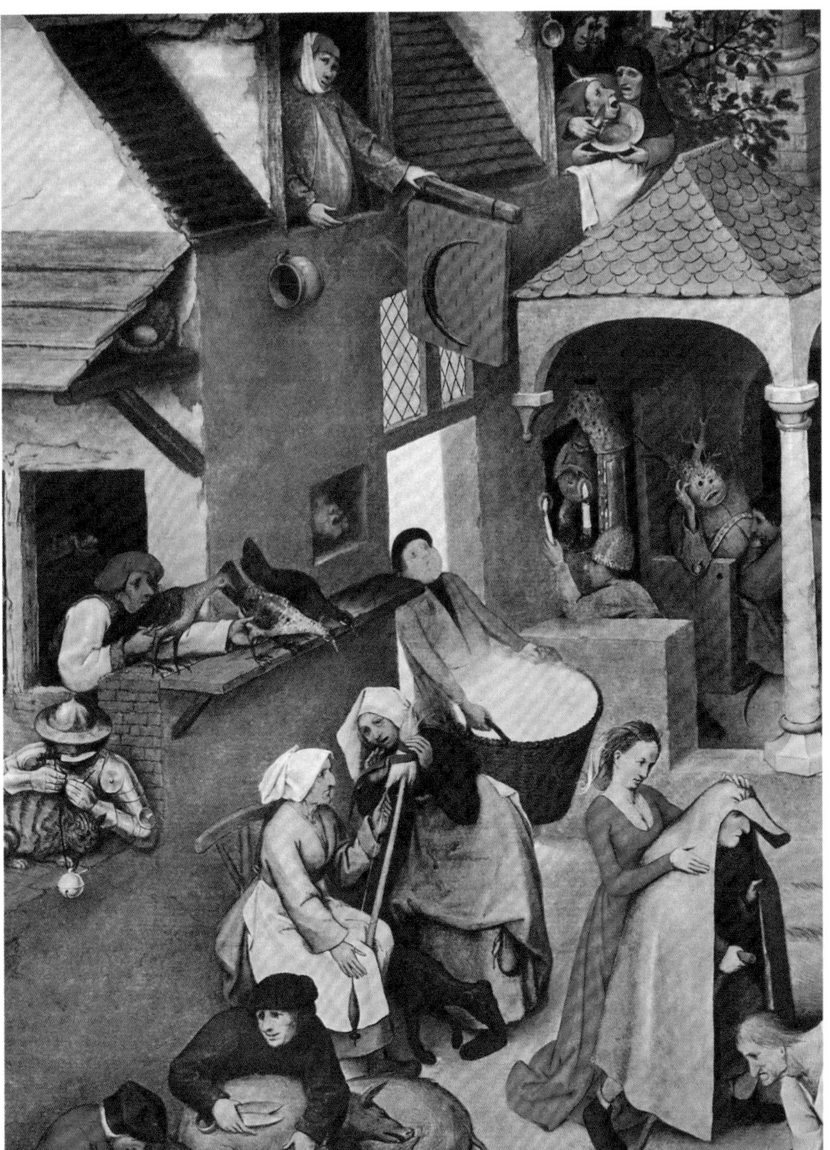

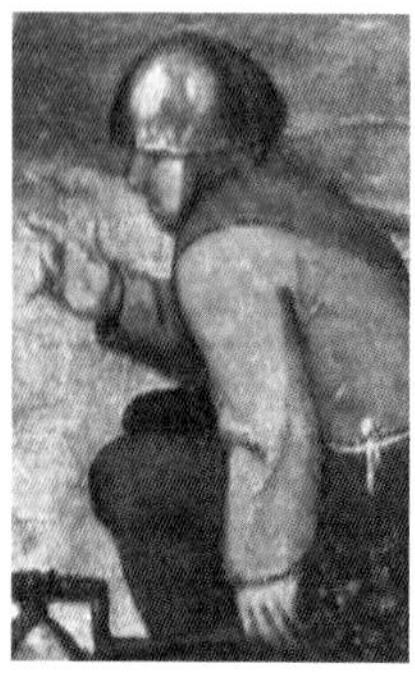

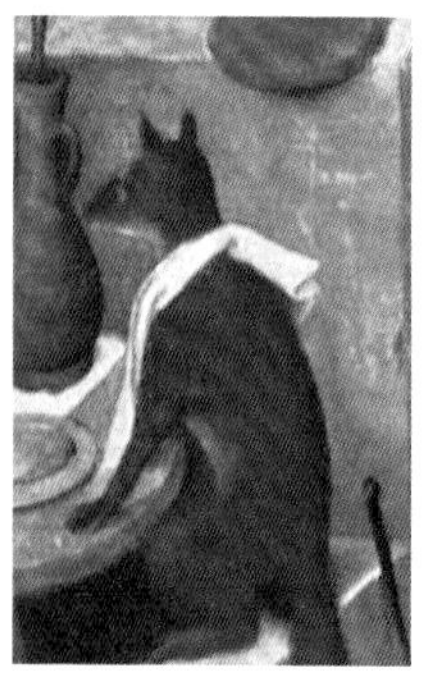

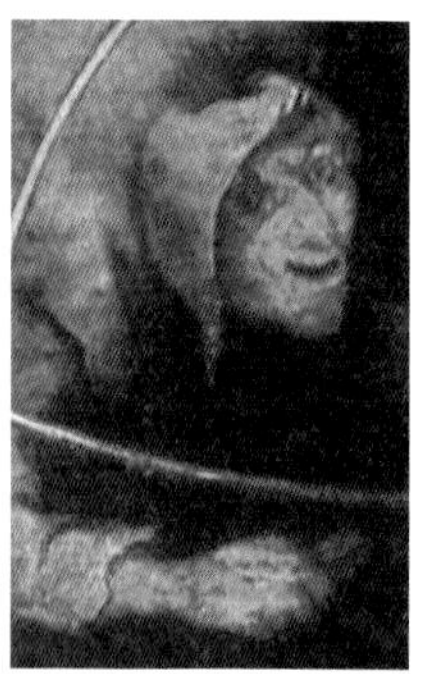

the era of Michelangelo, Raphael, and Leonardo da Vinci, who represented the most blinding brilliance of the blazing light of the Italian Renaissance. Yet, less than fifty years before, the Italians had borrowed aspects of the Flemish method of painting from nature, and the taut and powerful technique used by Jan de Bruges (as they called the elder Van Eyck),

Netherlandish Proverbs (detail)

1559
Oil on wood panel, 117 x 163.5 cm
Staatliche Museen, Gemäldegalerie, Berlin

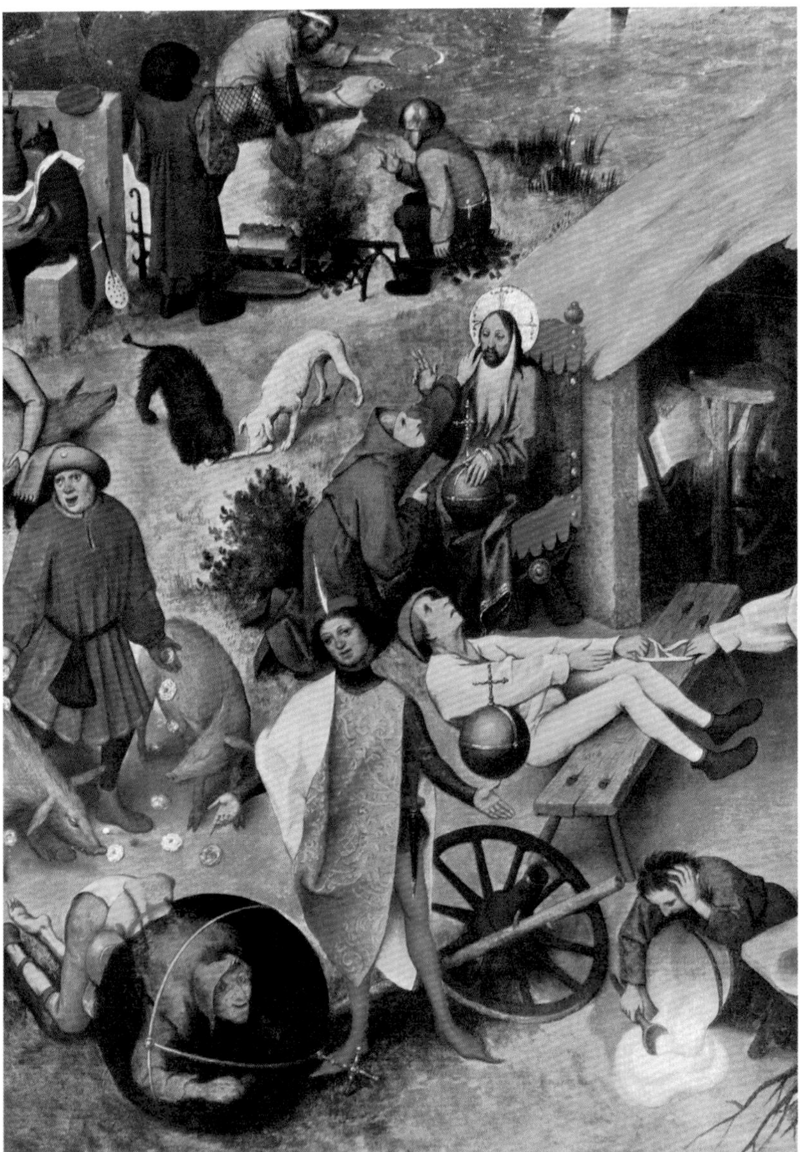

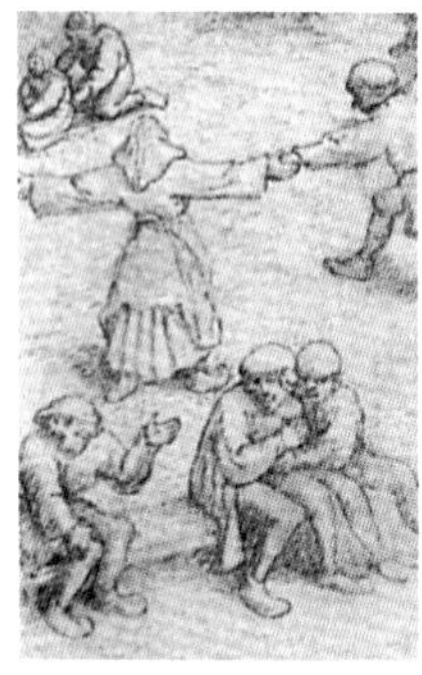

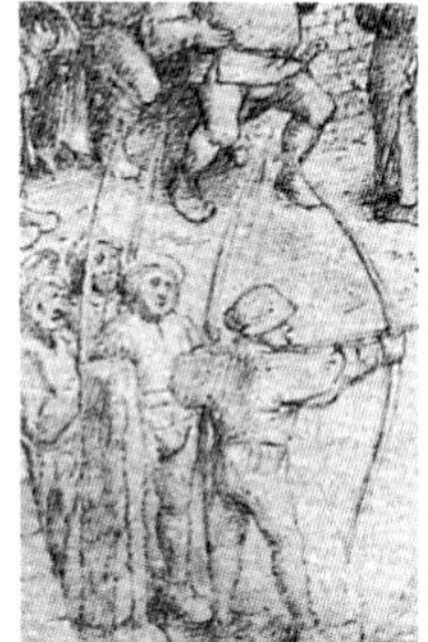

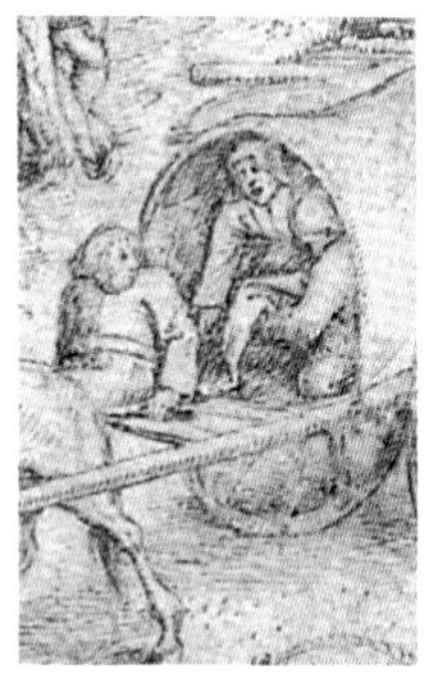

Hugues van der Goes, and Rogier van der Weyden. These borrowed techniques enabled the blossoming of Florentine art under Masolino da Panicale, Masaccio, and Andrea del Verrocchio, who were the direct precursors of the great Italian masters of the first half of the 16th century.

Bruegel's art is not the result of any particular school in the strict sense of the word. The best of his students,

The Fair at Hoboken

1559
Pen and brown ink, 26.5 x 39.4 cm
Courtauld Institute of Art, Lee Collection, London

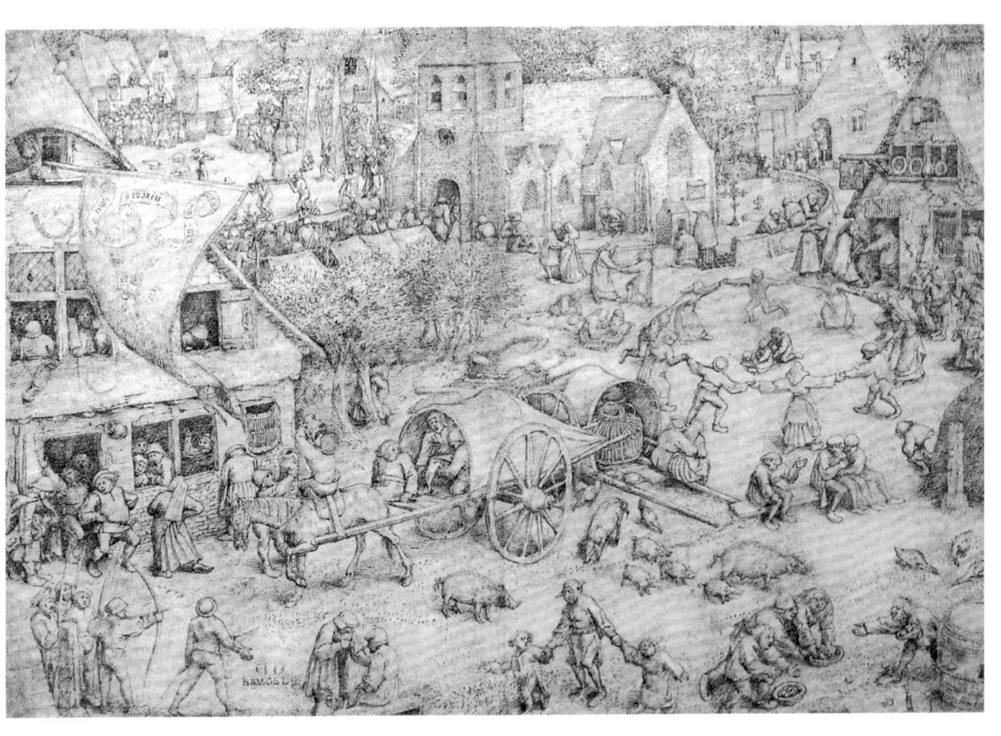

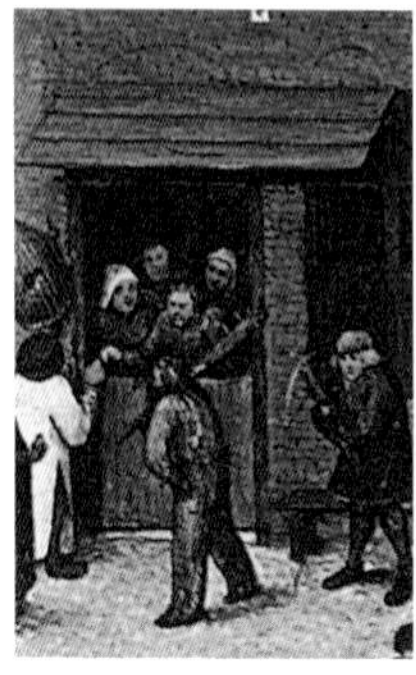

his son Pieter, known as the 'Hell Brueghel', simply copied him. Pieter Bruegel the Elder occupies an exceptional place in the history of Flemish painting, as much for the creative power of his genius as for his personal technique. It would be fair to consider him an extreme, a crowning achievement of the realist tendency that characterises Netherlandish painting.

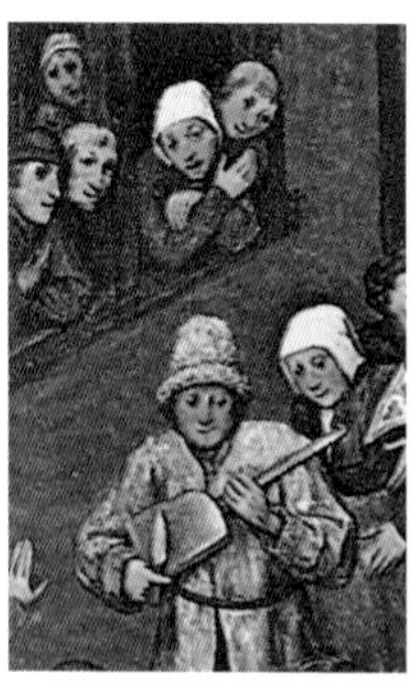

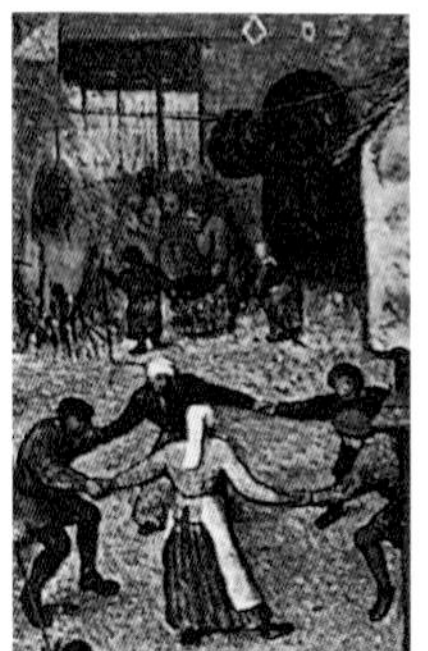

The Fight between Carnival and Lent

1559
Oil on oak panel, 118 x 164.5 cm
Kunsthistorisches Museum, Vienna

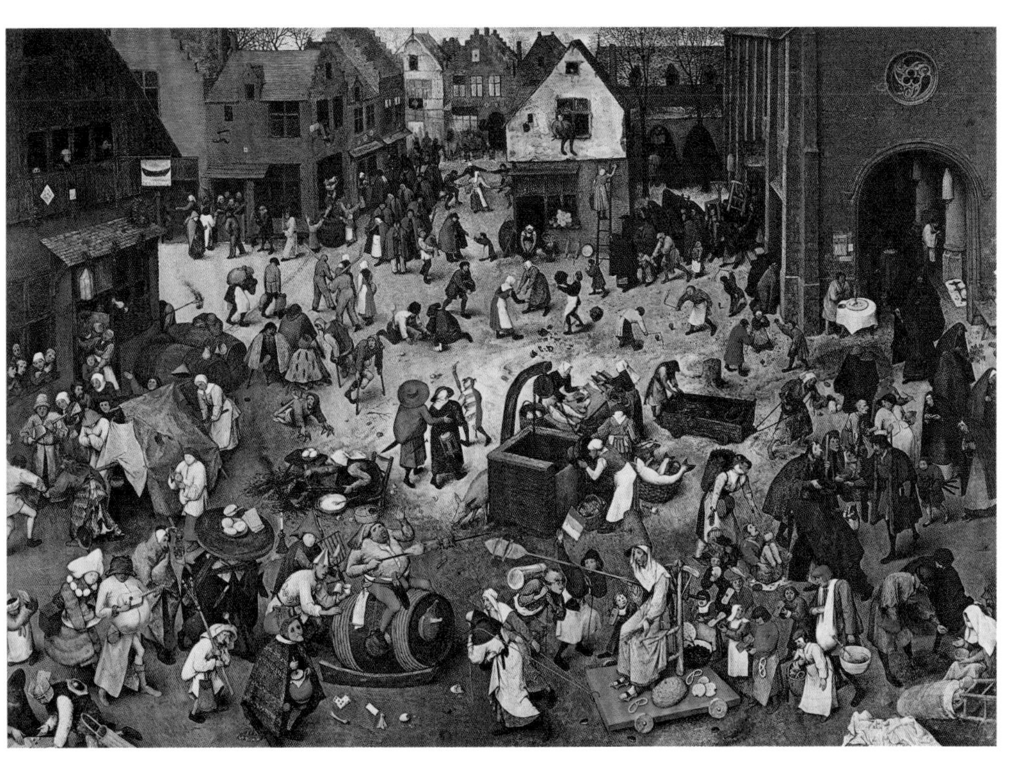

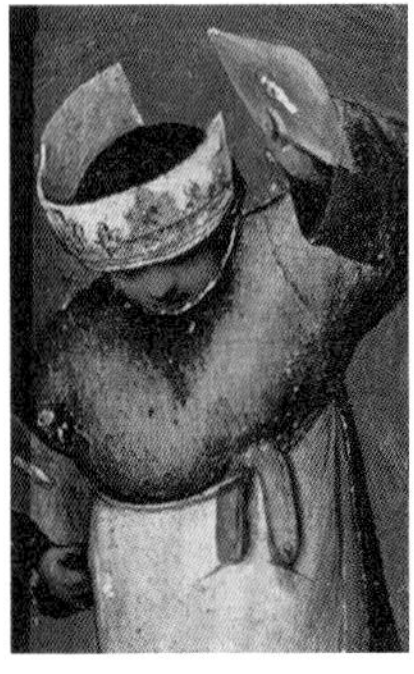

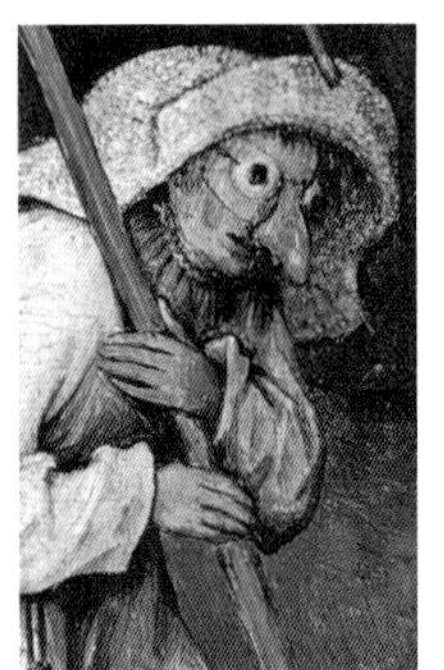

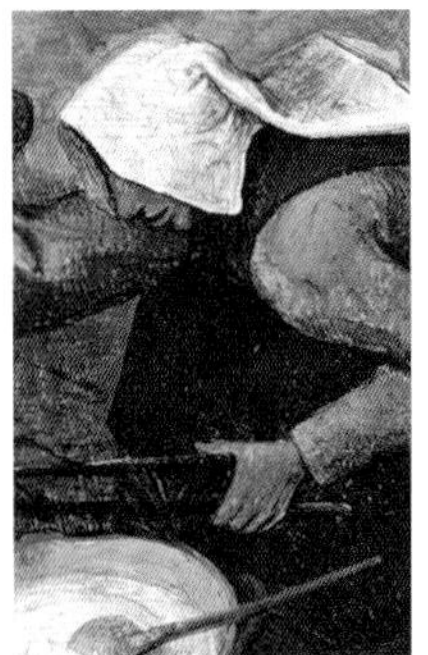

He applies himself to his subjects which are drawn from the daily lives of the Flemish people with a primary concern for sincerity before satire. It was only after completing a scene of daily life that he would attach a proverb or a certain moral sense to it. His work is so natural that he frequently does not seem to have set out with the preconceived idea of painting a particular moral lesson or proverb.

The Fight between Carnival and Lent (detail)

1559
Oil on oak panel, 118 x 164.5 cm
Kunsthistorisches Museum, Vienna

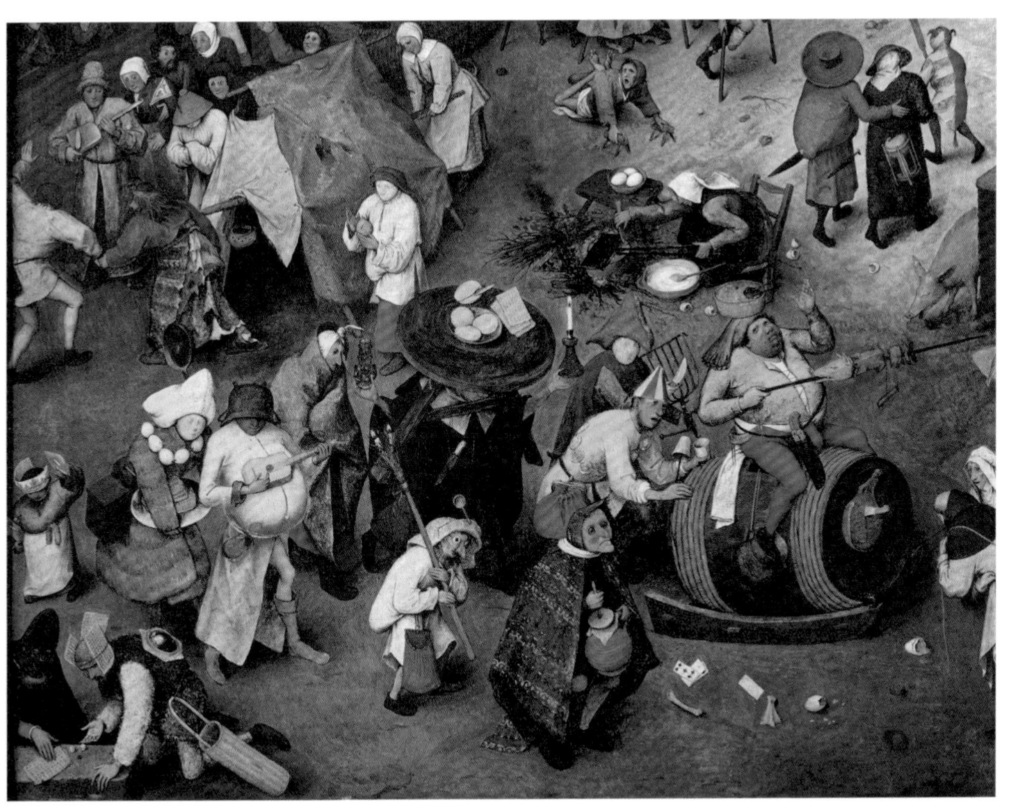

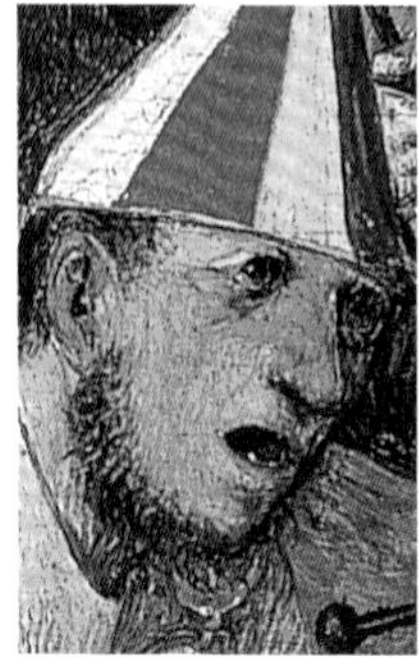

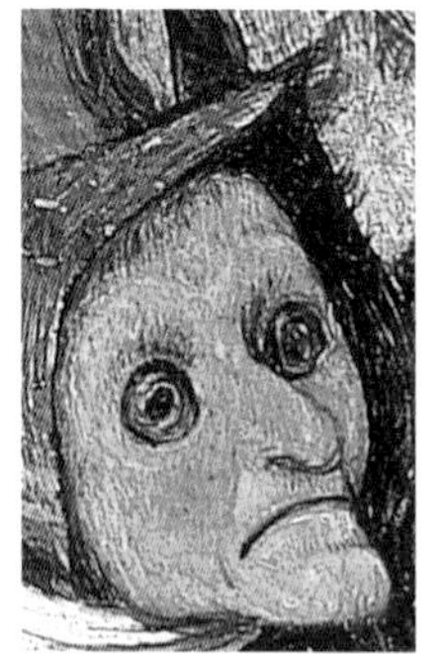

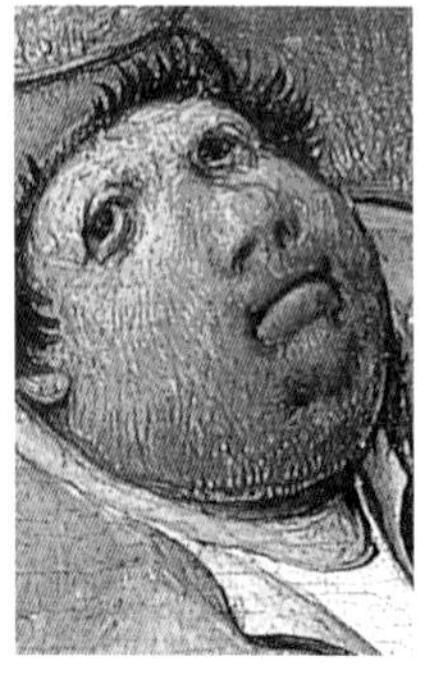

Pieter Bruegel the Elder's Beginnings

Nothing is less certain than Bruegel's date of birth, but there are also many questions regarding where he was born. Because he is recorded in the *liggeren* or 'Record of Artists' of the guild of Saint Luke in Antwerp under the name of 'Peeter Brueghels', it is concluded that he was from the village of Bruegel. Nevertheless, one fact is well known, Bruegel was the son of a peasant.

The Fight between Carnival and Lent (detail)

1559
Oil on oak panel, 118 x 164.5 cm
Kunsthistorisches Museum, Vienna

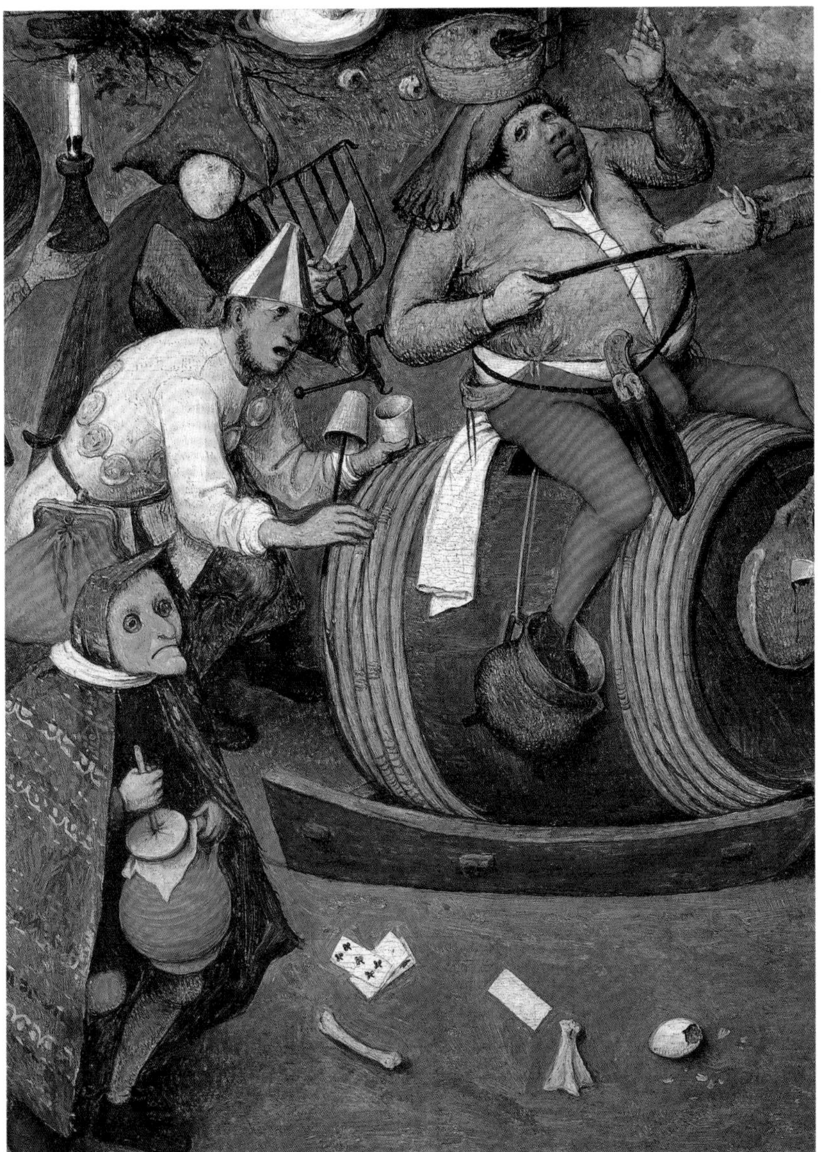

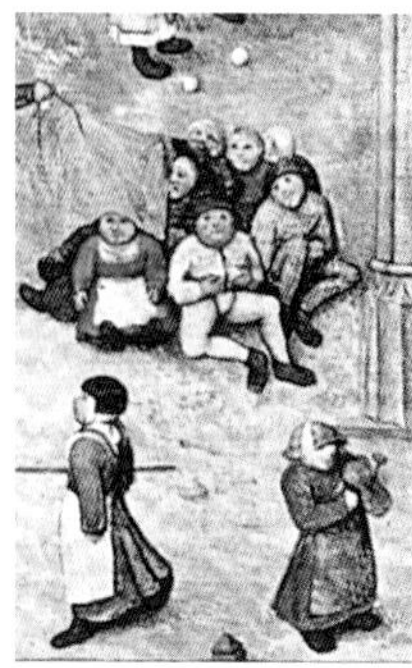

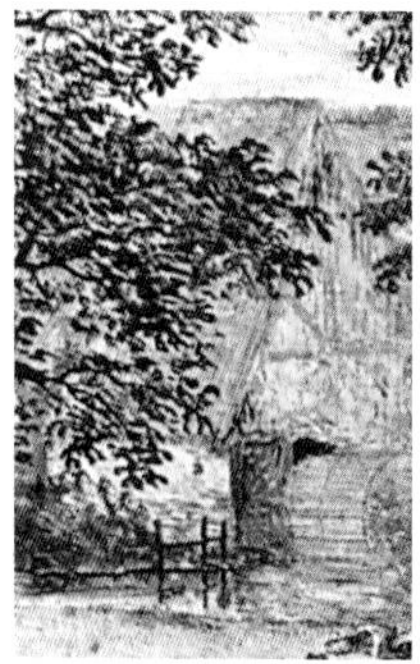

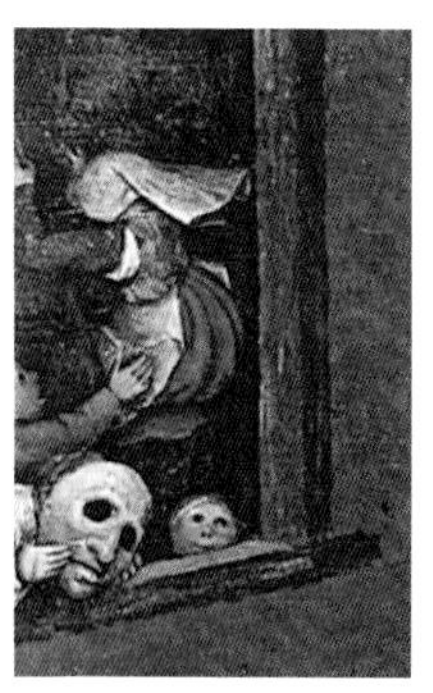

Only three dates are certain in the life of Bruegel the Elder: the date of his acceptance as a master in the Guild of Saint Luke, the date of his marriage, and that of his death. Only hypotheses exist regarding Bruegel's date of birth. It was in 1551 that Bruegel was added as a master to the *liggeren* of the Guild of Saint Luke in Antwerp. According to the same documents, the average length of an apprenticeship was six years.

Children's Games

1560
Oil on wood, 118 x 161 cm
Kunsthistorisches Museum, Vienna

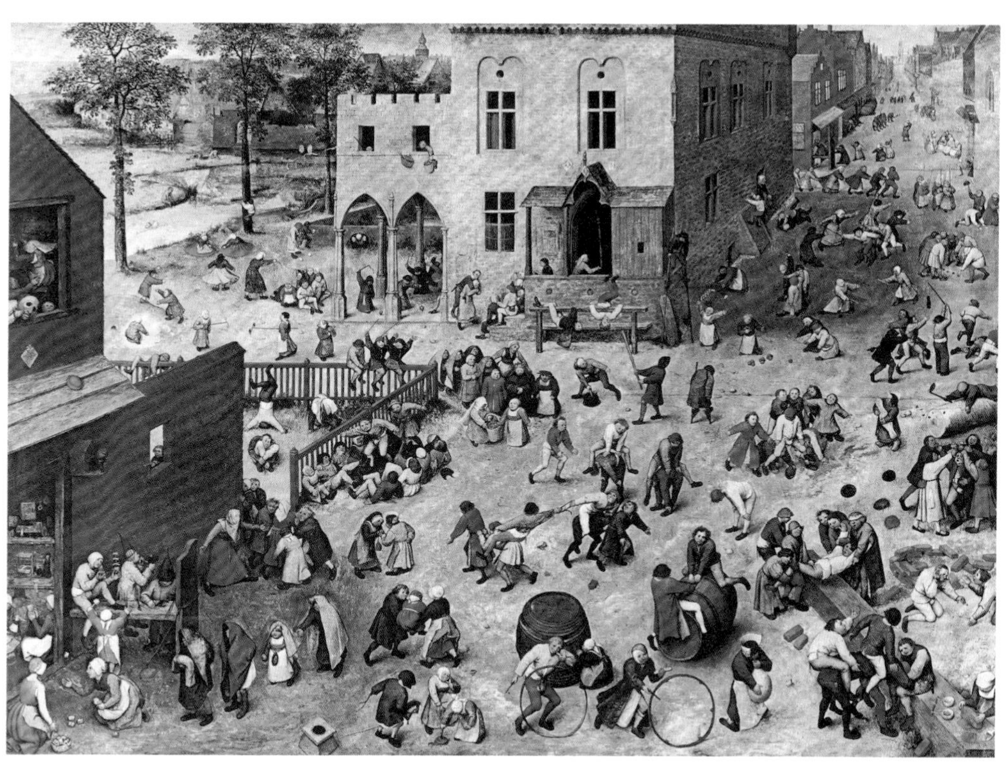

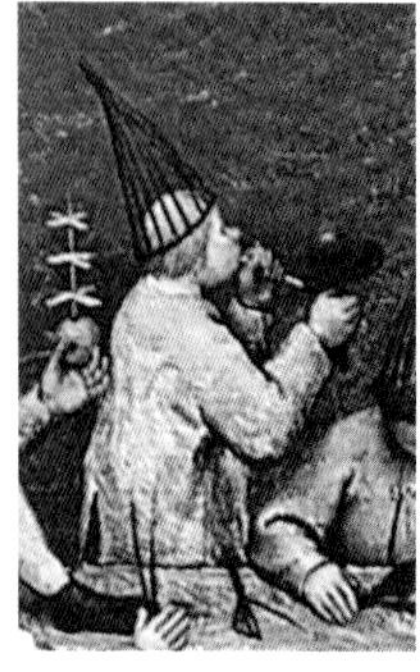

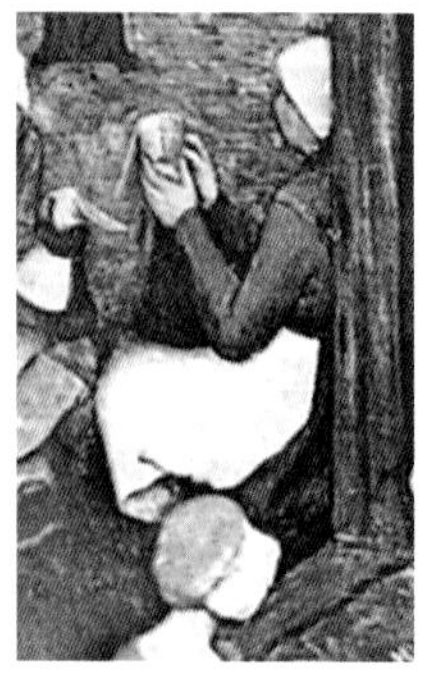

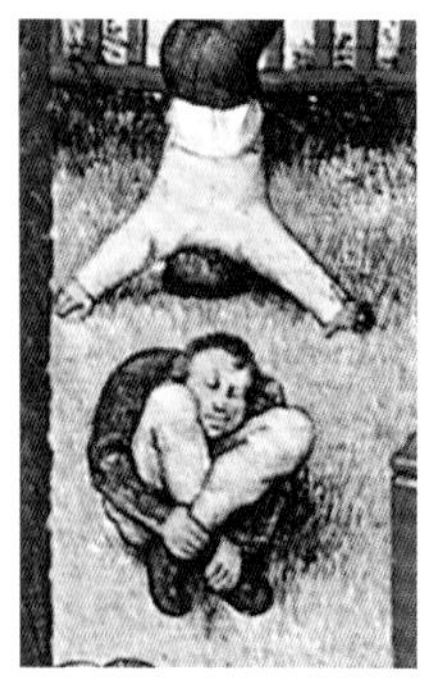

Thus, it was probably in 1545, between the ages of fifteen and twenty, that Bruegel became the apprentice of Pieter Coecke, his first master. His artistic calling was unquestionably awakened long before the end of his apprenticeship. Given his death in 1569, it seems unlikely that he began lessons with Coecke any earlier than 1545. Such a young age at death is hard to believe, given the significance of his work.

Children's Games (detail)

1560
Oil on wood, 118 x 161 cm
Kunsthistorisches Museum, Vienna

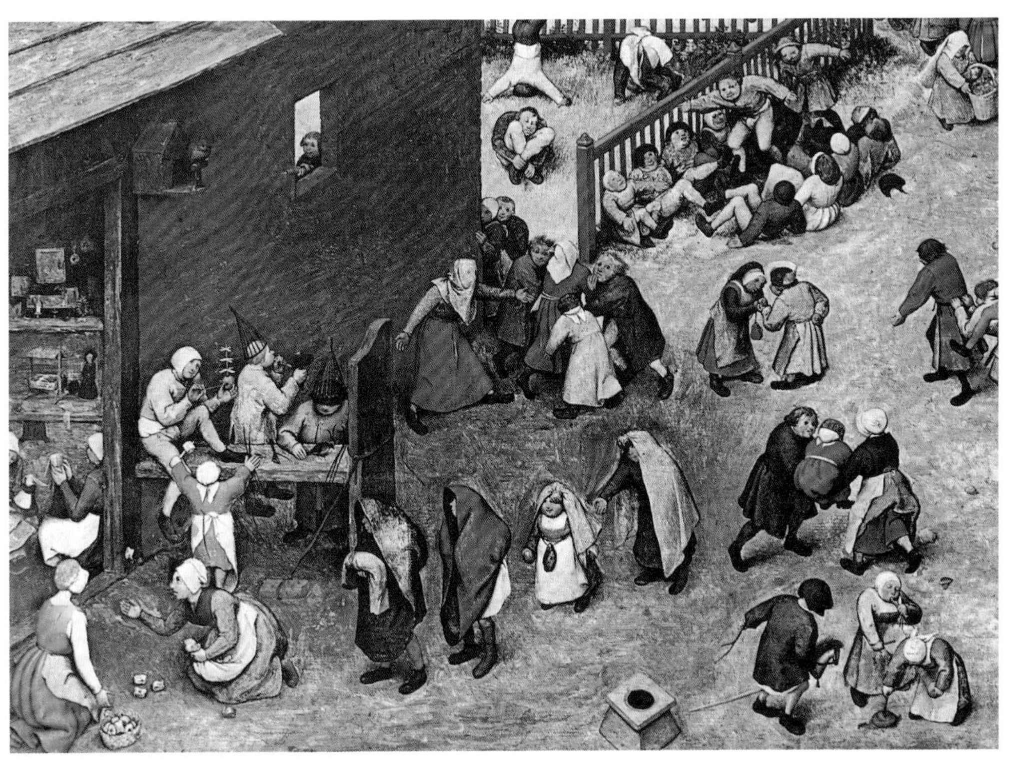

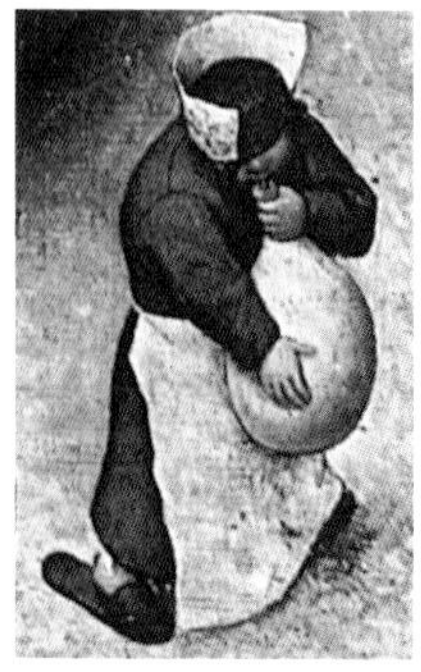

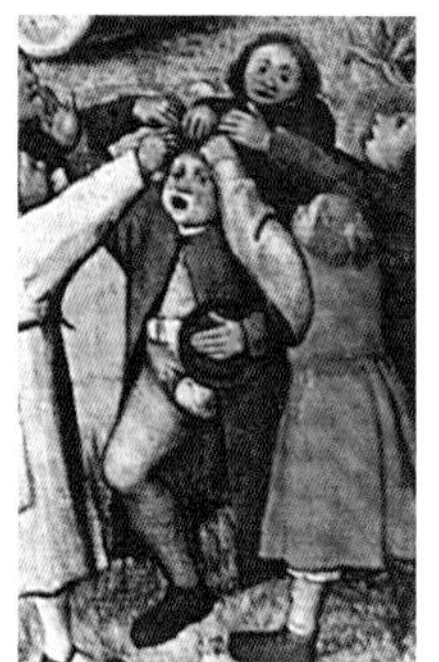

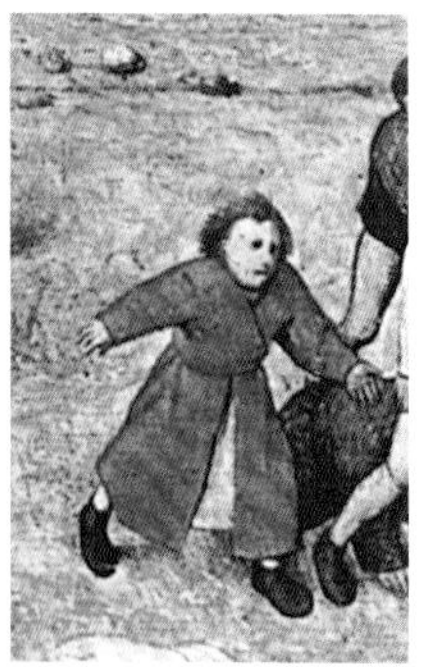

Pieter Bruegel the Elder had two sons and a daughter (Pieter, Jan, and Mayken) with his wife, Mayken Coecke, the daughter of his master Pieter Coecke. The elder son, Pieter, nicknamed 'Hell Brueghel', copied many of his father's works and treated similar subjects with variations. He was particularly known for his images of devilry and Hell, hence his nickname. It is difficult to ascertain the

Children's Games (detail)

1560
Oil on wood, 118 x 161 cm
Kunsthistorisches Museum, Vienna

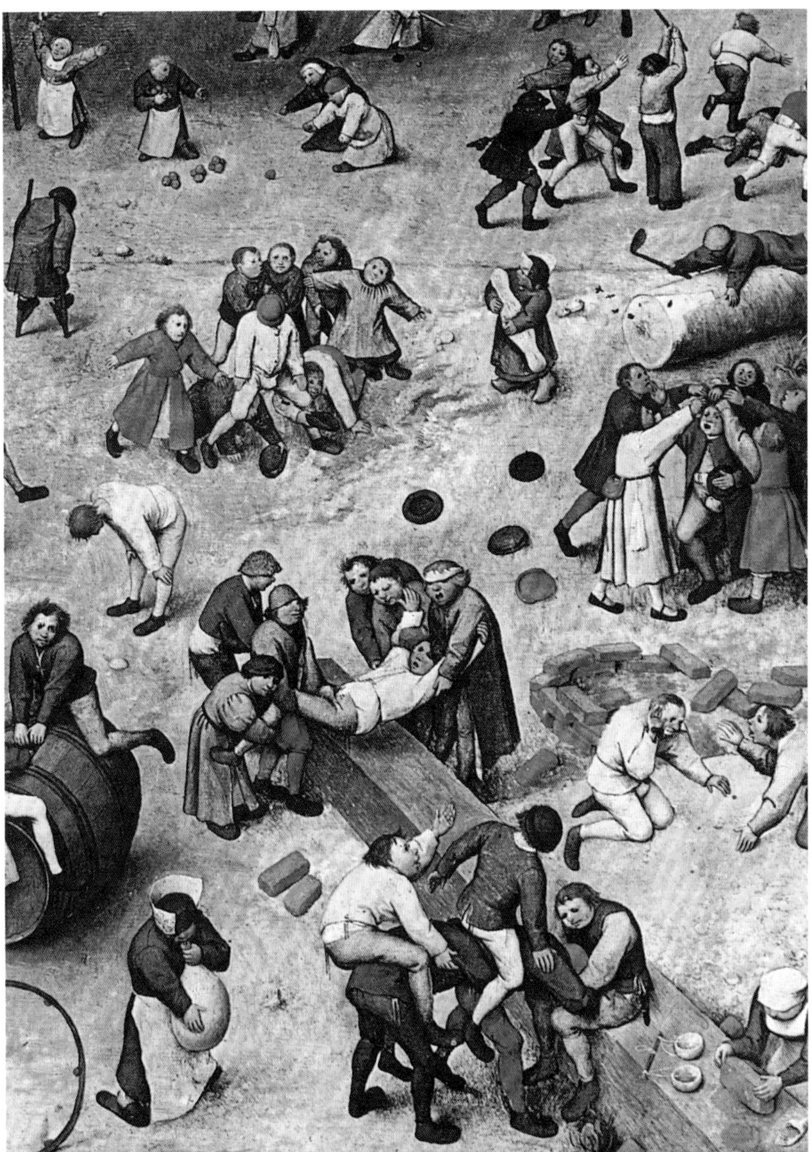

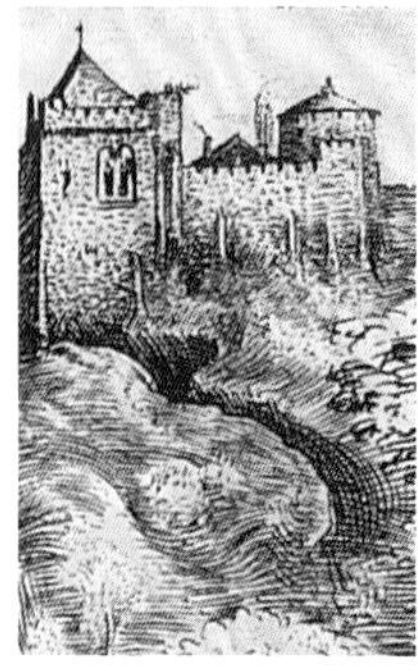

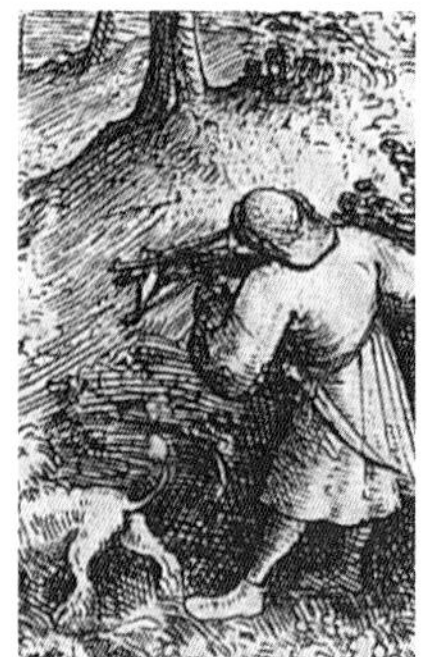

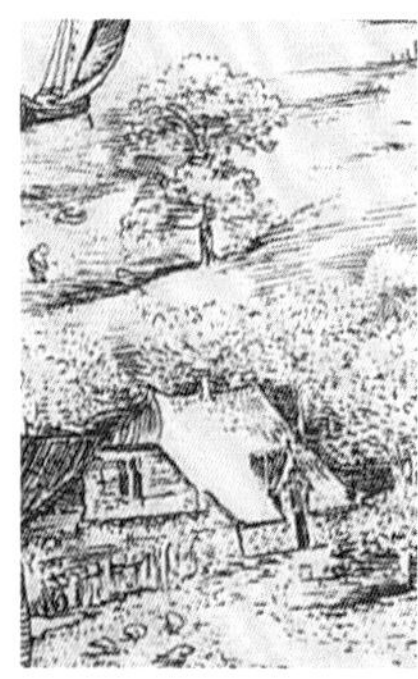

originality of his work where vulgarity seems to have replaced the careful observation and powerful realism of his father. Nevertheless, Pieter Brueghel the Younger was much appreciated by his contemporaries. Van Dyck painted his portrait and the excellent painter of animals, Frans Snyders, was one of his students.

His brother, Jan Brueghel the Elder, nicknamed 'Velvet Brueghel' for the richness of his palette, was by

The Rabbit Hunt

1560
Etching, 22.3 x 29.1 cm
The Royal Library of Albert I, Brussels

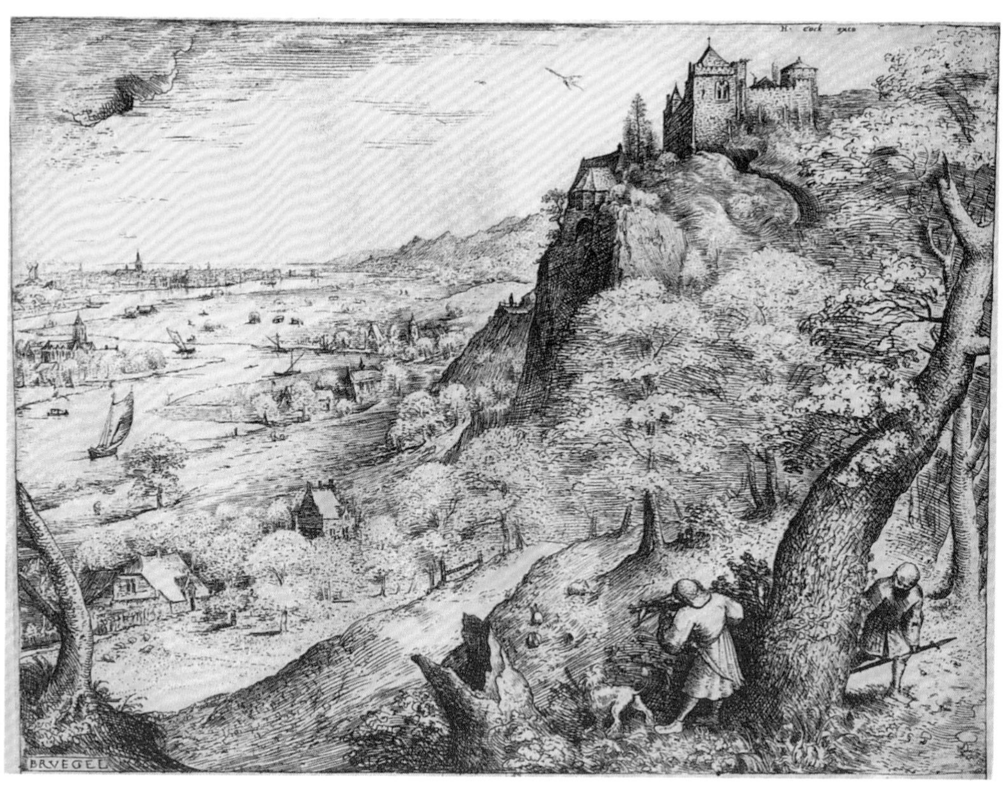
H. cock exc
BRVEGEL

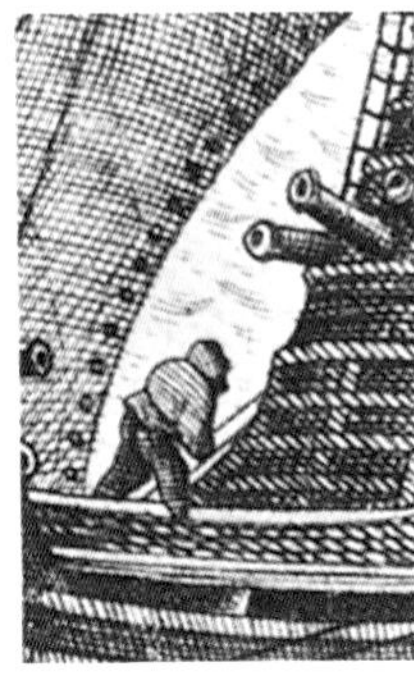

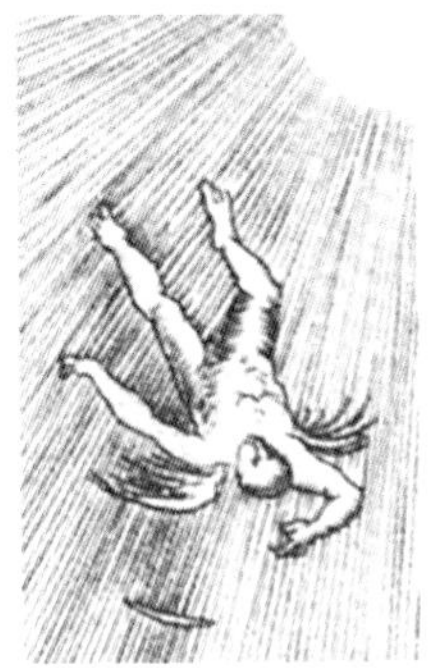

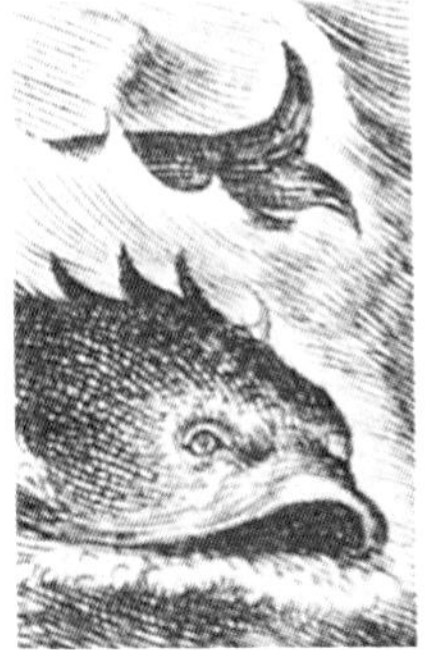

far the better painter. Jan's talent was very personal and full of charm, and he painted many canvases in collaboration with Rubens. He was an extremely talented painter of flowers, capturing their splendour and heady perfumed atmosphere. Pieter Brueghel the Younger and Jan Brueghel the Elder both had sons that also became painters. Pieter III, son of Pieter the Younger, and Jan the Younger, son of Jan the Elder.

Sailing Vessels

1560-1565
Engraving, 22.1 x 28.7 cm
British Museum, London

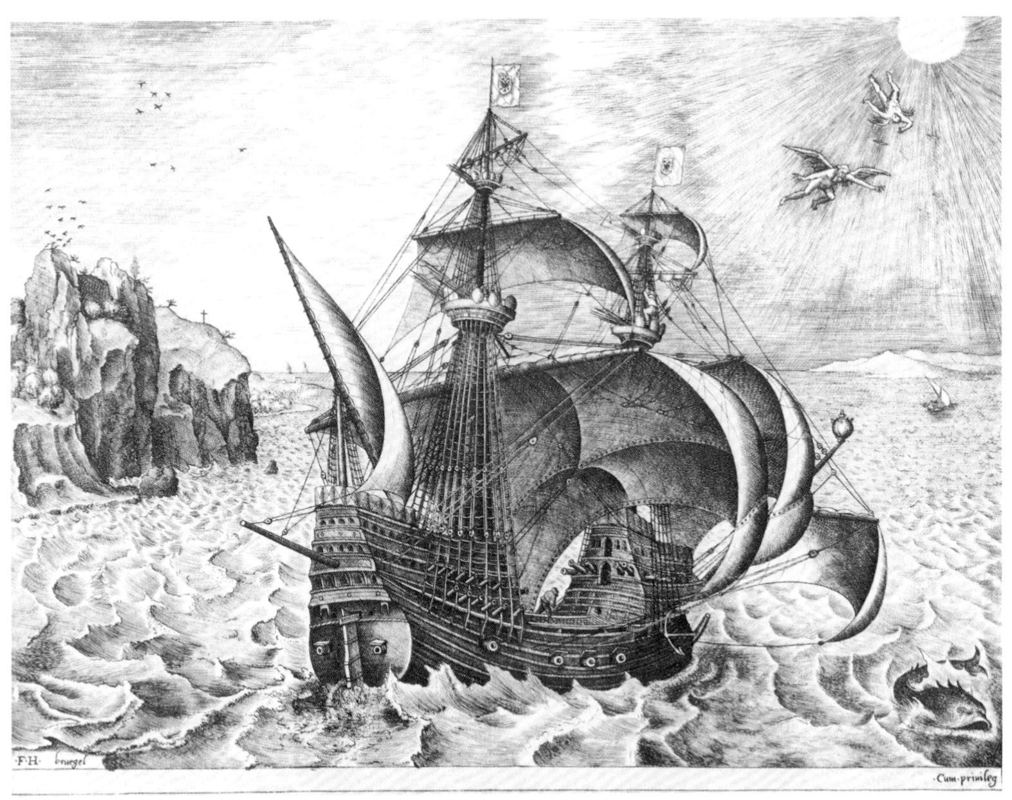

·F·H· bruegel
·Cum·priuileg

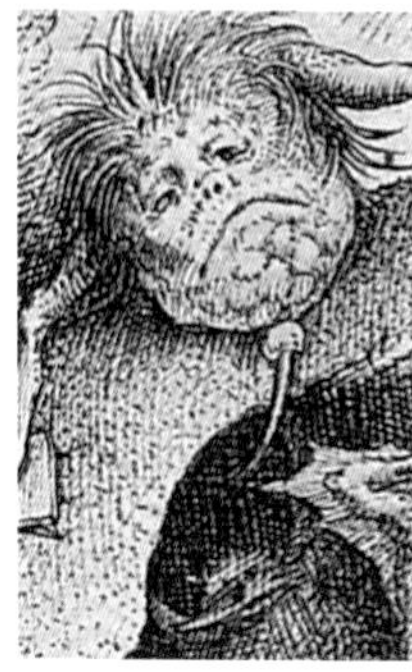

Anne Brueghel, the sister of Jan Brueghel the Younger, would marry David Teniers the Younger, thus assuring the continuation of one of the most numerous and glorious of the many dynasties of Netherlandish painters.

After learning the basics from Coecke, Pieter Bruegel the Elder left to work in the studio of Hieronymus Cock, who was more a merchant of paintings and engravings than he was painter. He acquired a great deal of fame

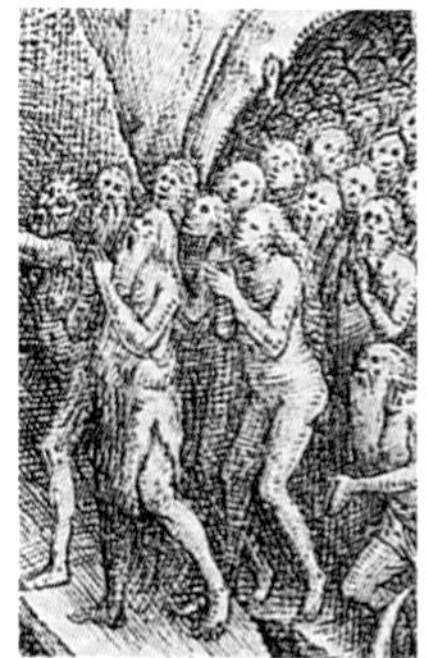

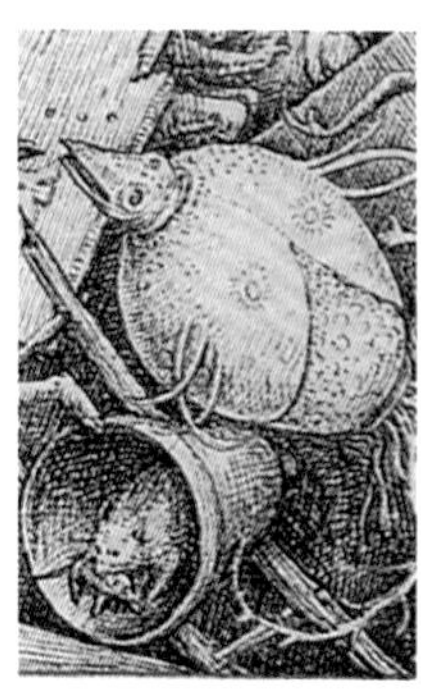

Christ's Descent into Limbo

1561
Pen and brown ink, 23.1 x 30.1 cm
Graphische Sammlung, Albertina, Vienna

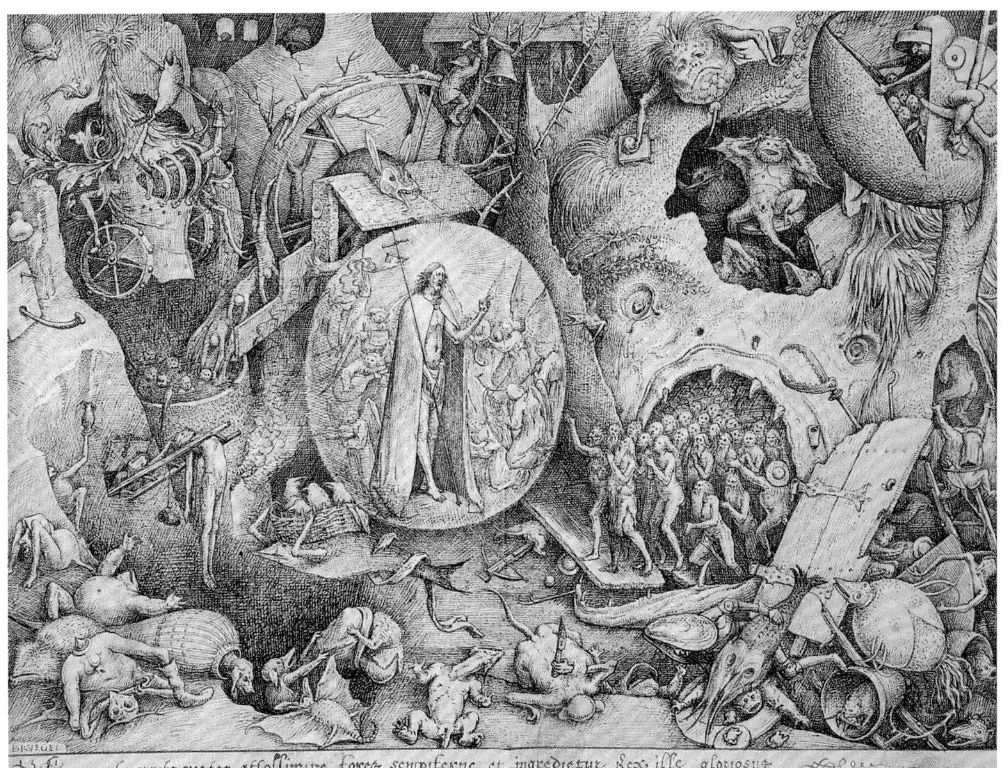
BRVEGEL
Tollite o porte capita vestra attollimine fores sempiterne et ingredietur Rex ille gloriosus

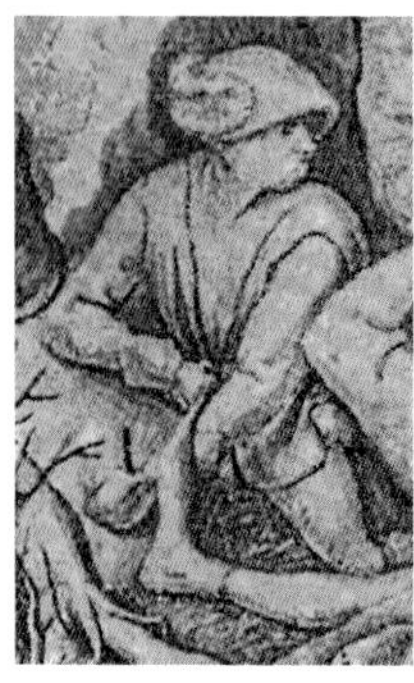

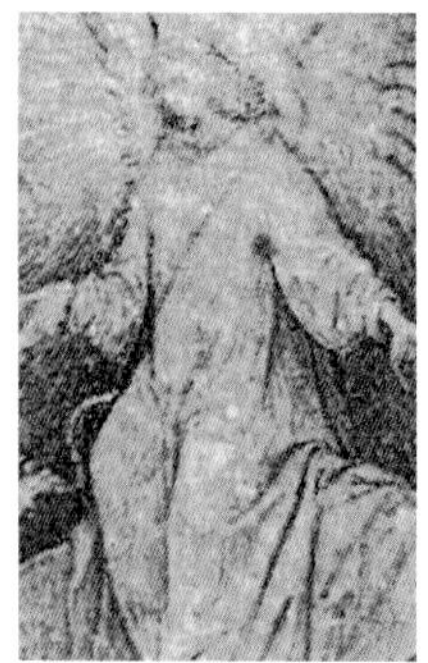

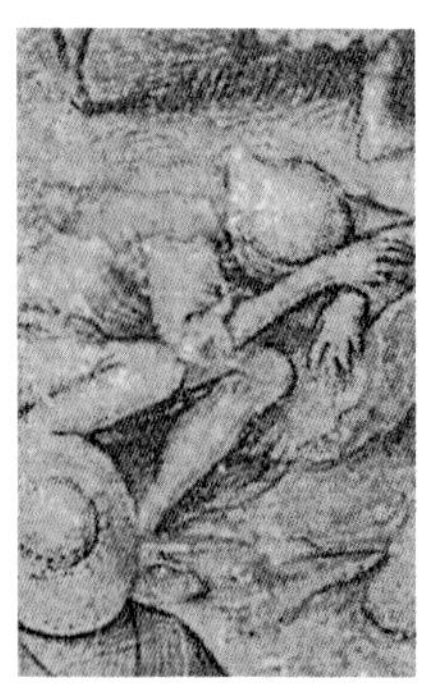

as an engraver and created a large number of plates for his shop.

At the beginning of his career, Bruegel composed many mountainous backgrounds that were complicated, picturesque, and imposing. He submitted to the influence of Cock's studio, docilely accepting the lessons that enabled him to properly interpret nature and already furnishing his master with a profitable product.

The Resurrection

c. 1562
Pen and brown ink highlighted with grey paint, 43.1 x 30.7 cm
Museum Boijmans Van Beuningen, Rotterdam

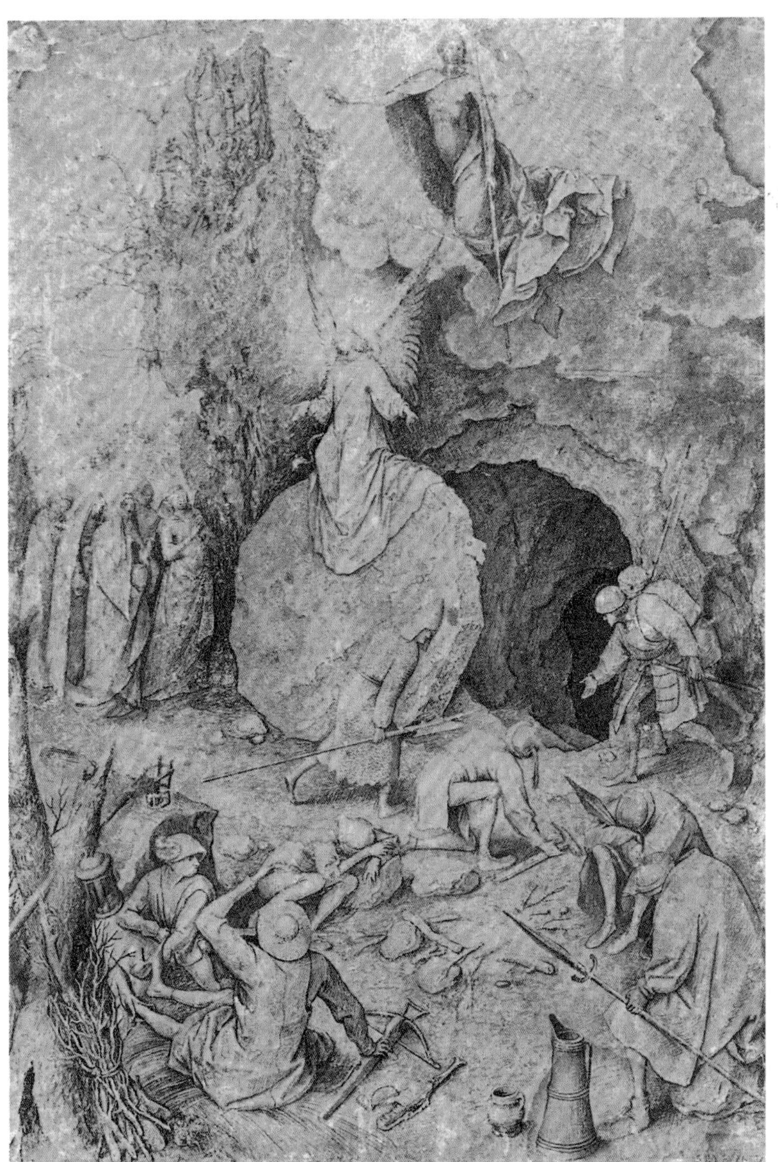

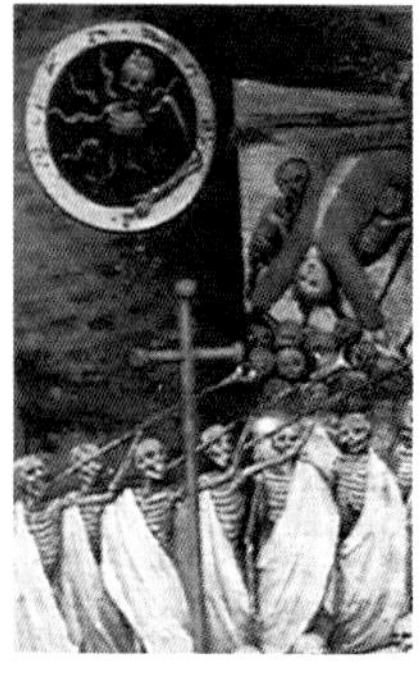

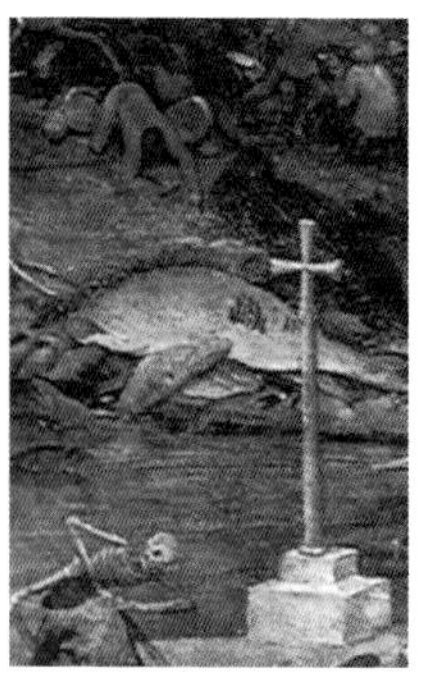

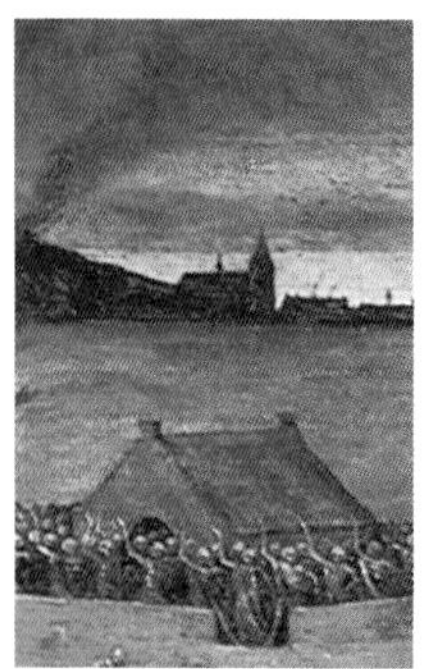

Among these, he must have sensed a natural attraction for the fantastical subjects of Hieronymus Bosch, and the comical popular scenes of Pieter Aertsen and Quentin Matsys, from which may have sprung the spark that would set his genius afire.

In keeping with the fashion of the times, Bruegel exhibited a strong and legitimate desire to study the Italian masterpieces in Italy. Two of his etchings,

The Triumph of Death

c. 1562
Oil on panel, 117 x 162 cm
Museo del Prado, Madrid

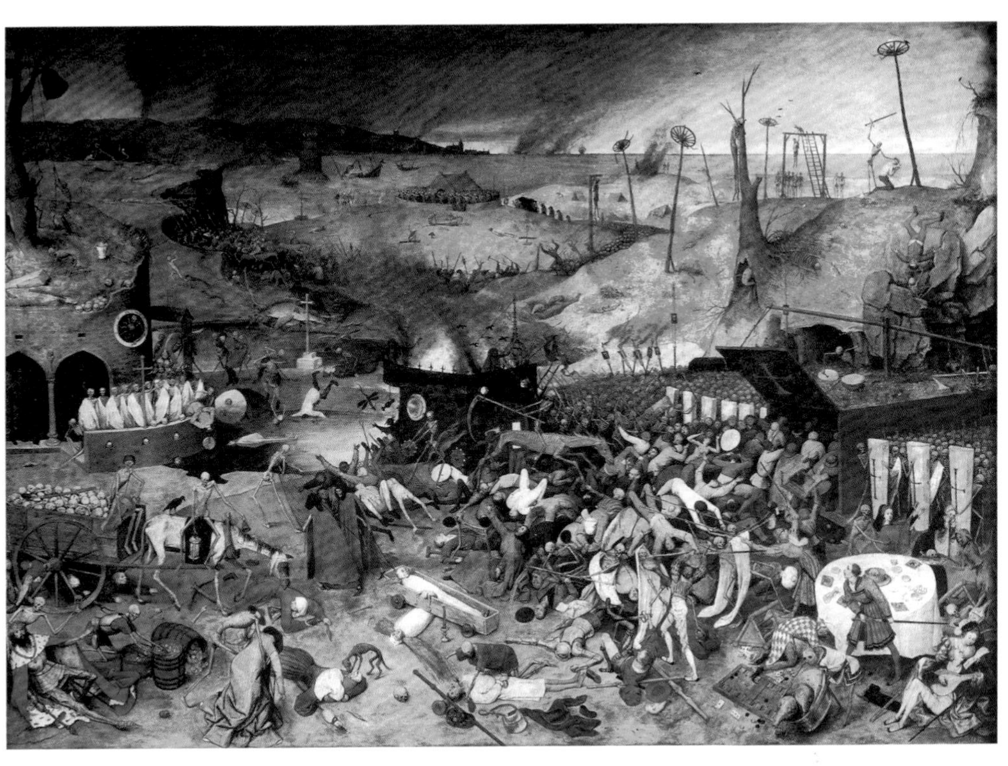

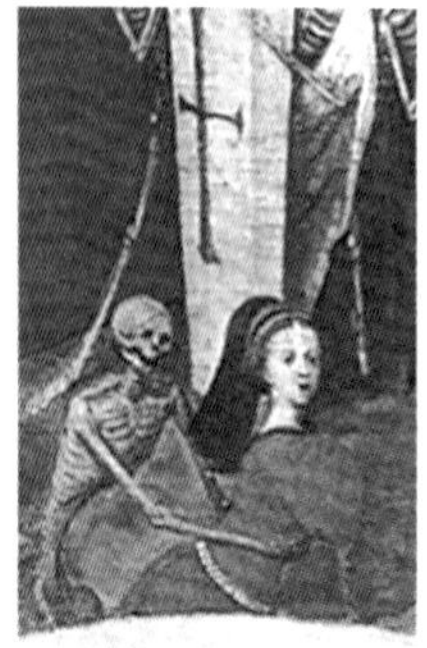

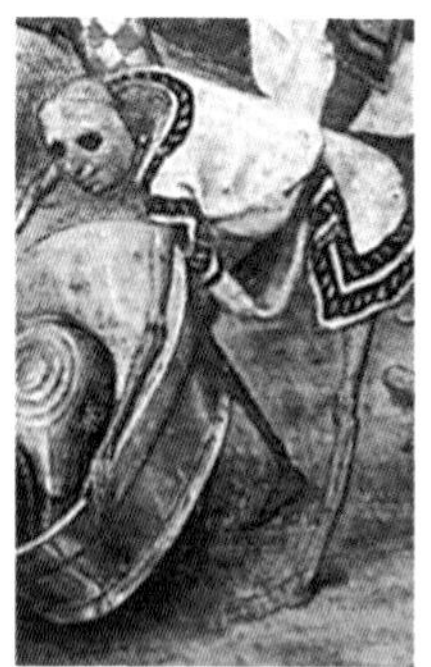

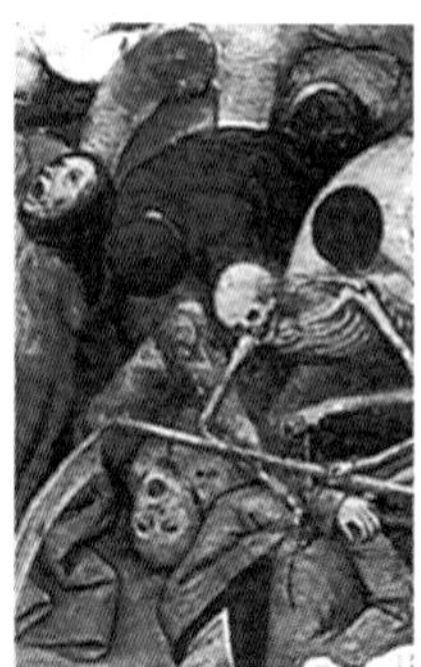

The Abduction of Psyche and *Daedalus and Icarus*, both signed and dated in Rome, are irrefutable evidence of his presence in the Eternal City. His work shows no trace of the influence that foreign beauty might have inspired, showing clear proof that he was not attracted to Italy by an invincible force. Bruegel was simply too artistic not to be curious to want to know Italy. In the aesthetic

The Triumph of Death (detail)

c. 1562
Oil on panel, 117 x 162 cm
Museo del Prado, Madrid

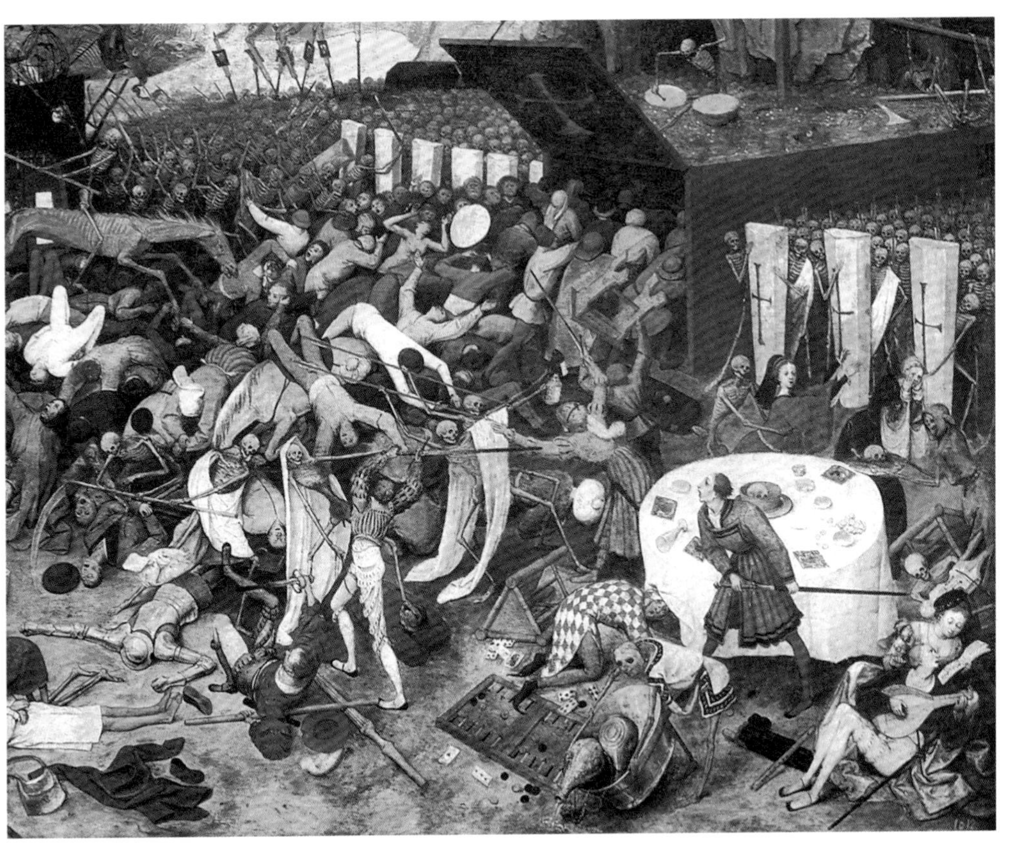

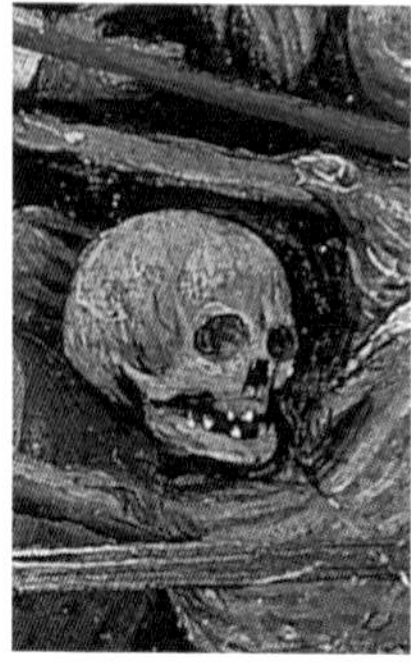

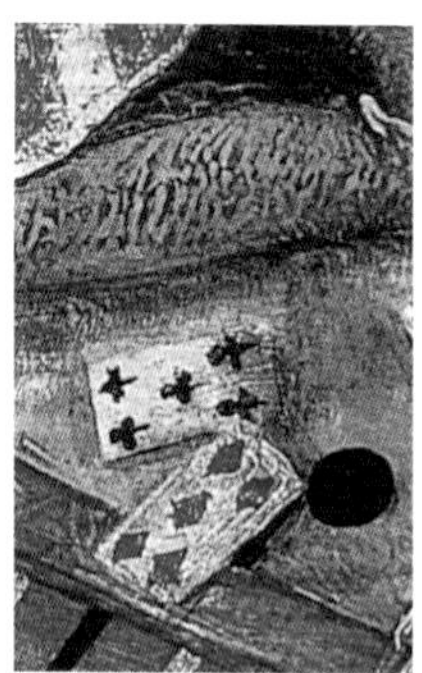

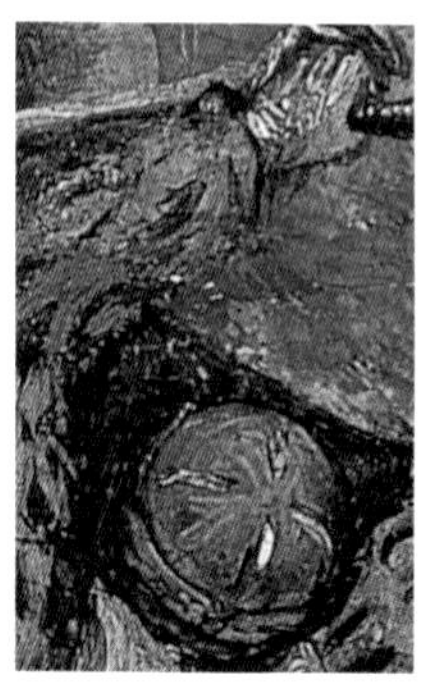

discussions in Hieronymus Cock's studio, the young Bruegel's spirit must have been excited to hear about the Italian masterpieces whose mastery he could not deny, even with his limited knowledge.

It is clear that Bruegel as a young peasant must have had an adventurous spirit to have left his village of birth to come to the city and find his fortune and career in the arts. Despite all of this, Bruegel set off with the money

The Triumph of Death (detail)

c. 1562
Oil on panel, 117 x 162 cm
Museo del Prado, Madrid

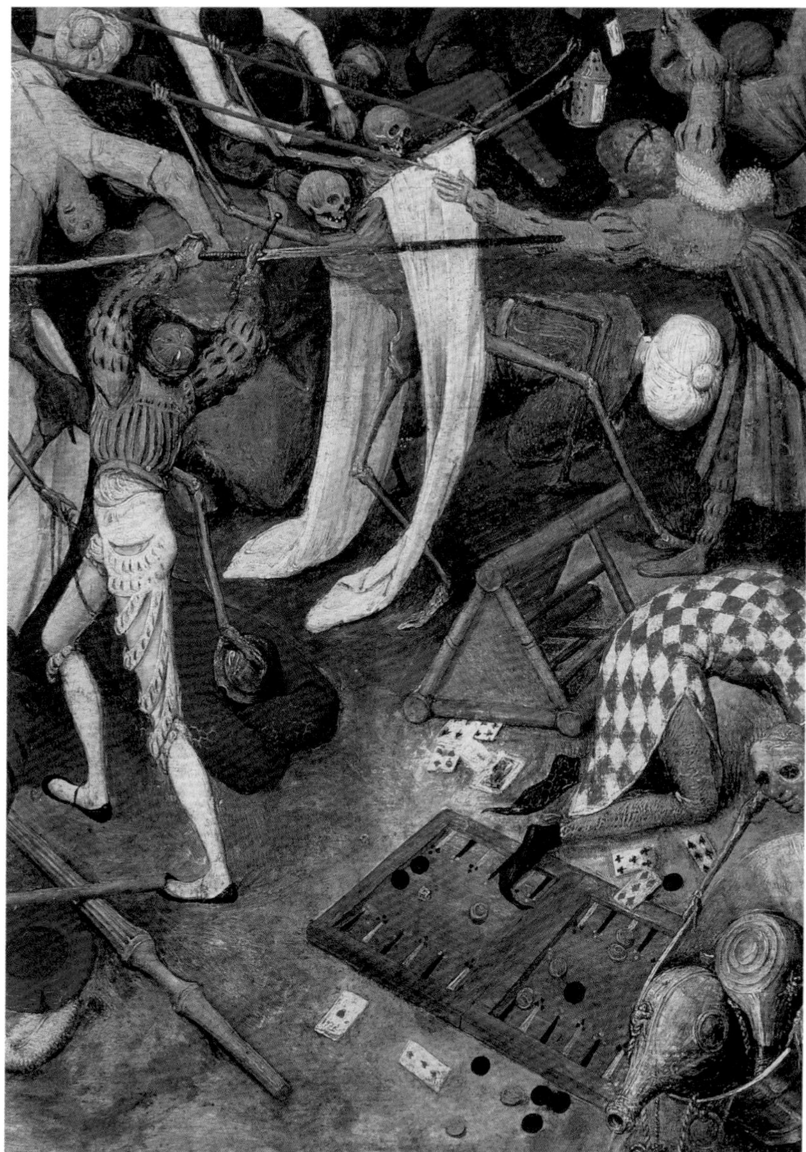

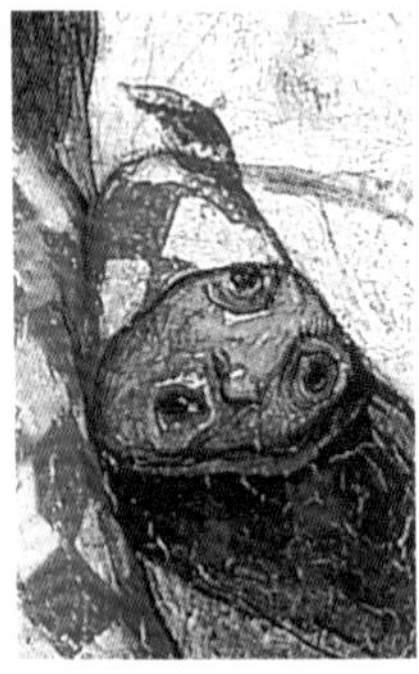

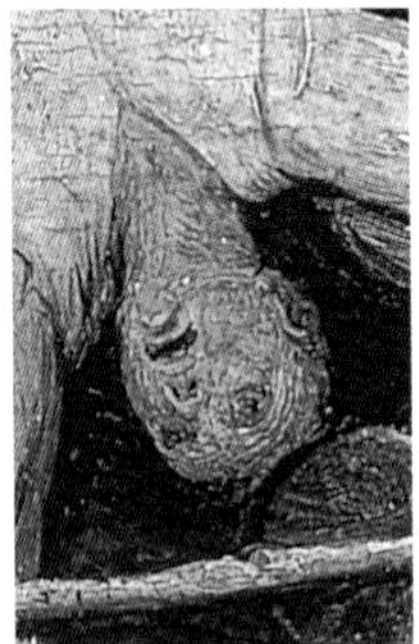

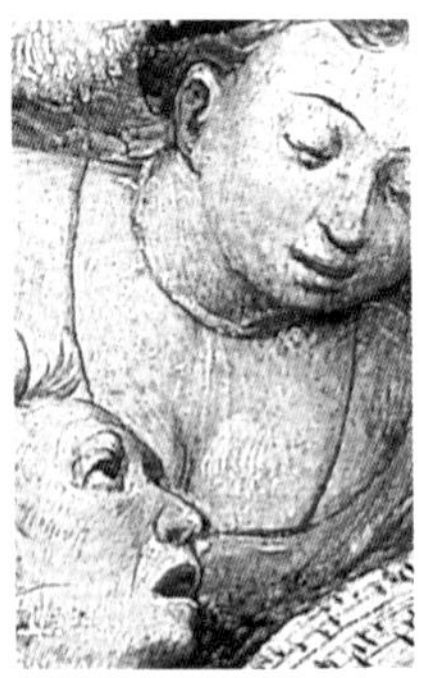

that he was able to save from what Cock had paid him for his work. Importantly and irrefutably, it should be remembered that Bruegel was added as a master to the register of the Guild of Saint Luke in 1551.

Bruegel, who decidedly did not go to Italy to copy its revolutionary masterpieces, was more interested by the changing landscape. Rome was not the goal of his peregrinations. He continued southwards to arrive at

The Triumph of Death (detail)

c. 1562
Oil on panel, 117 x 162 cm
Museo del Prado, Madrid

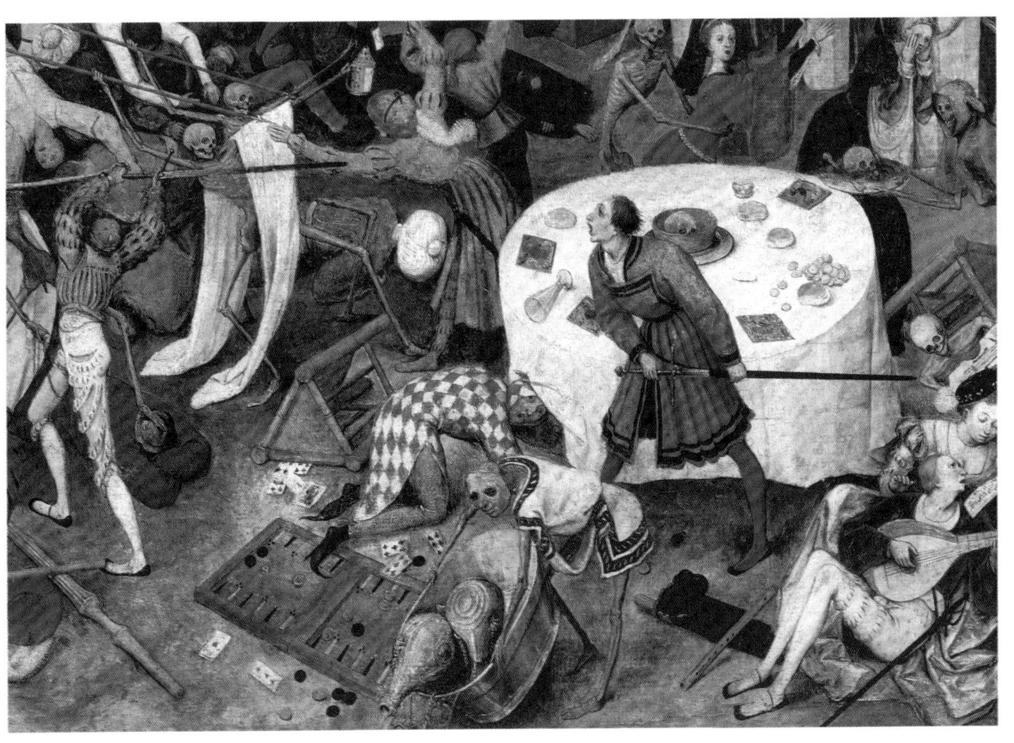

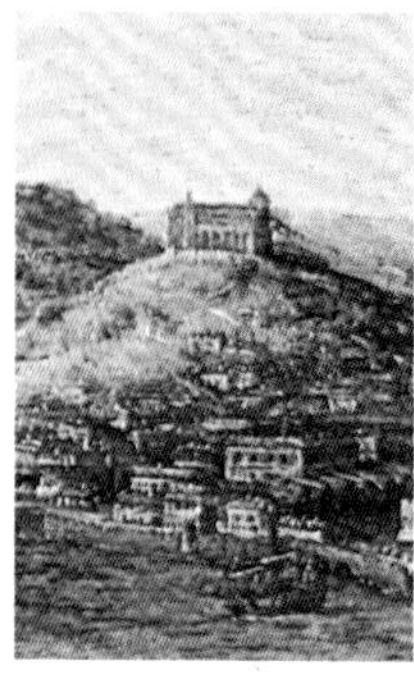

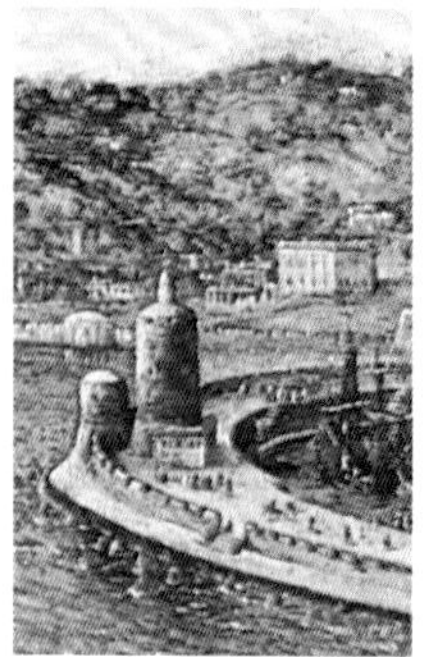

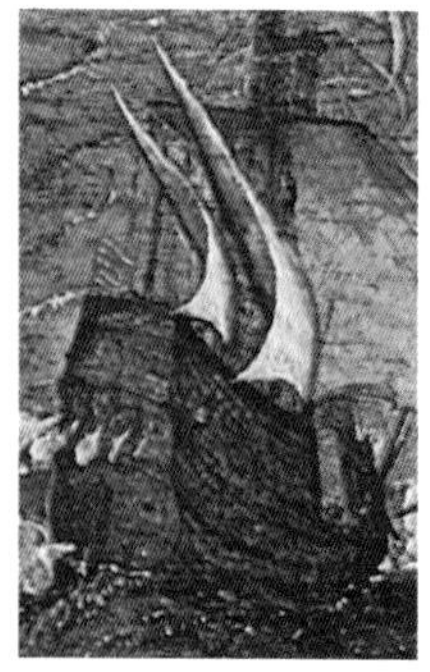

the Straits of Messina, where, after his months of mountain travel, he seems to have been filled with wonder by the sight of the Mediterranean, which was laid out like an azure blanket. He seized his tools and eagerly captured the general lines of the view, which he would later use in his *Naval Combat in the Straits of Messina*, engraved by Frans Huys in 1561, with its strange and varied warships.

Naval Battle in the Gulf of Naples

c. 1562
Oil on wood, 42 x 71 cm
Galleria Doria Pamphilj, Rome

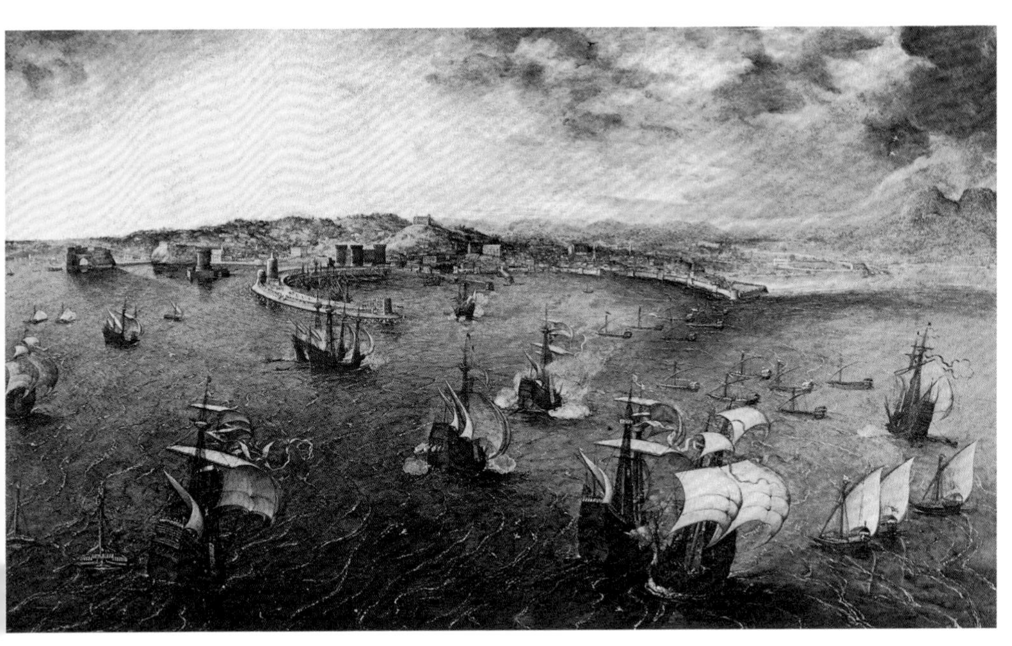

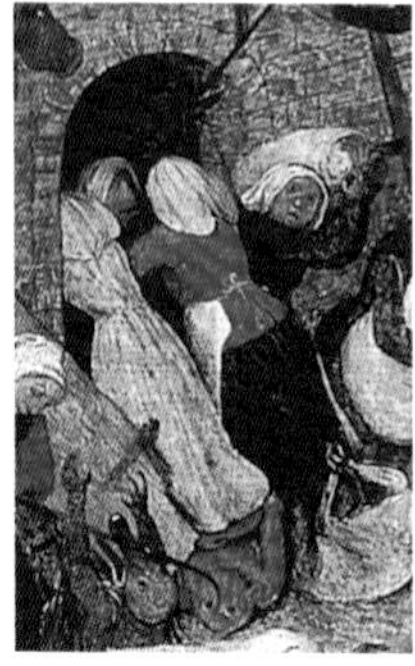

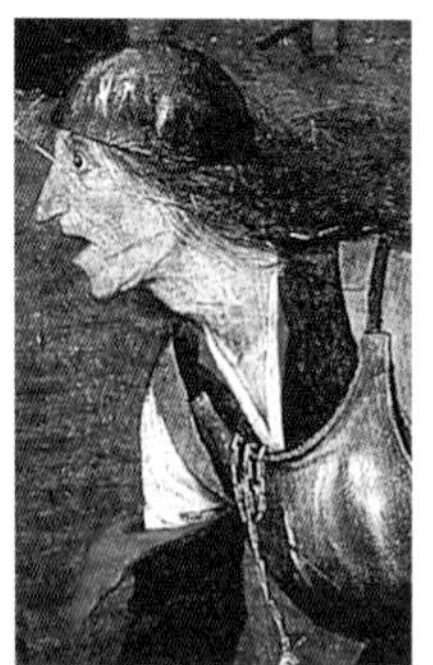

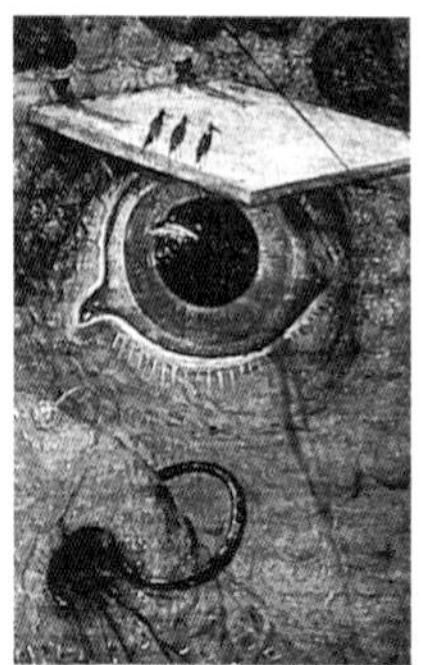

Bruegel returned to the studio of Hieronymus Cock in Antwerp at the end of 1553. By this time he had become a true collaborator, and Cock printed Bruegel's works which were produced during the period following his return. Given the great number of copies of Bruegel's engravings, his work must have been very popular. All the activity of the young artist was taken up by the creation of drawings, which were then rendered

Dulle Griet or Mad Meg

1562
Oil on wood, 117.4 x 162 cm
Museum Mayer van den Bergh, Antwerp

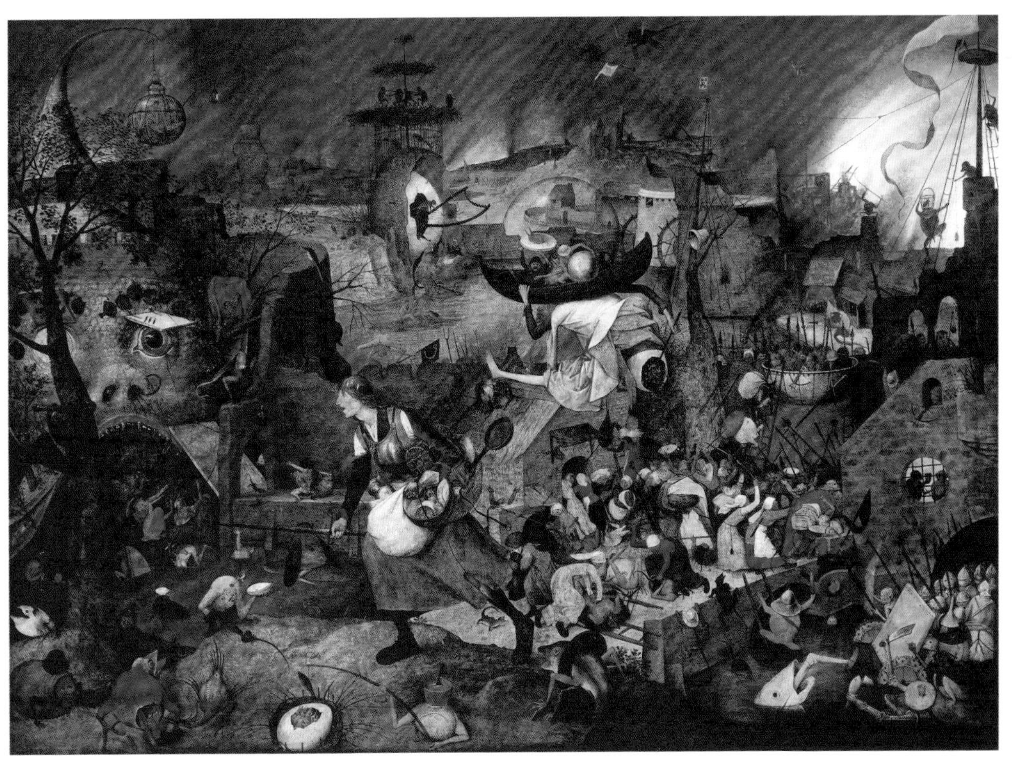

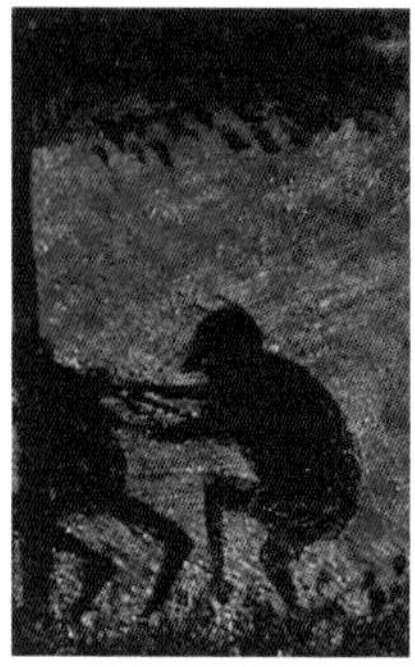
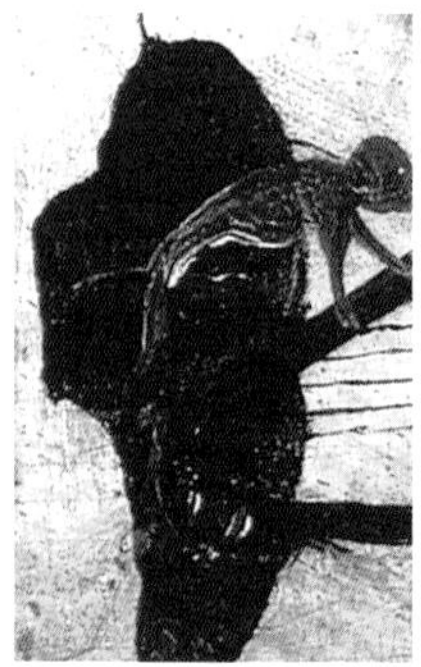
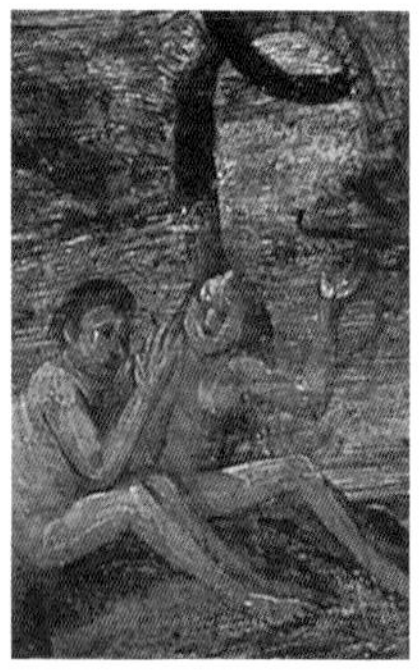

by the more or less skilled engravers employed by Cock. Cock's studio specialised in landscapes and diabolical imagery, so these were the genres in which Bruegel exercised his talent, particularly with landscapes in the beginning.

Upon his return, Bruegel was newly taken by the beauty of the countryside of the Brabant region, with its gently rolling fields, its refreshing little pools of water

Dulle Griet or Mad Meg (detail)

1562
Oil on wood, 117.4 x 162 cm
Museum Mayer van den Bergh, Antwerp

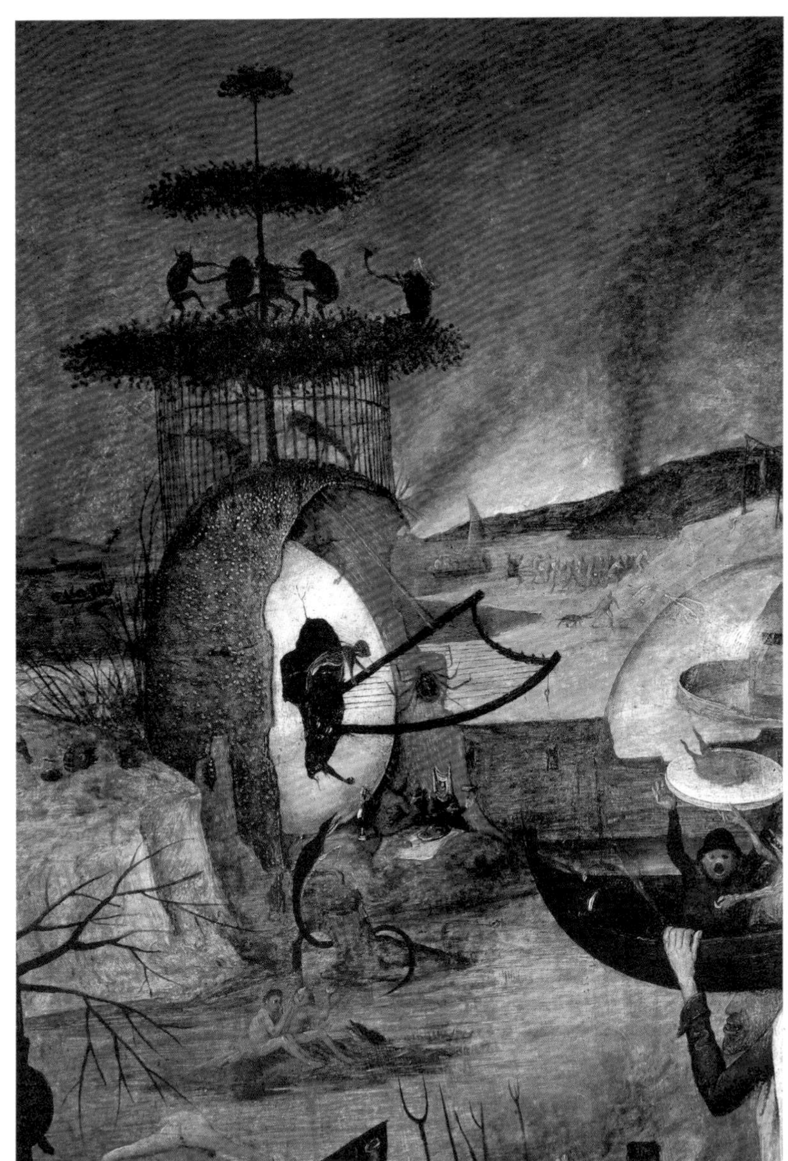

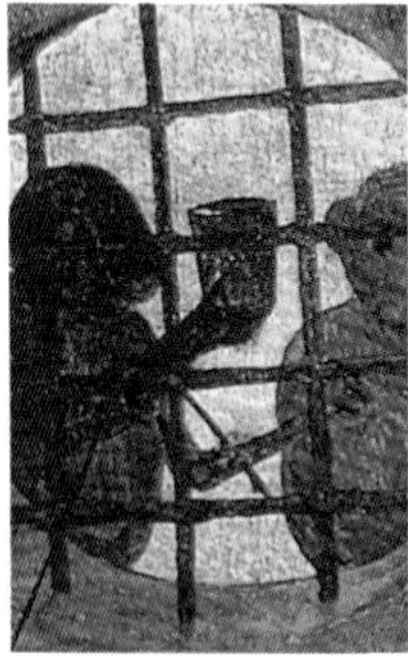

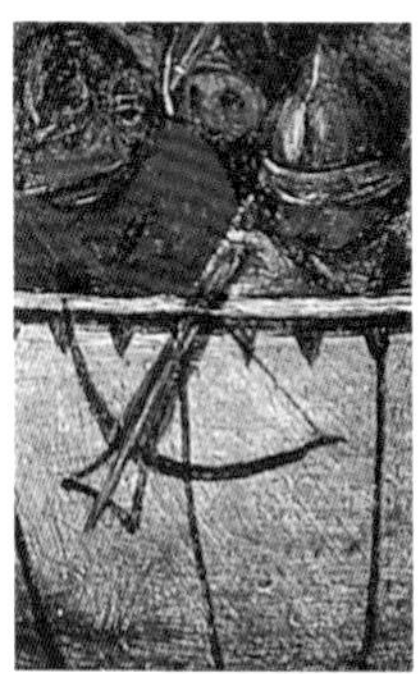

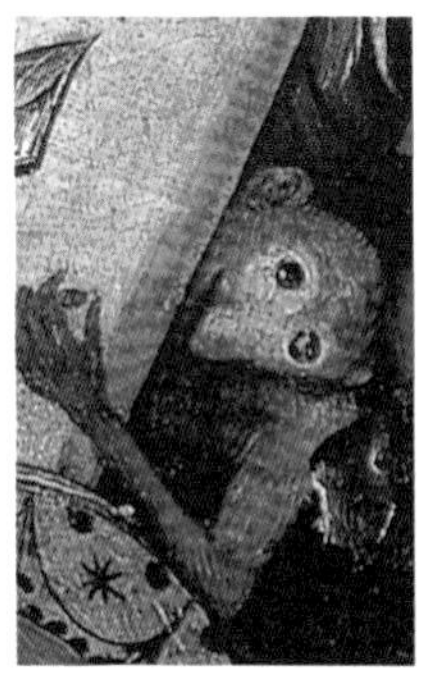

bordered by fringes of trees, and its arid and desolate moors. Even though he never completely banished his obsession with the rocky valleys of the Alps, it sufficed for him to see once more what the most sensitive of modern authors have described as "faces in the glow of their native land", for their invincible charm to disturb and erode the memory of the grandiose landscapes that he had brought back from abroad.

Dulle Griet or Mad Meg (detail)

1562
Oil on wood, 117.4 x 162 cm
Museum Mayer van den Bergh, Antwerp

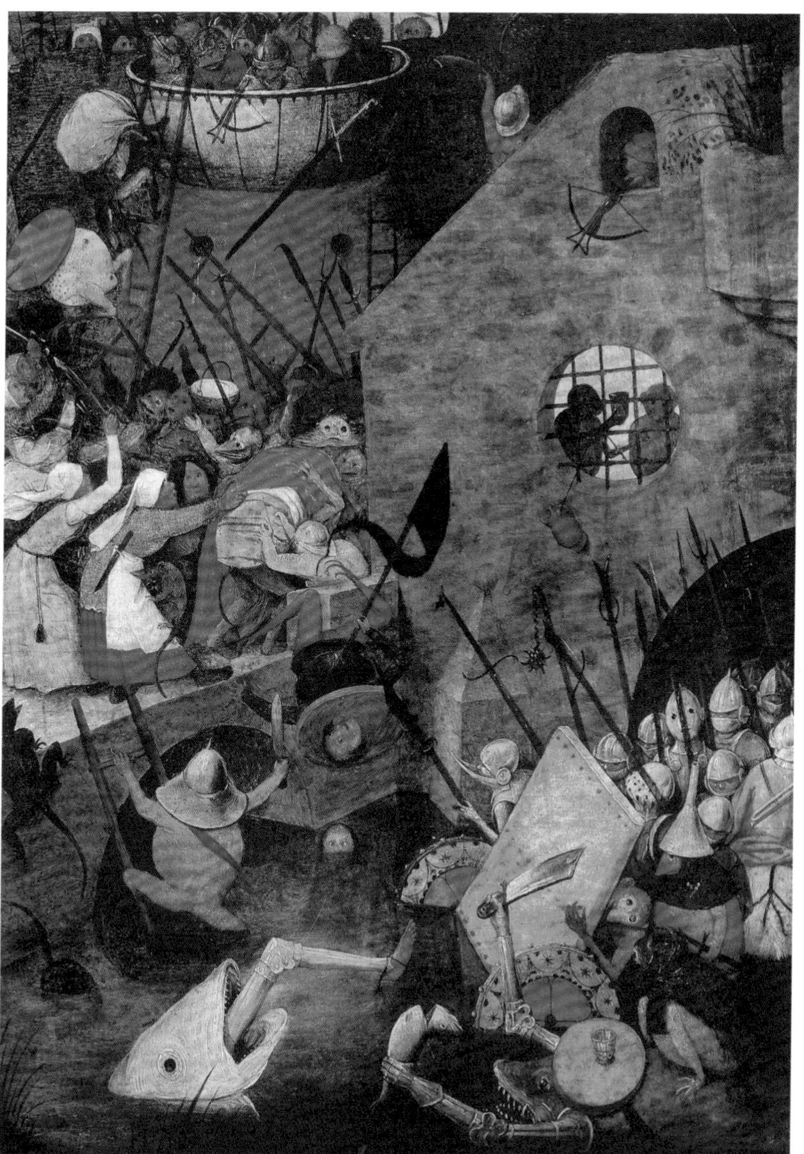

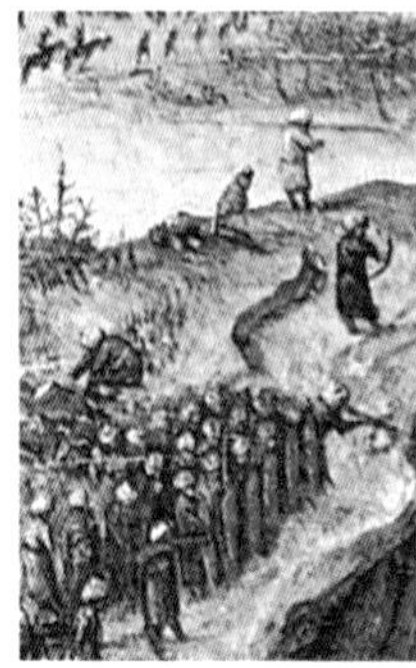

It was perhaps at his printer's request that Bruegel drew exclusively alpine landscapes based on the studies he brought back from the Tirol. The incontestable grandeur of these drawings is striking. The artist's eye encompasses immense reaches.

Before following the development of Bruegel's art that led him towards the Flemish landscape, the other aspect of his activity during his time in the studio of

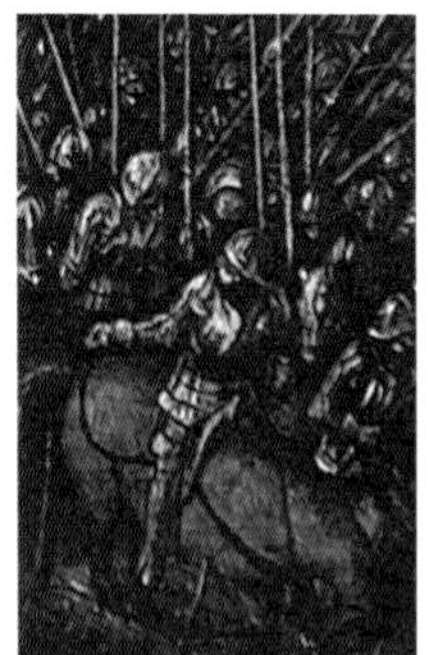

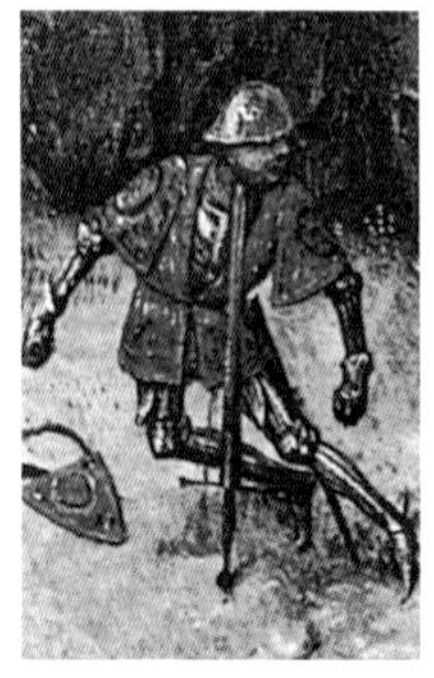

Battle between the Israelites and the Philistines

1562
Oil on wood panel, 33.5 x 55 cm
Kunsthistorisches Museum, Vienna

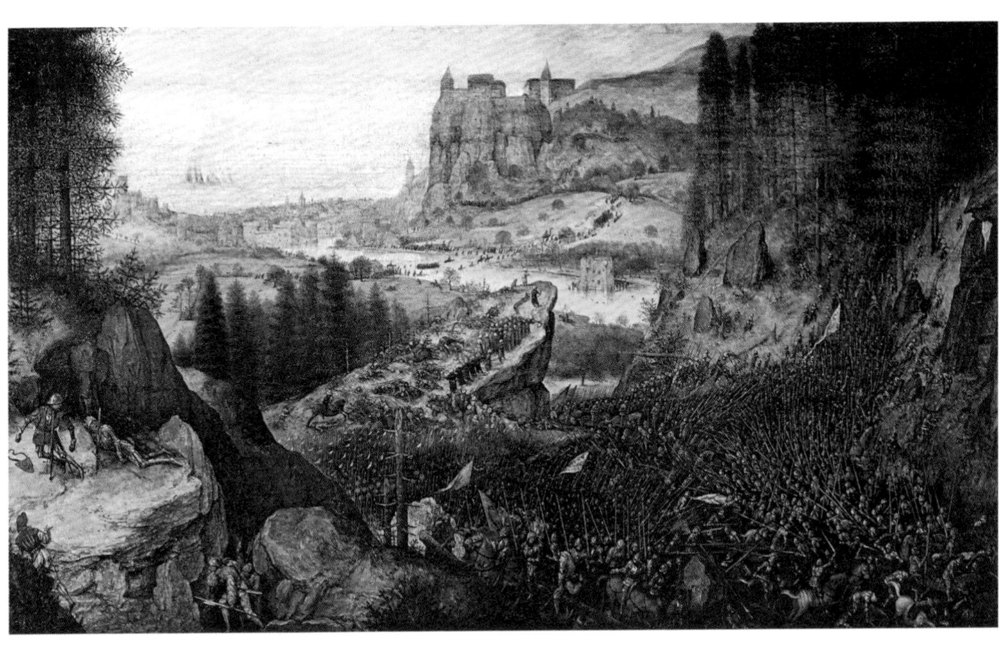

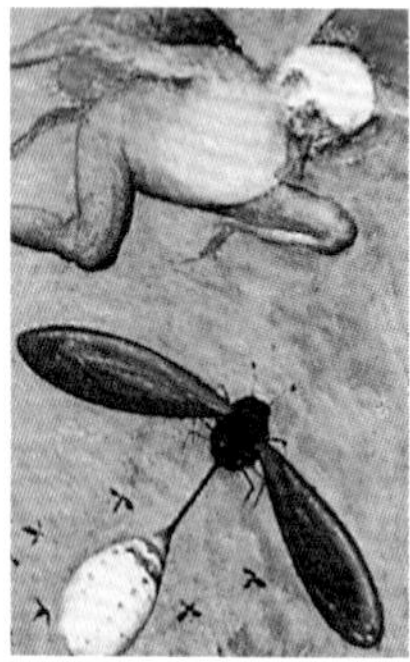

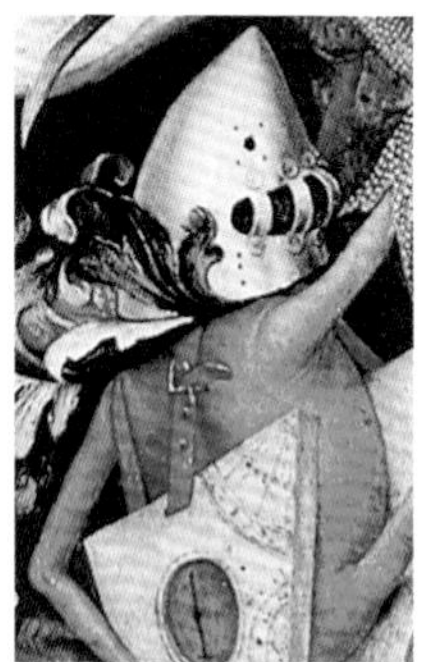

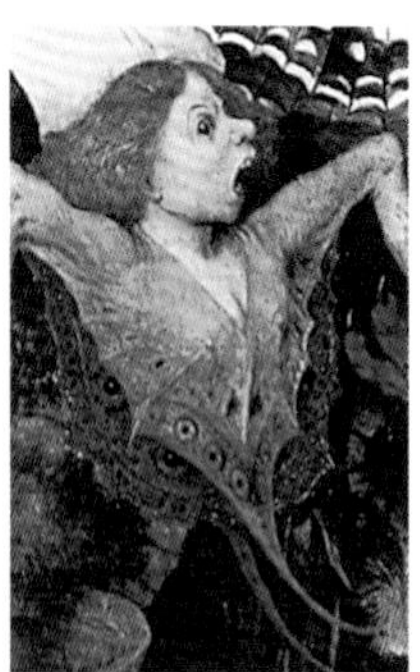

Hieronymus Cock needs to be examined. It should be noted that up to this time, Bruegel still had not expressed himself through painting, an act that would not occur for a few years to come. After returning from Italy and the humorous genre of Bosch and his school, Bruegel took into account the requests of his printer, Cock, and devoted himself entirely to the lucrative creation of drawings. Cock printed a great number of highly

The Fall of the Rebel Angels

1562
Oil on wood, 118.5 x 162.5 cm
Königliche Museen der Schönen Künste, Brussels

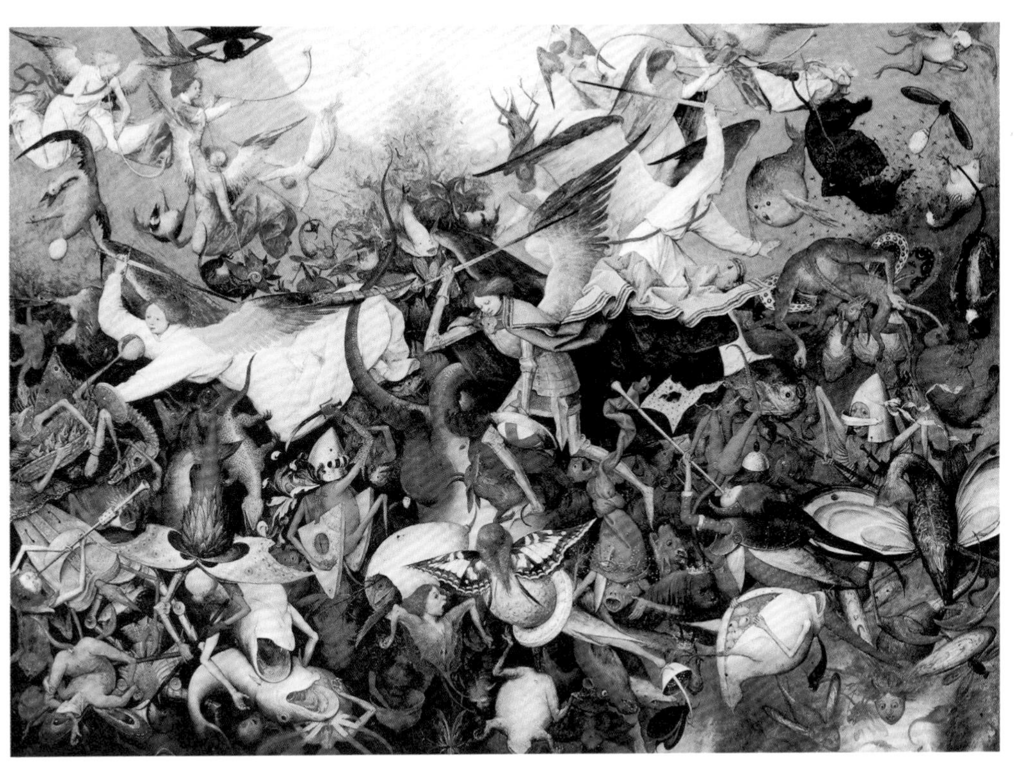

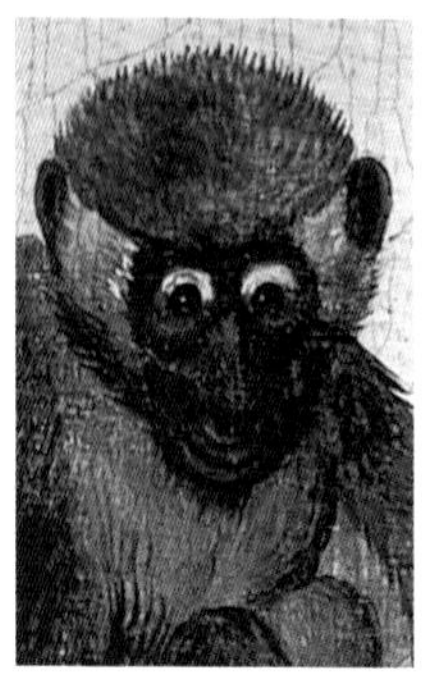

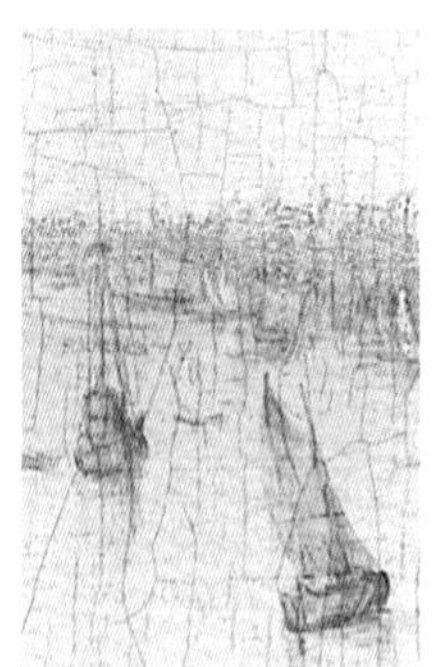

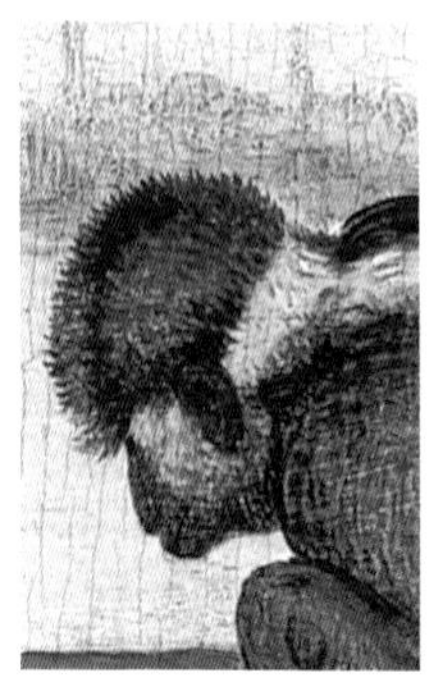

popular engravings of devilries. The naturally caustic and racy temperament of Bruegel led him to cultivate this genre, which was also a sure source of revenue.

As has already been mentioned, Bruegel's talent was particularly suited to this kind of work. Upon his return from Italy in 1553, he created the famous print *Skaters before the Gate of Saint George,* which was engraved by Frans Huys for Hieronymus Cock.

Two Chained Monkeys

1562
Oil on oak panel, 20 x 23 cm
Staatliche Museen, Gemäldegalerie, Berlin

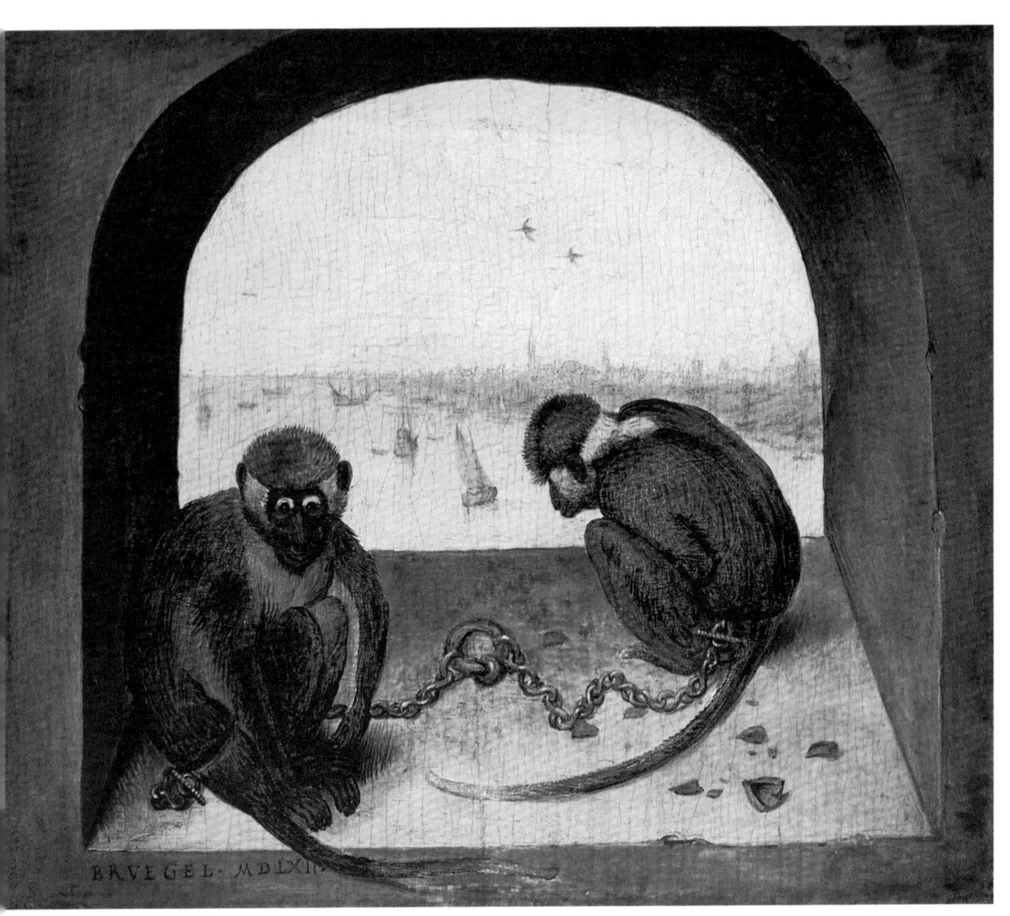
BRVEGEL·MDLXII

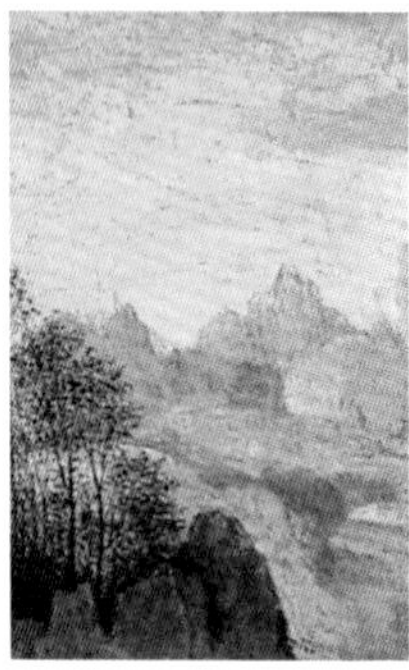

The scene takes place on the moat of the Saint George Gate in Antwerp. A great number of skaters, sketched from life, evolve across the ice in all directions. With a summary and accurate gesture, Bruegel is able to indicate a pose to characterise an attitude. He presents an entire crowd where each individual, while maintaining his individual characteristics, contributes to

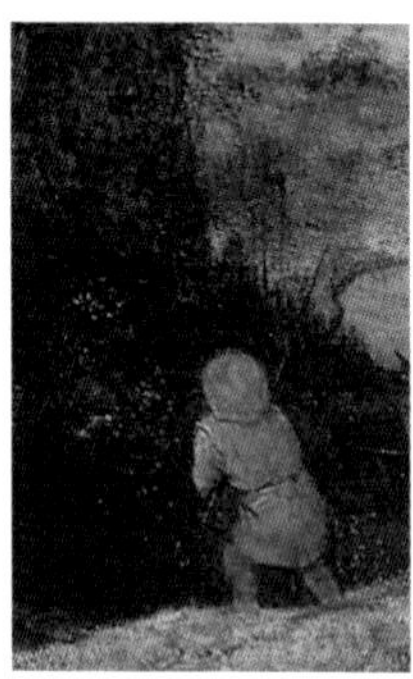

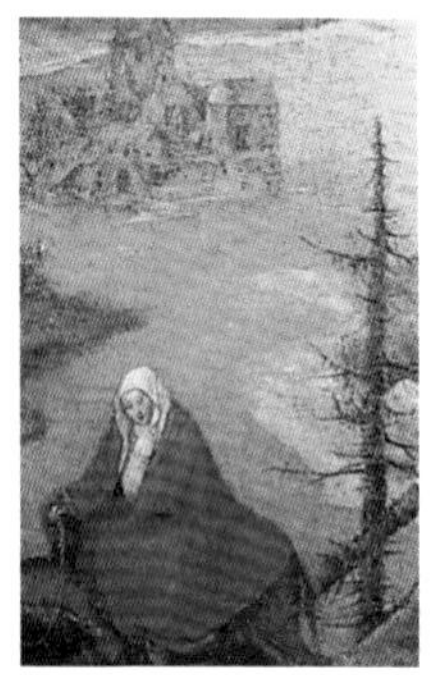

The Flight into Egypt

1563
Oil on canvas, 37 x 56 cm
Courtauld Institute of Art, London

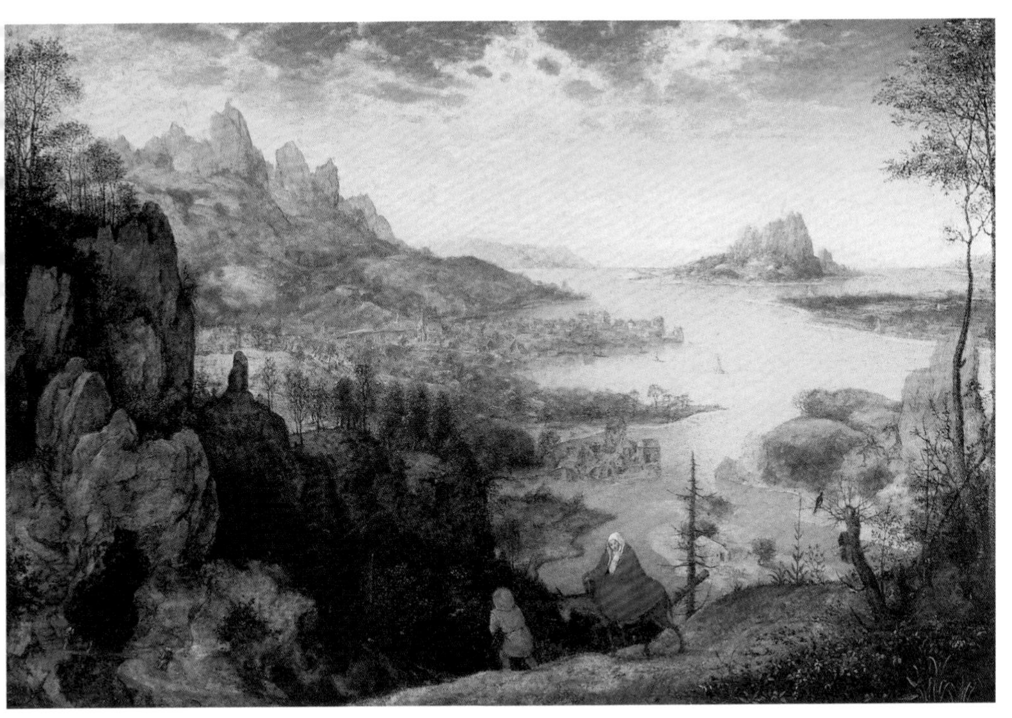

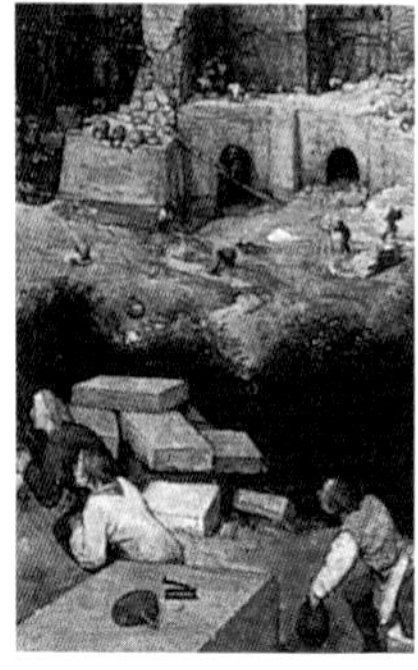

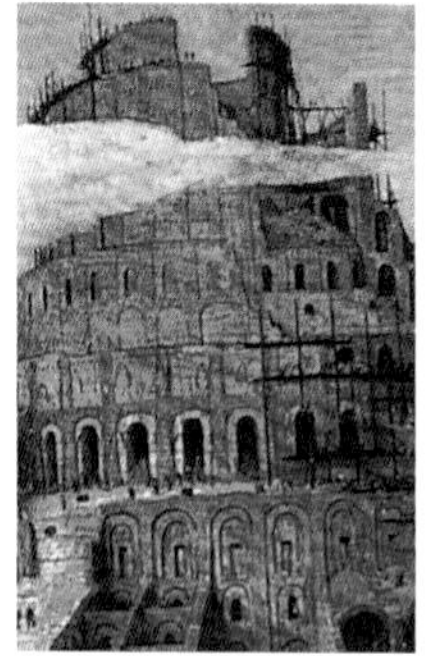

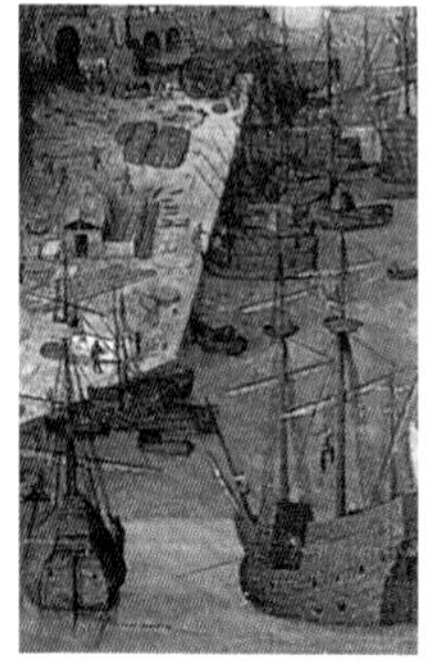

the creation of a collective soul. This is the first example in Bruegel's work of the technique that he would later develop to a high degree: the portrayal of a mass of people whose swarming he could render multiform and infinite. Yet there is no caricature in these figures who attempt to maintain their balance on the ice with varying degrees of success. The individual characters themselves contain a comical element marvellously

The Tower of Babel

1563
Oil on oak panel, 114 x 155 cm
Kunsthistorisches Museum, Vienna

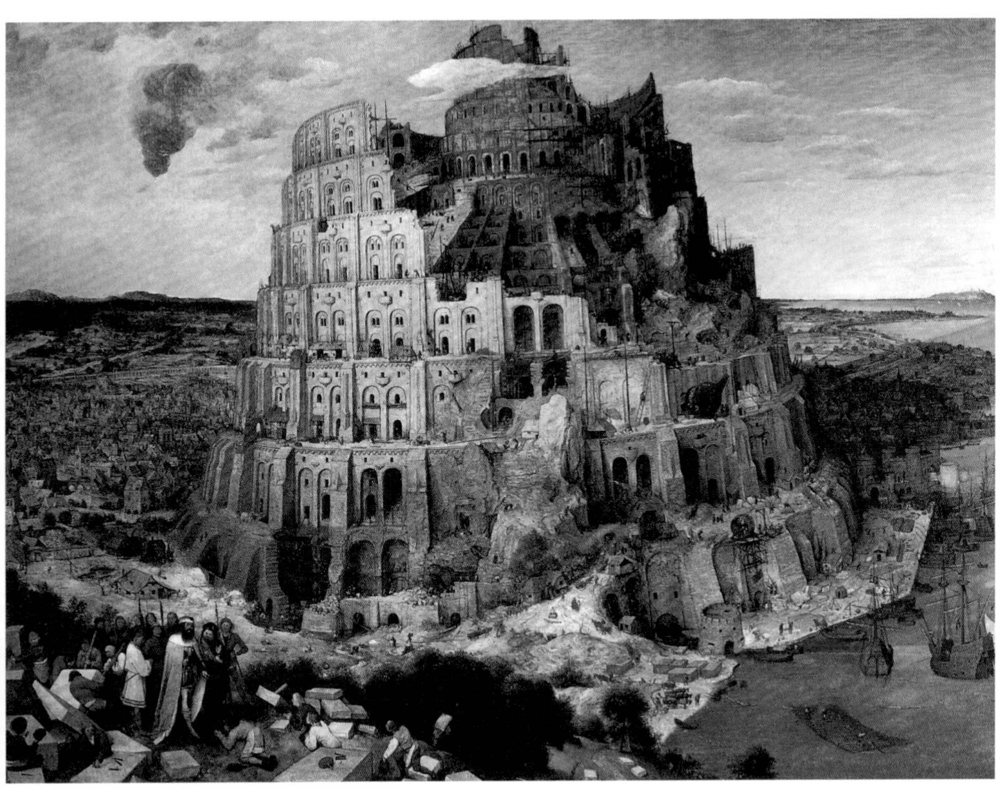

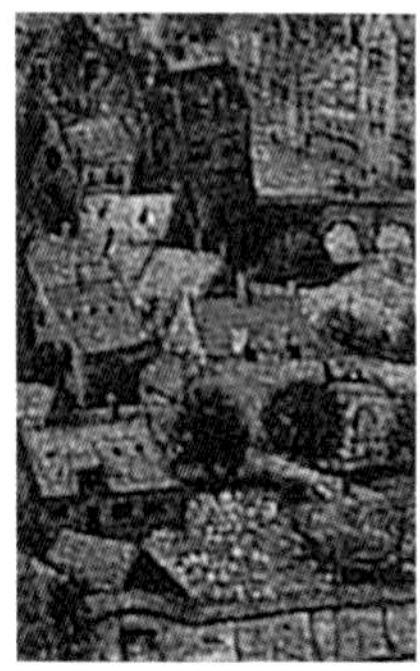

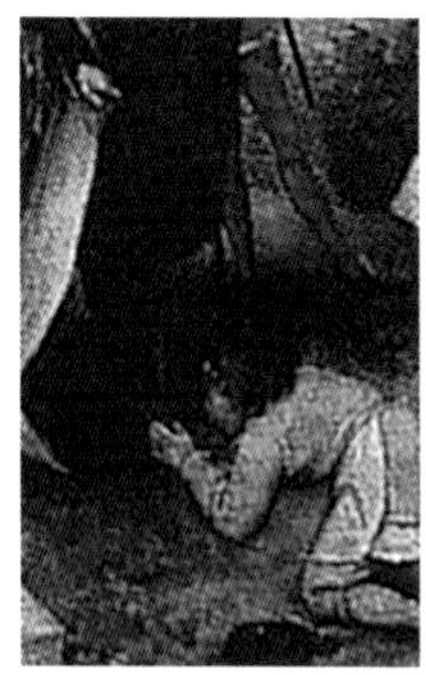

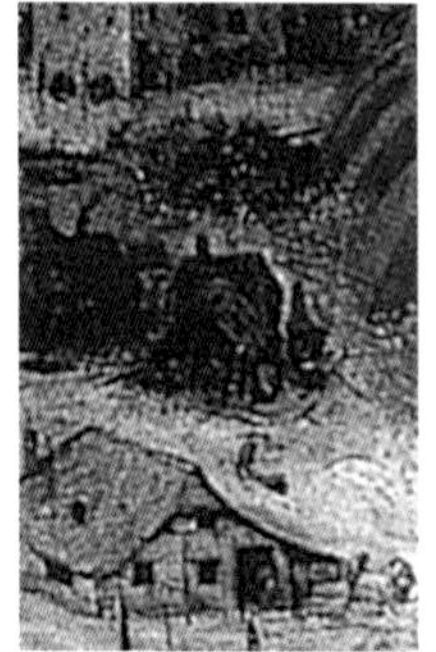

rendered by Bruegel. One contorts himself to keep his balance; another has fallen, spread out on the ice; a third stiffens all his muscles and grips the coattails of his companion, allowing himself to be pulled along. On the length of the sides of the moat there are people putting on their skates, as well as a waif seated on a sort of sled, pulling himself across the ice with two metal rods.

The Tower of Babel (detail)

1563
Oil on oak panel, 114 x 155 cm
Kunsthistorisches Museum, Vienna

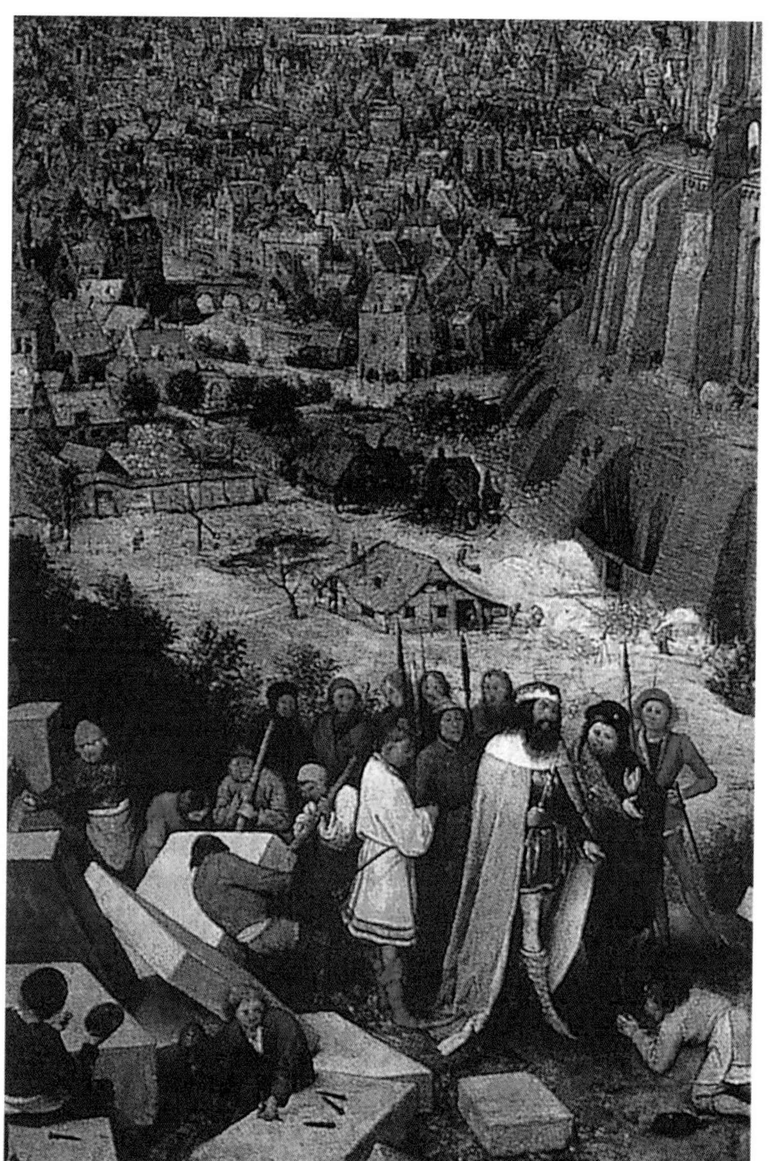

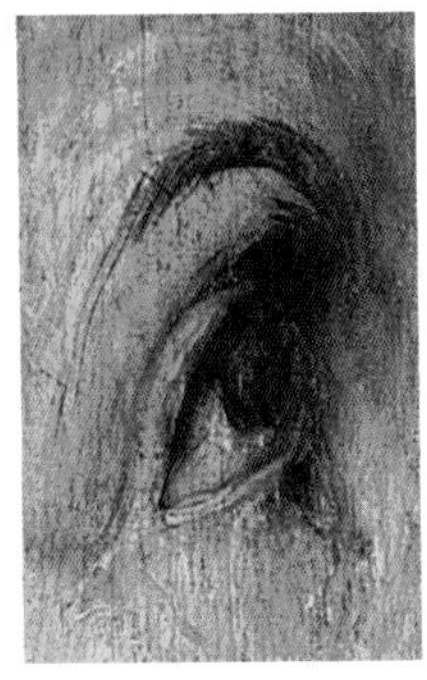

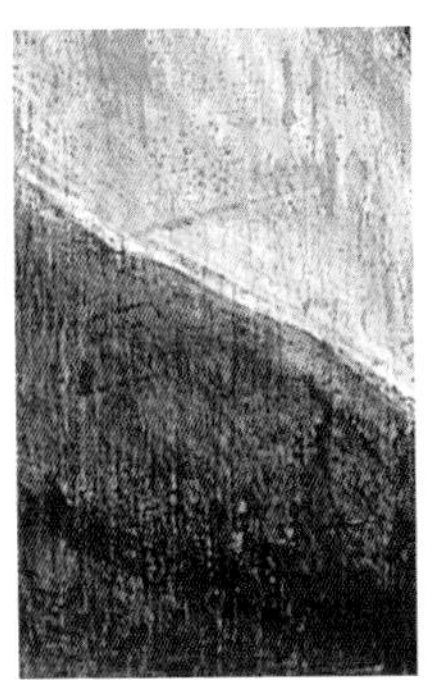

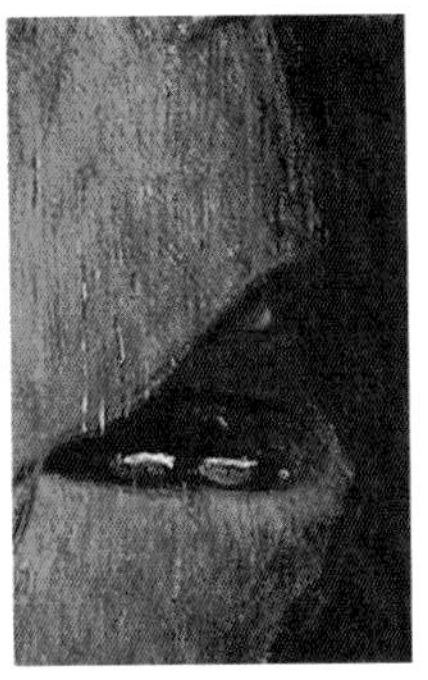

Each of these figures is outlined with an extraordinary vigour, as though conceived in a single strong line. The accuracy of the observation and the assured composition of this drawing reveal the work of a master.

Bruegel could not have been satisfied with the role of an imitator. His talent was too overt for him to not attempt original compositions merely inspired by the works of Bosch, a taste Bruegel acquired through imitation.

Portrait of an Old Woman

c. 1564
Oil on wood, 22 x 18 cm
Alte Pinakothek, Munich

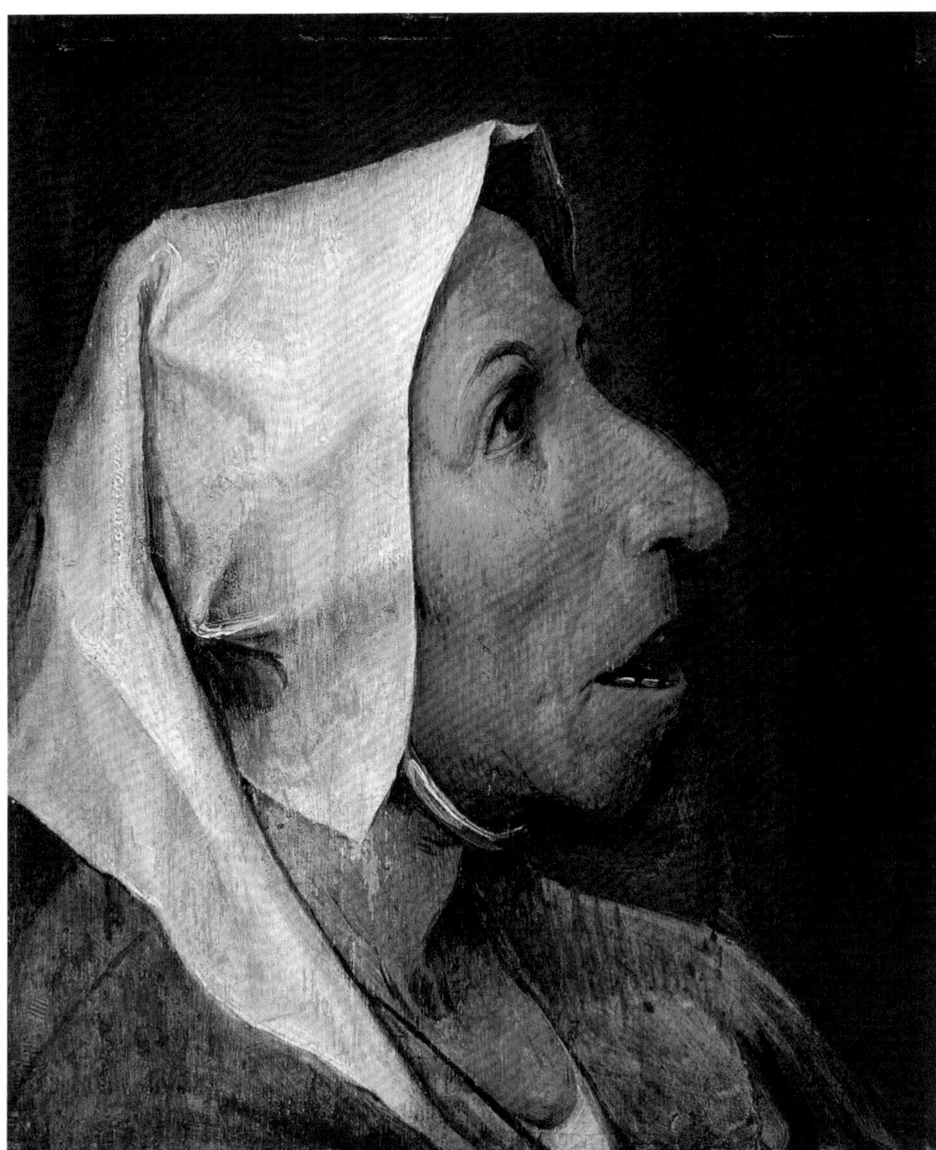

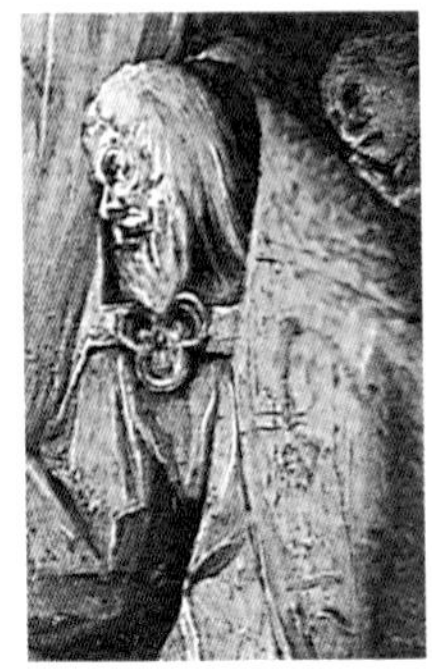

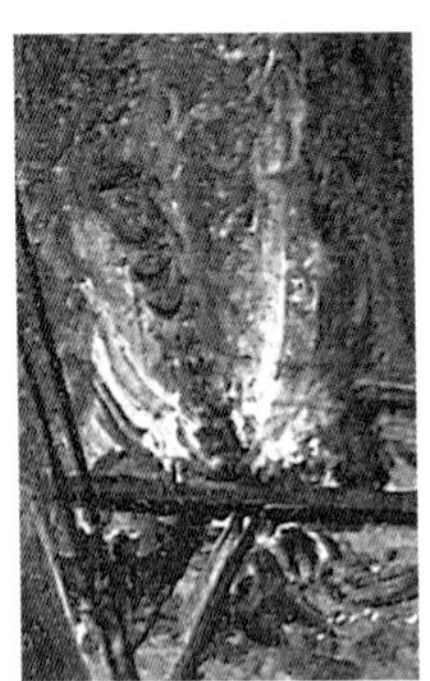

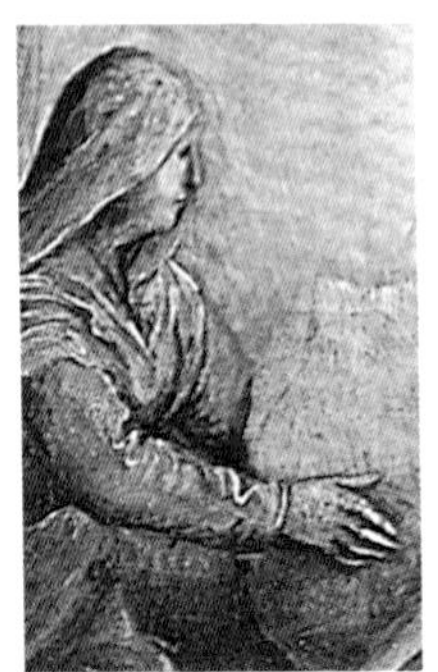

The public acclaim which these engravings received must have encouraged Bruegel to continue to work in a similar vein with his strange series *Seven Deadly Sins* and *Seven Virtues*, whose plates were engraved by Van der Heyden and printed by Cock. This kind of allegory, which gave free reign to his fantasy, was too popular at the time for it to have arisen spontaneously from Bruegel's spirit. From the point of view of their composition and rigorous detail, these engravings mark a step forward.

The Dormition of the Virgin

c. 1564

Oil in grey tones on oak panel, 36 x 55 cm

Upton House, National Trust, Banbury

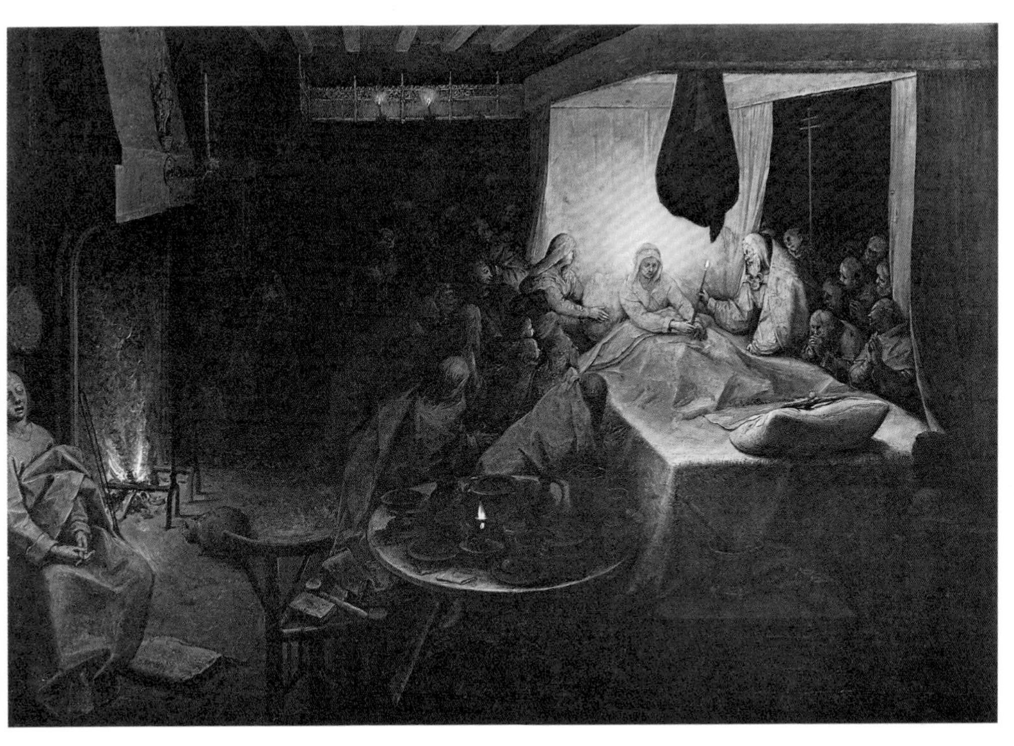

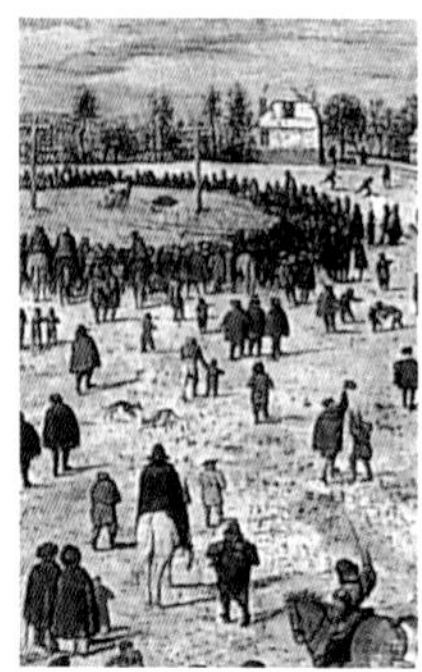

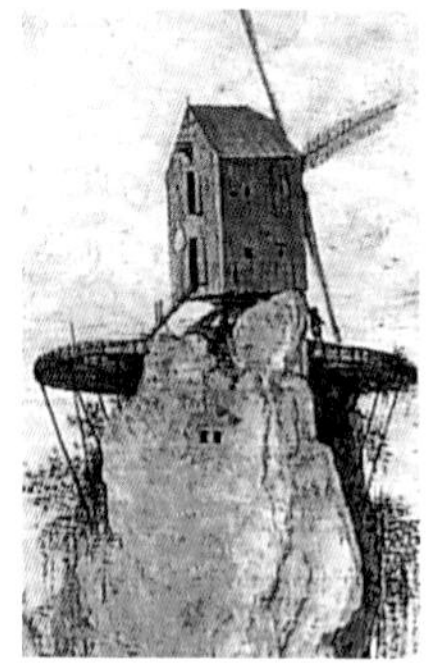

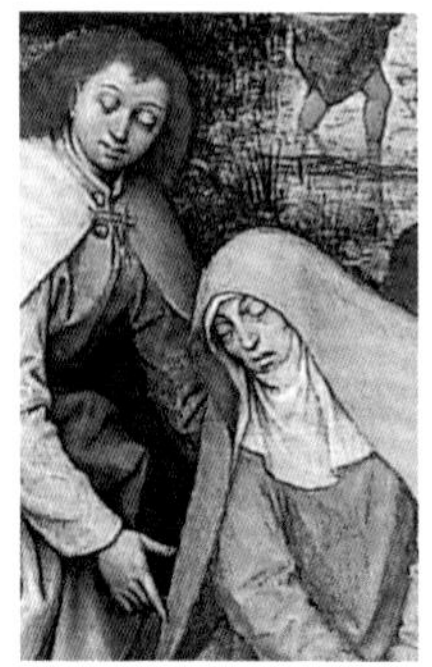

It is the Bruegel of *Skaters before the Gate of Saint George* that would prevail. Just as he re-embraced the landscapes of his native Brabant, he would also quickly rediscover his interest in the Flemish people. Curious about their customs and intrigued by their traditions, he became the interpreter of their daily lives.

Even more significant is the definitive version of *The Wedding Dance*, a clear sign of Bruegel's arrival as an artist. Its inspiration, draughtsmanship, and group of

Christ Carrying the Cross

1564
Oil on oak panel, 124 x 170 cm
Kunsthistorisches Museum, Vienna

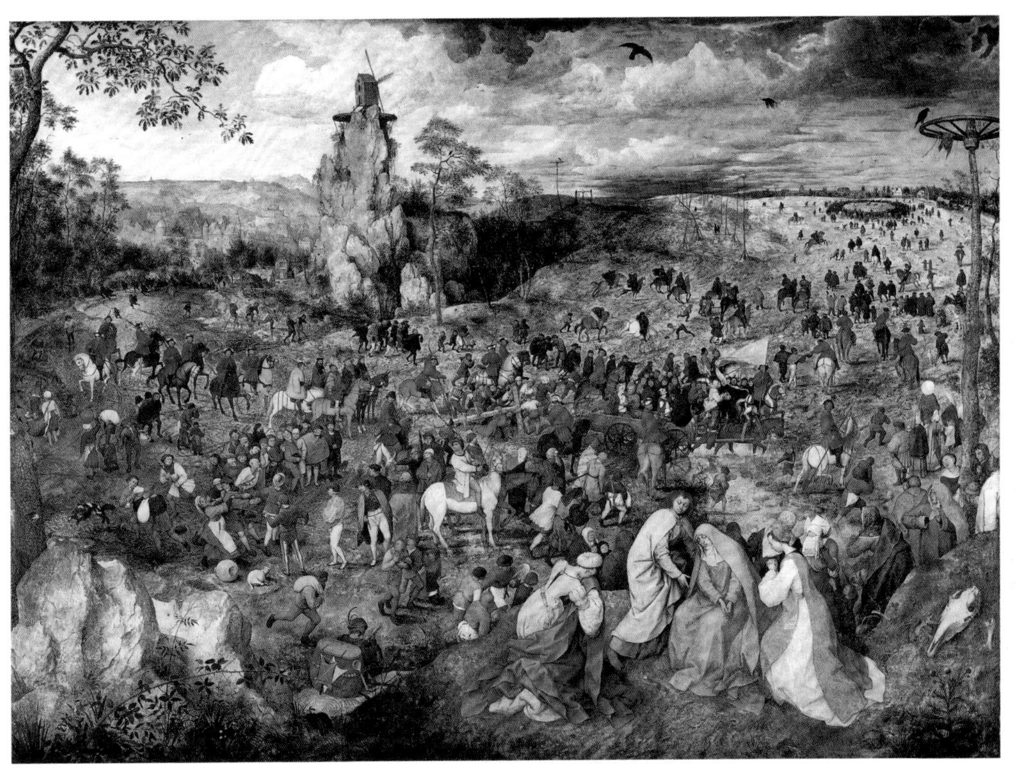

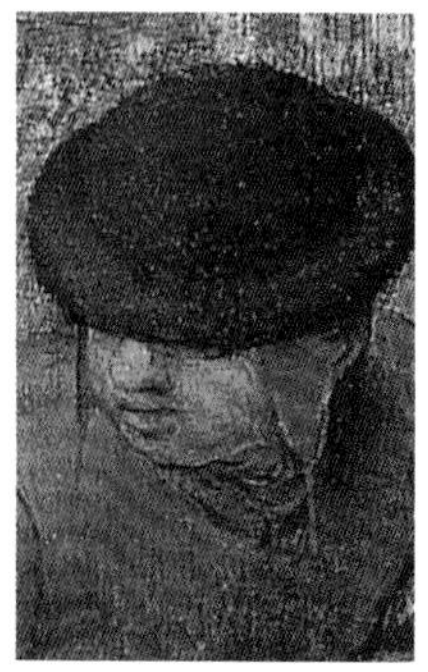

figures all carry the mark of the painter's personality. In the foreground, a peasant woman hikes up her skirt before her dancing partner, who advances with his shoulders thrown back, stomach thrust before him, and his hands behind his back. Farther back, an old peasant and his partner hold hands and mark a lively step. Couples embrace and crush their large and eager faces up against each other. Two musicians lean against a tree playing the bagpipes, while the bride, seated at a table in the

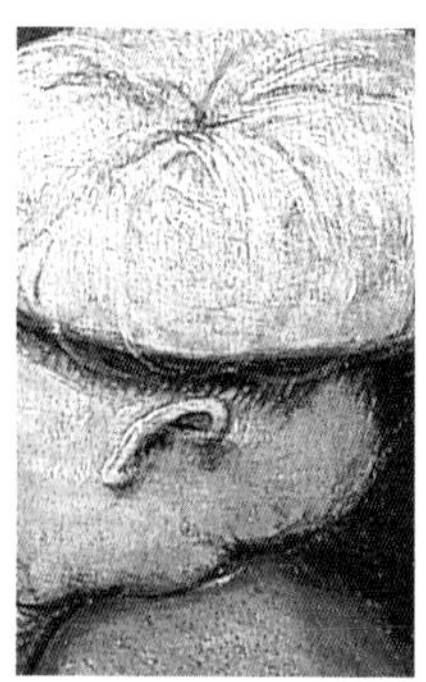

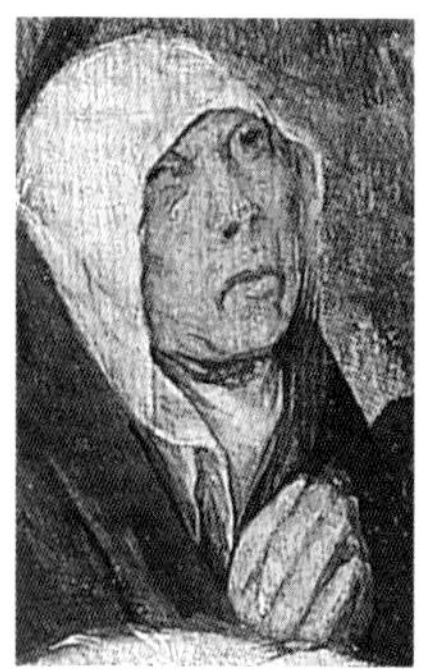

Christ Carrying the Cross (detail)

1564
Oil on oak panel, 124 x 170 cm
Kunsthistorisches Museum, Vienna

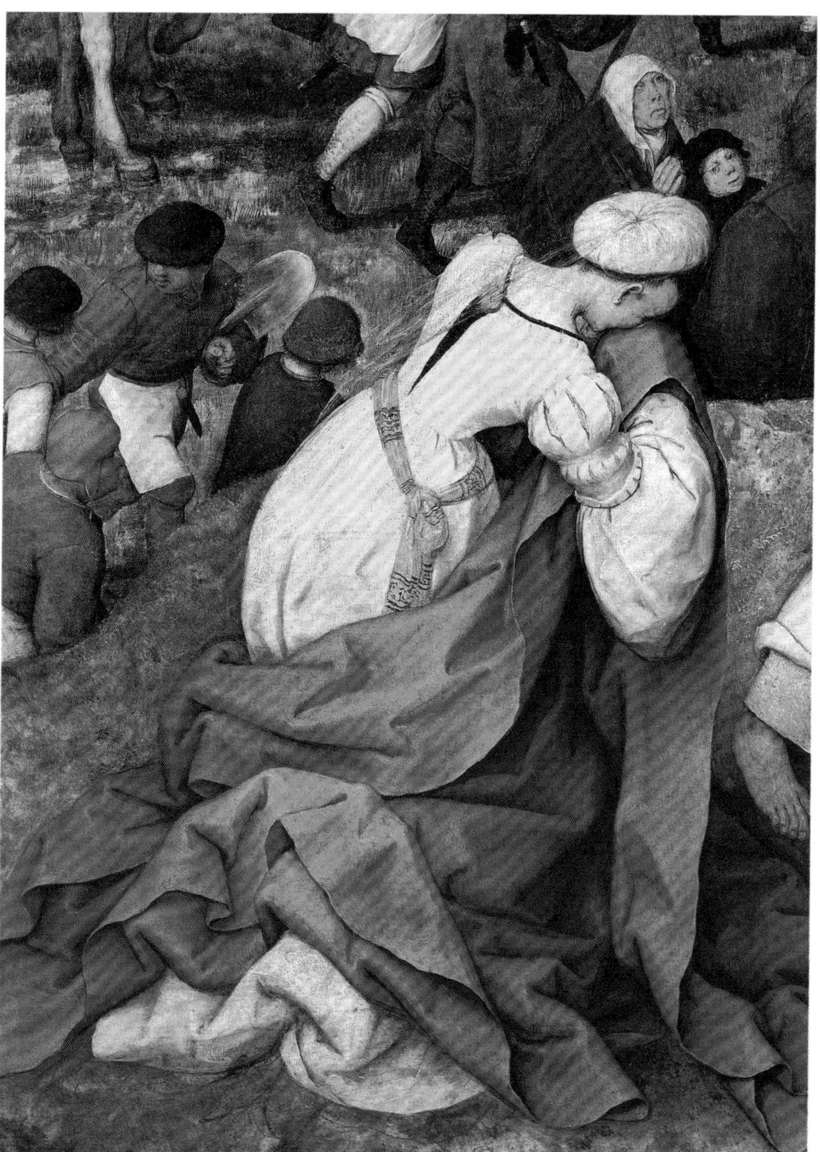

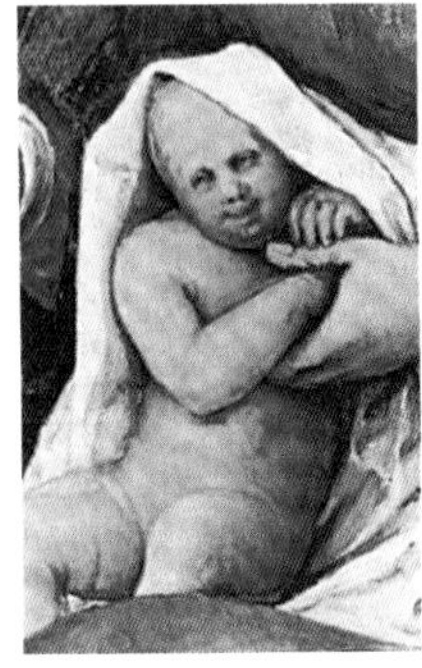

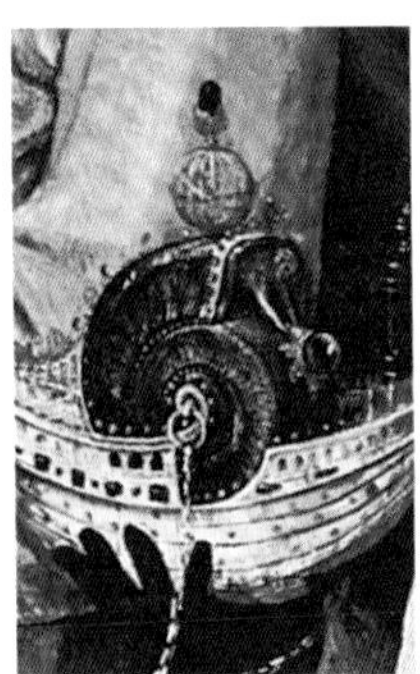

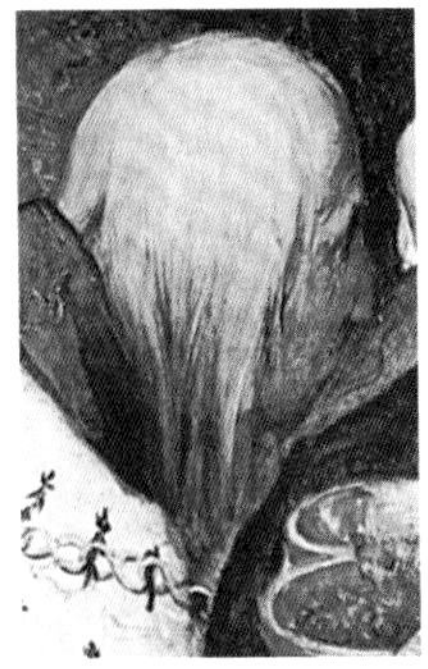

background, among a group of drunkards emptying their pots down their throats, receives her guests and their advice. One senses the breath of robust and healthy joy in this crowd of typical Flemish peasants given over to the pleasures of eating, drinking, and revelry. Until this moment, no painter, not even Quentin Matsys or Pieter Aertsen, had portrayed a popular scene with such energy and communicated the regional flavour. This was the birth of the great Pieter Bruegel of the Peasants.

The Adoration of the Magi

1564
Oil on wood, 111 x 84 cm
The National Gallery, London

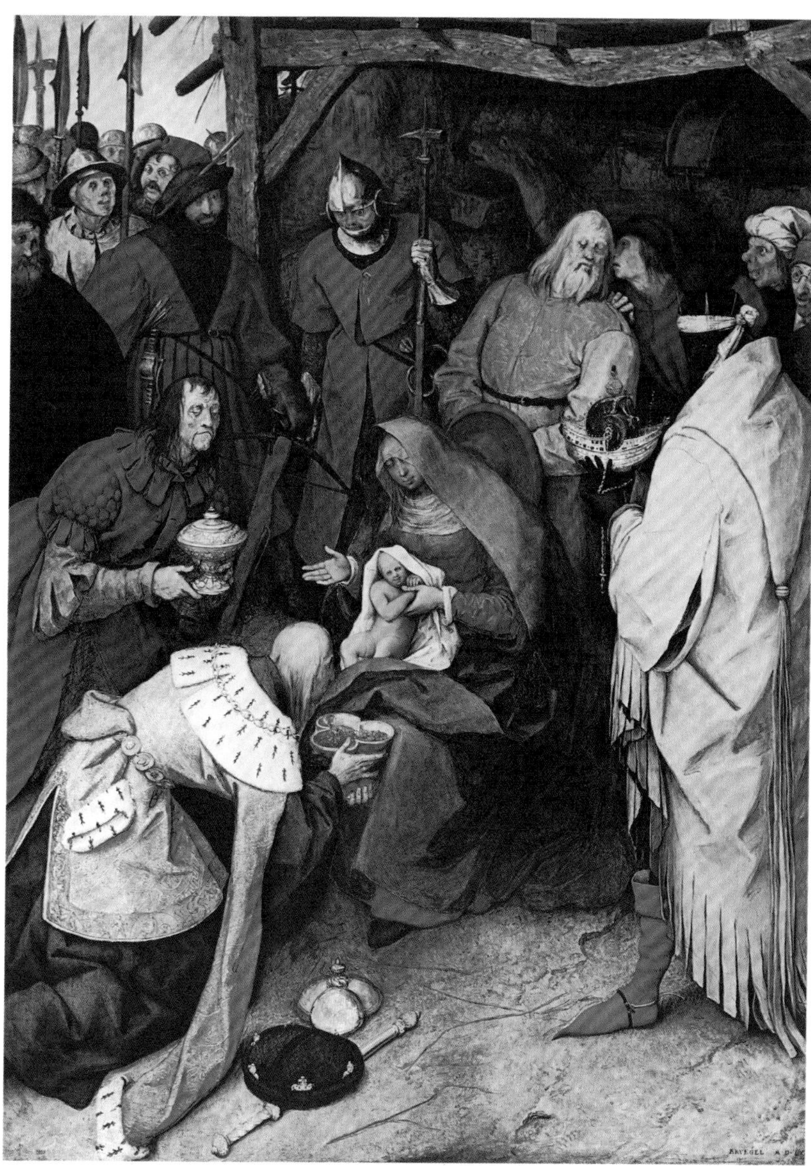

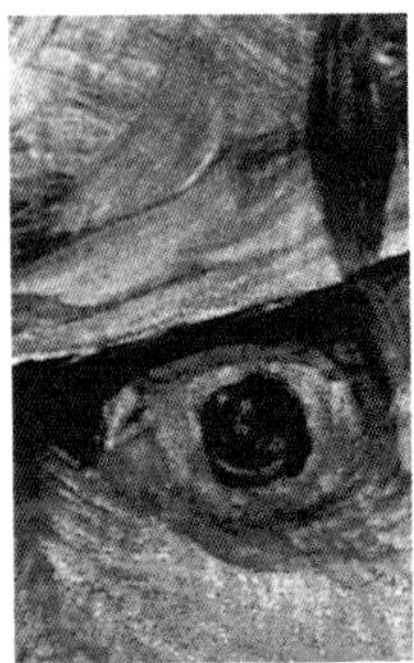

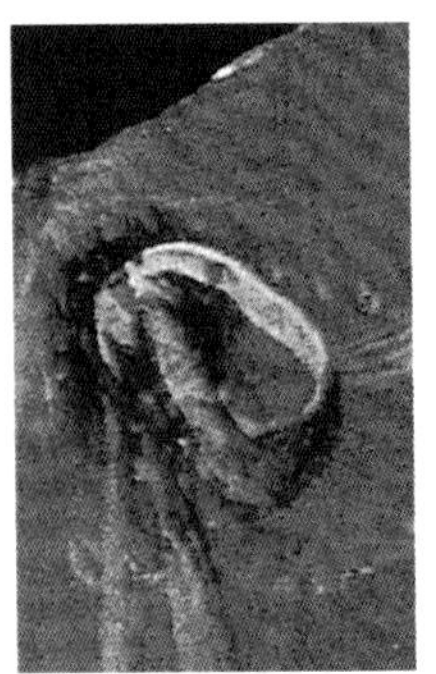

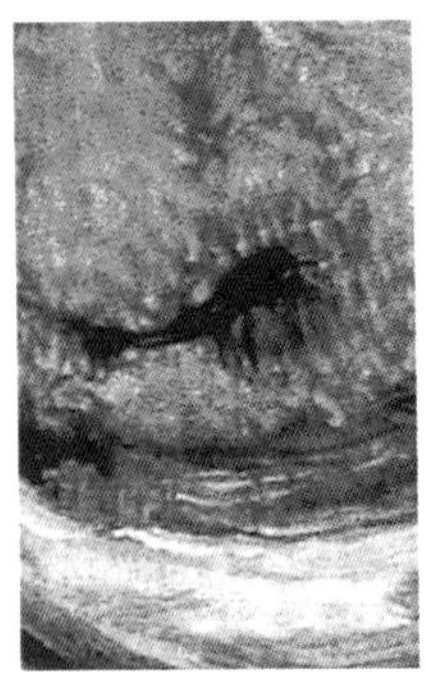

Pieter Bruegel the Elder's Mature Works

Obviously, Bruegel's evolution from the satirical and comic towards the purely realistic was a gradual one.

A short time after *The Wedding Dance*, Bruegel created the series *Seven Virtues* as a continuation of his *Seven Deadly Sins* printed by Hieronymus Cock. If some of the virtues, like *Patience*, are inspired by the work of Bosch, others have more in common with his new trend

The Adoration of the Magi (detail)

1564
Oil on wood, 111 x 84 cm
The National Gallery, London

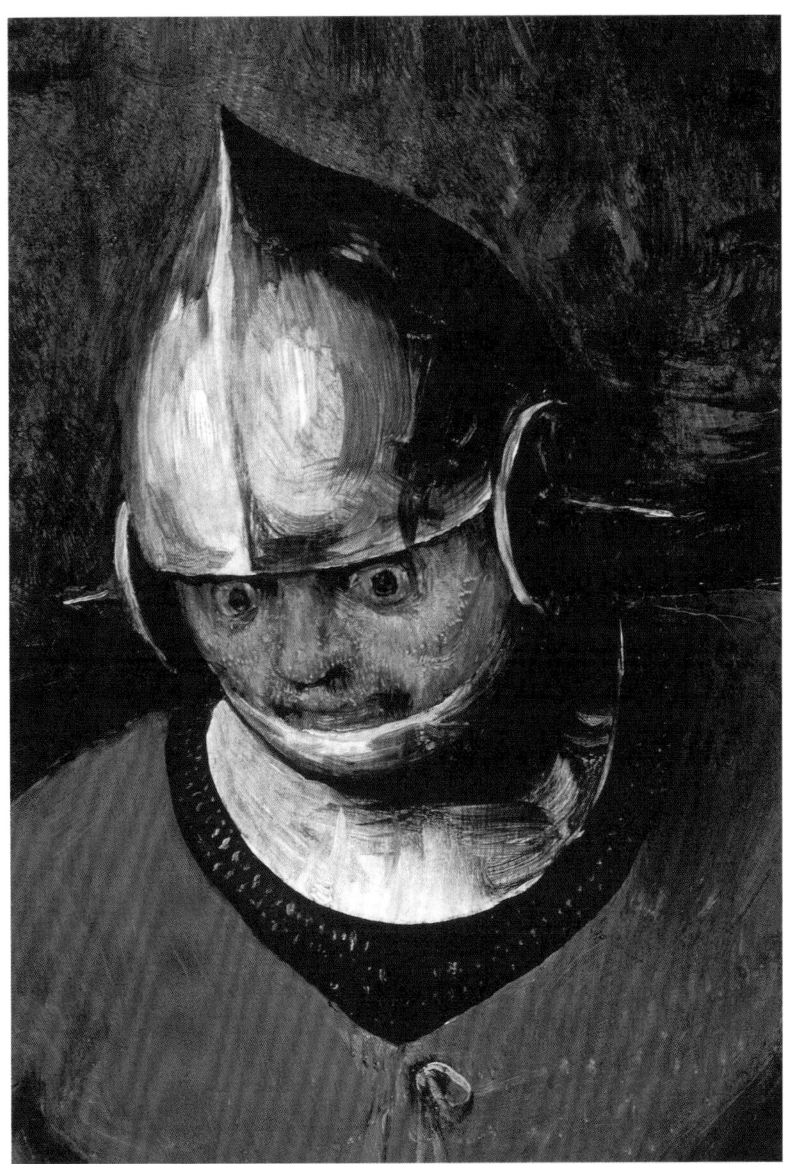

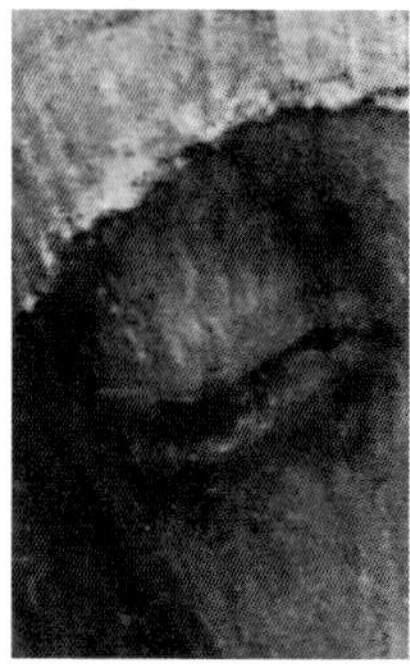

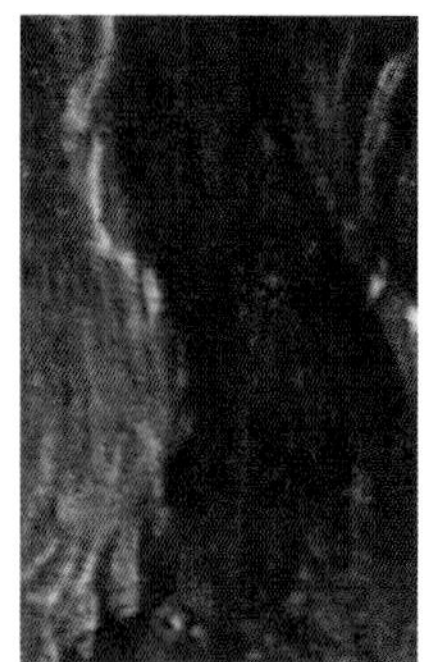

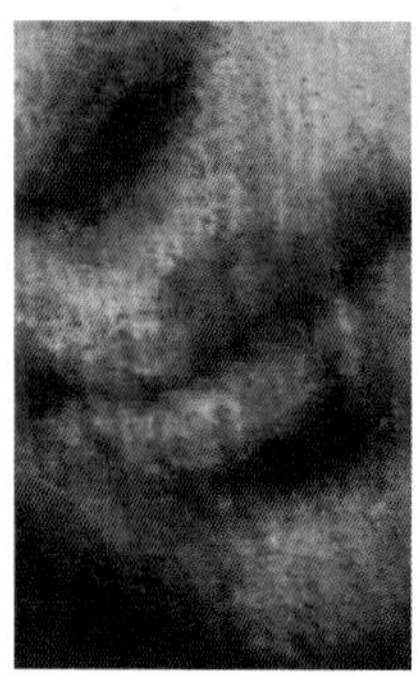

towards realism. The power of this change is most observable in *Charity*, which takes place in Bruegel's preferred setting, a village square. Charity occupies the centre of the foreground. Her right hand holds a flaming heart up to her chest, while a pelican with spread wings perched on her head pecks at itself. Around her bustles a crowd of miserable people to whom the charitable give alms. A group of the starving

The Adoration of the Magi (detail)

1564
Oil on wood, 111 x 84 cm
The National Gallery, London

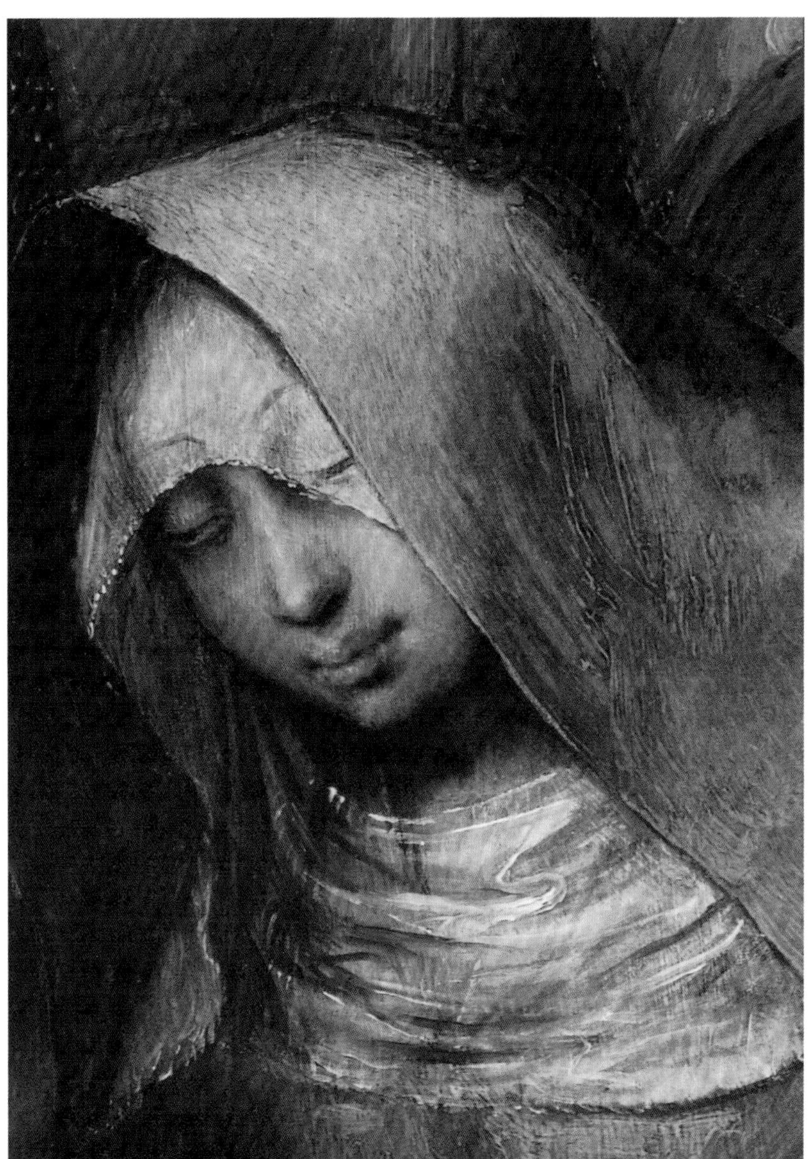

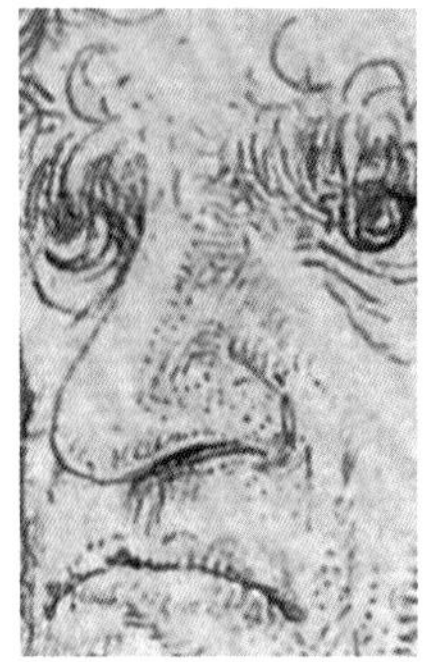

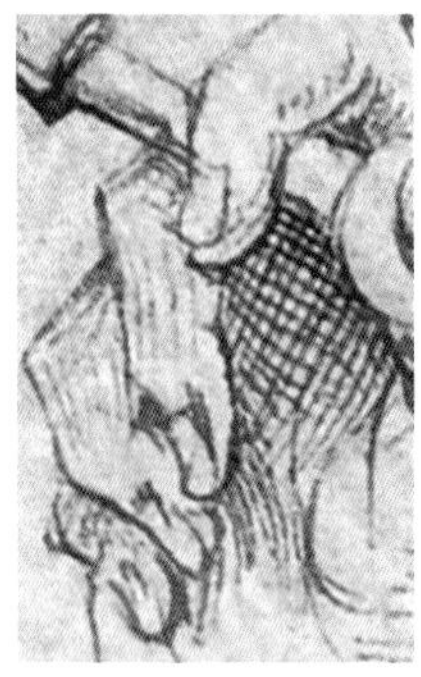

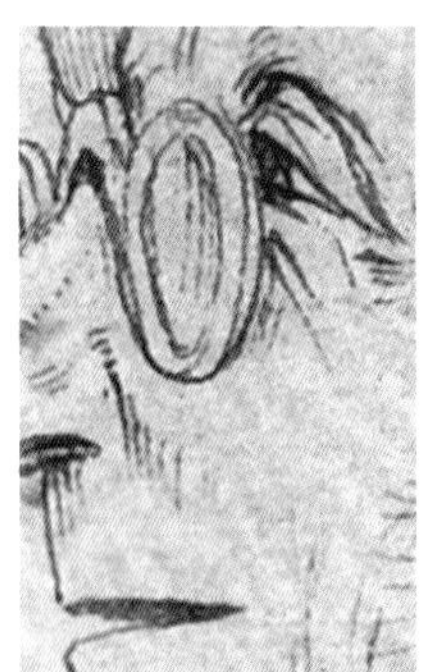

rush towards baskets full of bread; elsewhere, women distribute linen and clothing, while farther back, a group of unfortunates jostle around a barrel from which beer is drawn. Inside a jail, two women can be seen ministering to prisoners whose feet are fixed in some kind of torture device. Across the way, in a miserable slum, a woman with a swollen leg propped up on a tripod accompanies a man lying on a pallet.

The Painter and the Collector

c. 1565

Pen and black ink on brown paper, 25.5 x 21.5 cm

Graphische Sammlung, Albertina, Vienna

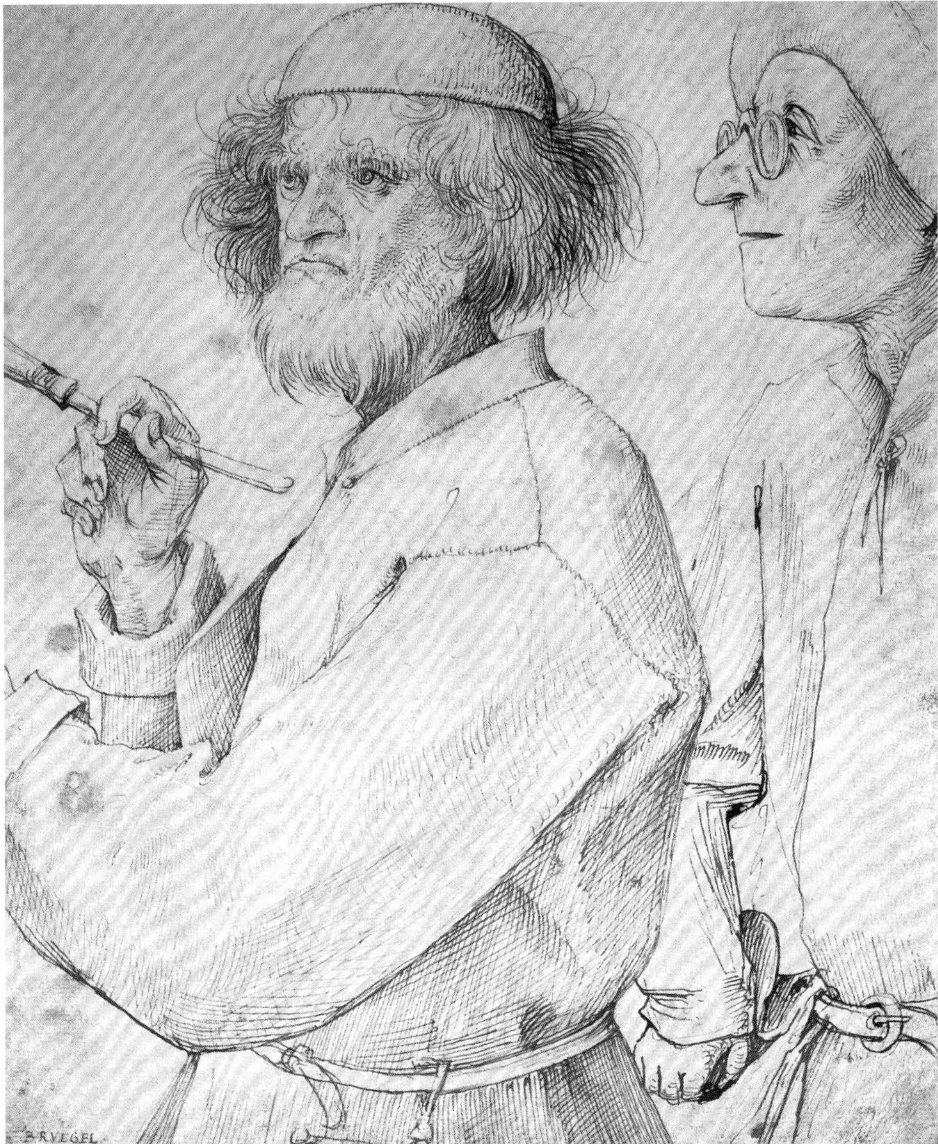
BRVEGEL

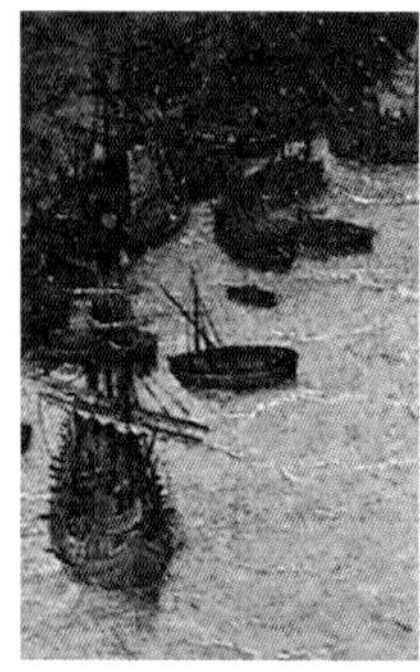

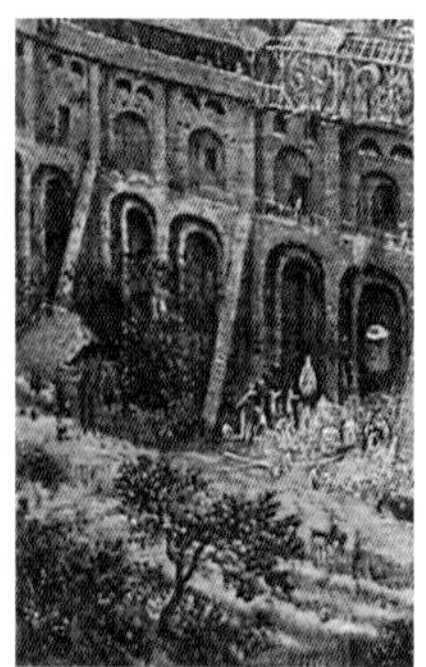

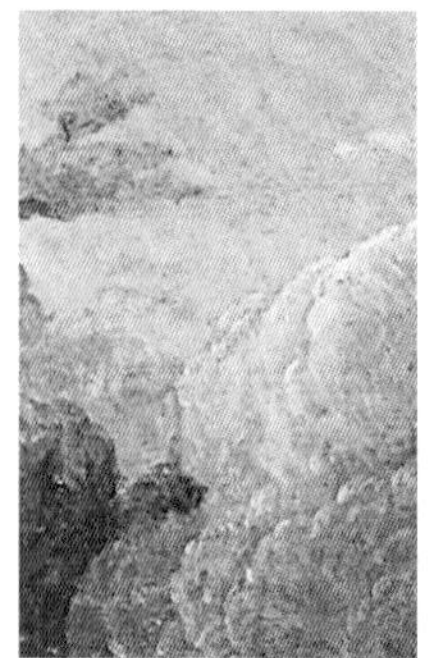

In number, the unfortunate overwhelm those who come to their aid with blessings.

Nothing in this scene is caricatured or clownish. Even the crippled man in the foreground, a sort of beggar whose frail legs are drawn up to his neck, remains profoundly human. It is clear that sincere emotion guided him in the creation of this work, and one recognises the marvellous artist revealed by the

The Tower of Babel

c. 1565
Oil on wood, 60 x 75 cm
Museum Boijmans Van Beuningen, Rotterdam

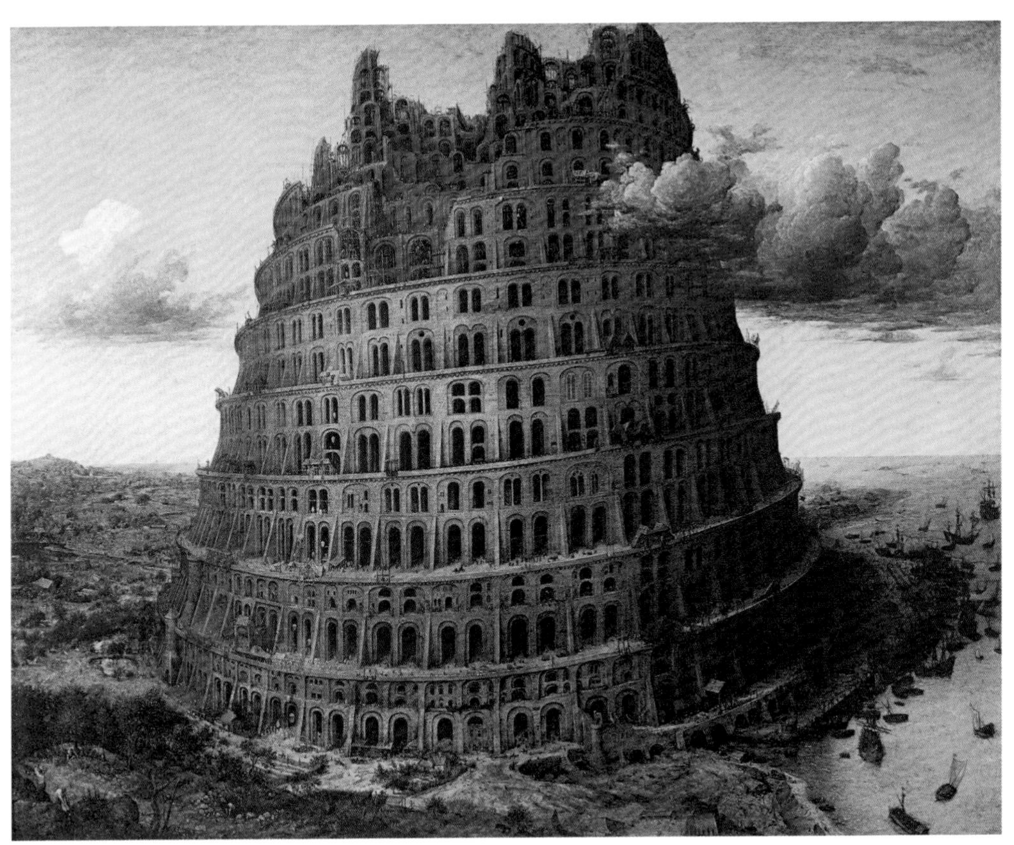

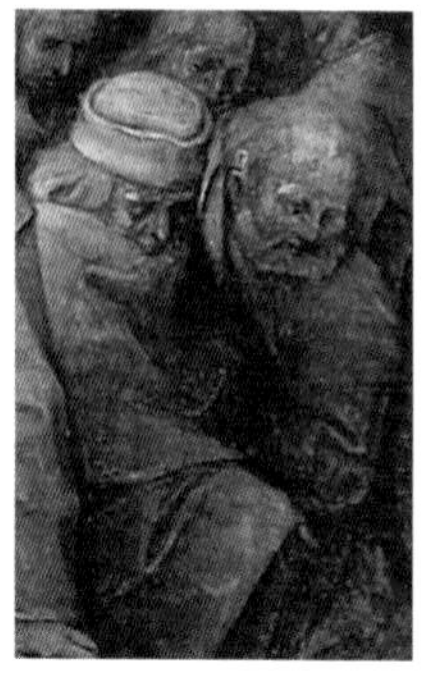

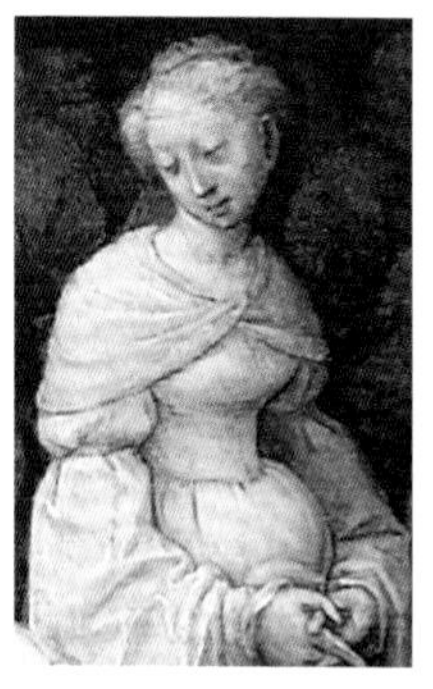

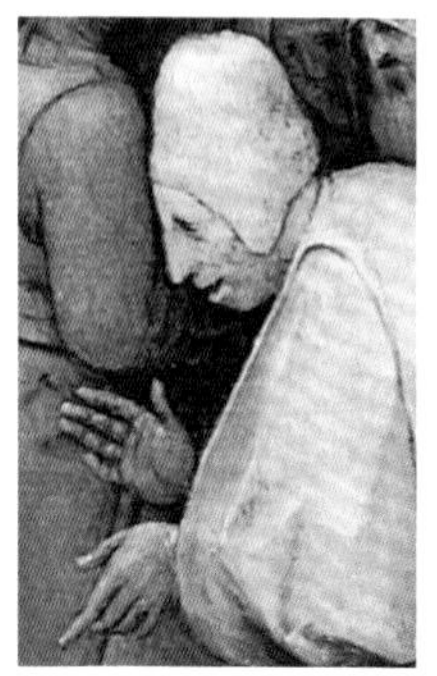

Skaters before the Gate of Saint George. Each of these characters, drawn from life and composed with powerful lines, holds an astonishing allure. These are no longer rocks spitting out on to paper, as goes the powerful expression of Van Mander, but the very life of the people transported into his work.

In passing, it should be remarked that Bruegel also painted in tempera, a widespread practice in his time.

Christ and the Woman Taken in Adultery

1565
Oil in grey tones on panel, 24.1 x 34.4 cm
Courtauld Institute of Art, London

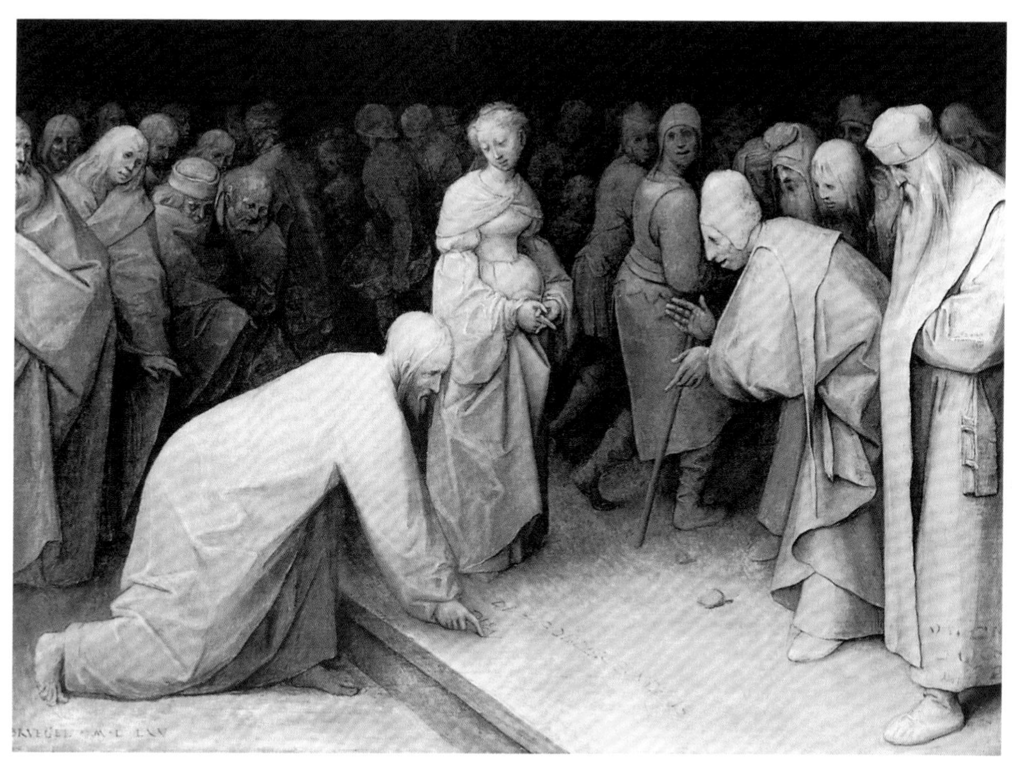

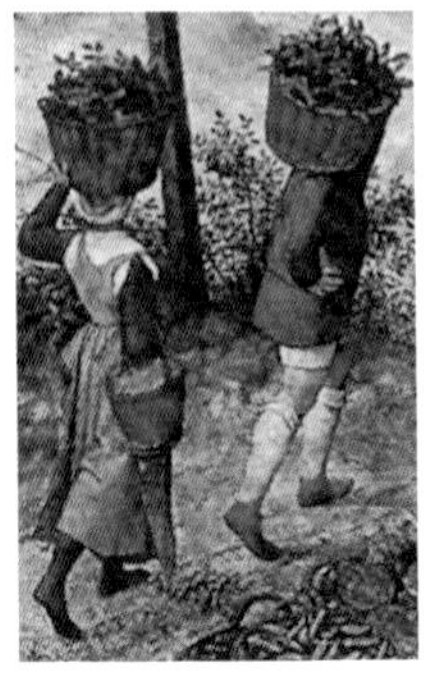

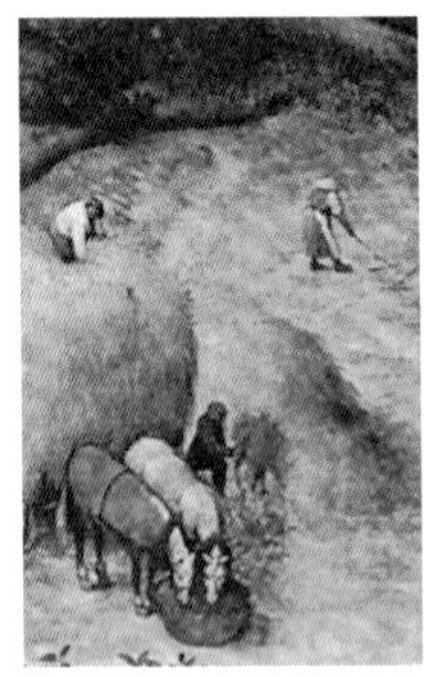

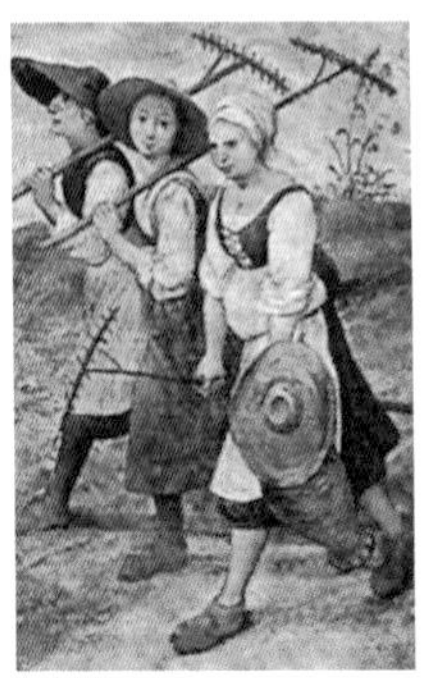

This fragile process was undoubtedly responsible for the loss of many of his works. Nevertheless, a few of Bruegel's tempera paintings survive, including *The Parable of the Blind Leading the Blind,* in the Museum of Naples, reproductions of which hang in Parma and at the Louvre. (The Louvre's copy was acquired in 1891 at an auction held in Antwerp). Other examples of Bruegel's work in tempera include *The Misanthrope,*

Haymaking (July)

1565
Oil on panel, 117 x 161 cm
Národní Galerie, Prague

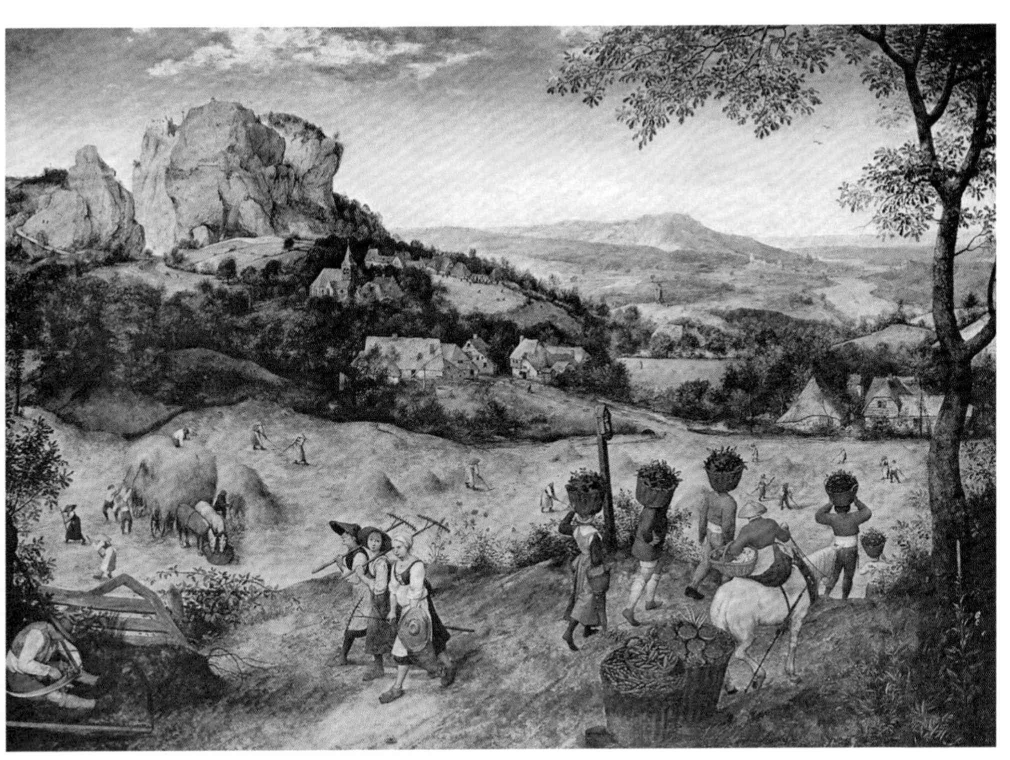

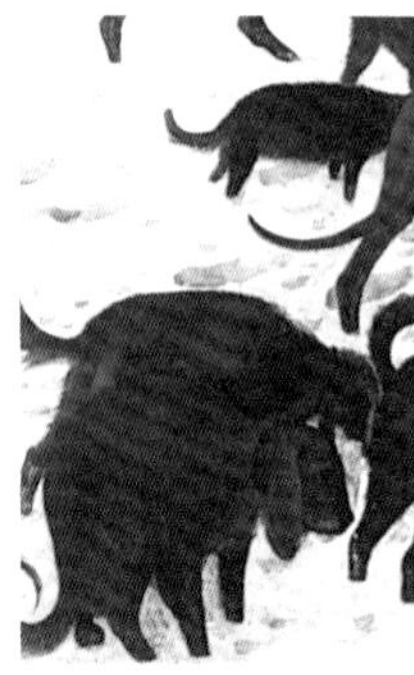

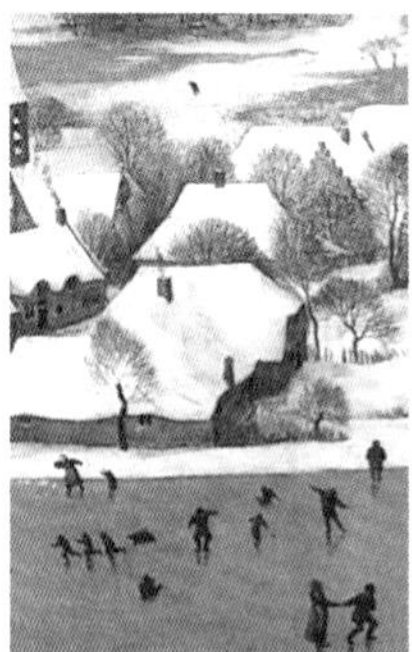

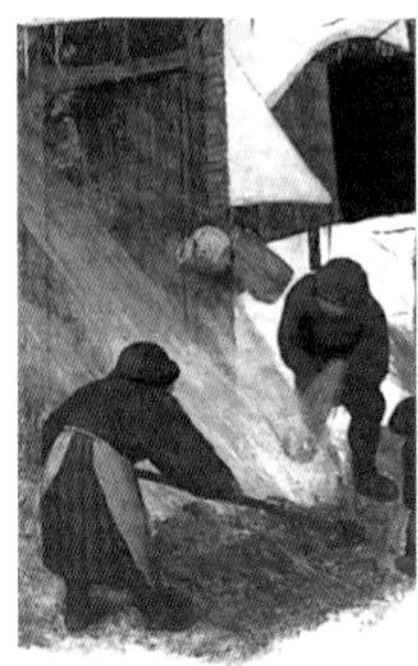

also held in Naples, and *The Adoration of the Magi*, in a private collection in Brussels. *The Dancing Peasant* in the collection of M. Van Valkenburg of The Hague can also be cited, but its attribution remains uncertain.

At this point it is as well, before continuing in the study of Bruegel's oeuvre, to examine the artist's life in Antwerp, for his life was closely related to his work. According to Van Mander, Bruegel lived "with a girl

The Hunters in the Snow (January)

1565
Oil on wood, 117 x 162 cm
Kunsthistorisches Museum, Vienna

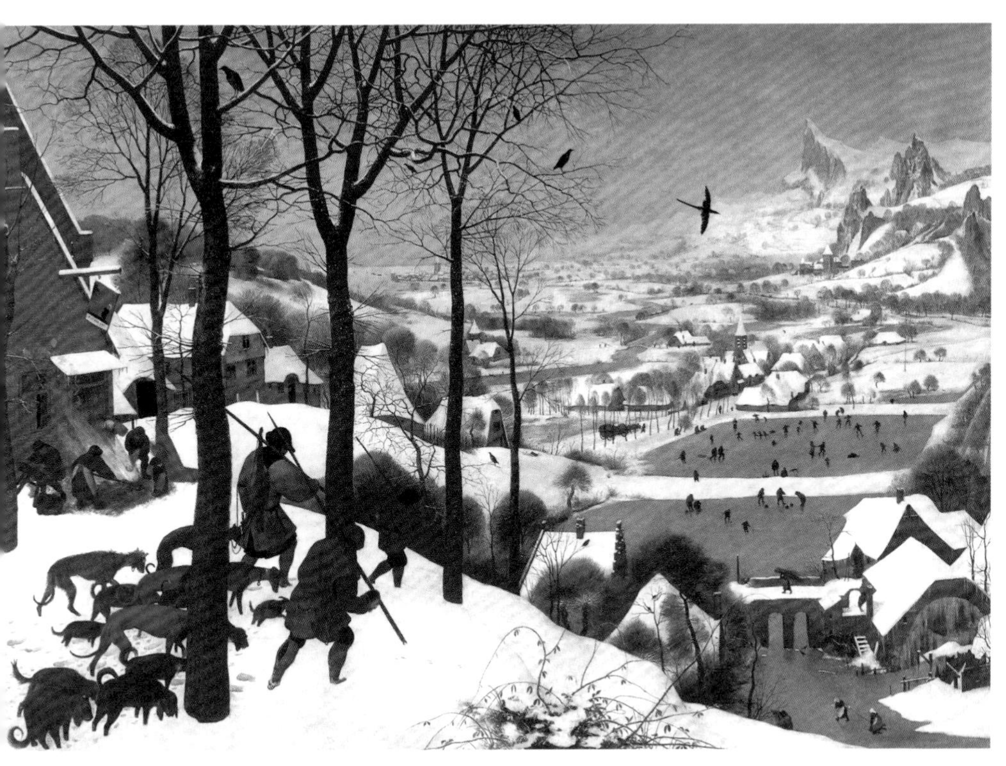

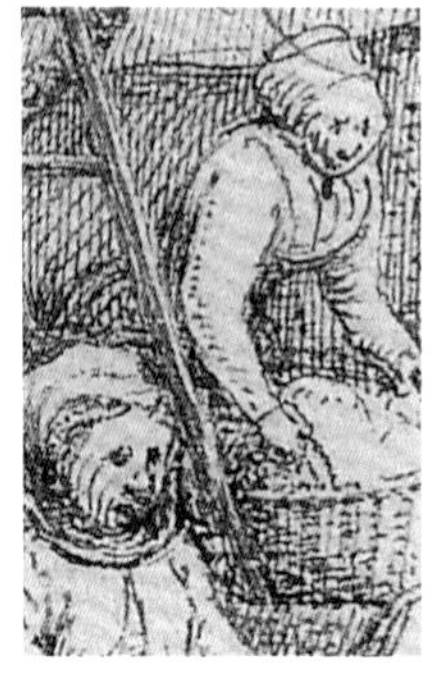

whom he would have liked to marry, had she not been such an incorrigible liar. He made a bargain with her that he would note each of her lies on a long belt that he had chosen. If the belt filled up, the idea of marriage would be abandoned. This came to pass not long afterwards". The important part of this anecdote is that Bruegel lived a rather carefree life on the margins of bourgeois society, but eventually this

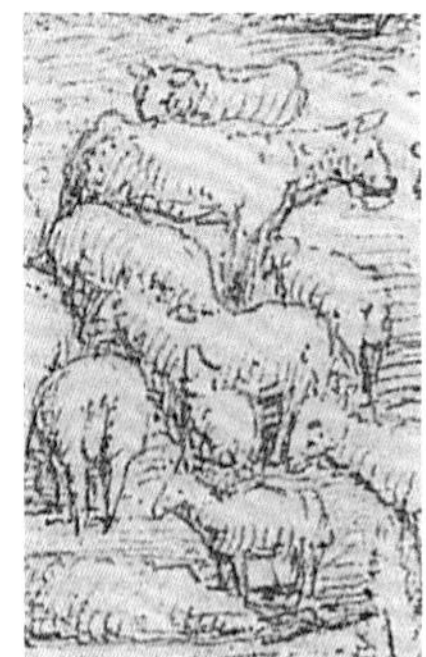

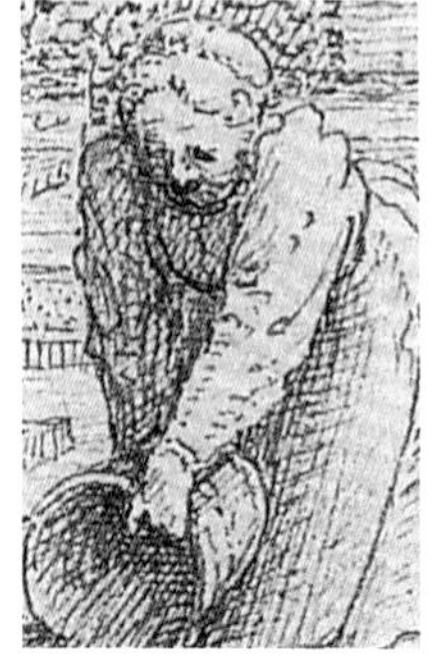

Springtime

1565
Pen and brown ink, 22.3 x 28.9 cm
Graphische Sammlung, Albertina, Vienna

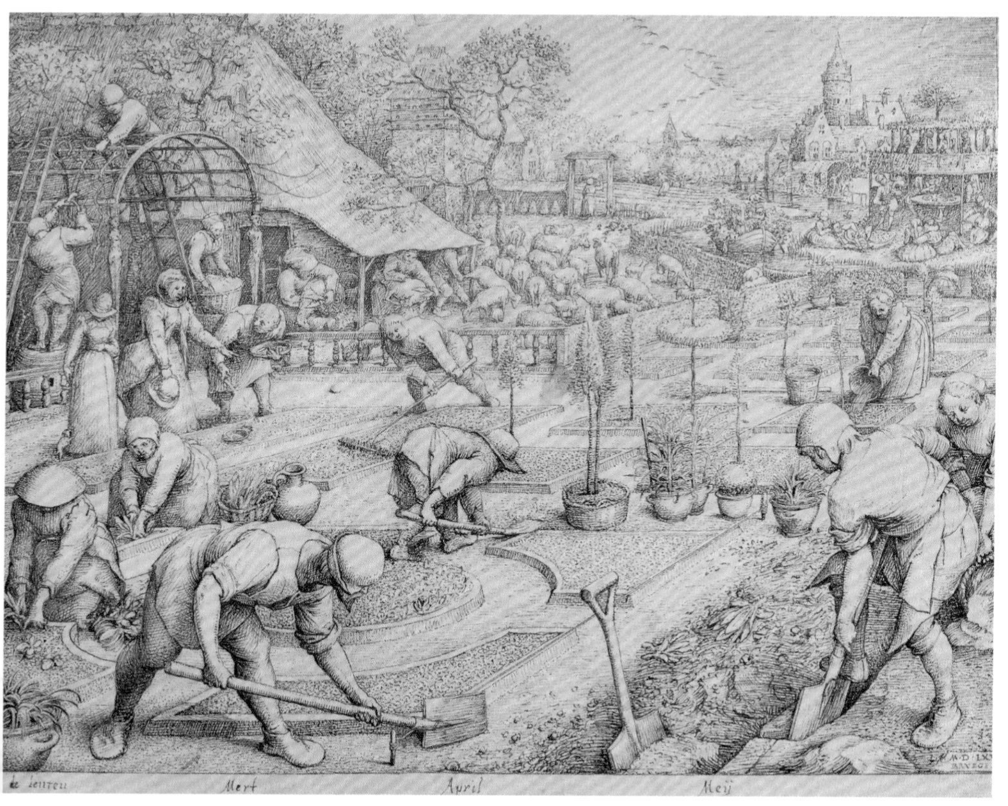
de lenten
Mert
April
Meij

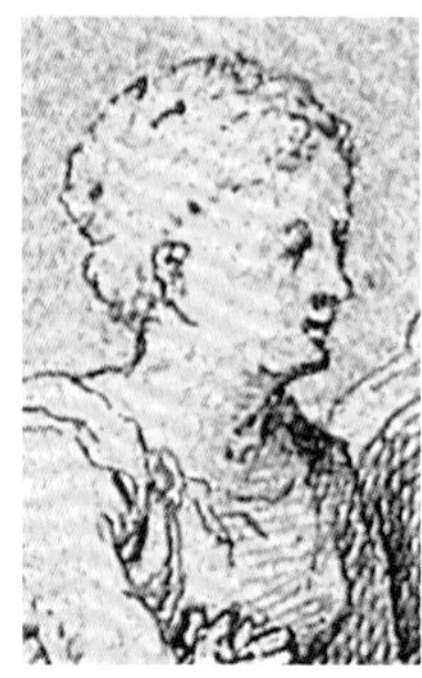

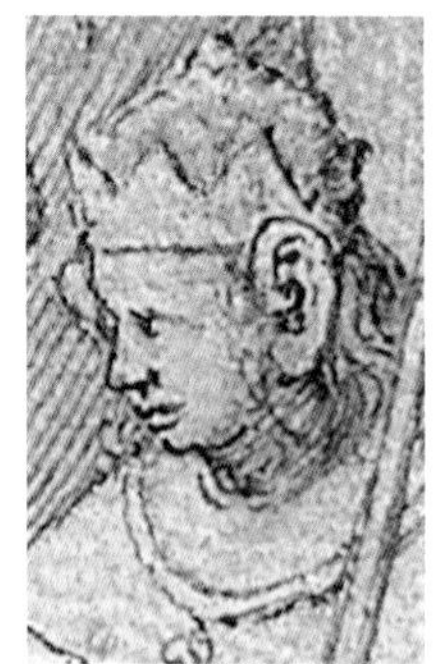

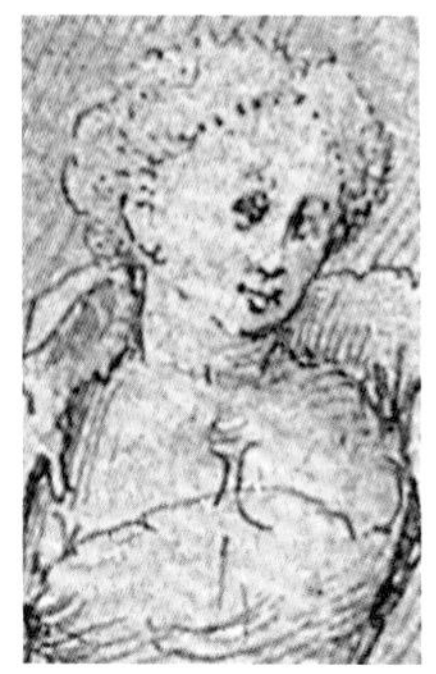

bohemian existence became untenable to him, so he went to Brussels to marry Mayken Coecke, the daughter of his first master, "the same girl he had held so often in his arms".

More pertinent from the point of view of the correlation between the man and his work are these lines which illuminate the character of the painter. "Bruegel was a quiet and steady man, who spoke little

The Calumny of Apelles

1565
Pen and brown ink, with white highlights on brown paper, 20.4 x 30.7 cm
British Museum, London

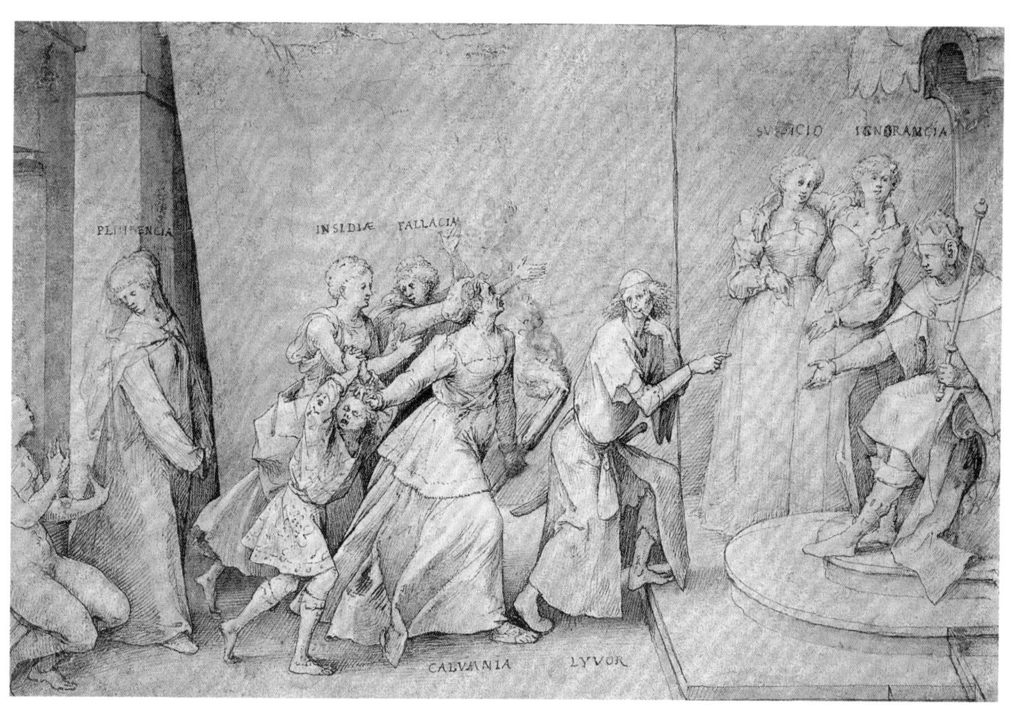
INSIDIÆ
FALLACIA
CALVMNIA
LYVOR

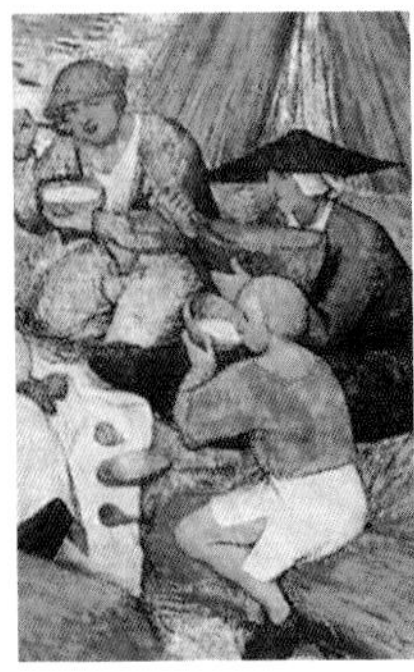

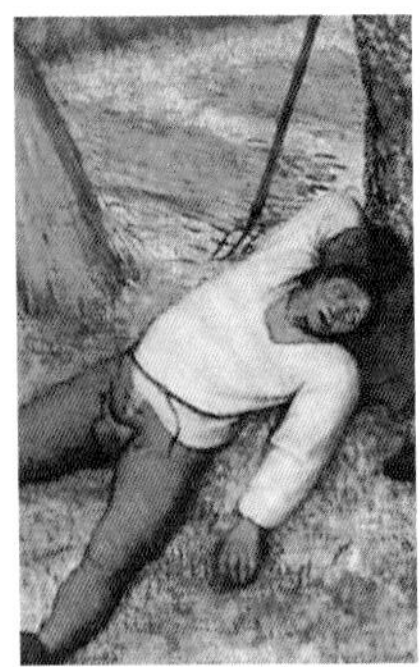

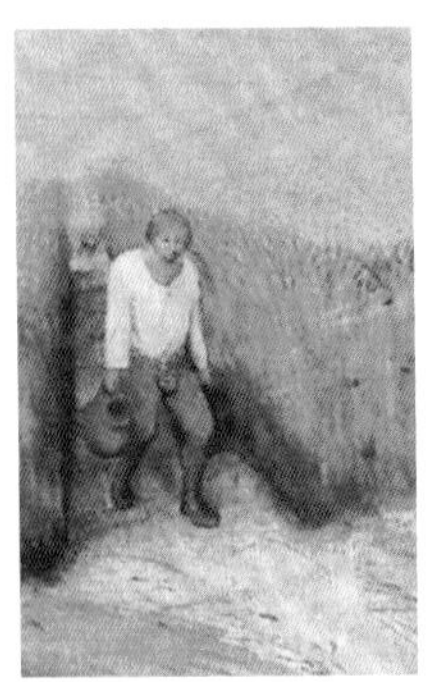

but was amusing in good company, taking pleasure in scaring his companions, particularly his students, with stories of ghosts and noises of the supernatural."

It is easy to imagine the stubborn Bruegel, quiet and given over to dreaming, with abundant reserves of robust gaiety hidden beneath his silence. When he was under the right influence, his weakness for fantasy brimmed over in an excessive and extravagant manner.

The Harvesters (August)

1565
Oil on wood, 119 x 162 cm
The Metropolitan Museum of Art, New York

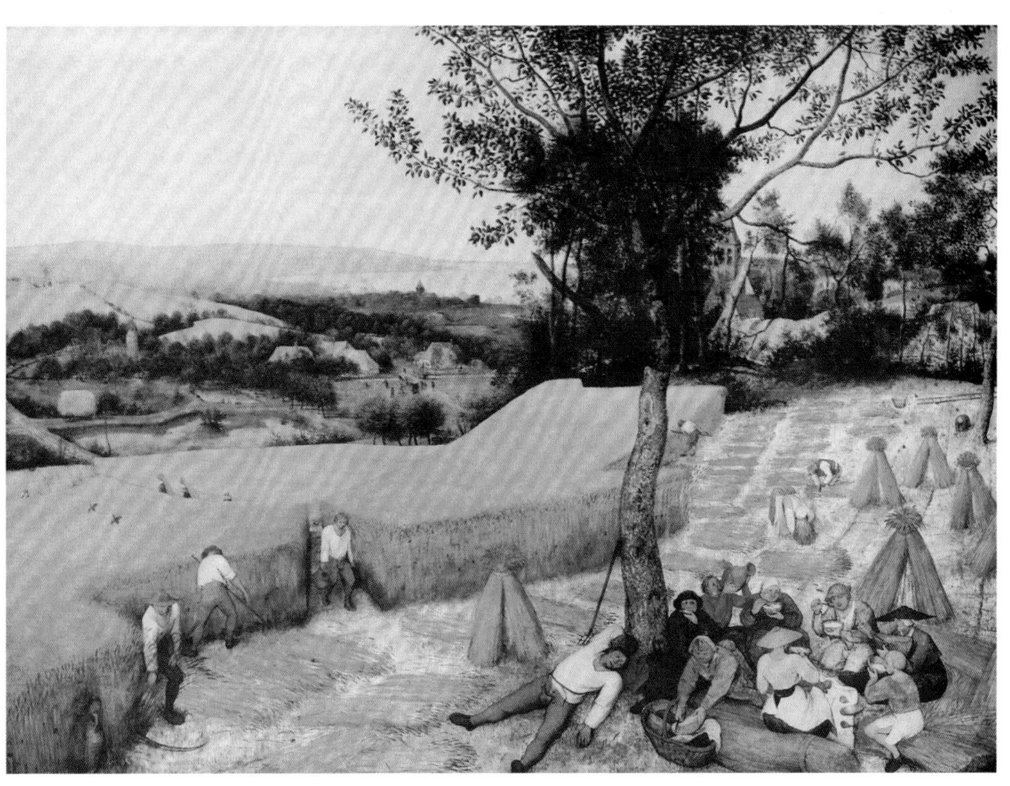

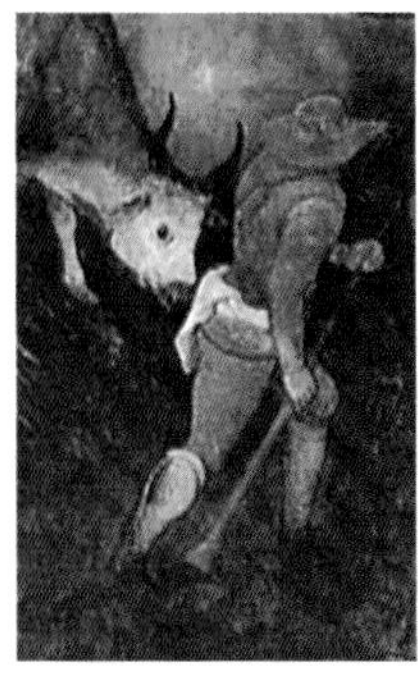

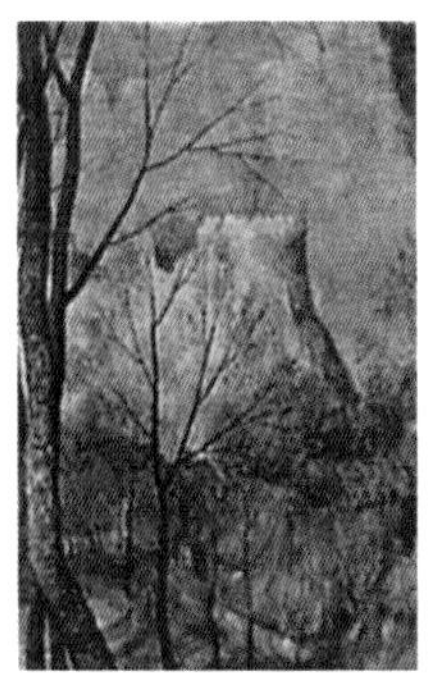

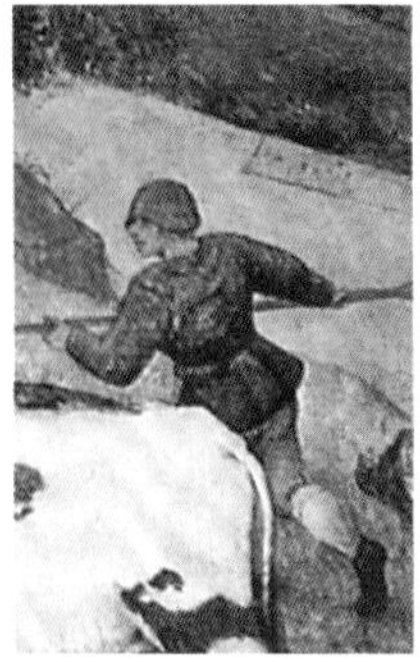

He was jovial, had a wild imagination, and was a practical joker and a hoaxer. These moments were the inevitably violent reactions of his otherwise contained personality.

Just as quickly, Bruegel would become silent and attentive, watching and listening with his ever wakeful and marvellous faculties of observation. A permanent facet of his life was the study of the intense and colourful

The Return of the Herd (November)

1565
Oil on panel, 117 x 159 cm
Kunsthistorisches Museum, Vienna

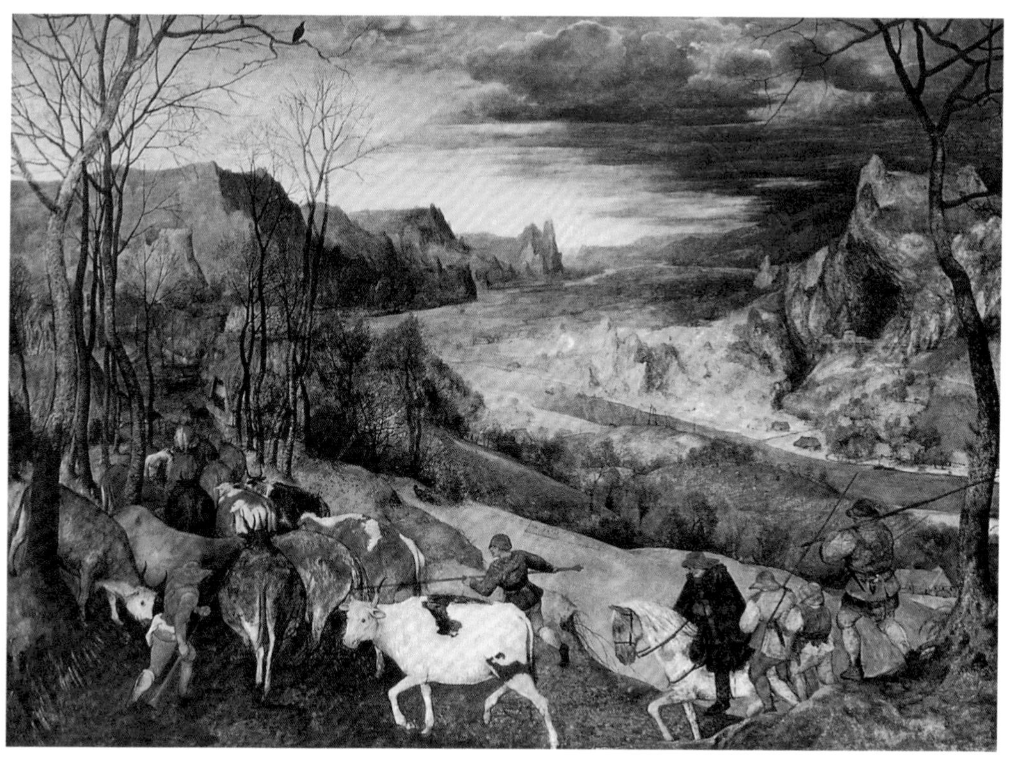

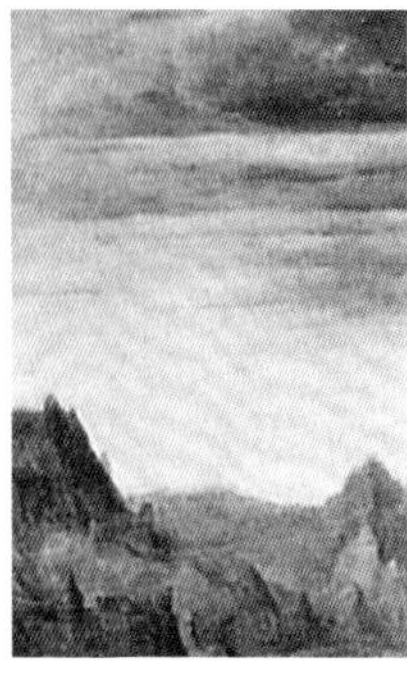

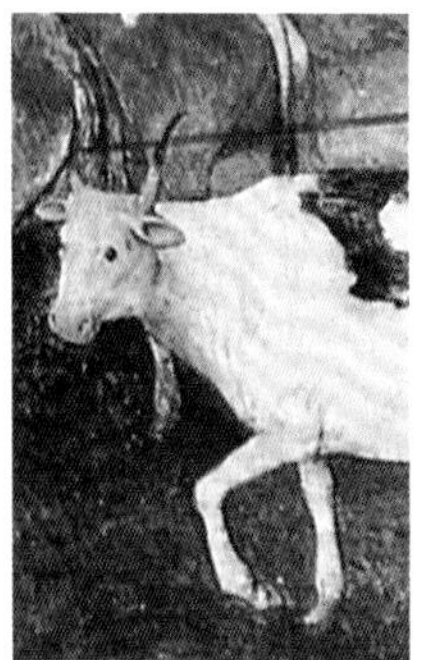

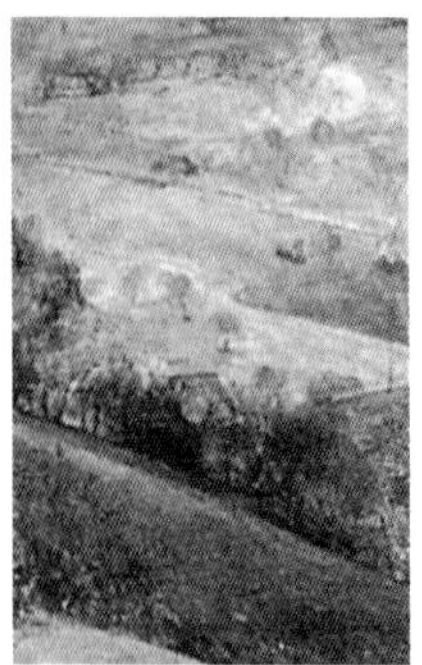

faces of the populace that surrounded him and their essentially miserable daily lives. He would note a spicy detail here, a salient feature there, and the synthesis of a work would be born out of the interior accumulation of his multiple and profound visions of the men, women, and objects of his time.

Van Manders completes this image of Bruegel's personality with a brief anecdote. "A merchant named

The Return of the Herd (November) (detail)

1565
Oil on panel, 117 x 159 cm
Kunsthistorisches Museum, Vienna

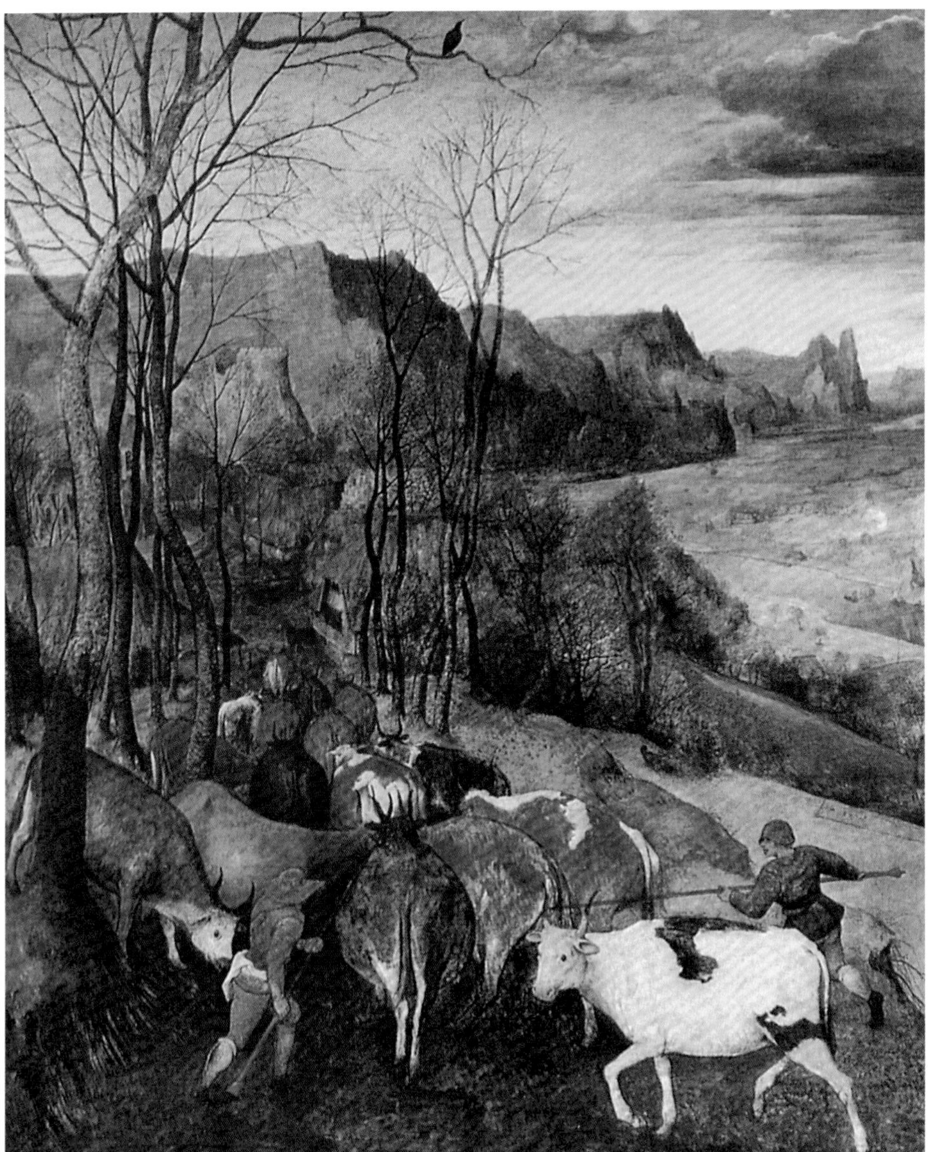

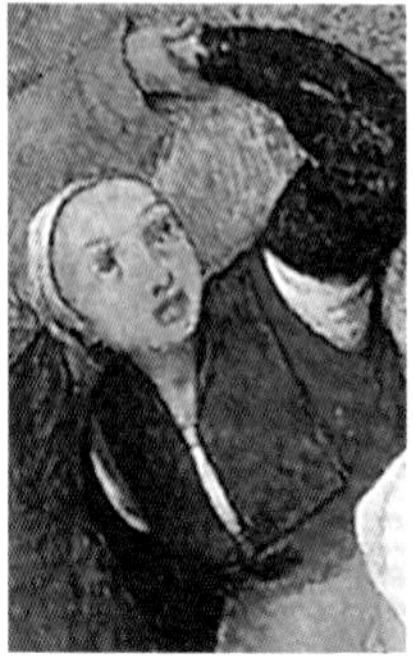

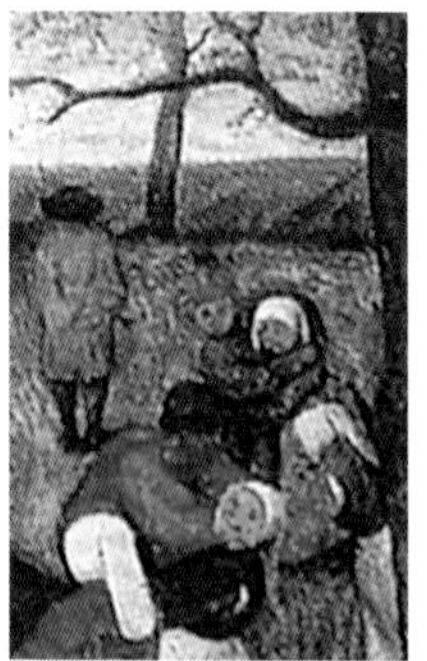

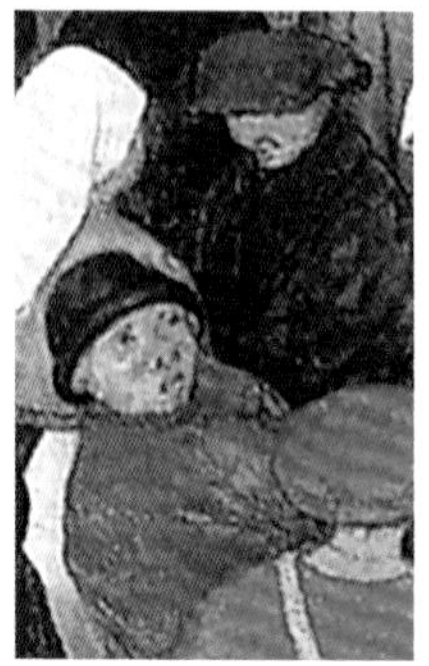

Hans Franckert had commissioned many paintings from Bruegel. He was an excellent man who was very attached to the painter. The two of them used to take great pleasure in disguising themselves as peasants to attend village fairs and weddings, offering presents like the other guests and pretending to be from the family of the bride or the groom. It was Bruegel's pleasure to study the rustic customs, celebrations,

The Wedding Dance

c. 1566
Oil on panel, 119.4 x 157.5 cm
The Detroit Institute of Art, Detroit

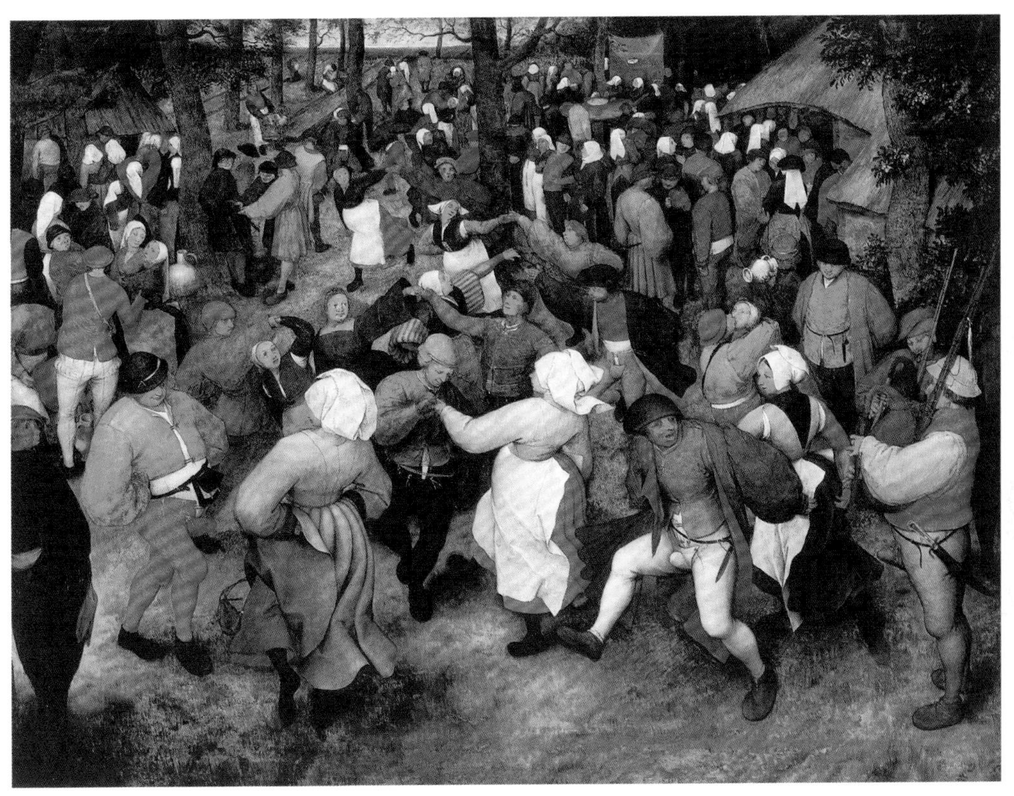

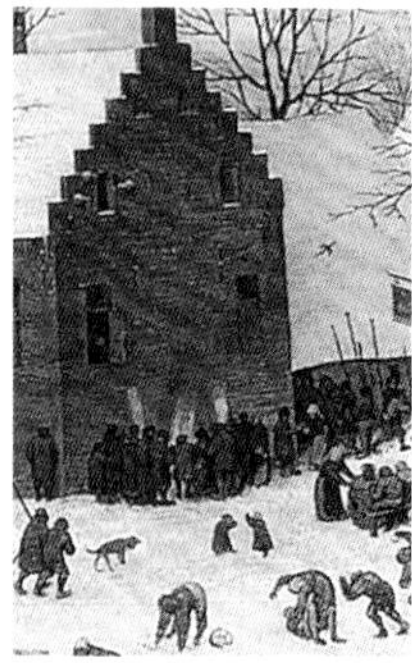

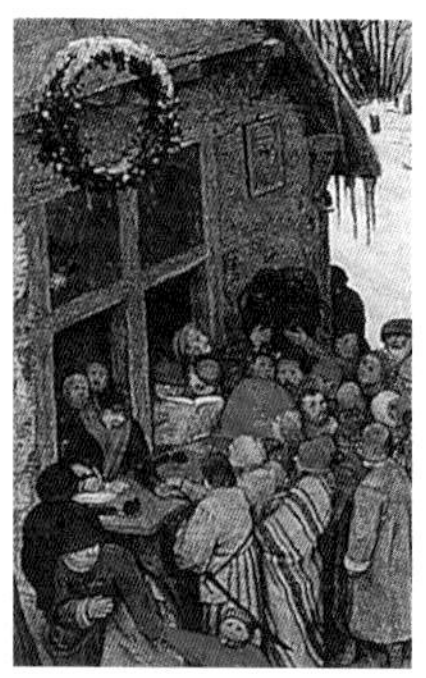

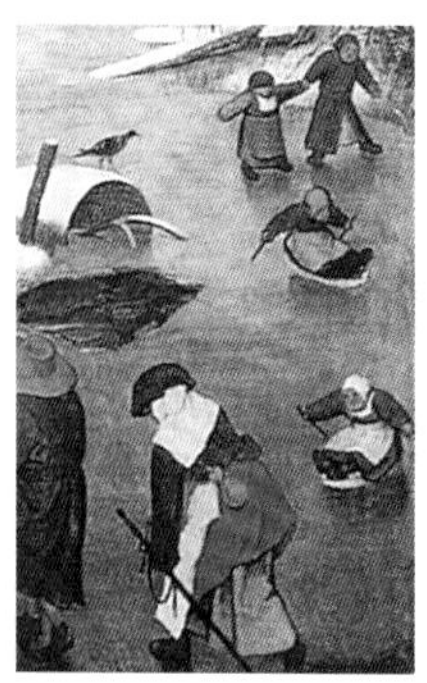

dances, and pastoral romances at which he excelled in translating with his paintbrush in both oil and tempera, for he was familiar with both techniques."

Pieter, from Breugel, the little hamlet in the north of Brabant, seems to have been irresistibly attracted to these peasants of the Campine region to whom he felt a deep affinity. His city life and contact with artists, the rich bourgeois, and the lords that frequented the shop

The Census at Bethlehem

1566
Oil on oak panel, 115.5 x 163.5 cm
Königliche Museen der Schönen Künste, Brussels

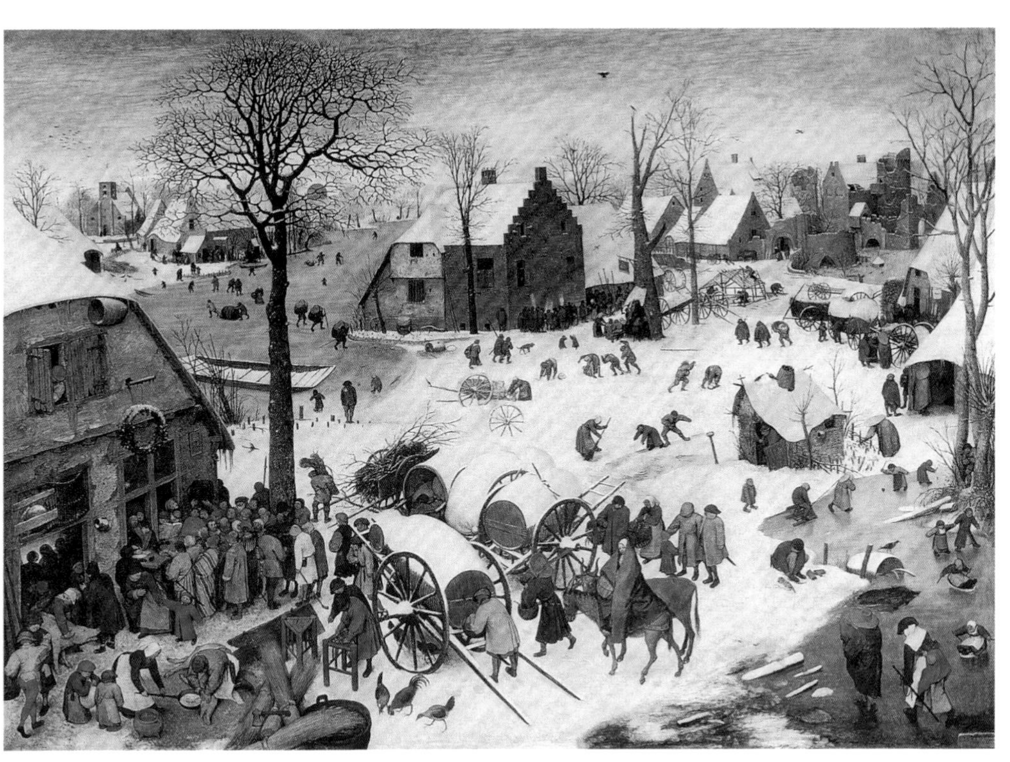

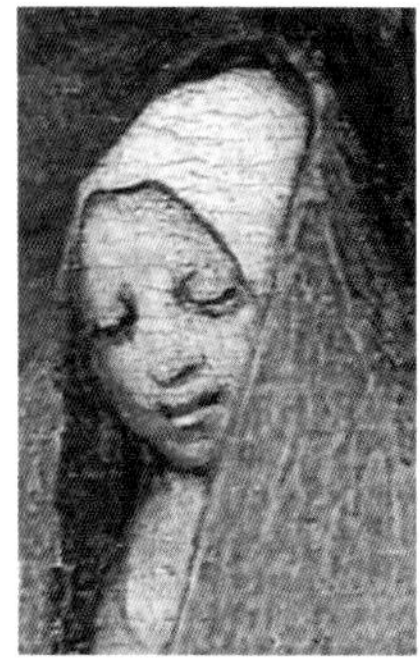

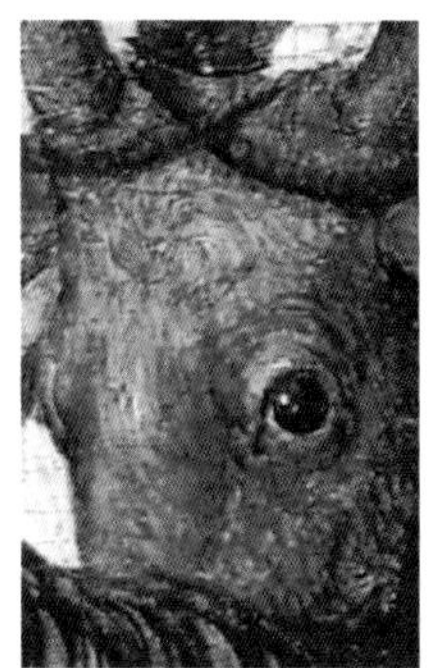

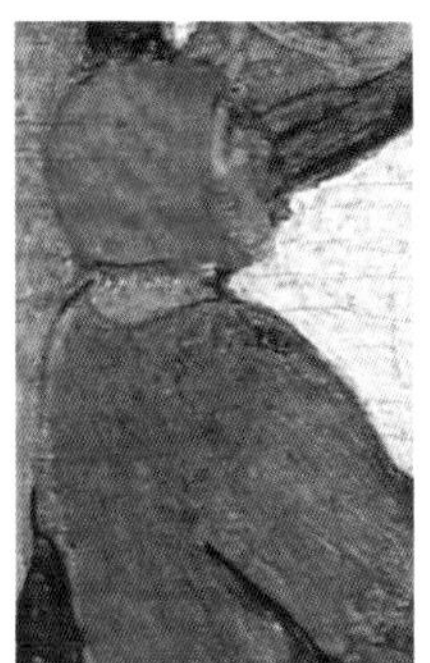

of his patron Hieronymus Cock, and even his travels in Italy must have refined his intelligence and developed the impeccable taste that every true artist carries within himself. Yet it seems that he also retained the timidity typical in people of rural origins and that he always felt a bit disoriented in big cities. When he was among his friends, his good humour would reappear with all its fantasy and excesses.

The Census at Bethlehem (detail)

1566
Oil on oak panel, 115.5 x 163.5 cm
Königliche Museen der Schönen Künste, Brussels

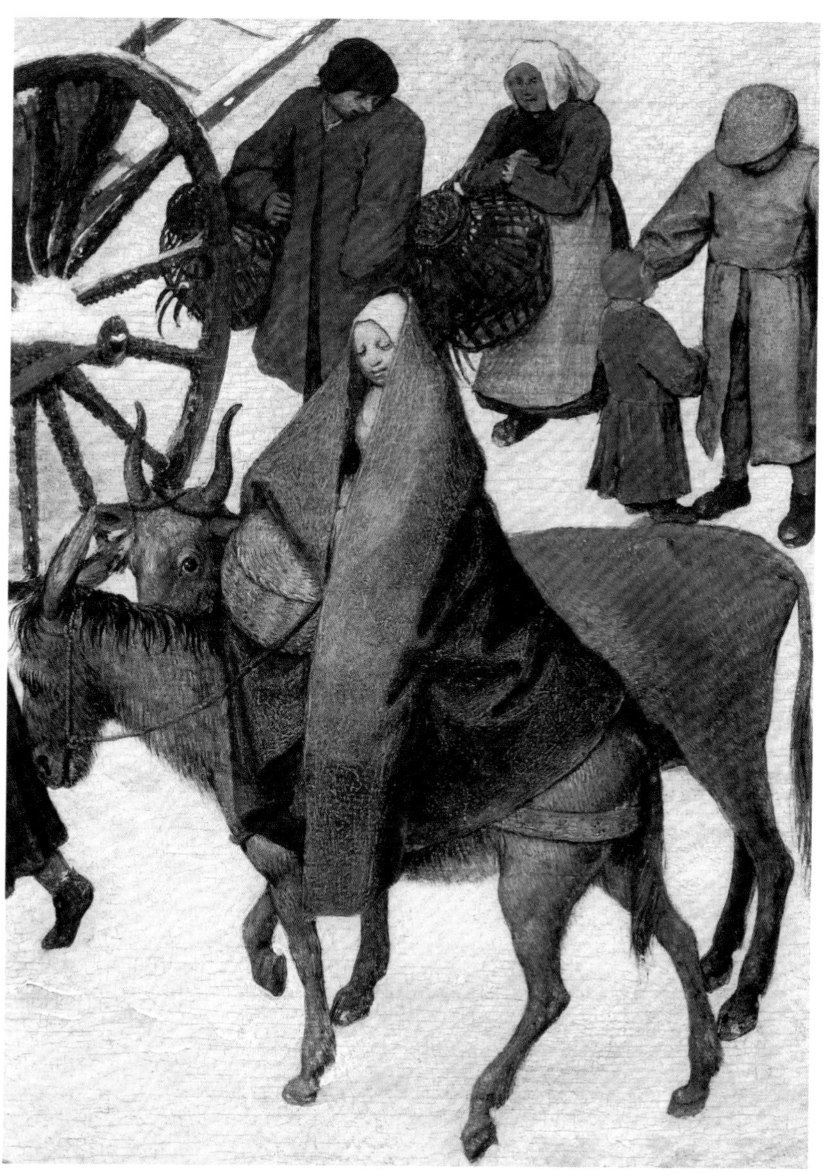

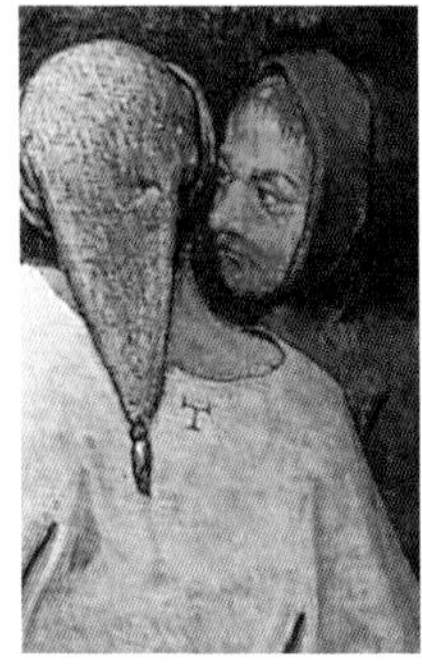

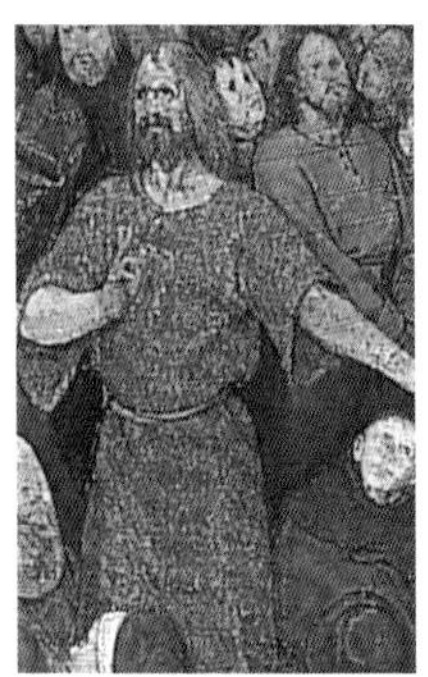

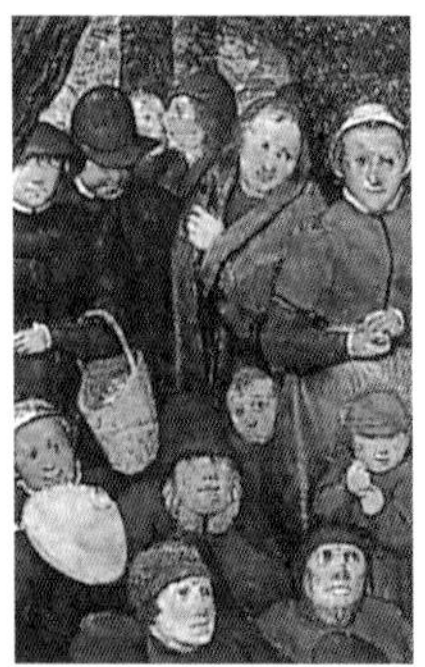

He liked nothing better than to return to his native region, to the peasants and squires of his origins. This is where the secret of his art can be found, this is the hidden stimulant of his genius. Bruegel expressed himself through his art, but he returned frequently to what could be described as the source of his ego. Like the mythical Antaeus, Bruegel was constantly renewing himself through continued contact with the earth from which he was issued.

The Sermon of Saint John the Baptist

1566
Oil on wood, 95 x 160.5 cm
Szépmüvészeti Múzeum, Budapest

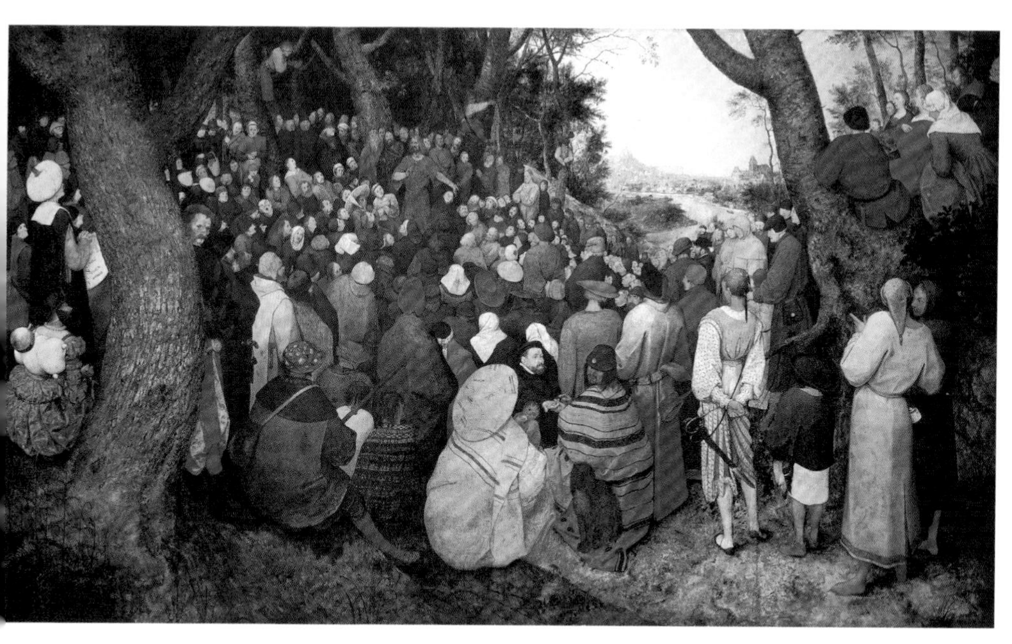

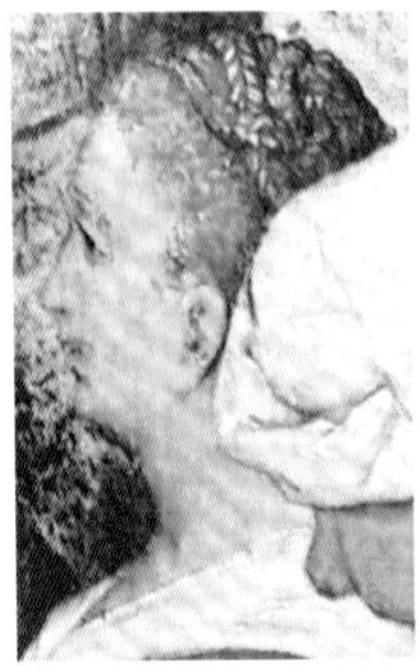

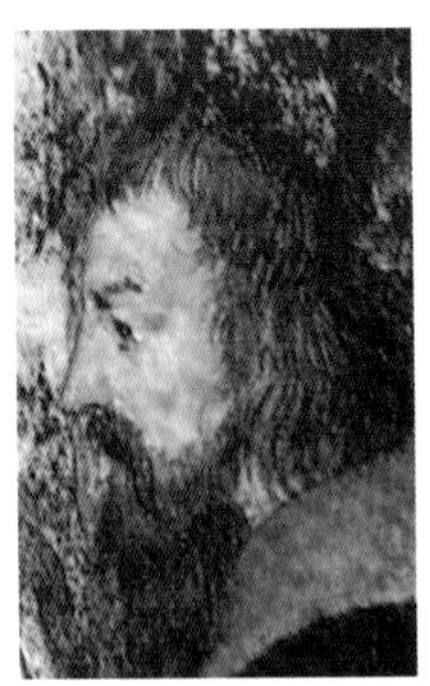

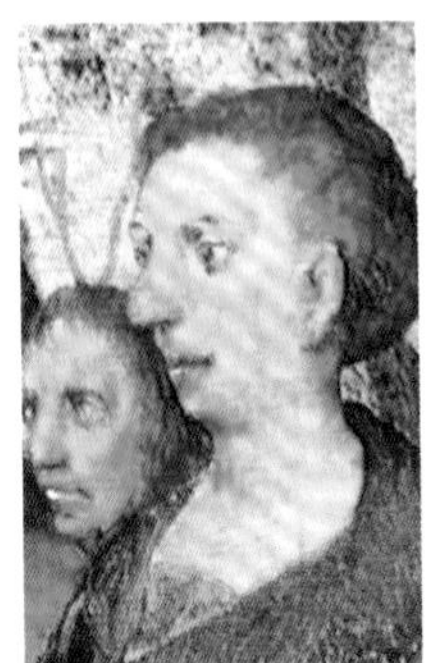

Bruegel did not only attend weddings, banquets, and festivals to observe peasant customs. He also captured men while they were at work and in repose. As he was not only a sharp observer, but also a talented draughtsman, his lines are broad and vigorous, supple and free. He mercilessly traces the silhouettes of his models, pruning out useless details and capturing the essentials of their personalities. Each gesture and pose

The Sermon of Saint John the Baptist (detail)

1566
Oil on wood, 95 x 160.5 cm
Szépmüvészeti Múzeum, Budapest

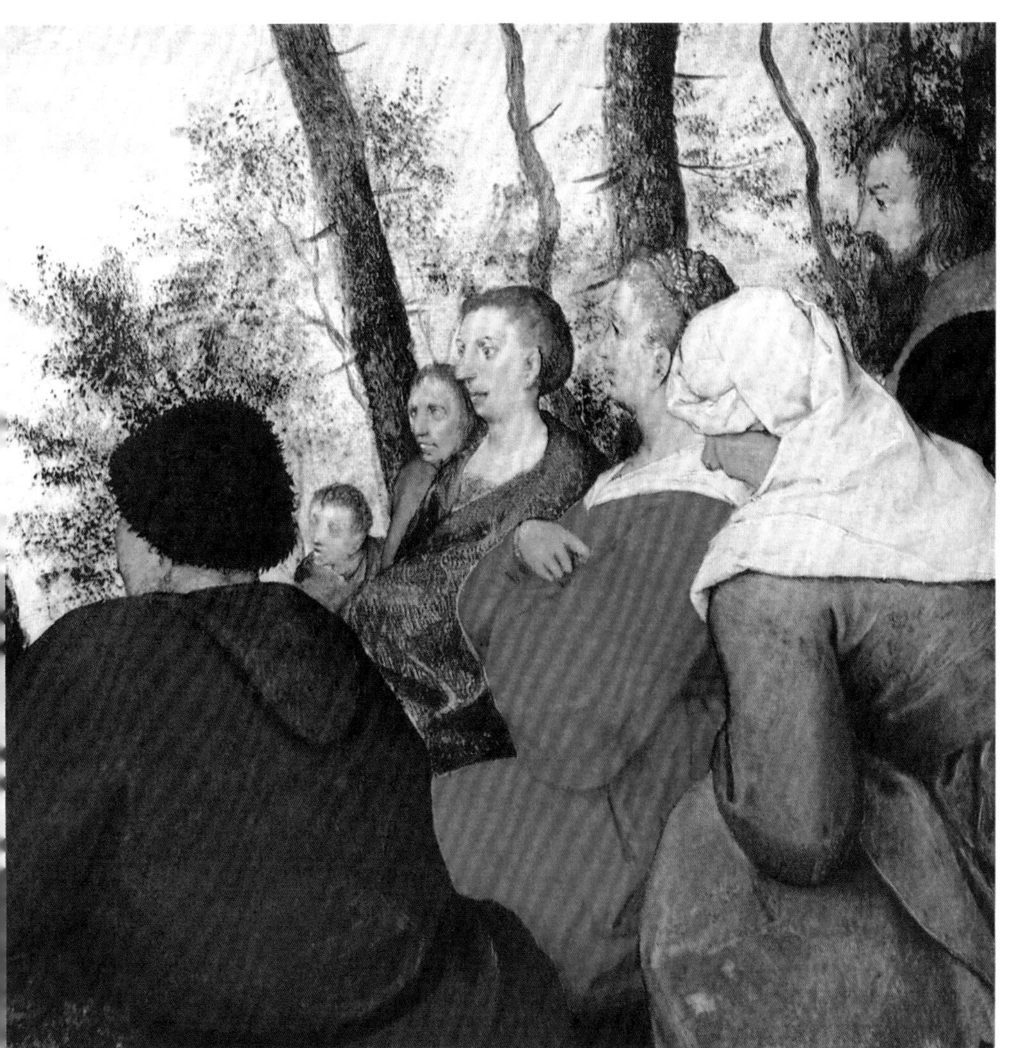

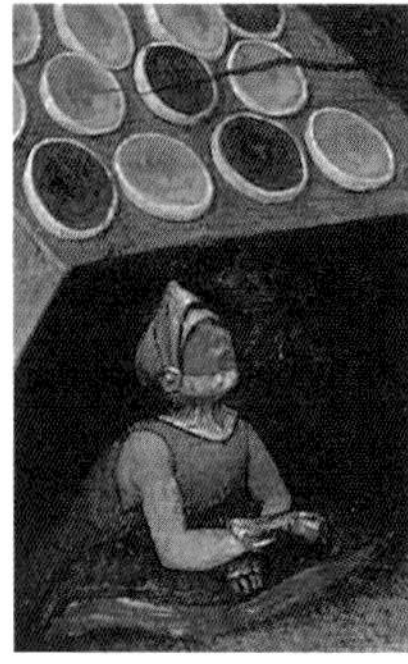

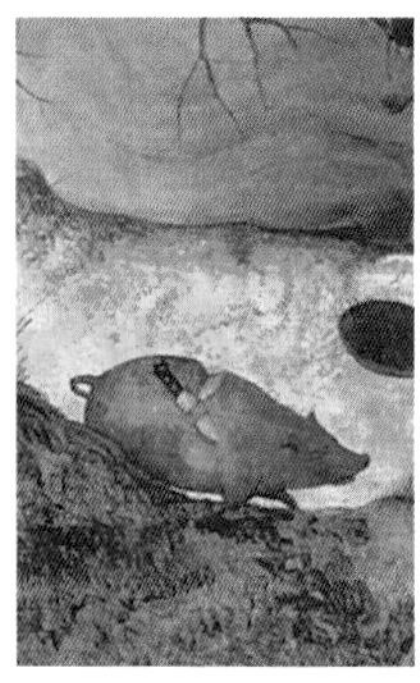

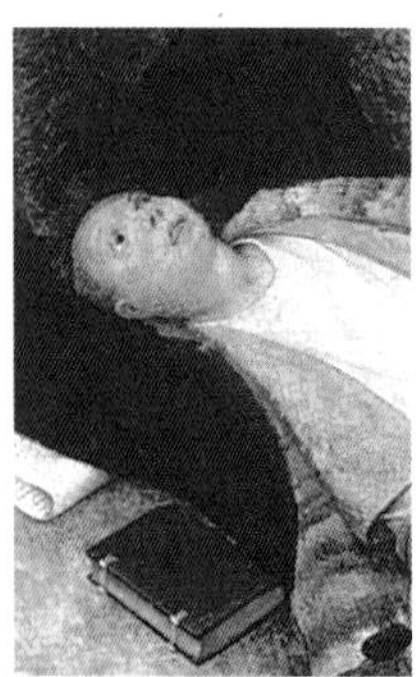

is faithfully interpreted. When he captures the image of a man in action, the movement is not interrupted, and has neither a beginning nor an ending: it simply happens. This is the source of the life that animates even his smallest compositions. His *Hunters in the Snow* and *The Return of the Herd* are astonishing in their naturalism and their profound attractiveness. Bruegel was also a keen observer of animals. His horses and cows, like those

The Land of Cockaigne

1566
Oil on wood, 52 x 78 cm
Alte Pinakothek, Munich

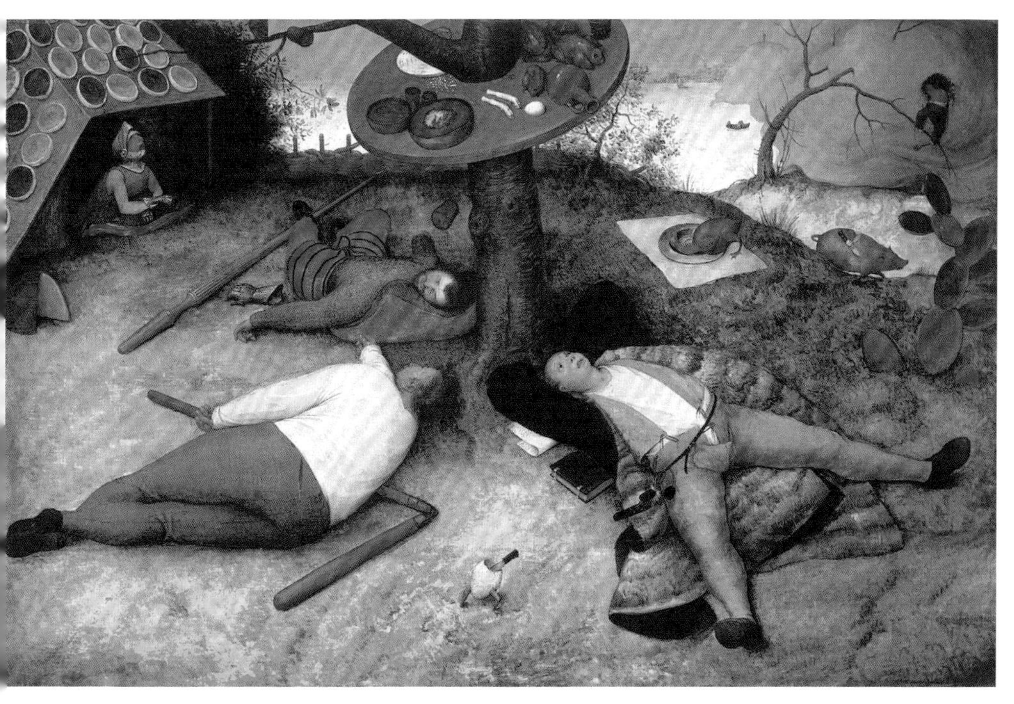

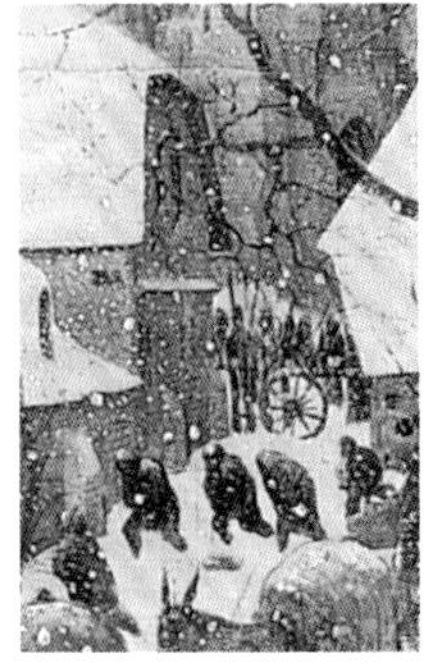

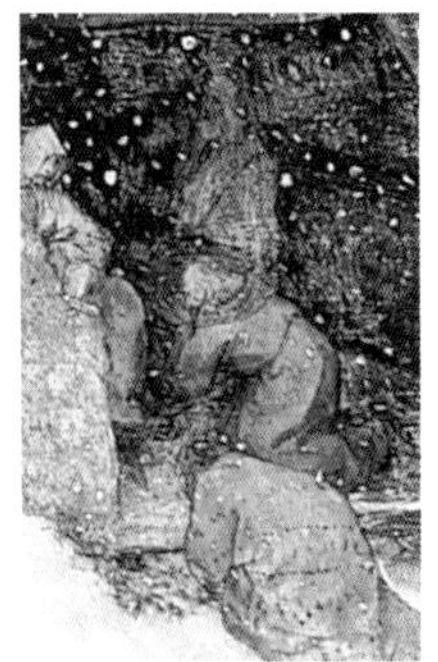

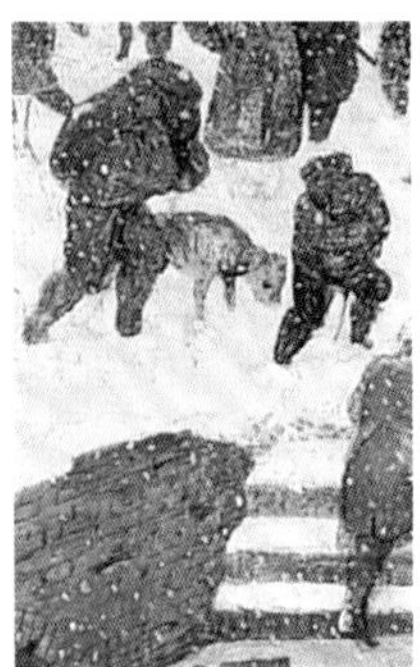

in *The Return of the Herd*, and his dogs, like those in *Hunters in the Snow*, are very distinctive. A pen and ink drawing of a team of two harnessed workhorses in the Albertina Museum in Vienna is sufficient proof that Bruegel was a talented artist of animals.

It was nature that seduced Bruegel, and it was in nature that he found his inspiration and the secret driving force of his art. He sought to penetrate the

The Adoration of the Magi in the Snow

1567
Tempera on panel, 35 x 55 cm
Oskar Reinhart Collection, Winterthur

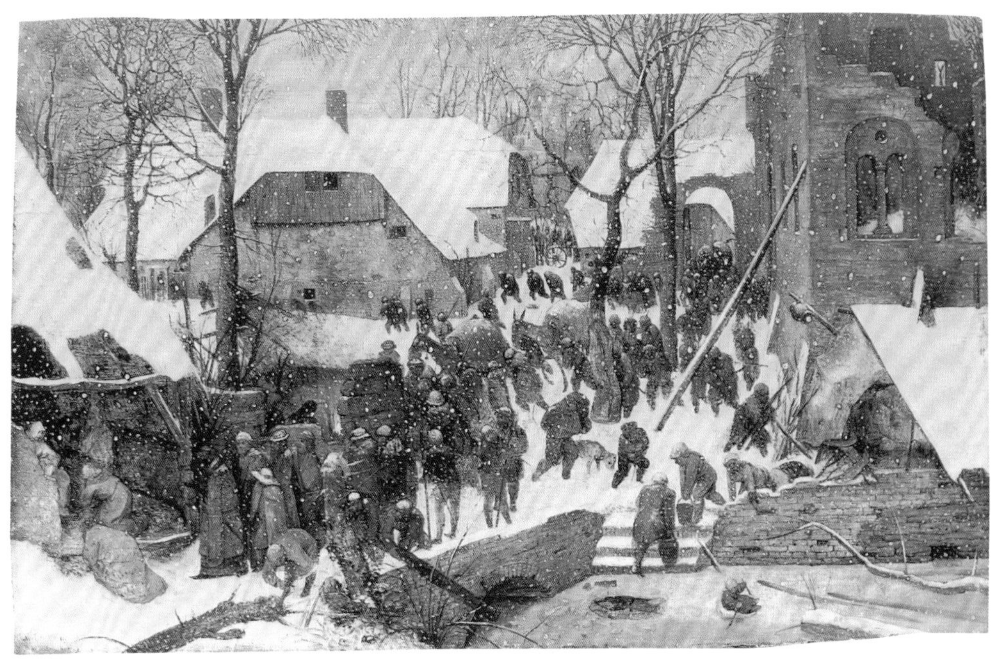

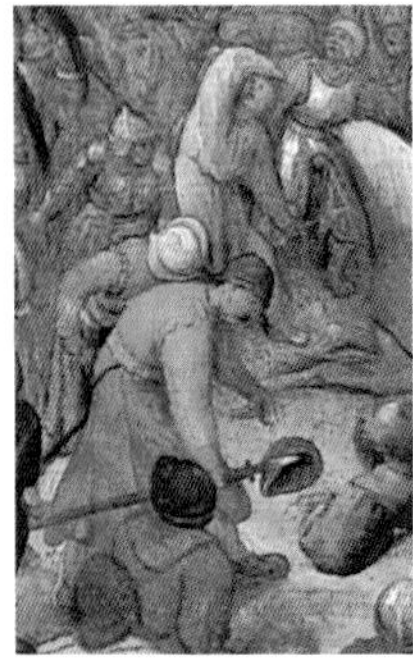

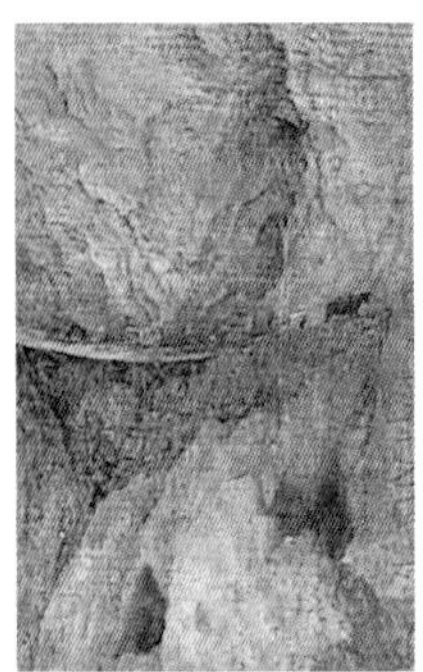

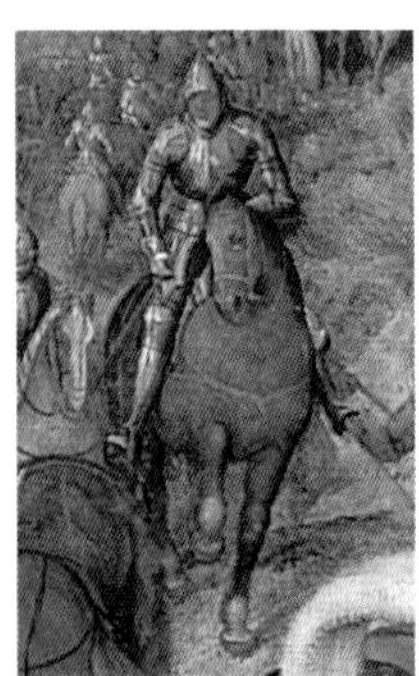

essence of objects just as he strove to capture their many aspects. At the same time, he studied the rudimentary but elusive psychology of the people he portrayed, his alert eyes breaking down their movements, noting the salient lines of their faces, and retaining their expressions. The sum of his works, like each of his individual figures, shines with a sincerity that is at once powerful and troubling.

The Conversion of Saint Paul

1567
Oil on wood, 108 x 156 cm
Kunsthistorisches Museum, Vienna

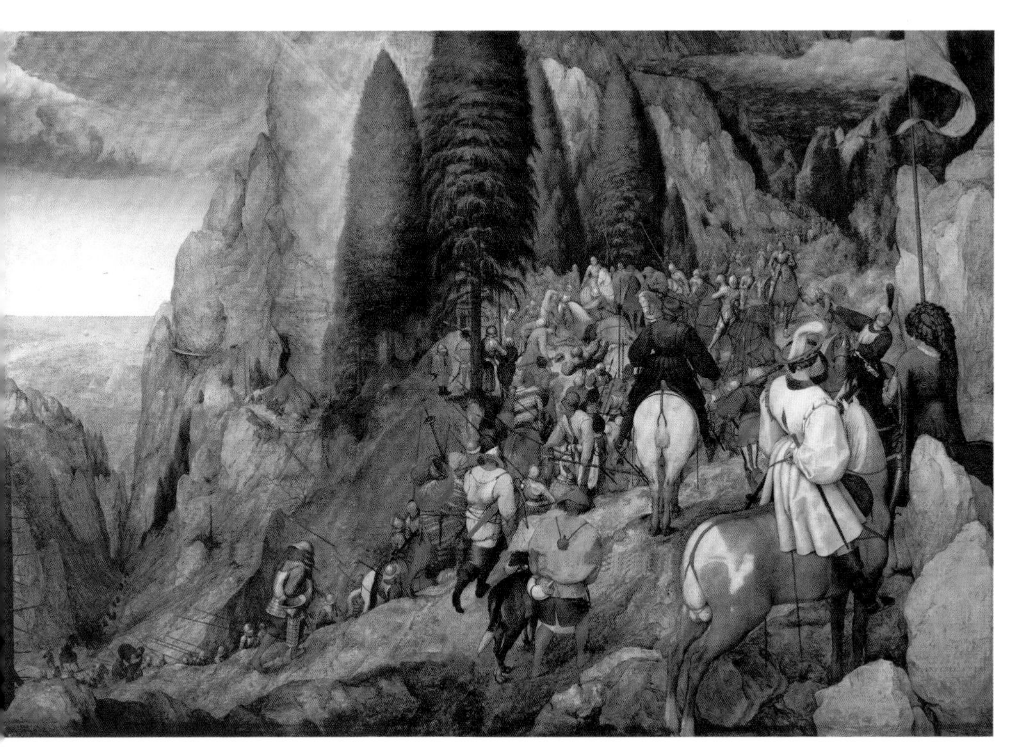

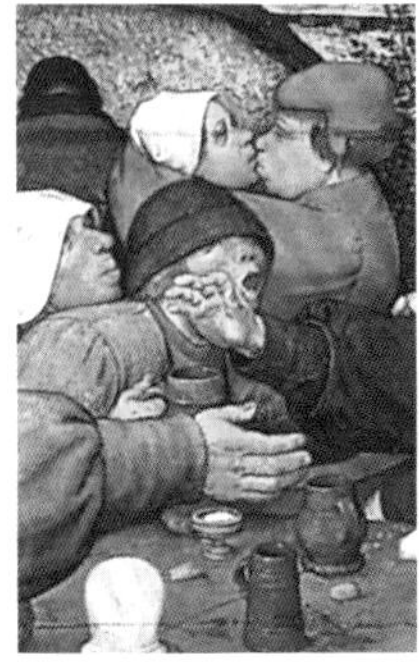

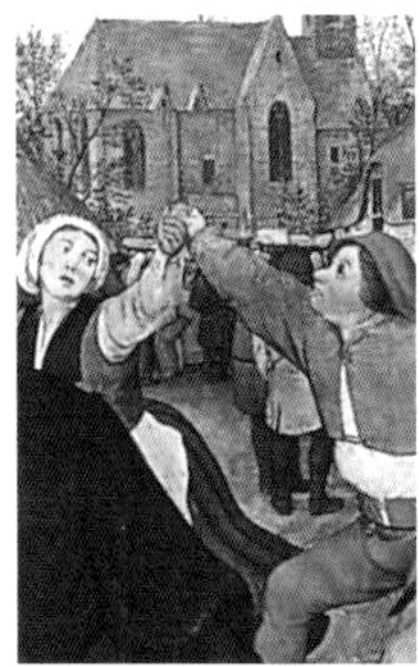

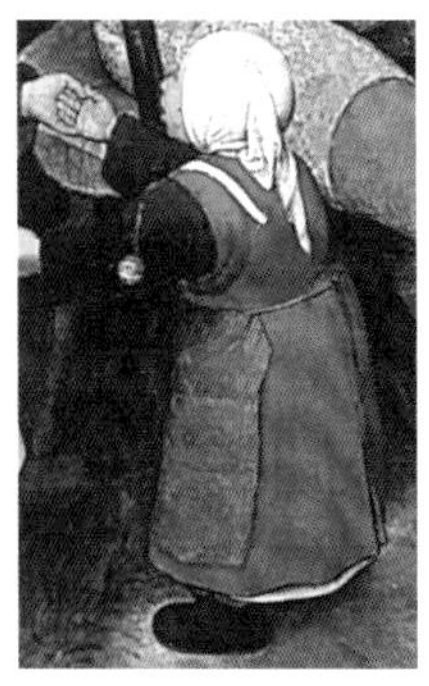

Christ's Descent into Limbo, a pen and ink drawing from 1561, plunges back into devilry. Set at the centre of an oval, Christ, nude beneath a tunic, in the manner that the glorious Christ was always portrayed in that time, advances upon the mouth of Hell from which the crowd of delivered patriarchs escapes. Around him bustles a mass of ghosts and demons whose forms are borrowed from toads, fish, and bats, while the damned are made to suffer refined and morbidly humorous tortures.

The Peasant Dance

c. 1568
Oil on wood, 114 x 164 cm
Kunsthistorisches Museum, Vienna

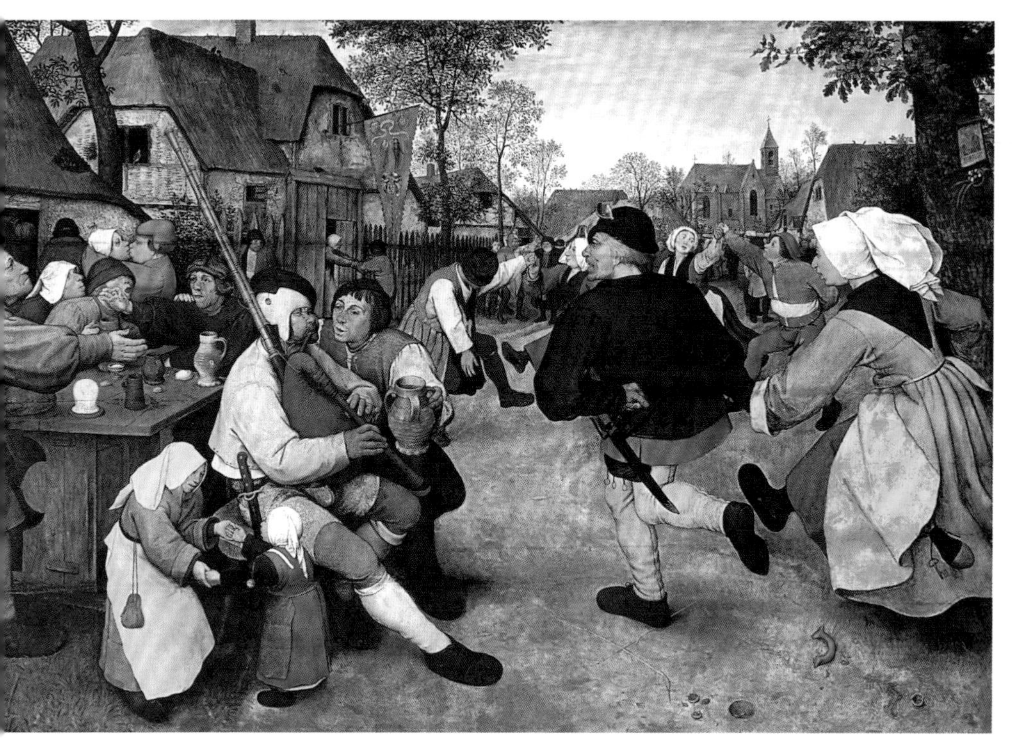

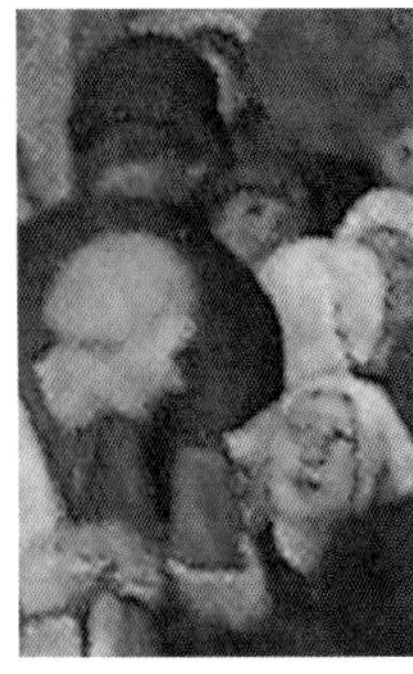

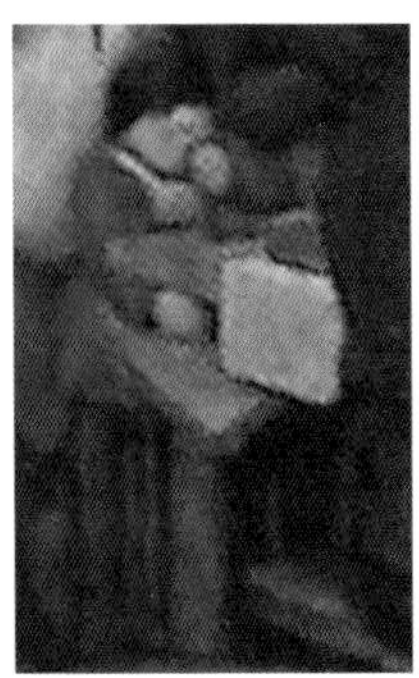

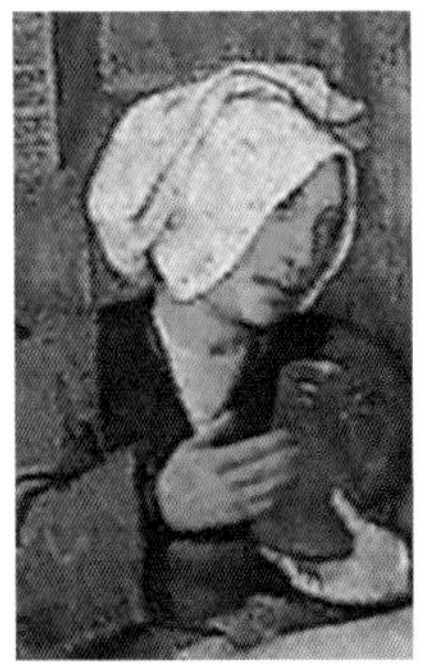

This drawing is a preparation for *The Fall of the Rebel Angels* painted the following year, the most impressive effort by Bruegel in this genre. The richness of colour is particularly striking with its knowledgeable harmony between whites, yellows, ochres, and browns which melt into one another and lighten as they fade into the distance. At the summit in the centre, the archangels descend from above with harsh blows of their

Peasant Wedding

c. 1568
Oil on wood, 114 x 164 cm
Kunsthistorisches Museum, Vienna

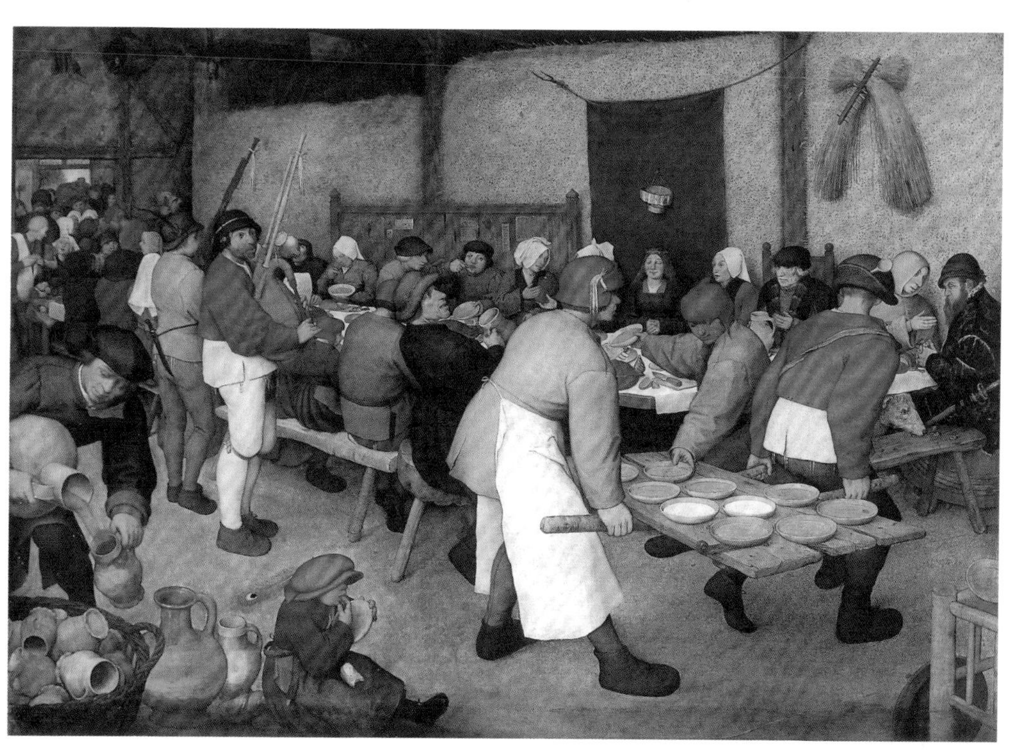

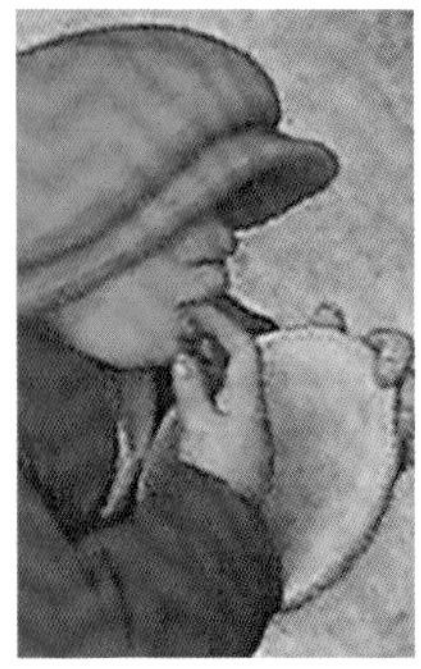

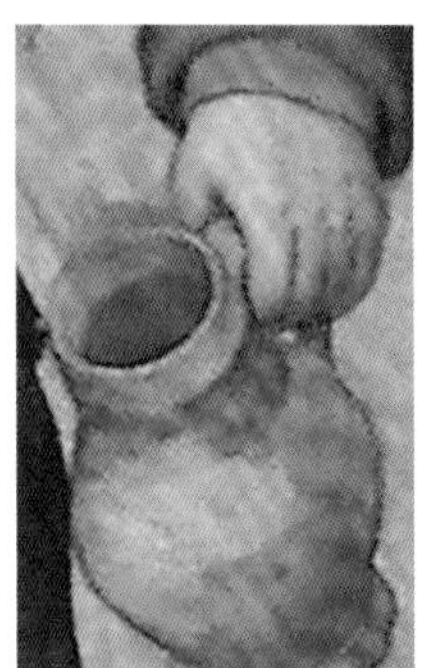

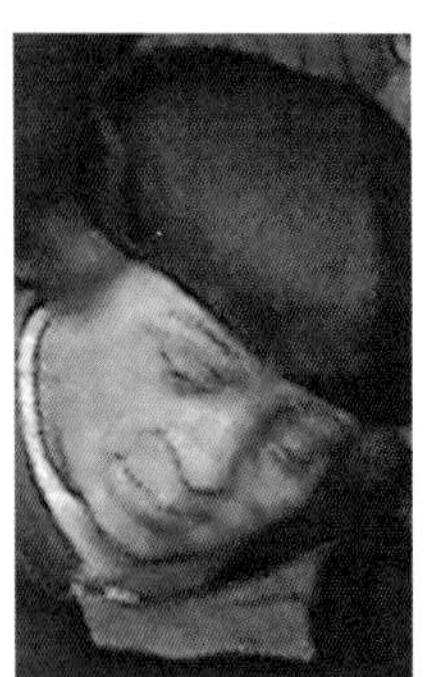

broadswords. The white robes of the first, who turns to the left, illuminate the scene with a blinding burst of light. At the centre, a long-limbed and bare-headed Saint Michael, wearing golden armour, his blue cape floating behind him, lowers his shield at the end of his outstretched arm towards a veritable tangle of frightful heads, arms, tentacles, and jaws that surge up and twist beneath his feet. In the upper corners, angels wearing

Peasant Wedding (detail)

c. 1568
Oil on wood, 114 x 164 cm
Kunsthistorisches Museum, Vienna

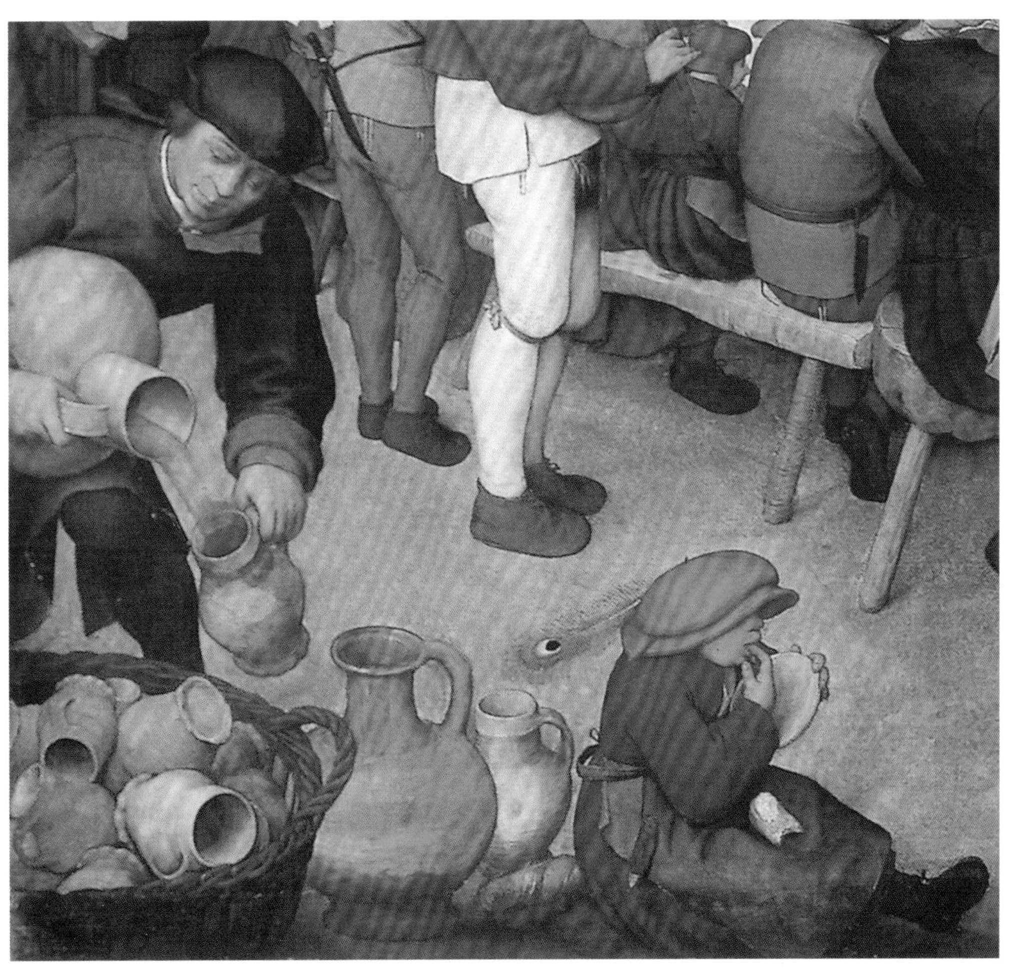

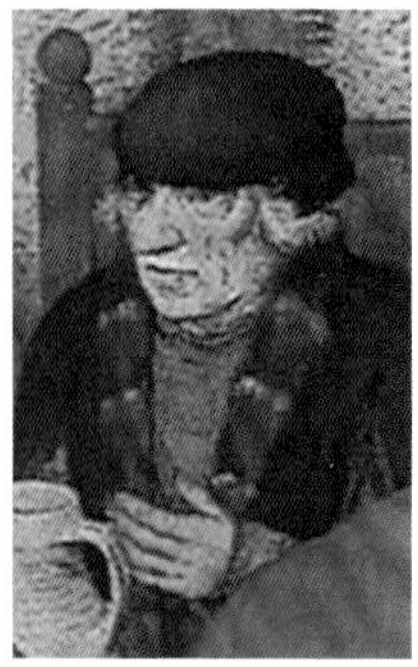

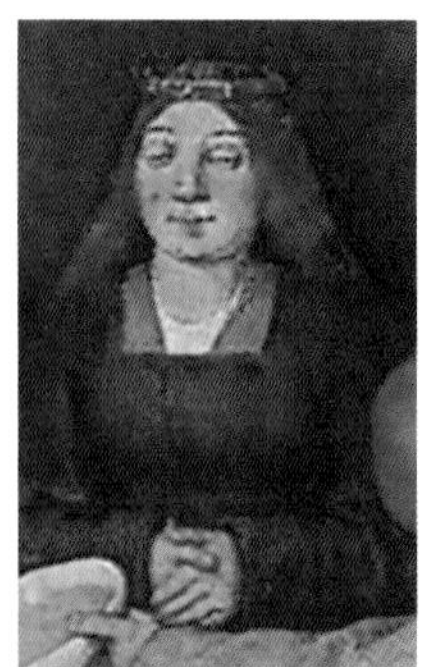

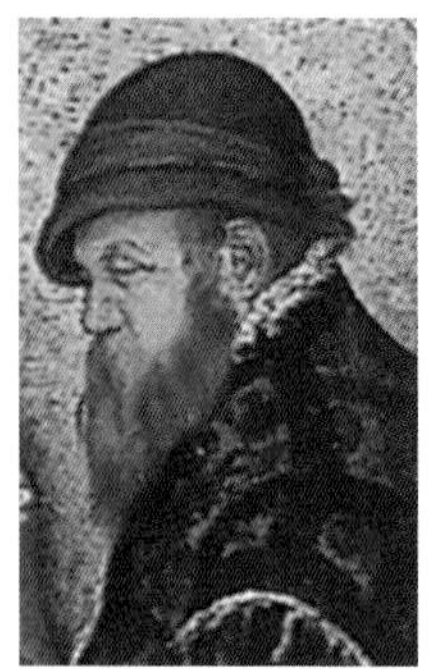

white, blue, yellow, and pink sound their trumpets. From the sides and in the lower corners an incredible mass of monsters and unearthly beasts surge. Here, Bruegel is just as imaginative as Bosch, yet more accurate in his execution, with the strange life he breathes into his unreal creatures. Each part of which they are composed – such as frog bellies, reptile tails, lizard or fish heads – is full of life and admirably observed.

Peasant Wedding (detail)

c. 1568
Oil on wood, 114 x 164 cm
Kunsthistorisches Museum, Vienna

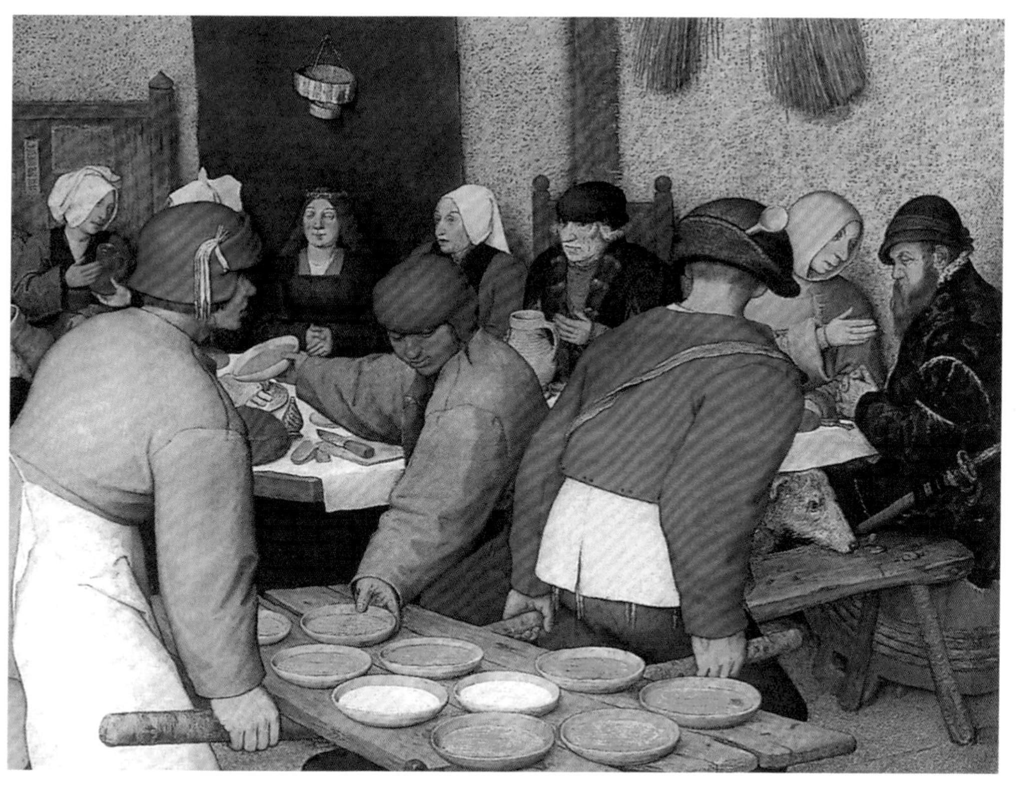

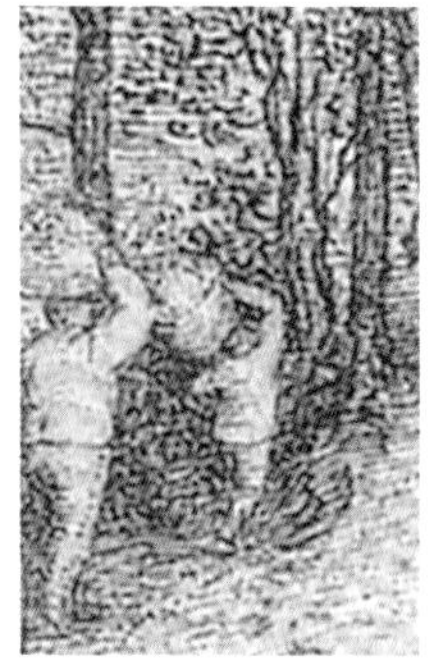

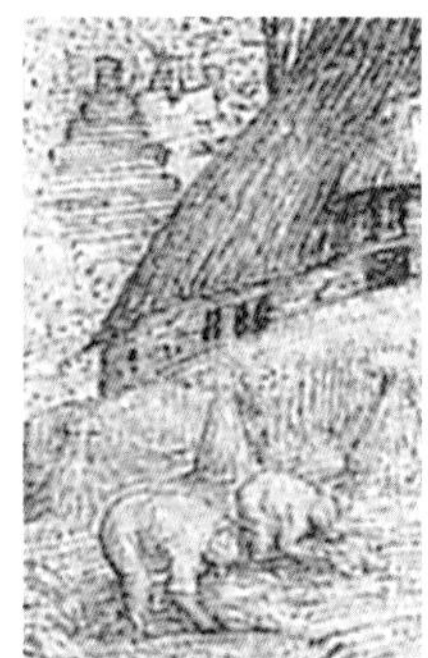

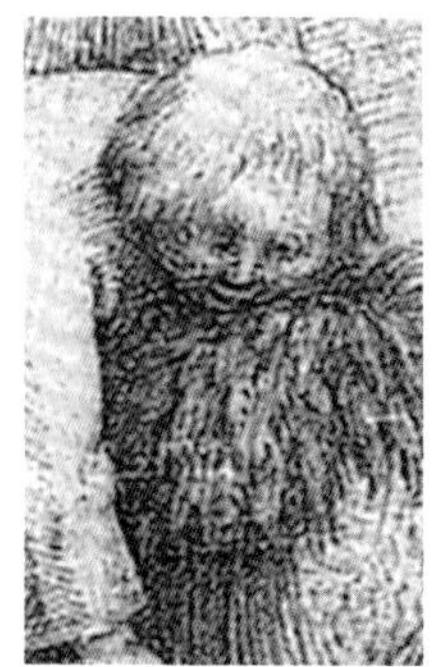

Bruegel borrows from all the kingdoms of life: he couples animals with plants, even inanimate objects. On the left, in the mass of demons that pursue the white archangel, one creature has a turnip for a head, an artichoke for a body, and a carrot for a tail. Between its head and body are a butterfly's wings and two thin arms, one protected by arm and elbow armour, the other terminating with pincers. Elsewhere, from a sort of

Summer

1568

Pen and Indian ink, 22 x 28.6 cm

Hamburger Kunsthalle, Kupferstichkabinett, Hamburg

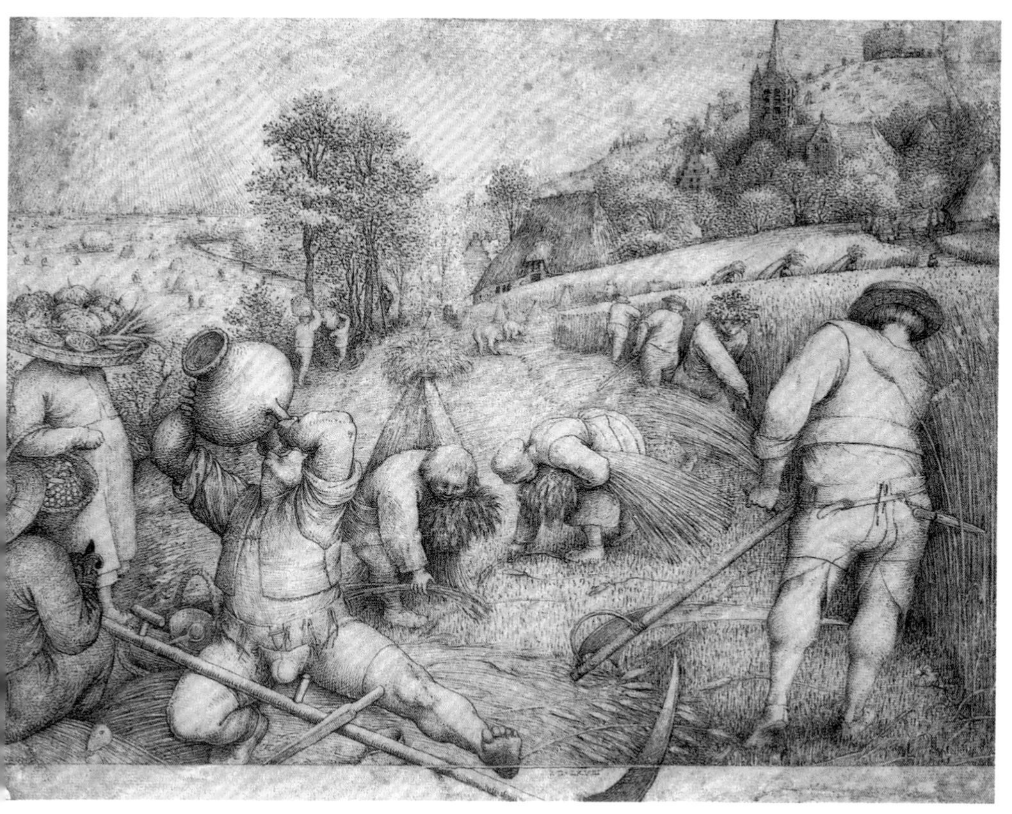

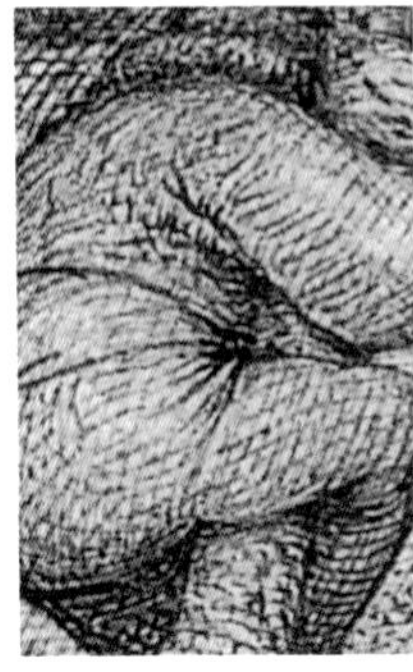

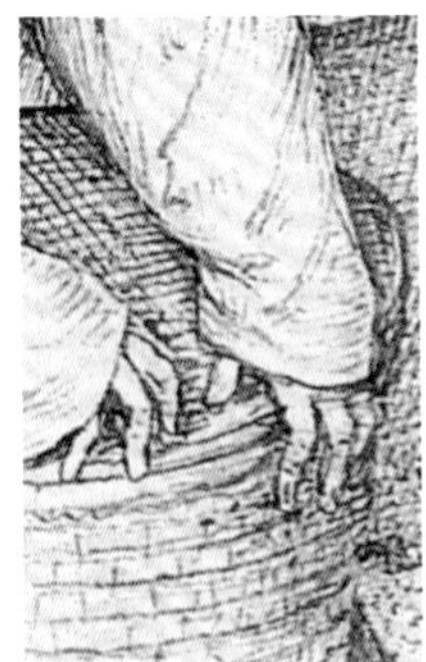

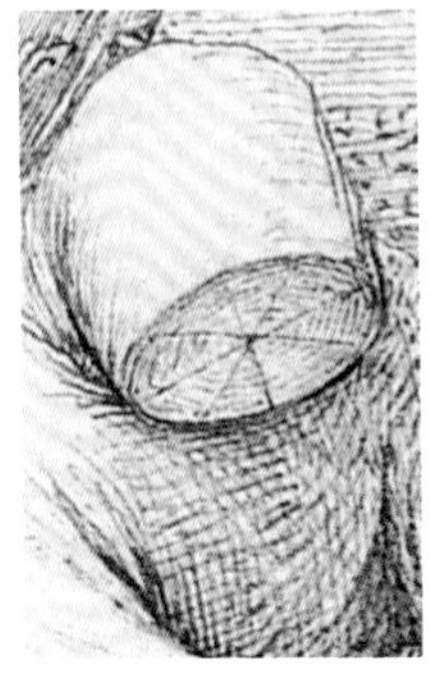

guitar, sprout the head and legs of a monstrous beetle. An upside-down demon has arms in place of his legs and bites its wrists. Another, with a mouth crossed between a wolf and a crocodile, carries a basket full of frightful baby birds with long gaping beaks. There are sharks, helmet-wearing frogs, foetuses, and gigantic molluscs. A toad undoes the buttons on its stomach to reveal the eggs swelling inside.

The Beekeepers

1568
Pen and Indian ink, 20.3 x 30.9 cm
Staatliche Museen, Berlin

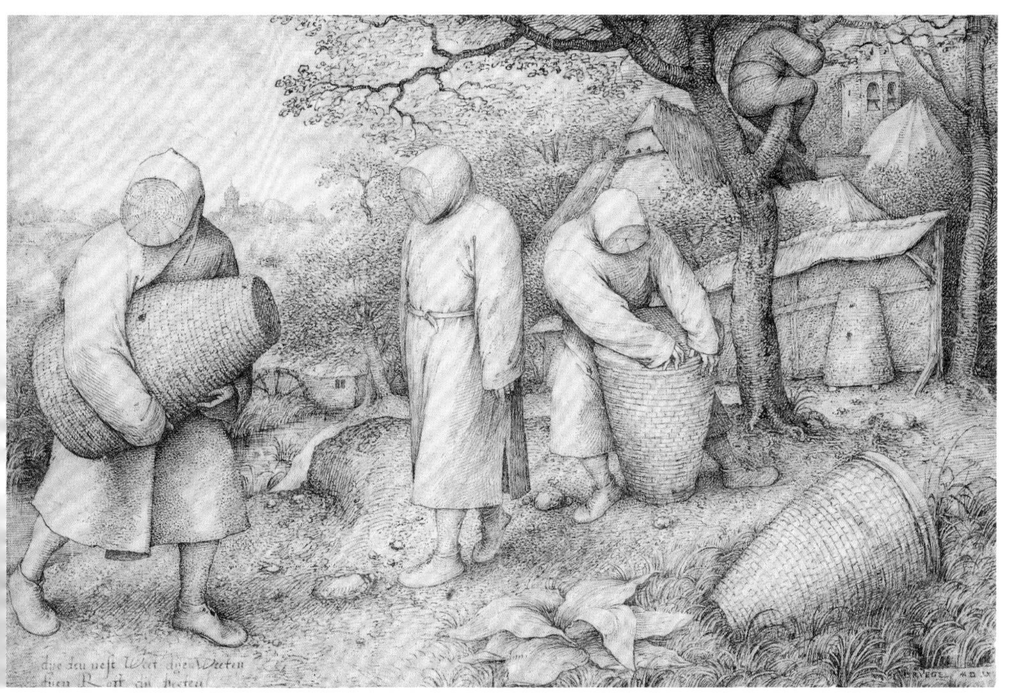

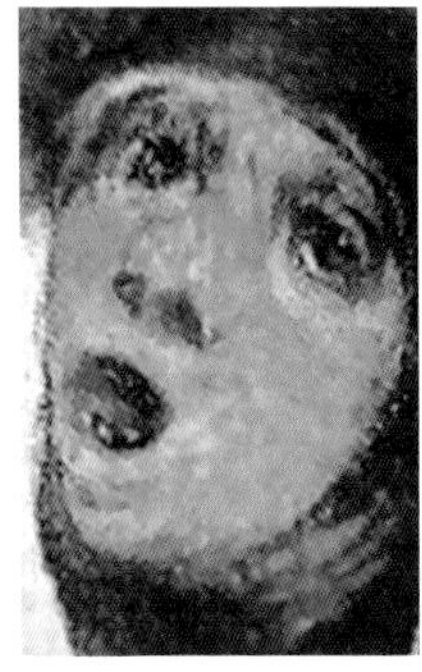

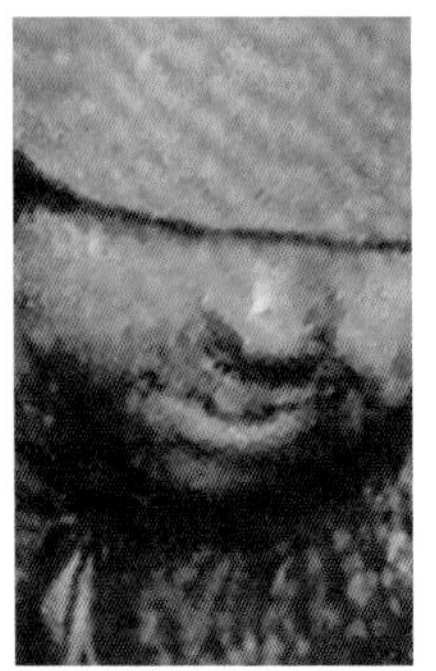

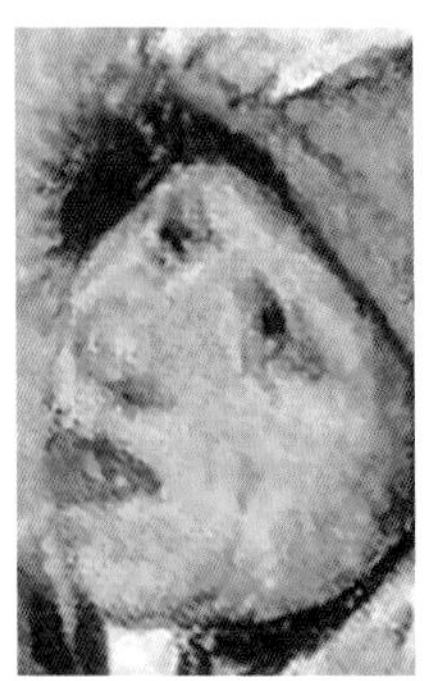

Flying fish, bats, and moths take flight amid a swarm of flies, and here and there grimacing human heads fixed to the bodies of monkeys or insects complete the exasperation of this nightmarish vision.

Two years later, in 1564, Bruegel created the original drawing known by the name *The Fall of the Magician* or *Saint James and the Magician Hermogenes*, depending upon which of these two legends is seen by the viewer. The same year was

The Beggars

1568
Oil on wood panel, 18.5 x 21.5 cm
Musée du Louvre, Paris

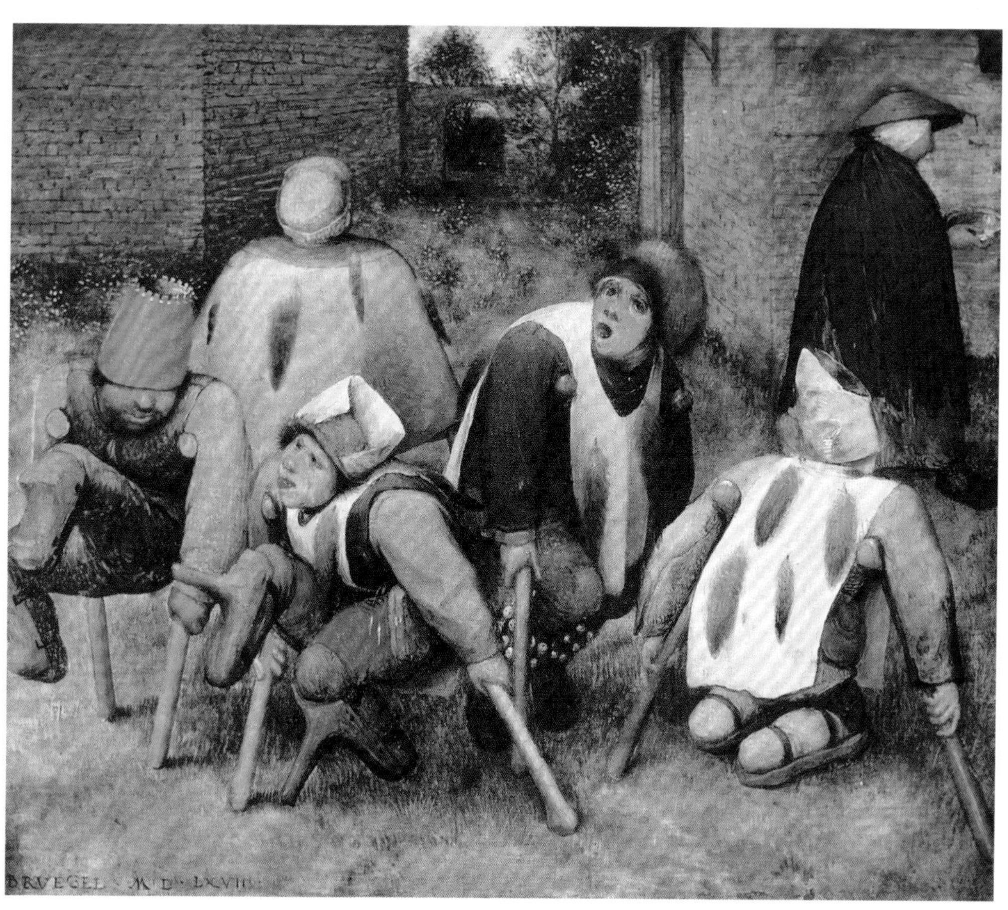
BRVEGEL · M · D · LXVIII

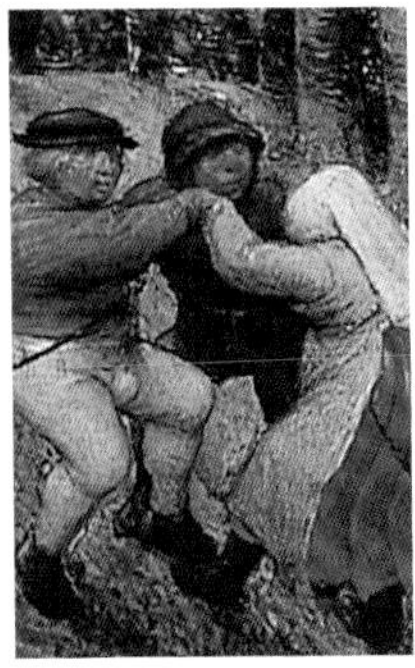

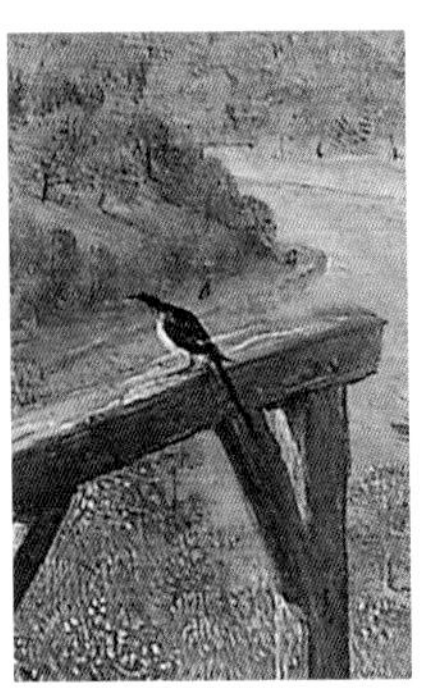

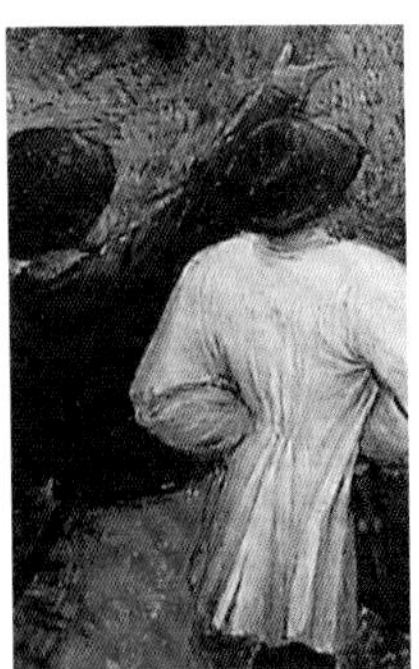

marked by the completion of a much more important work, *Dulle Griet*, which is, in a sense, the crowning achievement of Bruegel's diabolical imagery. *Margaret the Mad* and *Margaret the Terrible* are two possible translations of the name of this woman that personifies the straying and furious insanity of evil. For example, the large cannon of Ghent was baptised Dulle Griet. Zwarte Griet, which means the same thing in Flanders,

The Magpie on the Gallows

1568
Oil on wood, 46 x 51 cm
Hessisches Landesmuseum, Darmstadt

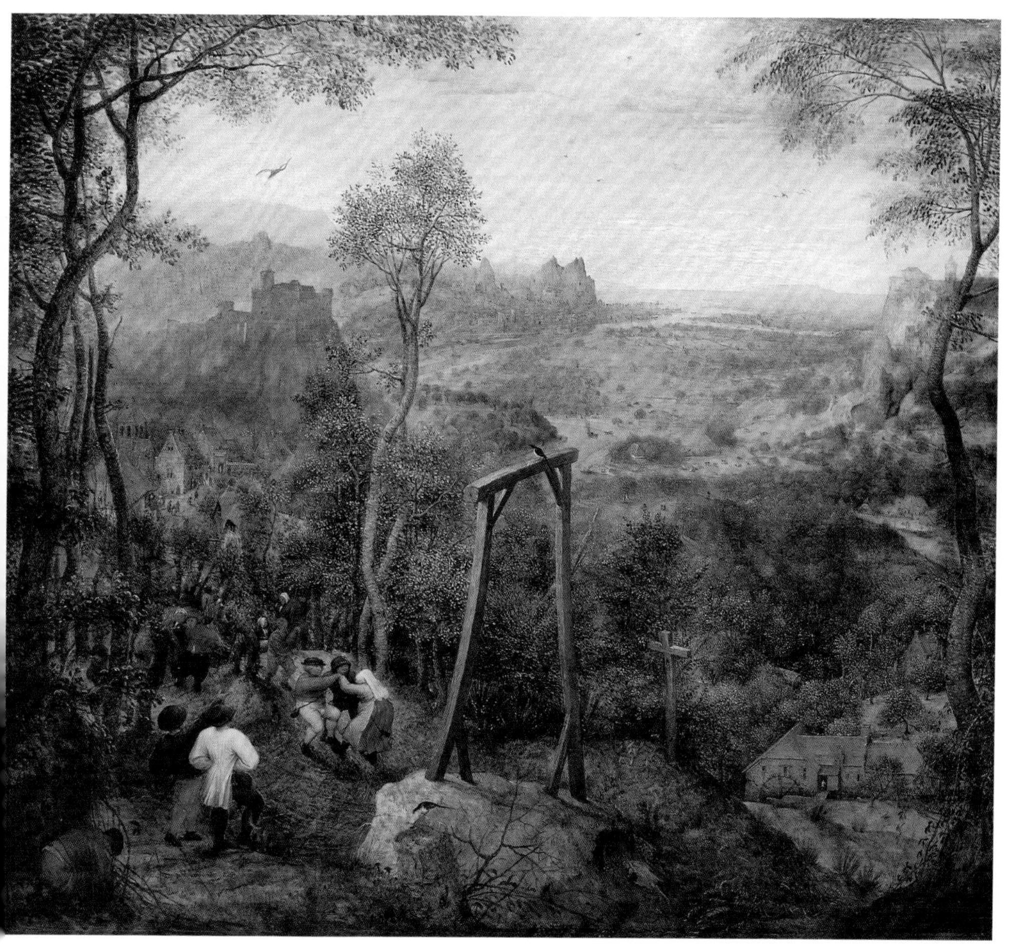

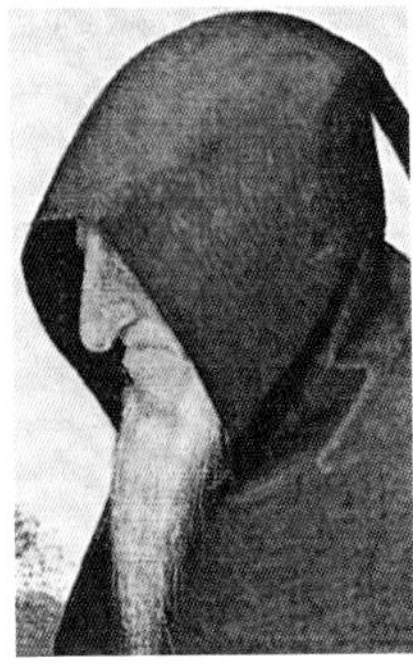

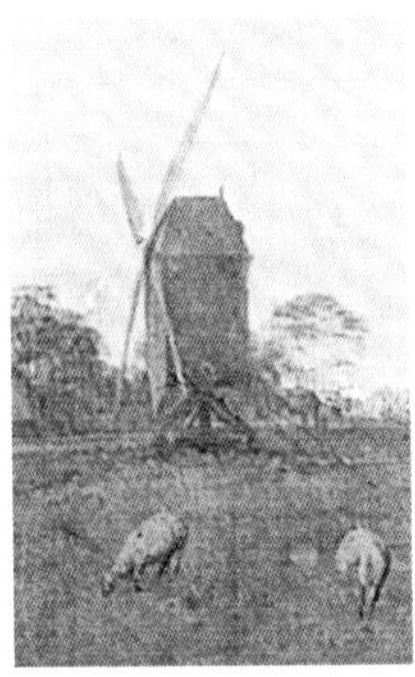

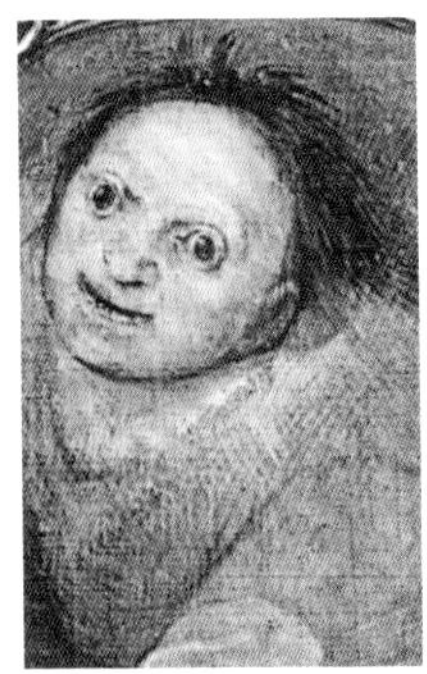

Holland, and part of Germany, was the personification of an evil woman before whom even the Devil is afraid.

In this work, Bruegel returns to his favourite style of composition. Around a large central figure that attracts the viewer's attention, which is set among a vast and complicated decor, unfold countless smaller related scenes acted out by smaller figures. Dulle Griet, with her sword in one hand, advances towards the Mouth of Hell.

The Misanthrope

1568
Oil on canvas, diameter: 86 cm
Museo Nazionale di Capodimonte, Naples

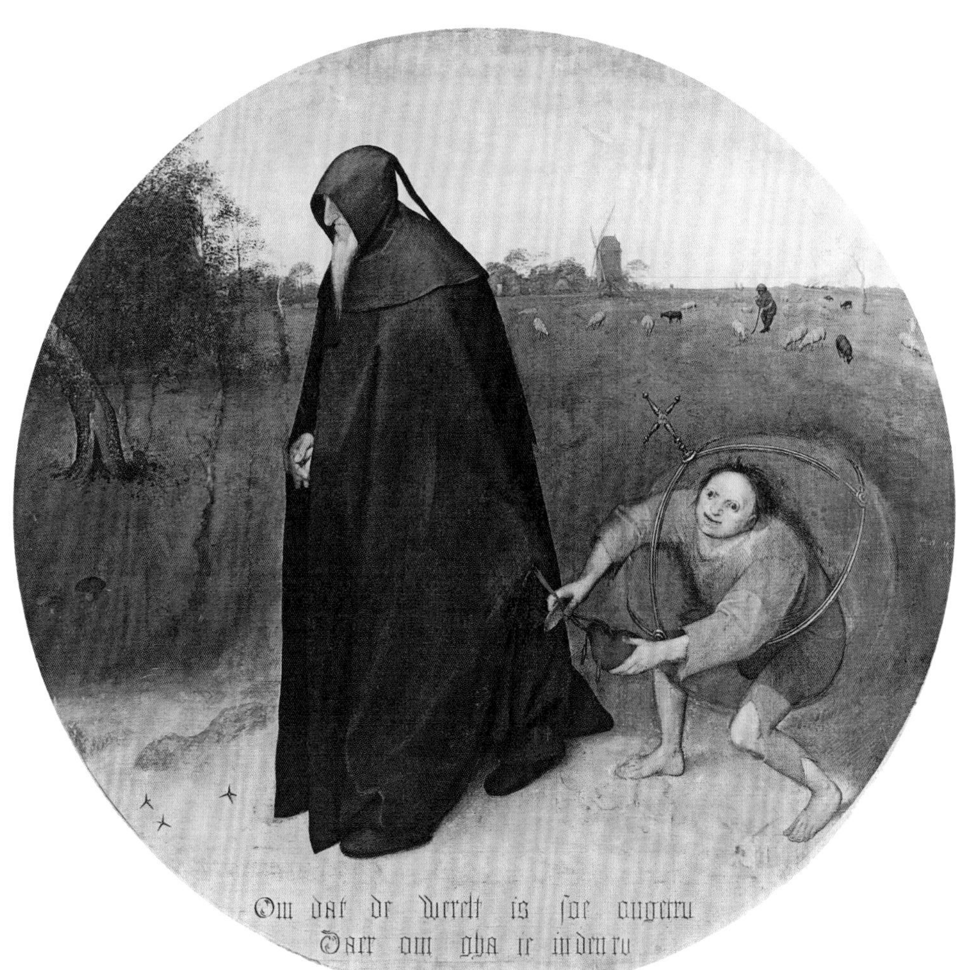
Om dat de werelt is soe ongetru
Daer om gha ic in den rou

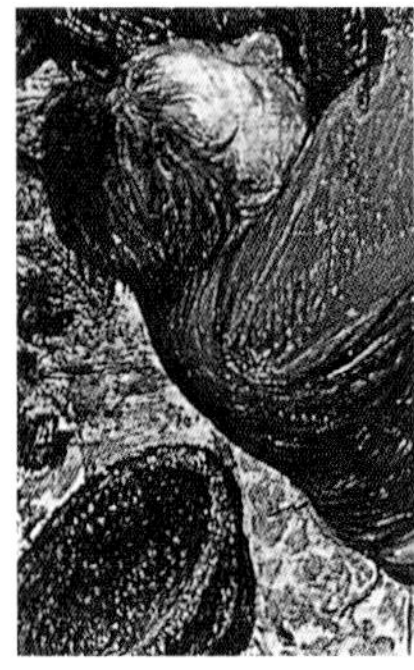

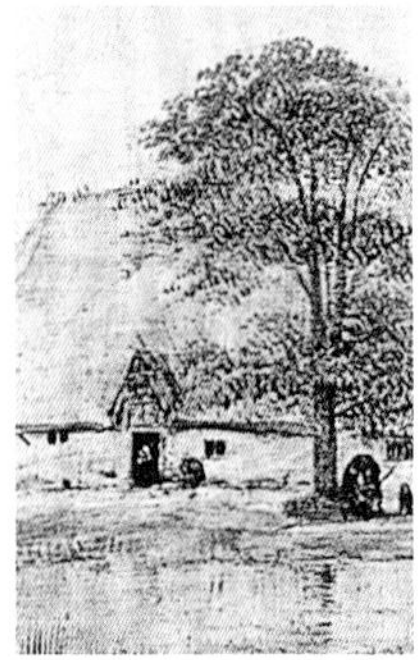

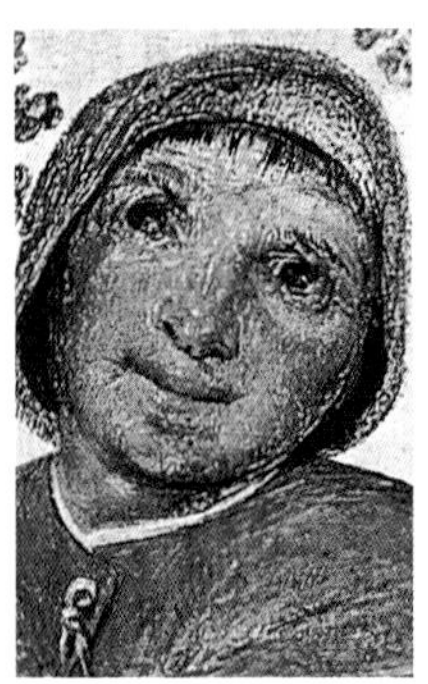

Her profile, sharp as though cut by a hatchet, her small hard eye, and the rictus of her mouth are infused with ferocious alacrity. She hurries forth with long strides, wearing a helmet without a visor and with a breastplate hanging from her shoulders. Under her left arm she holds a disparate plunder: a chest, a bundle, two baskets full of dishes, and a frying pan. Demons with fantastic forms like those described in *The Fall of the*

The Peasant and the Birdnester

1568
Oil on panel, 59.3 x 68.3 cm
Kunsthistorisches Museum, Vienna

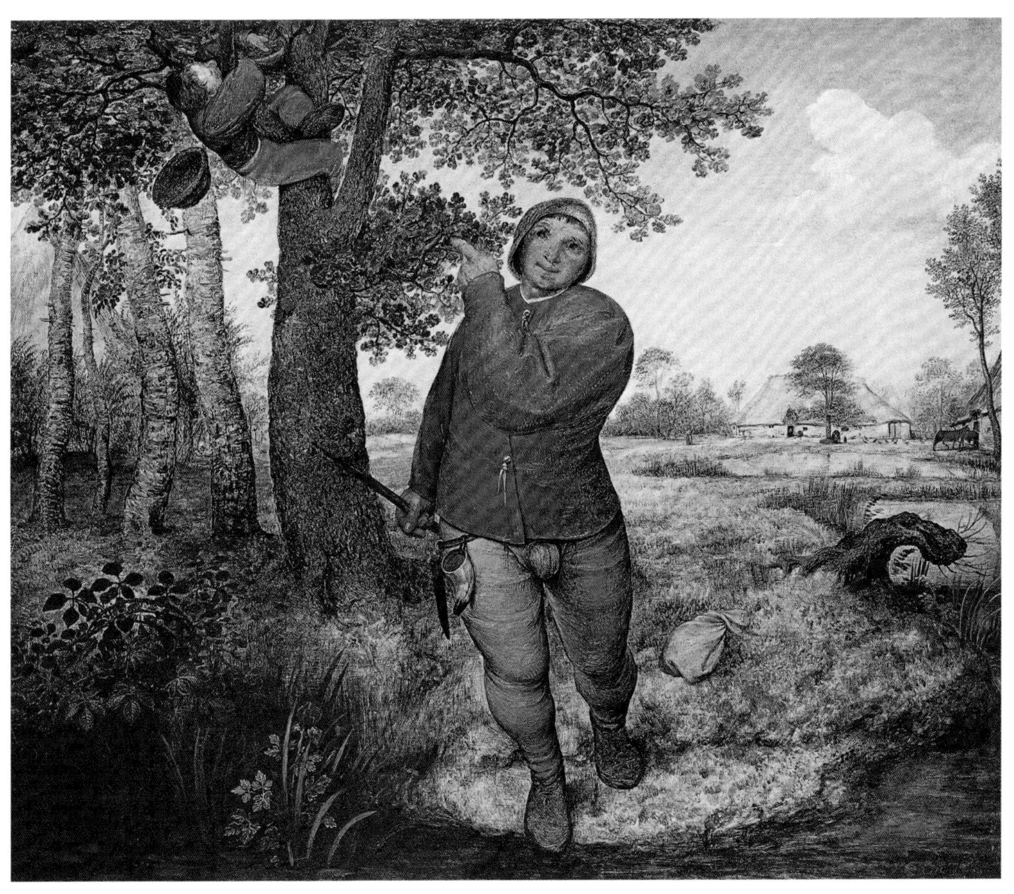

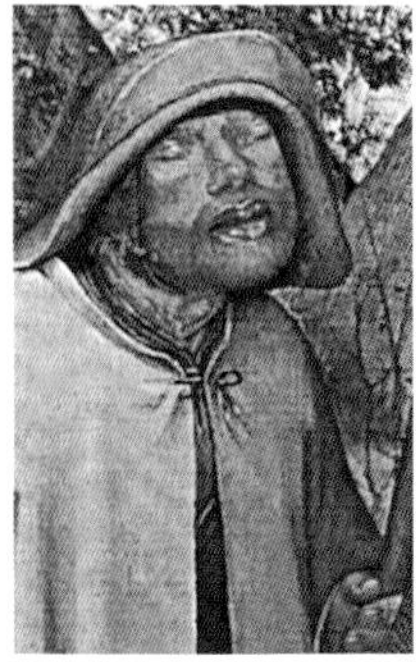

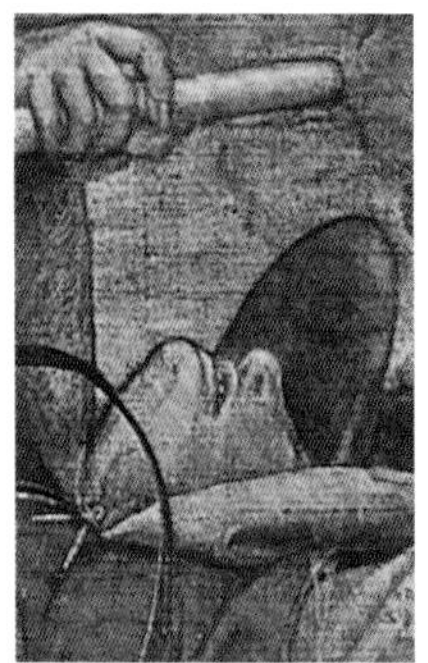

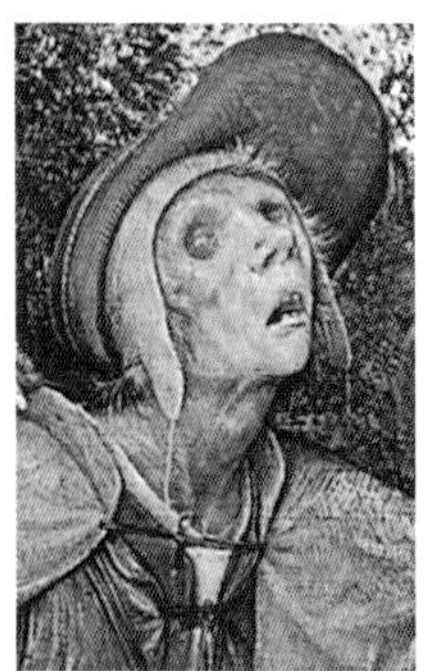

Rebel Angels flee before her, but the Mouth of Hell still seems off-limits. The mouth regards the madwoman with a dilated eye of terror that wears a sort of awning in the place of an eyelid. At the summit of her pointed hat hangs a transparent globe inside of which writhe the damned. To the right, demons spring out of a partially destroyed fortress, some descend in a sort of basket, while others, newly armoured, take their place

The Parable of the Blind Leading the Blind

1568
Tempera on canvas, 86 x 154 cm
Museo Nazionale di Capodimonte, Naples

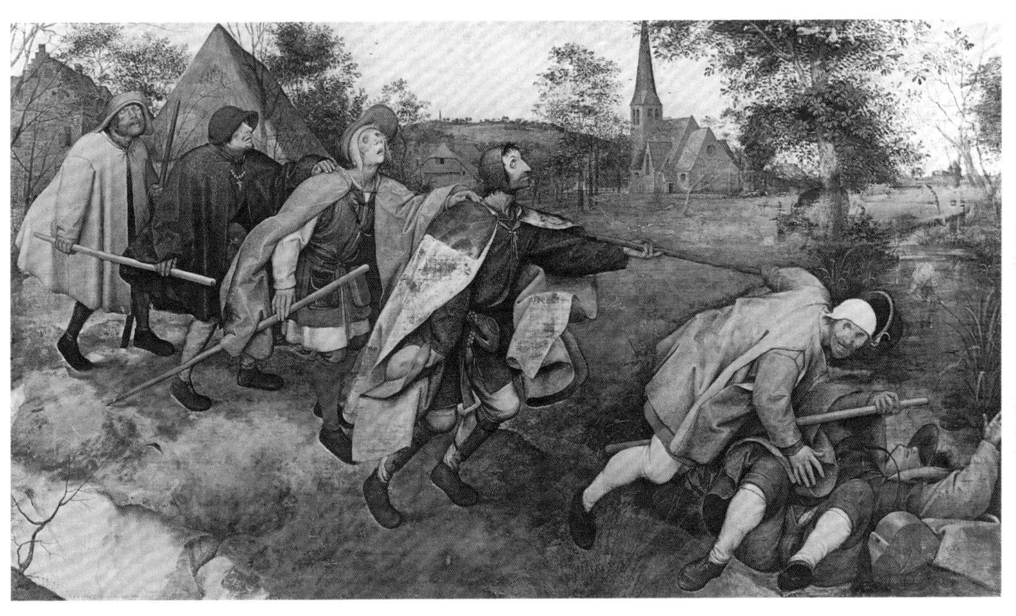

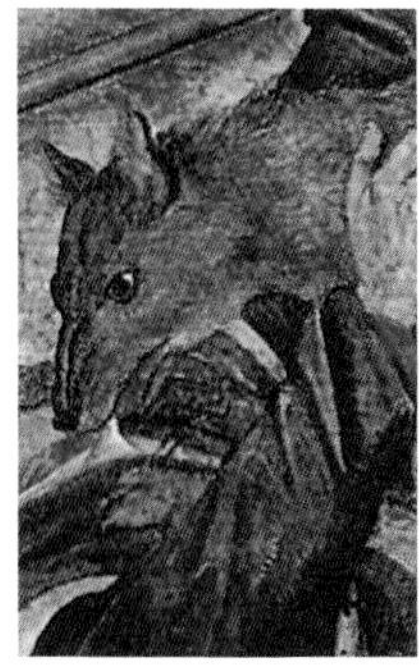

in a sort of boat which is a demon itself, and which advances on the moat. A horde of madwomen armed with clubs pushes them back. Some streak the uncovered backside of one of their companions with blows of their rods, and others amuse themselves by tying a prisoner to a mattress, following the old Flemish proverb that one should tie the Devil up in such a way to show that one is more powerful than he.

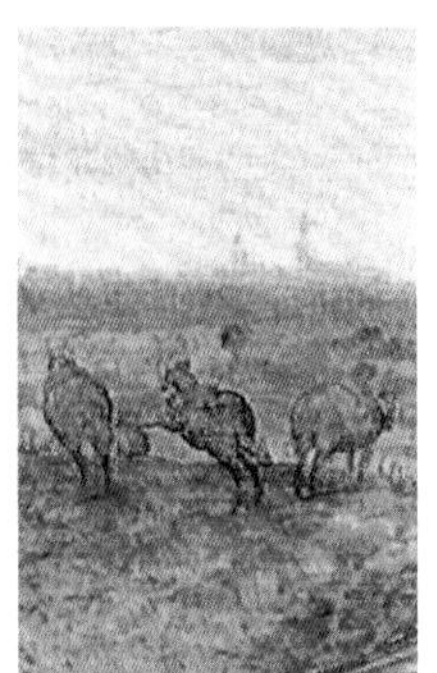

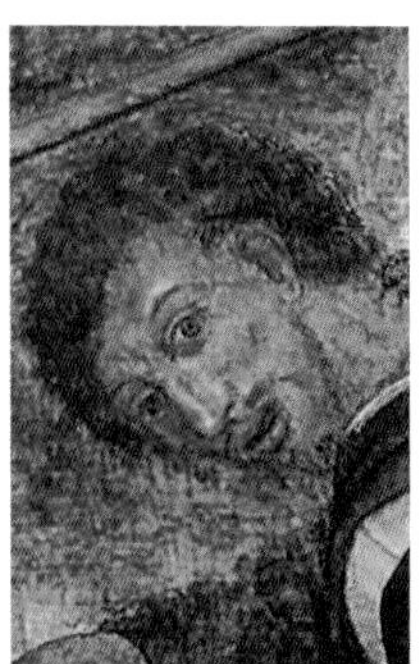

The Good Shepherd

Pieter Brueghel the Younger
Oil on wood, 40 x 57.8 cm
Private collection

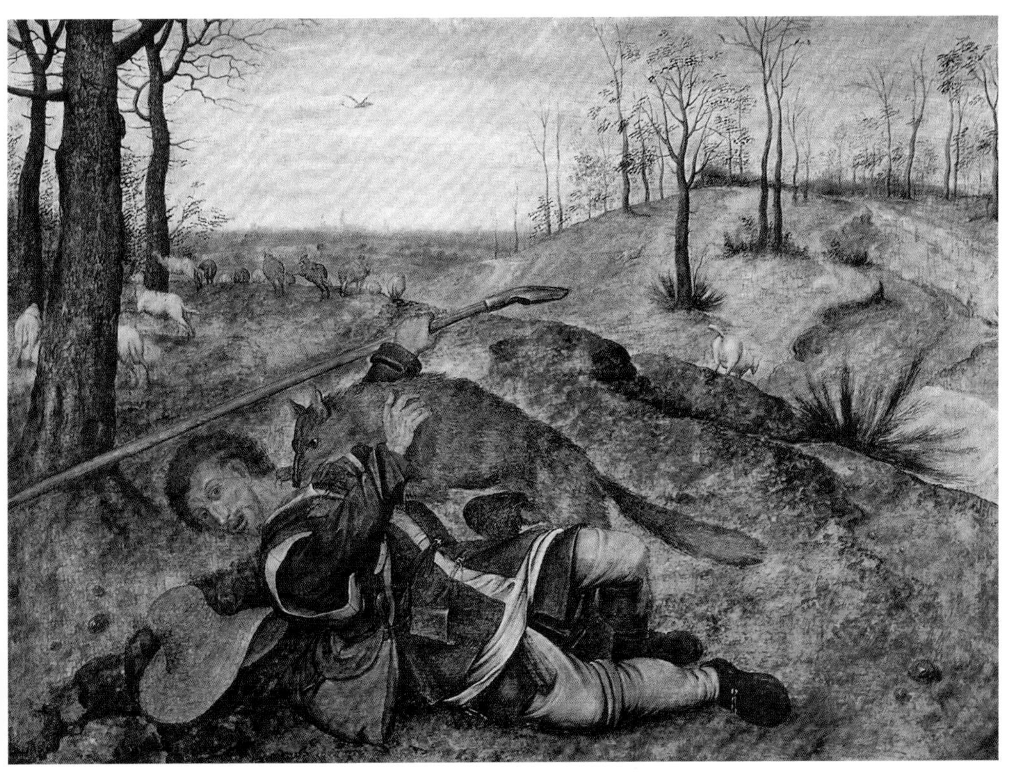

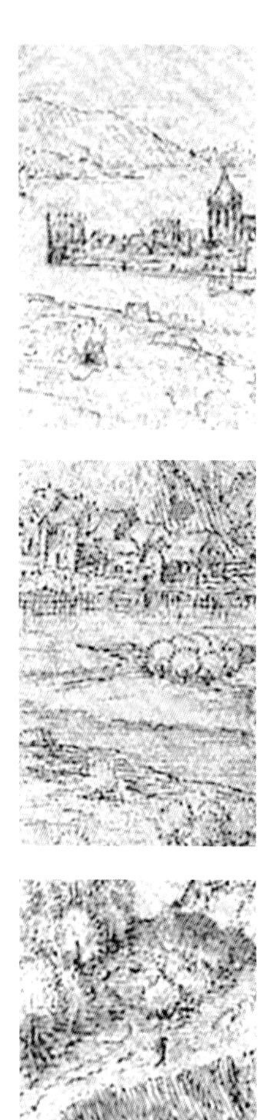

At the centre of the scene, a clownish figure is partially crushed by a tub in which other demons agitate. More demons can be seen in a sort of tower rising in the distance next to black waters expanding beneath a fiery sky. Nothing is more tragic than this horizon of mountains from which rise columns of red vapour, which tops off the fiery decor of this fantastical composition. A wide purple- and wine-coloured band completes this hot symphony of ochres, yellows,

Solicitudo Rustica

Pieter Bruegel the Elder (?), c. 1575-1600
Preparatory drawing for the series *Large Landscapes*
Pen and brown ink over black chalk, 24.4 x 35.1 cm
British Museum, London

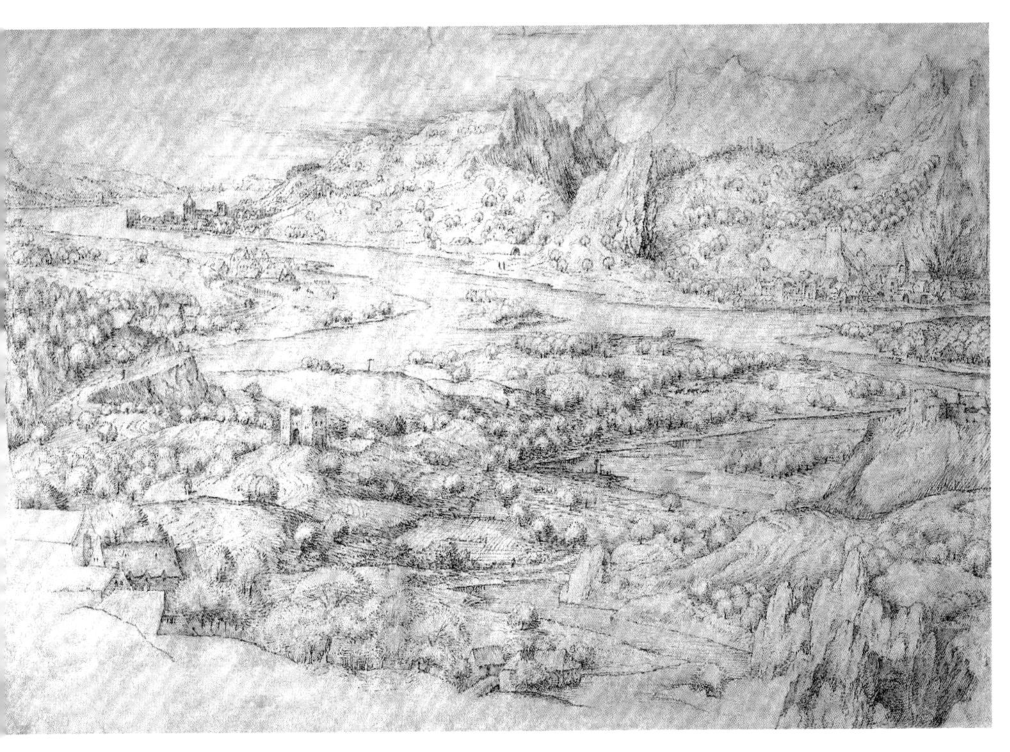

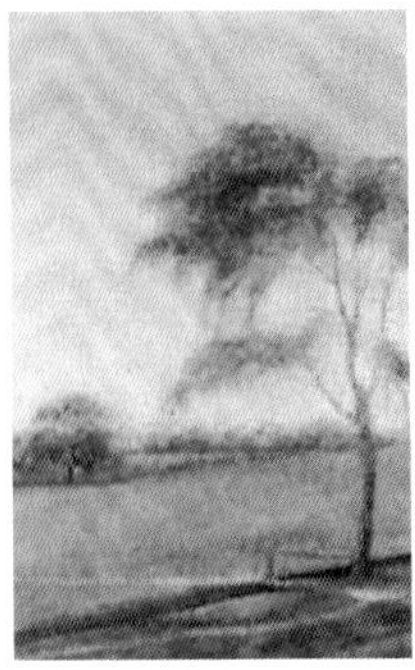

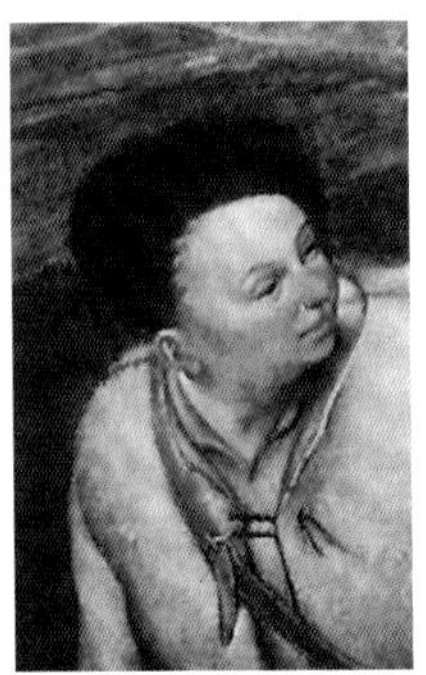

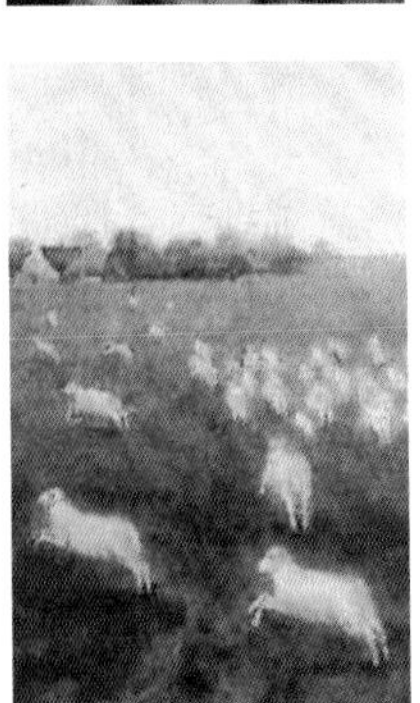

and browns, of a hue even richer than in *The Fall of the Rebel Angels,* in which the soft blue tones of Dulle Griet's skirt, the shining of her helmet and armour, and the folds of her crimson velvet sleeves acquire admirable relief. As Van Mander observed, from the point of view of the unity and variety of composition, as well as the power and harmony of colours, this work should be considered among Bruegel's most important.

The Unfaithful Shepherd

c. 1575-1600
Oil on panel, 61.6 x 86.7 cm
The Philadelphia Museum of Art, Philadelphia
Probably after a lost painting of 1567-1569

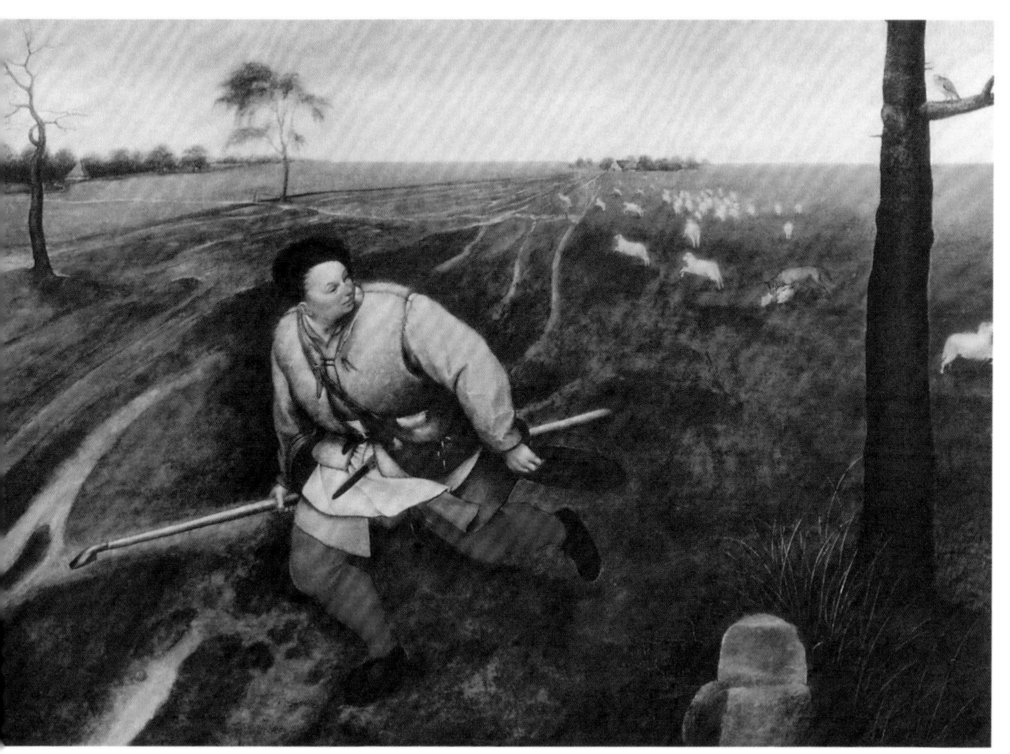

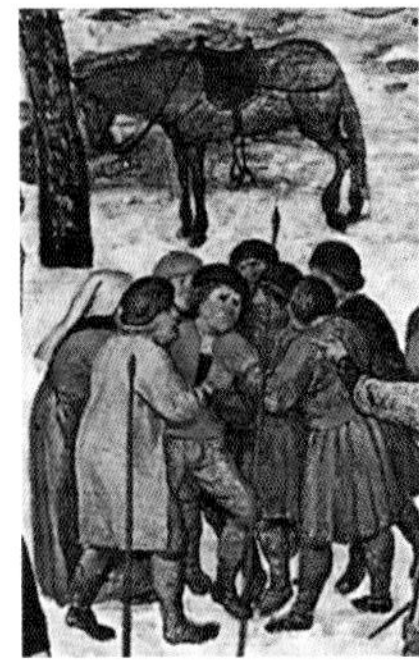

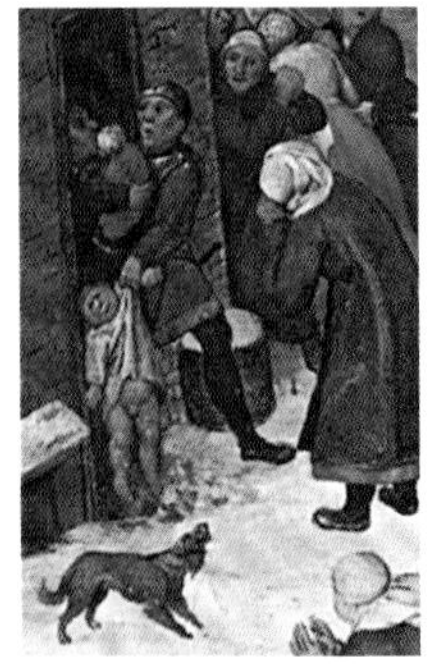

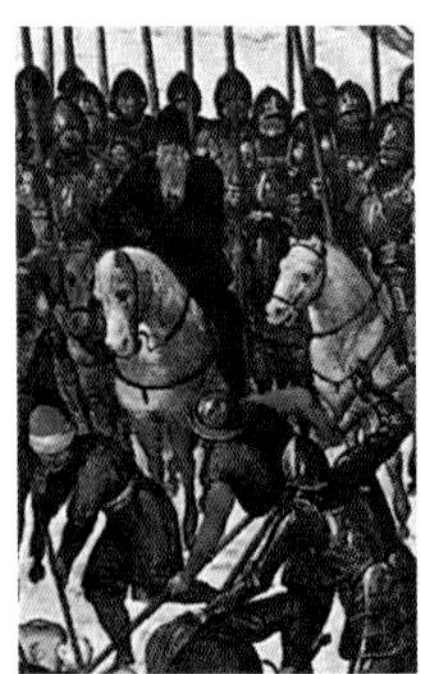

Dulle Griet is more than the simple development of a subject taken from folklore, or the paraphrase of two or three popular proverbs. There seems to be a deeper idea animating this image. Dulle Griet personifies brutality, the passion of destruction, the sanguine folly that had begun to spread in the Low Countries during the period at the start of the Reformation. Not only the harshness of the gestures, the vigorous movements of

The Massacre of the Innocents

Pieter Bruegel the Elder (copy after), late 16th century
Oil on panel, 116 x 160 cm
Kunsthistorisches Museum, Vienna

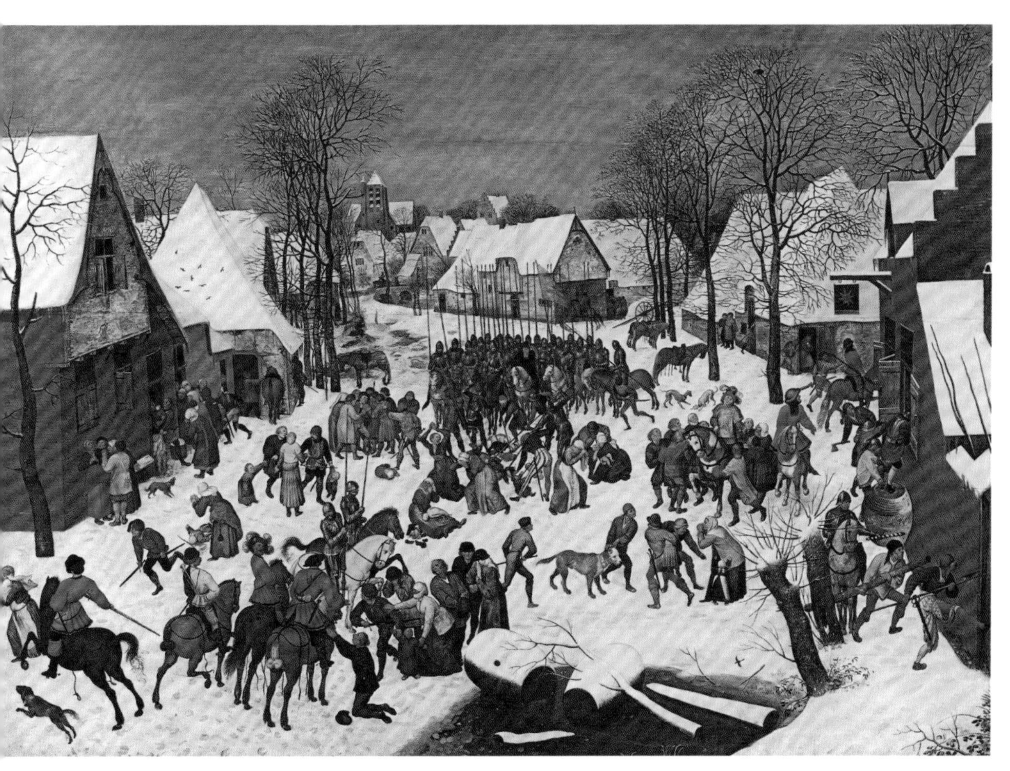

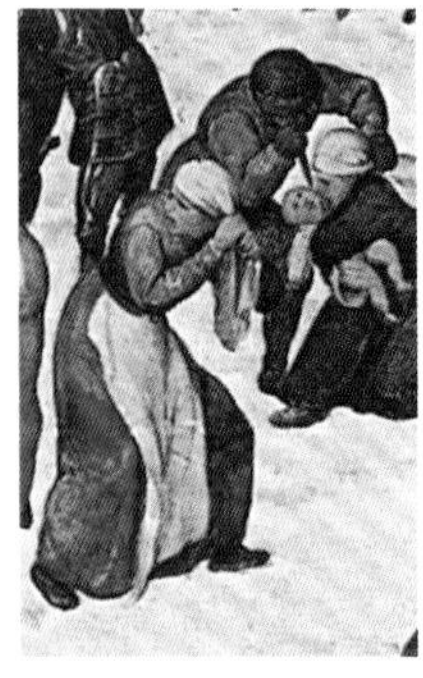

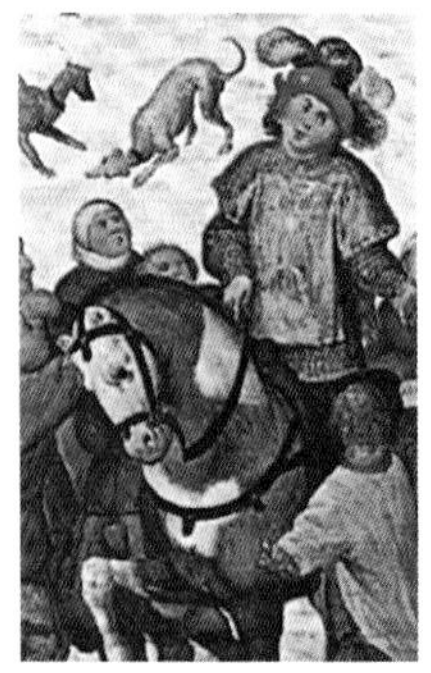

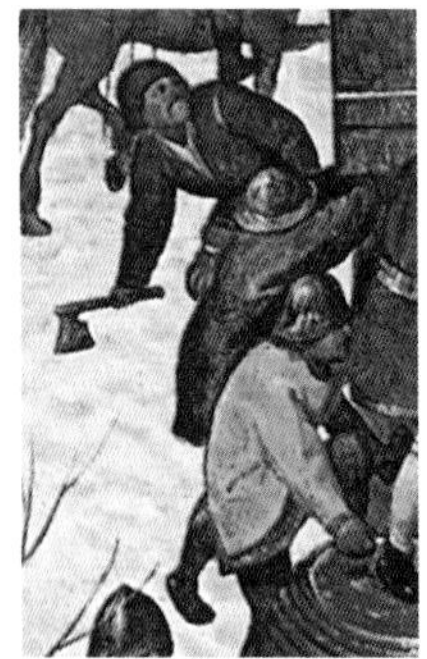

the devils and tartars, but the terror and tragic horror that hangs over the scene, despite the fact that it is populated by unreal beings and an incredible accumulation of fantasy, combine to make it a painting of terrifying reality. Bruegel's *The Triumph of Death* is of a similar inspiration. This work is a measure of Bruegel's genius, distant from that of Hieronymus Bosch, and one in which quivers a profound, painful, and intense humanity.

The Massacre of the Innocents (detail)

Pieter Bruegel the Elder (copy after), late 16th century
Oil on panel, 116 x 160 cm
Kunsthistorisches Museum, Vienna

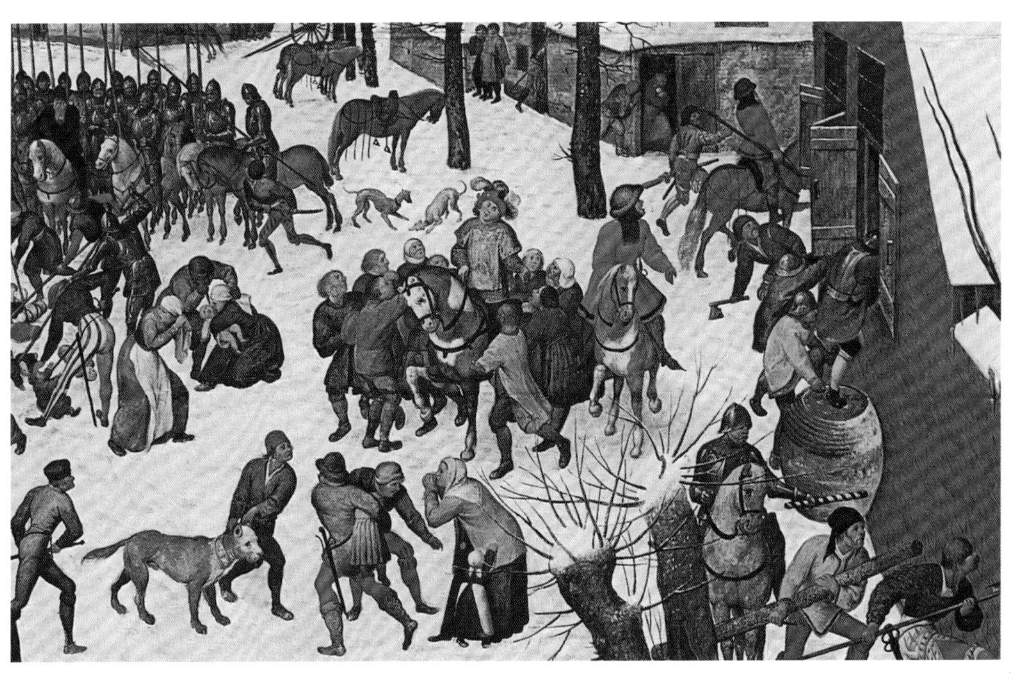

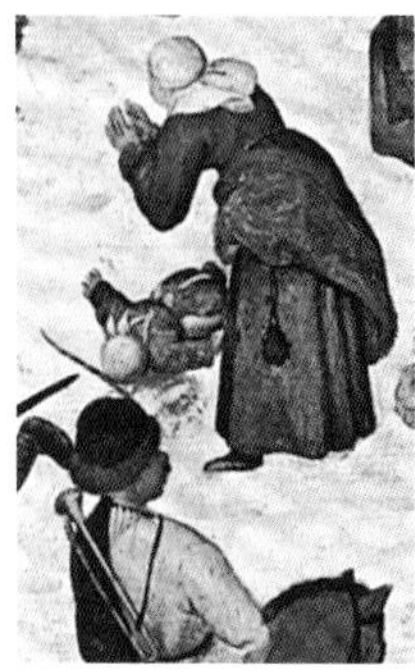

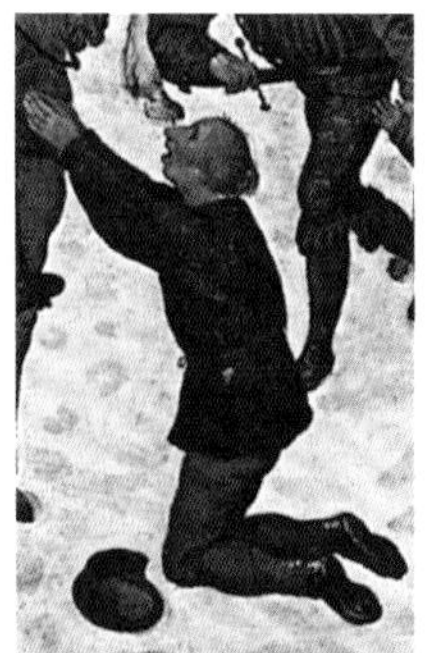

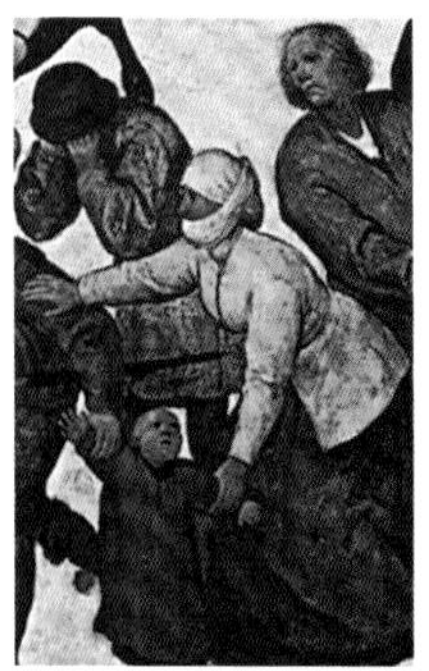

In 1563, an important change occurred in Bruegel's life. The spicy anecdote of the break with his mistress, whom he could not dissuade from lying, has already been mentioned. Bruegel did not have a flighty personality and was not the womaniser that many have made him out to be. He needed the support of a sincere and durable relationship, for the solitude of his selfish and cowardly bachelor's life

The Massacre of the Innocents (detail)

Pieter Bruegel the Elder (copy after), late 16th century
Oil on panel, 116 x 160 cm
Kunsthistorisches Museum, Vienna

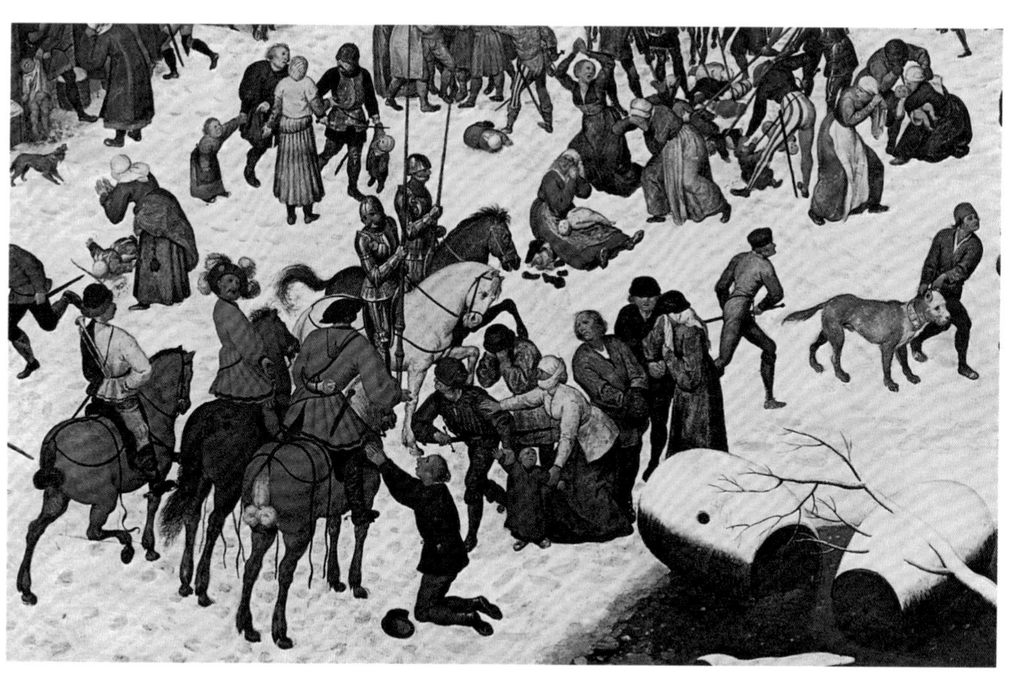

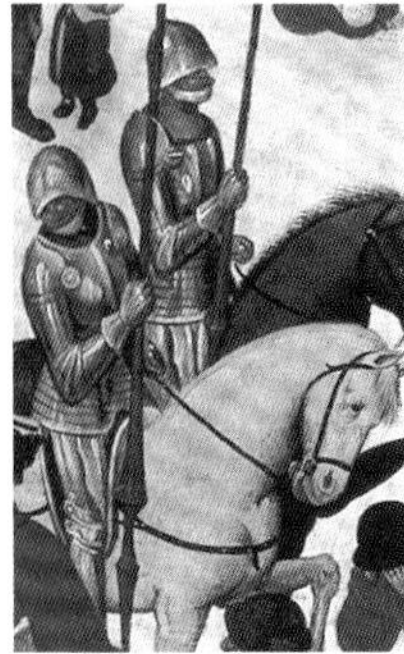

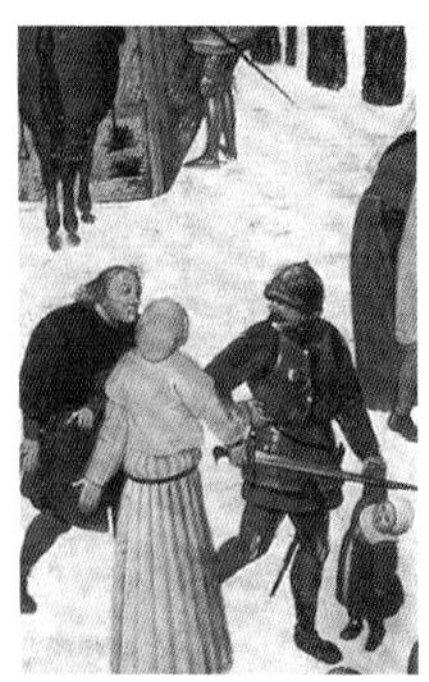

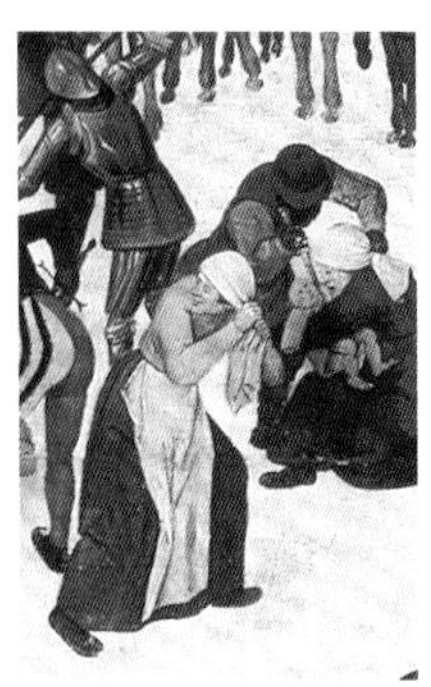

disgusted him. He dreamt of marriage and his thoughts ran naturally to Mayken Coecke, the daughter of his first master.

For some time, the widow of Pieter Coecke, Mayken Verhulst (also known as Marie Bessemers) had lived in Brussels. Her condition for the proposed marriage between Bruegel and her daughter was that her son-in-law would come to Brussels to live in her household, "so that he might pull away from his former relationship",

The Massacre of the Innocents

Pieter Brueghel the Younger, late 16th century
Oil on wood, 116 x 160 cm
Kunsthistorisches Museum, Vienna

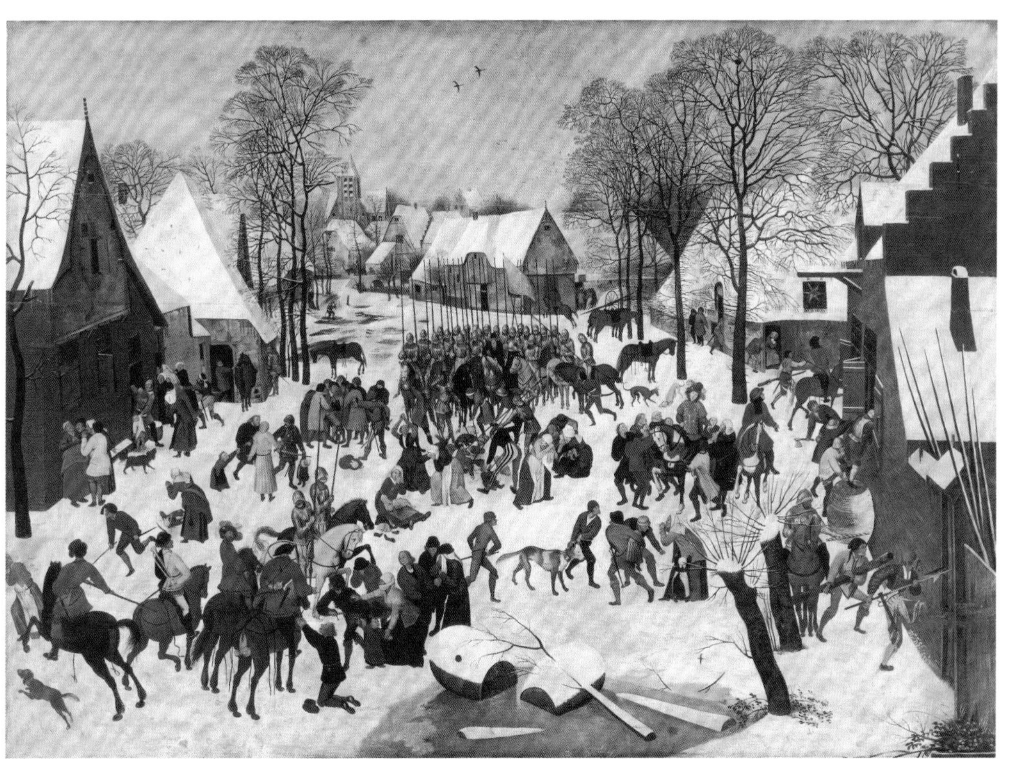

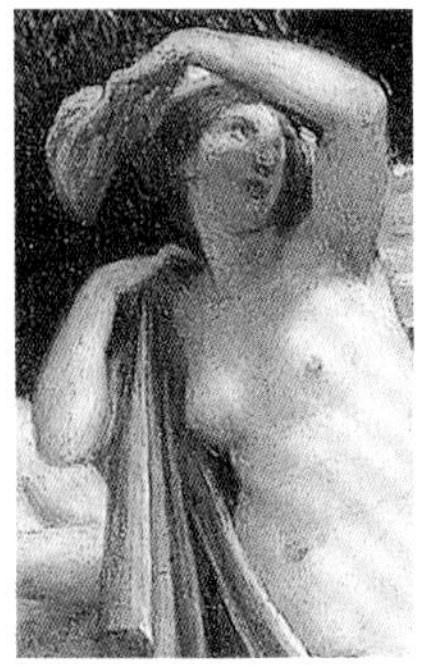

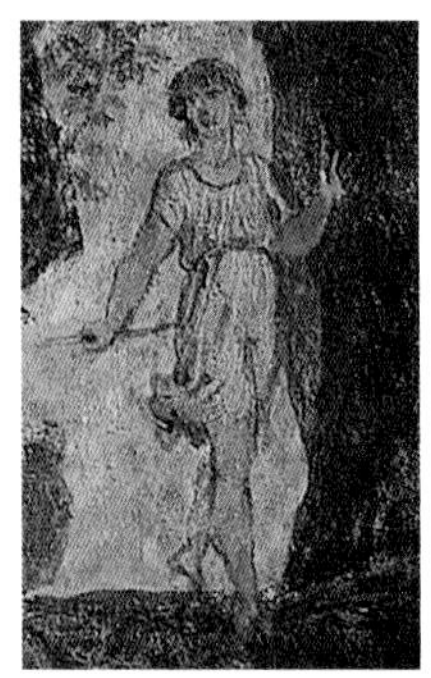

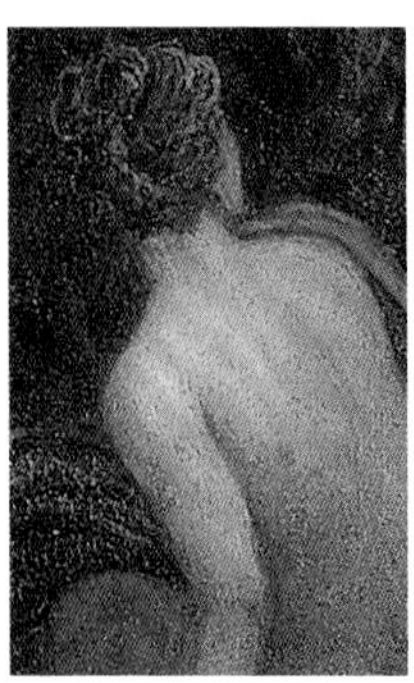

as Van Mander puts it. It is clear that Mayken Verhulst was not only a talented miniaturist but also a shrewd mother-in-law. Bruegel surrendered to his desires and Antwerp saw the departure of the most original and powerful of its artists.

He was welcomed with open arms in Brussels, and shortly there after the magistrate honoured him with an official commission. Bruegel was asked to render the

Landscape with Diana and Actaeon

Jan Brueghel the Elder, c. 1591
Oil on copper, 37 x 27 cm
Nationalmuseum, Stockholm

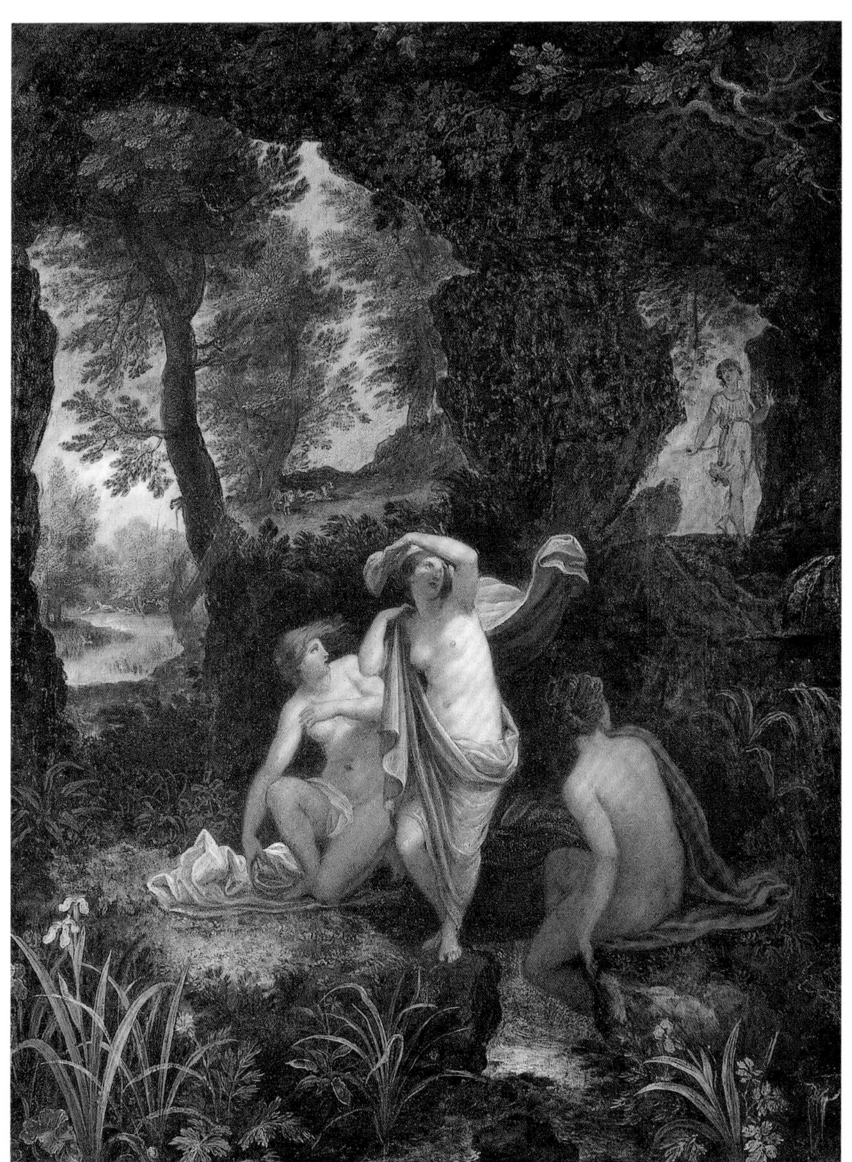

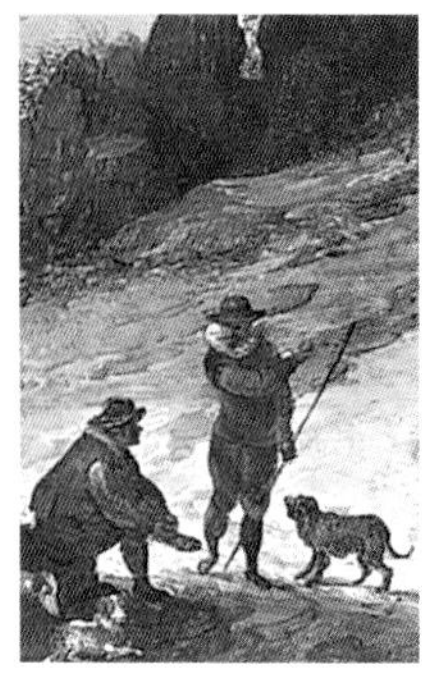

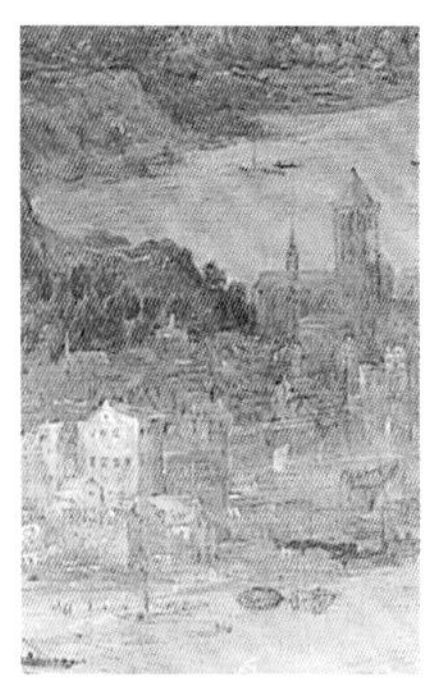

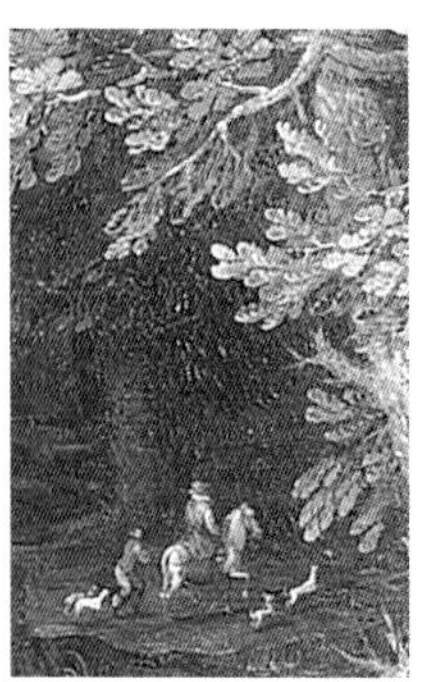

scene of the inauguration of the new canal between Brussels and Antwerp, whilst the painter Jan Leys from Antwerp was charged with realising the decorations on the boats and the banks of the canal. The organisers of the commission must have imagined that this picturesque and animated scene would tempt Bruegel's brush. Knowing his sincere love for the realism and the proud picturesque aspect of life that springs forth

River Landscape with Resting Hikers

Jan Brueghel the Elder, 1594
Oil on copper, 25.5 x 34.5 cm
Private collection

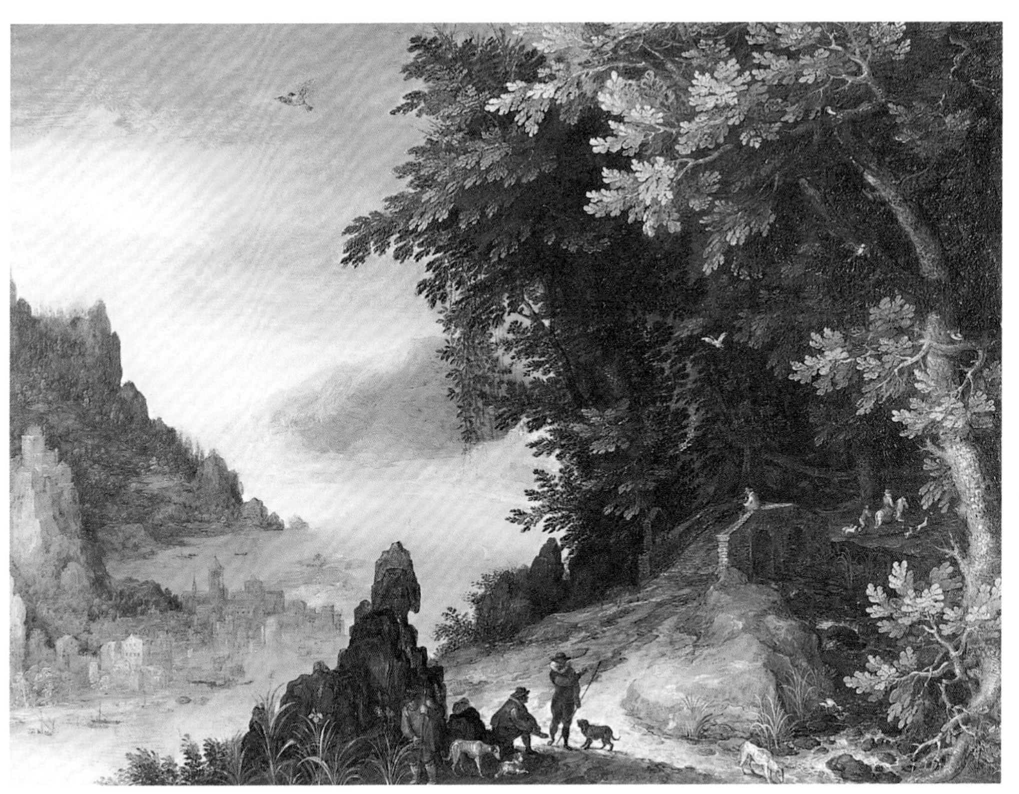

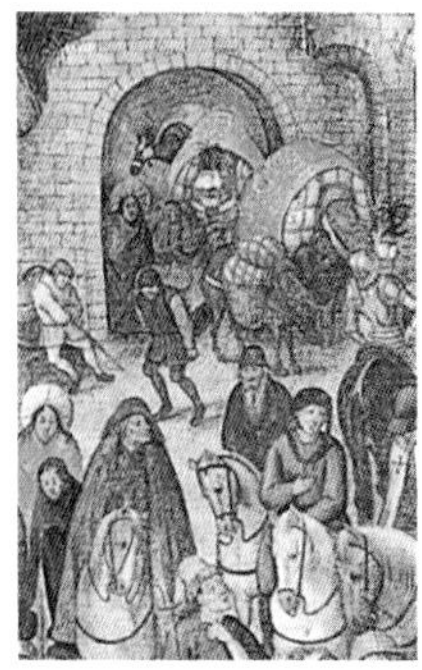

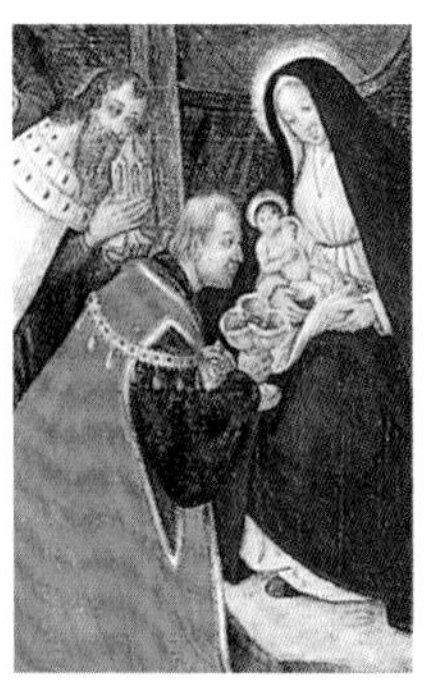

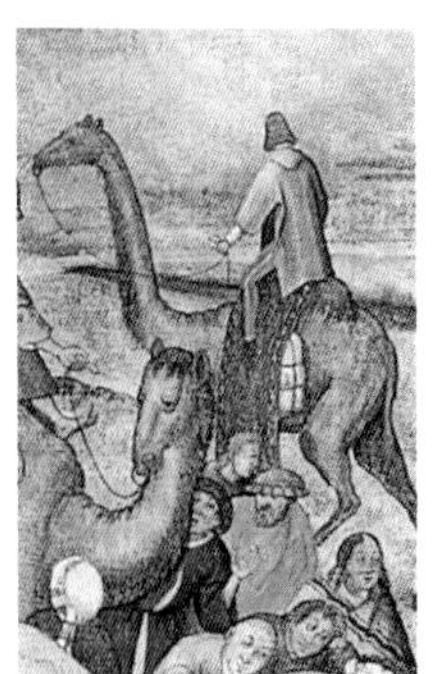

naturally without official preparation, it is not astonishing to note that Bruegel had not yet begun work on this commission at the time of his unexpected death four years later. The critic B. Hymans wondered about possible studies existing for this painting, referring to an auction in Amsterdam on 6 May 1716. On this occasion, a painting of a boat going to Brussels, titled *View of the Escaut*, signed P. Brueghel was sold.

The Adoration of the Magi

Pieter Brueghel the Younger, 1595 (?)
Oil on canvas, 123.2 x 161 cm
The Philadelphia Museum of Art, Philadelphia

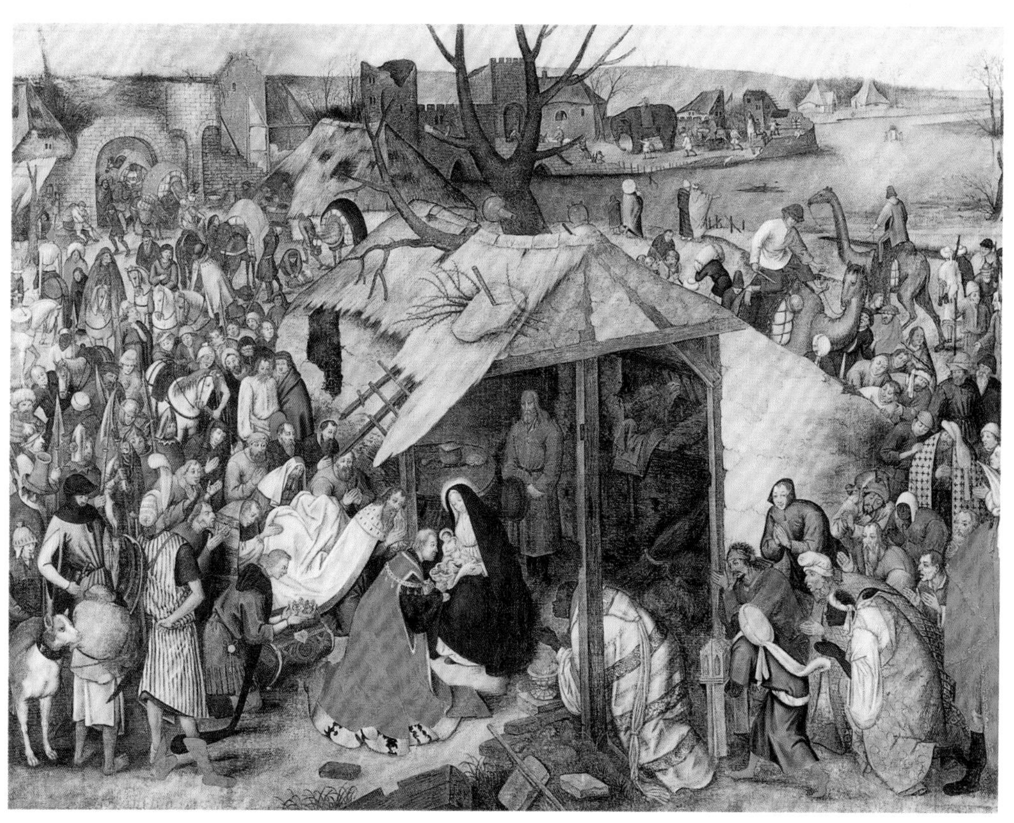

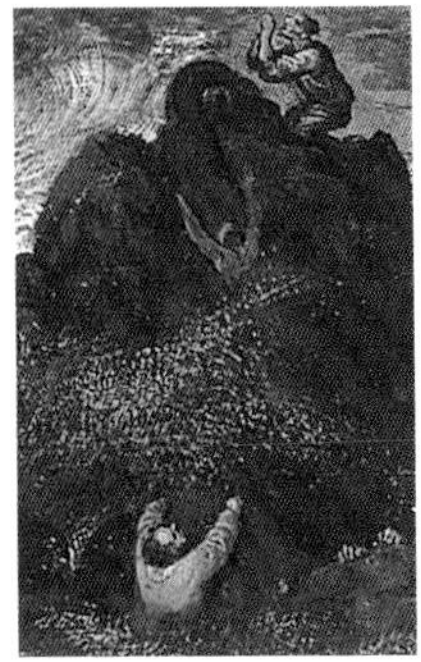

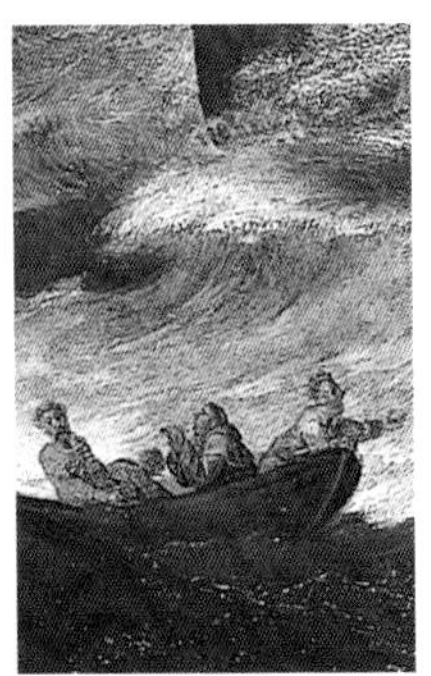

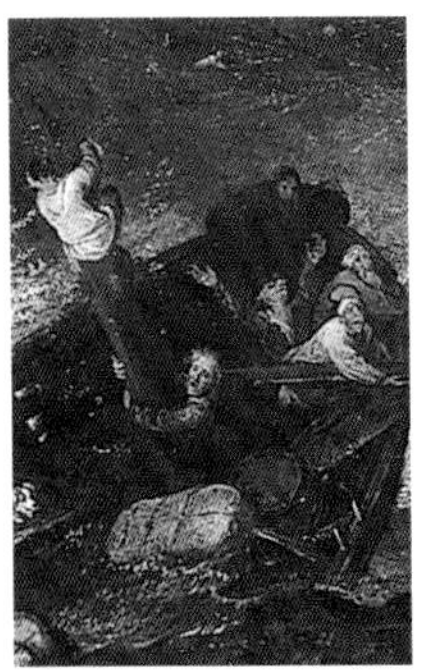

René Van Bastelaer proposes that Bruegel's time in Brussels influenced him to abandon satirical and humorous figures. He left behind the gleeful rhetoricians who had also become his daily companions. Despite the lack of biographical detail, one senses, nevertheless, that Bruegel had a natural gravity and tendency to daydream, which would have combined easily with a playful and even excessive

Storm at Sea with Shipwrecks

Jan Brueghel the Elder, c. 1595-1596
Oil on copper, 25.5 x 34.5 cm
Private collection

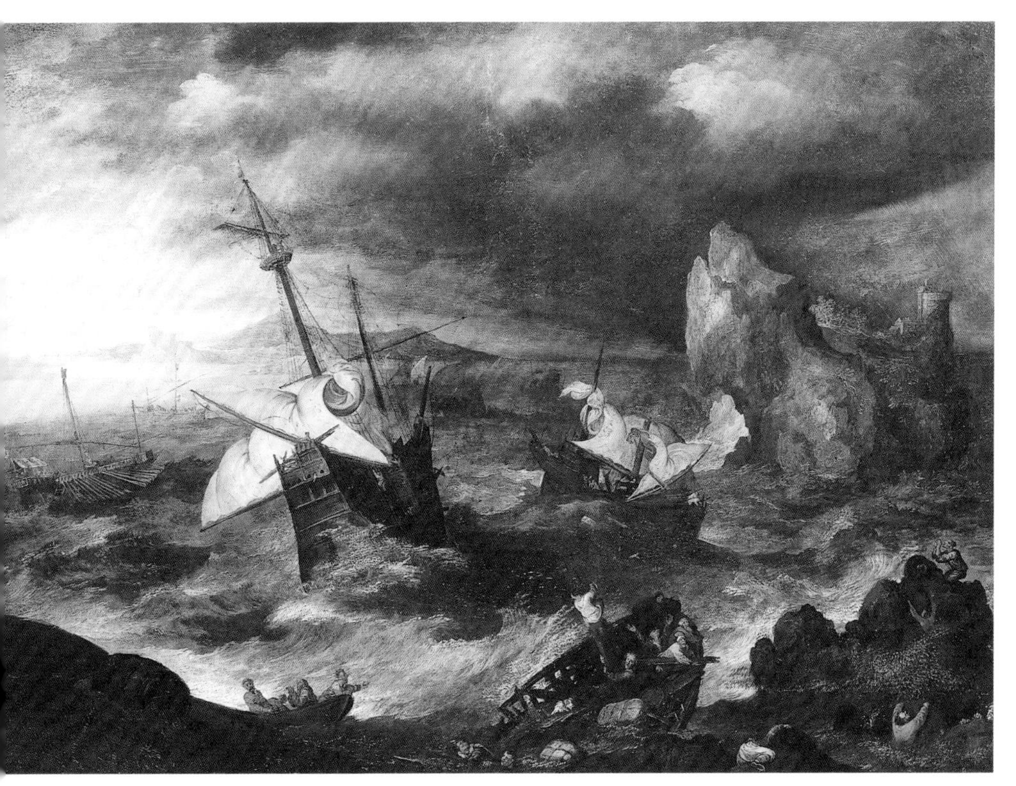

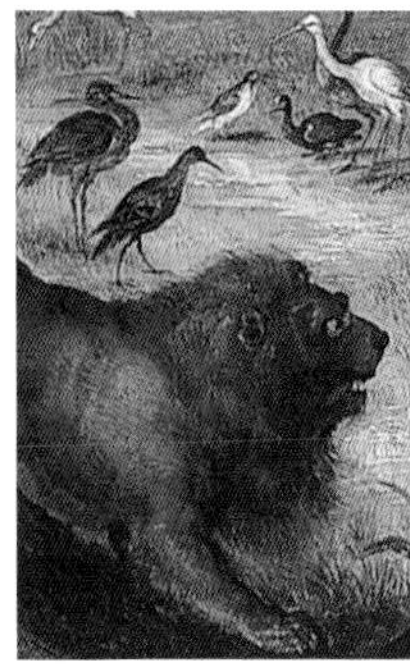

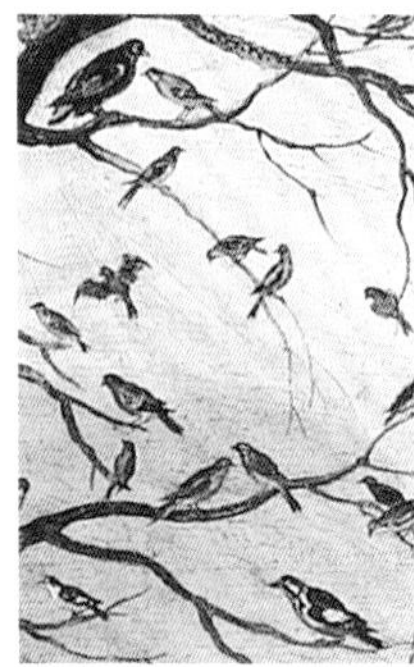

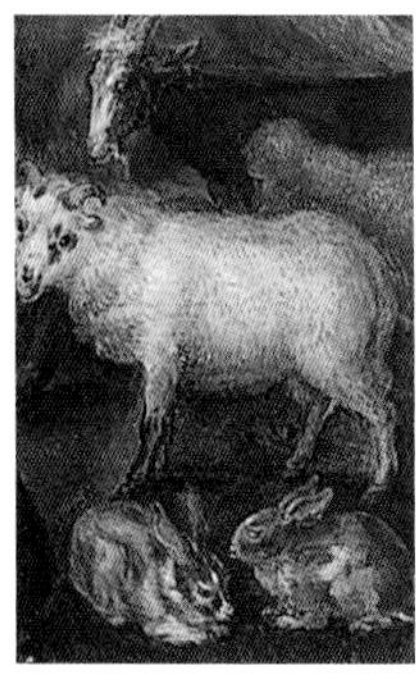

good humour, as would be expected in a personality given over to extremes.

The steps of Bruegel's evolution towards serious and purely human subjects had begun ten years before, upon his return from Rome in 1553. His increasing inclination towards gravity and reflection, which led him to marry, allowed him to cultivate his taste for the serious and eliminate the intermediaries between

The Garden of Paradise with
the Embarkment of the Animals into Noah's Ark

Jan Brueghel the Elder, 1596
Oil on copper, 27 x 35 cm
Private collection

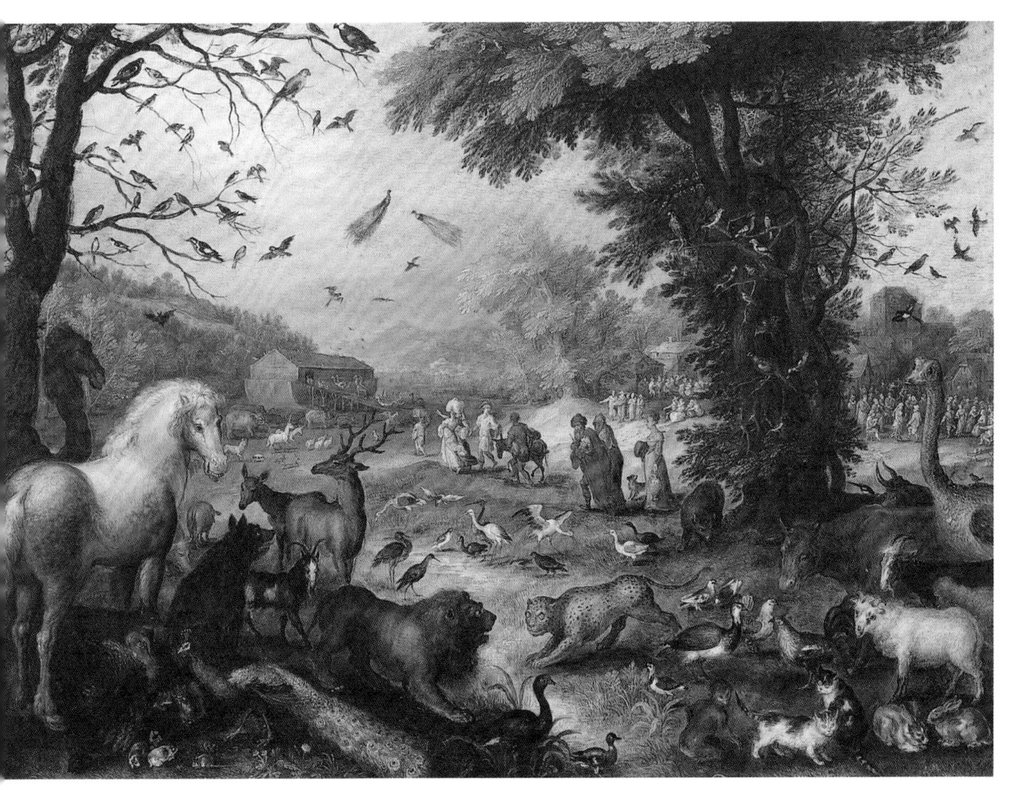

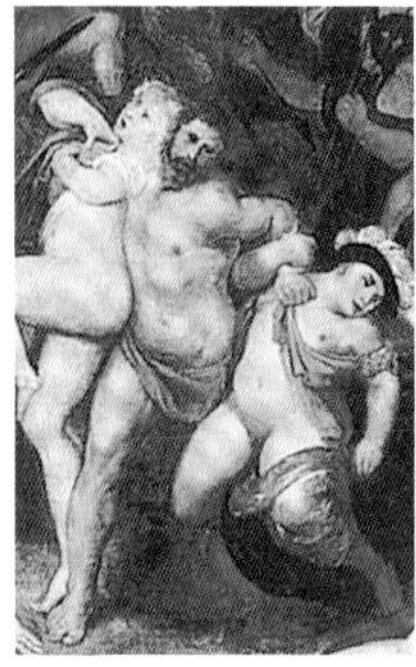

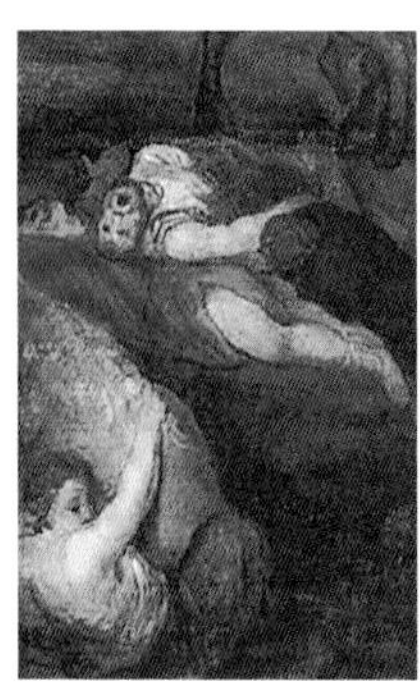

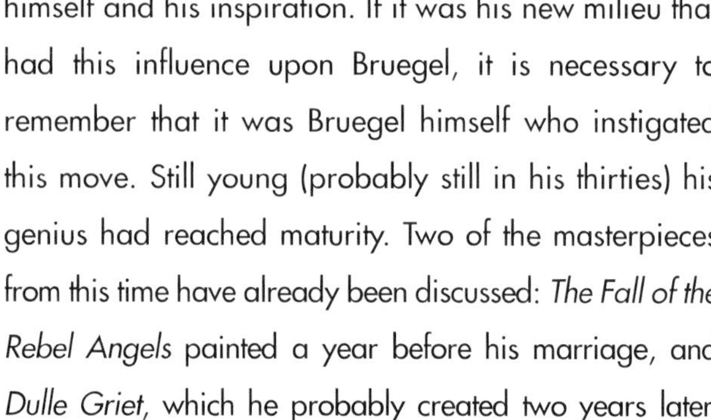

himself and his inspiration. If it was his new milieu that had this influence upon Bruegel, it is necessary to remember that it was Bruegel himself who instigated this move. Still young (probably still in his thirties) his genius had reached maturity. Two of the masterpieces from this time have already been discussed: *The Fall of the Rebel Angels* painted a year before his marriage, and *Dulle Griet*, which he probably created two years later.

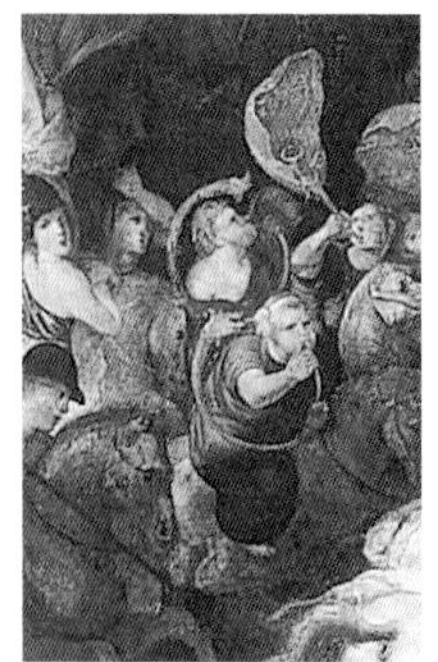

The Battle of the Amazons

Jan Brueghel the Elder and Peter Paul Rubens, c. 1597-1599
Oil on wood, 102 x 120 cm
Private collection, Antwerp

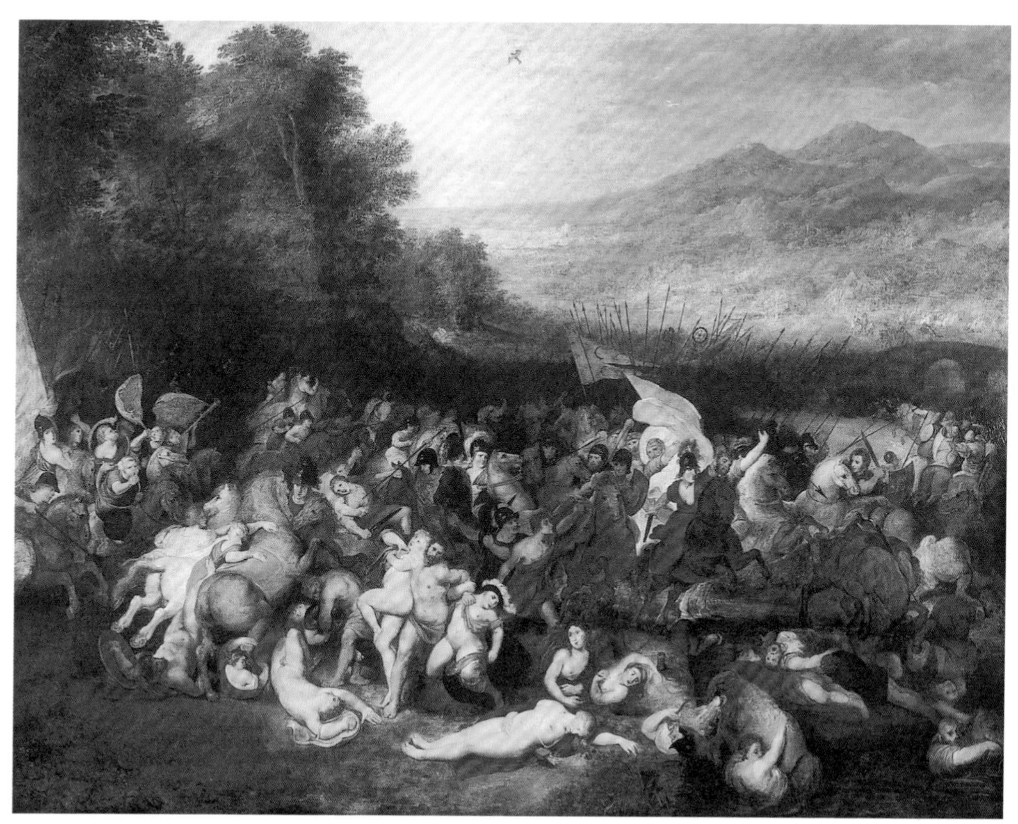

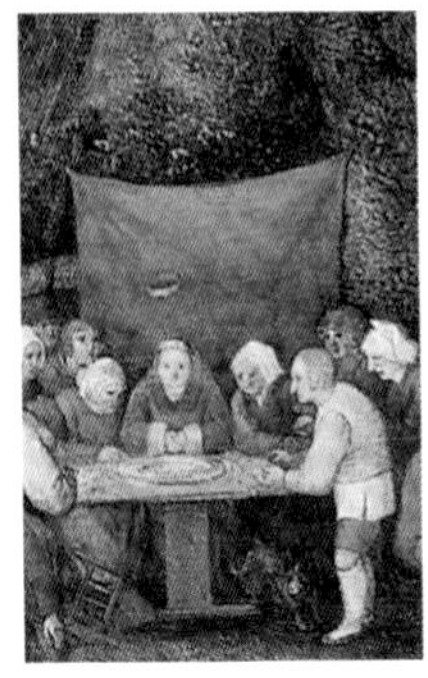

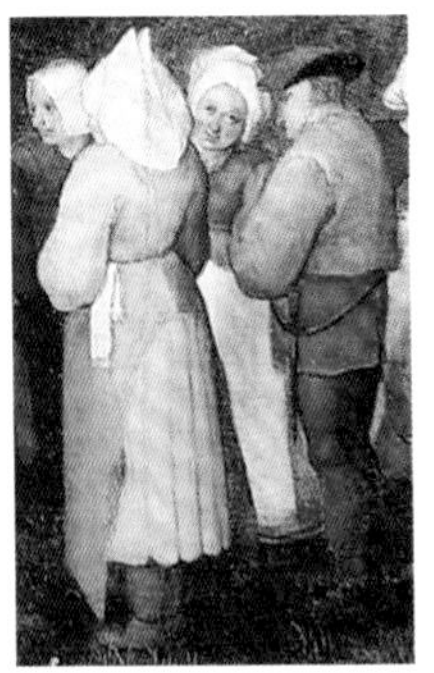

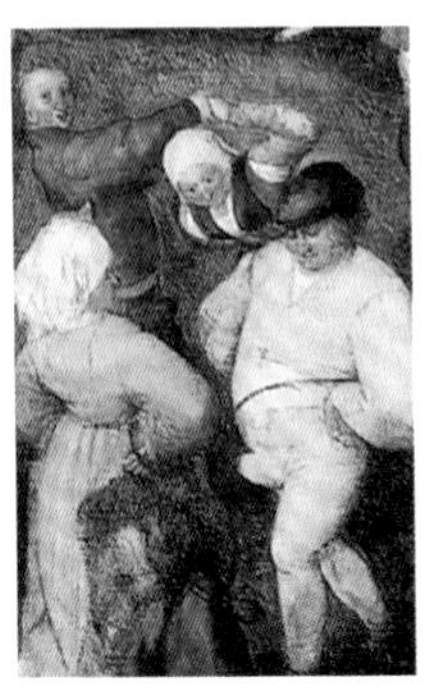

Two paintings, *The Battle of the Israelites and the Philistines* and *The Tower of Babel*, date from the year of his marriage, 1563.

Neither his fantasies nor his studies of village customs distracted Bruegel from the illustration of landscapes. His taste for nature had already caused him to ignore numerous masterpieces during his trip in Italy. Seduced by the harshness of the Alps and the

The Wedding Dance

Jan Brueghel the Elder, c. 1597
Oil on wood, 37.4 x 55.2 cm
Private collection, England

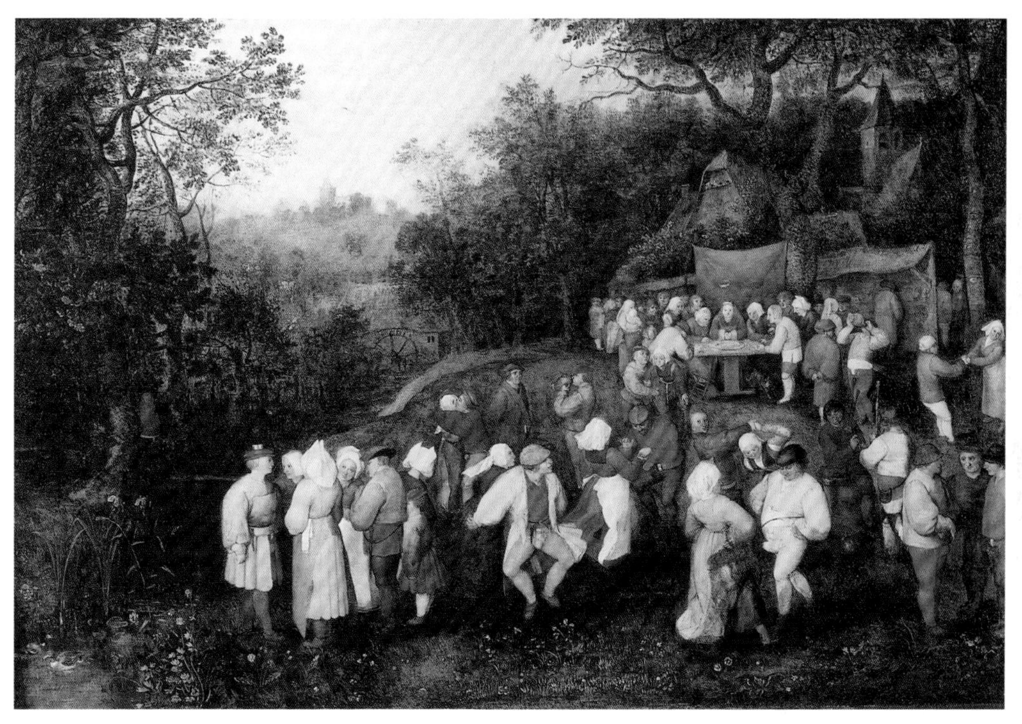

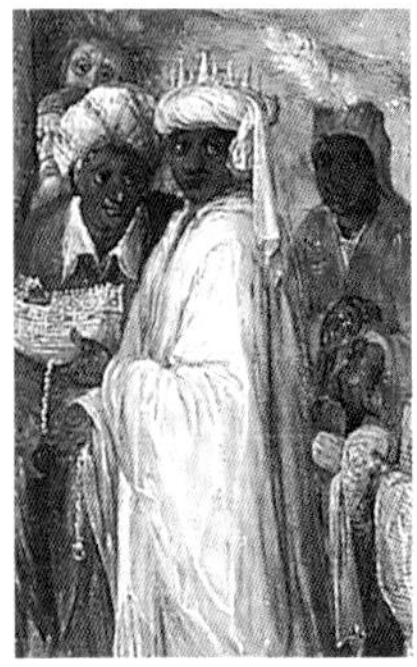

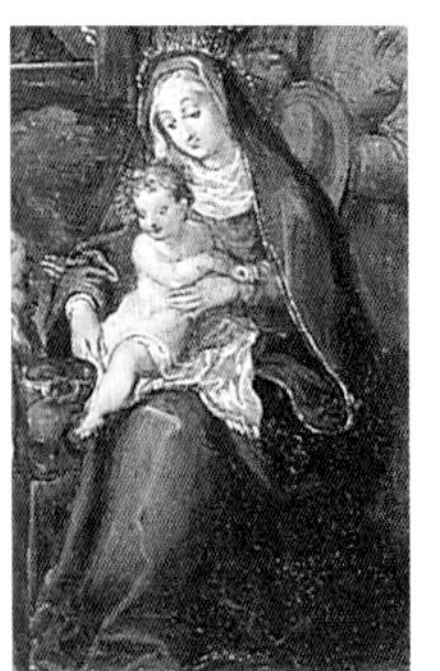

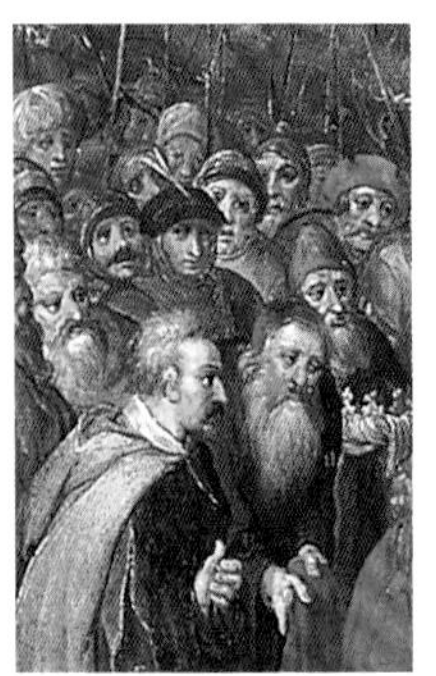

joyful scenery of his native Brabant, he captured their immutable lines and shifting souls. He had an incredible manner of juxtaposing these two contrasting countries in hybrid landscapes with an indefinable beauty. He would surround the Flemish countryside with amphitheatres of rock until he realised that he no longer needed to employ borrowed Italian beauty. He increasingly composed fresh little drawings of the

The Adoration of the Magi

Jan Brueghel the Elder, c. 1598-1600
Oil on copper, 27.4 x 36 cm
Museum Mayer van den Bergh, Antwerp

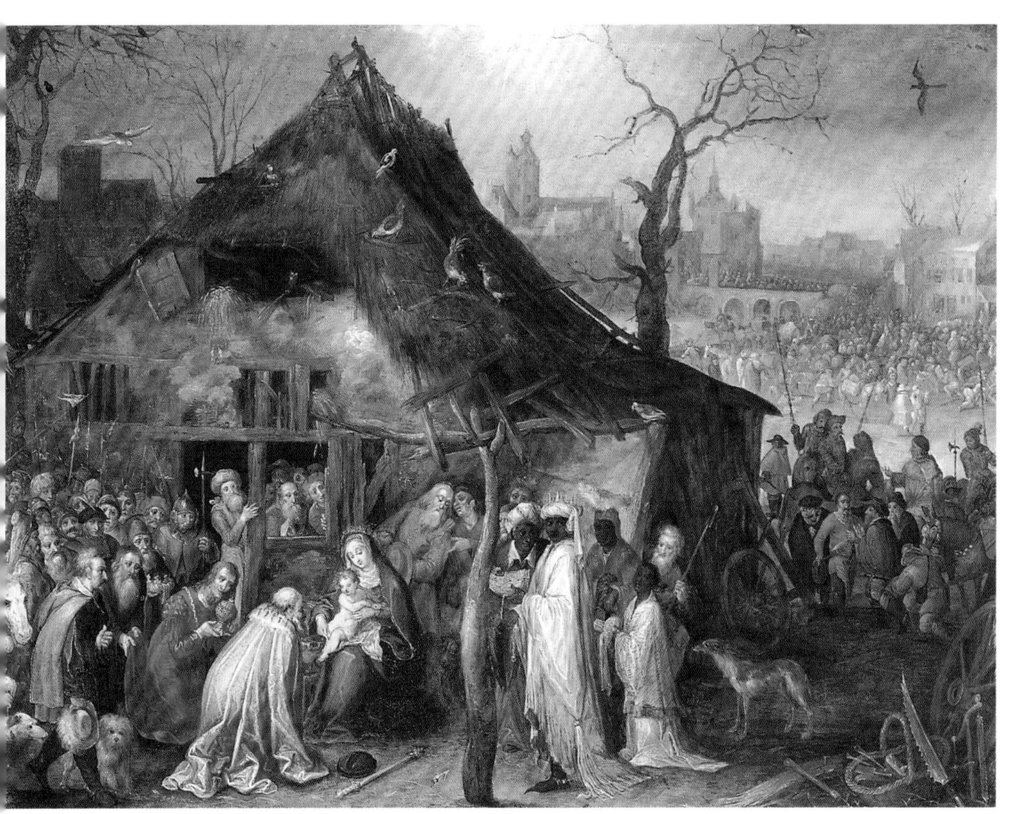

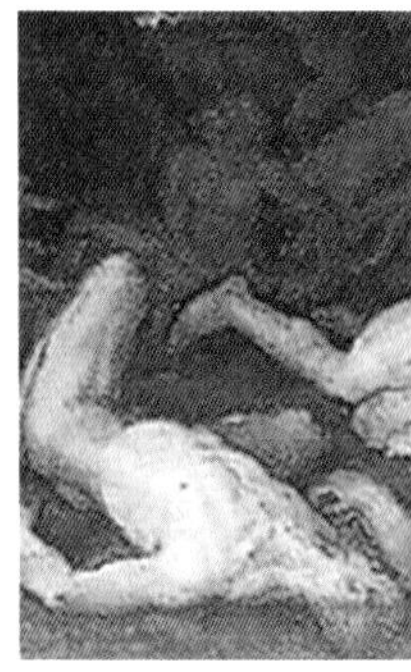

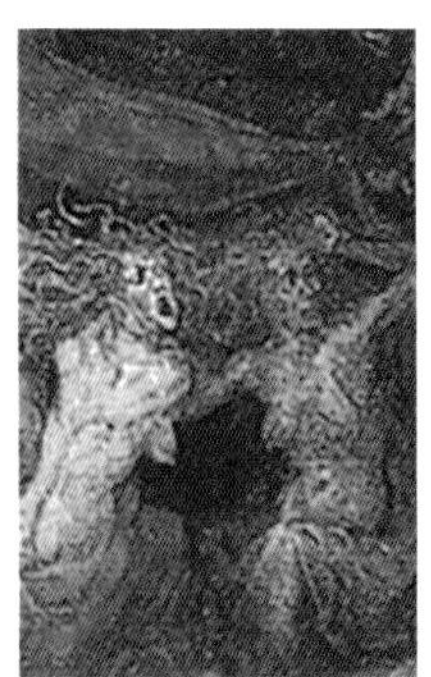

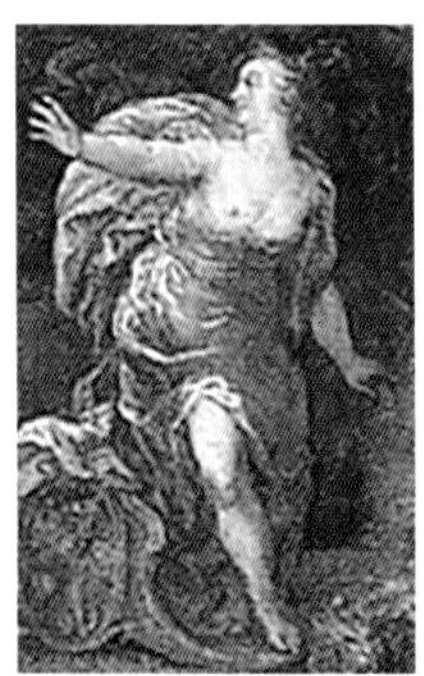

Flemish countryside, which are today found in the print collections of the Louvre, and in the museums of Berlin, Munich, London, and Vienna.

The corner of a pond, a thatched cottage, and a grove of trees became sufficiently attractive subjects, and his line, without losing its rigour, managed to capture their impalpable movement. A pearly atmosphere quivers about the curtain of willows and

Juno in the Underworld

Jan Brueghel the Elder, c. 1598
Oil on copper, 25.5 x 35.5 cm
Staatliche Kunstsammlungen,
Gemäldegalerie Alte Meister, Dresden

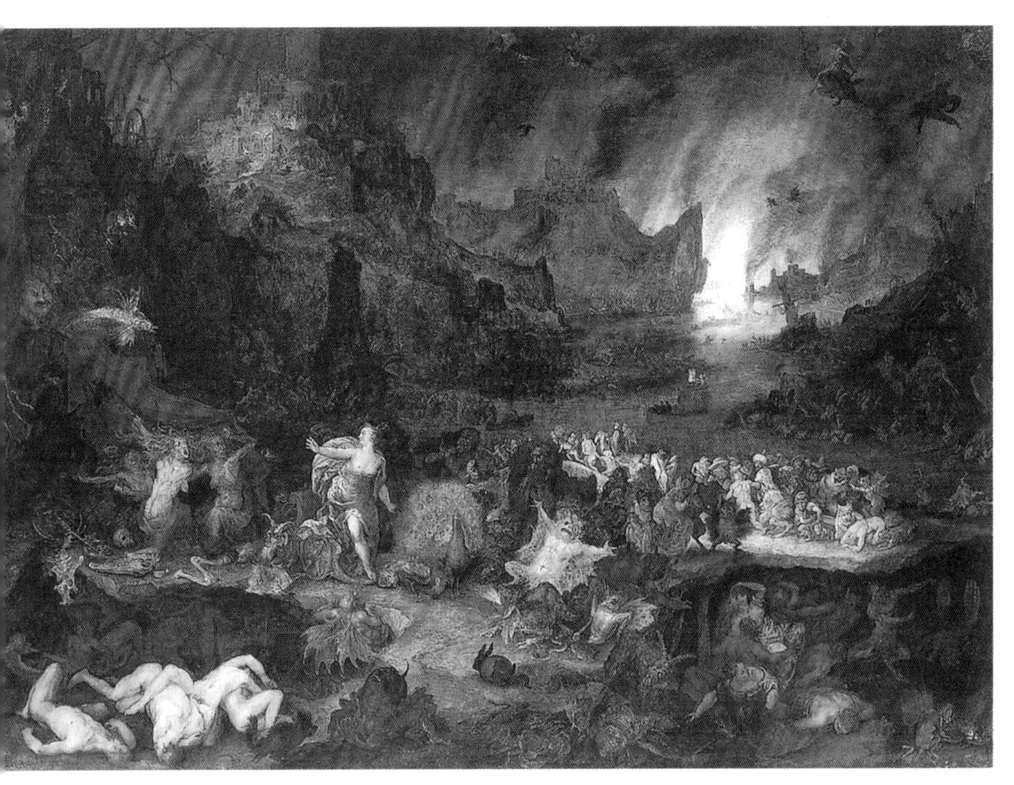

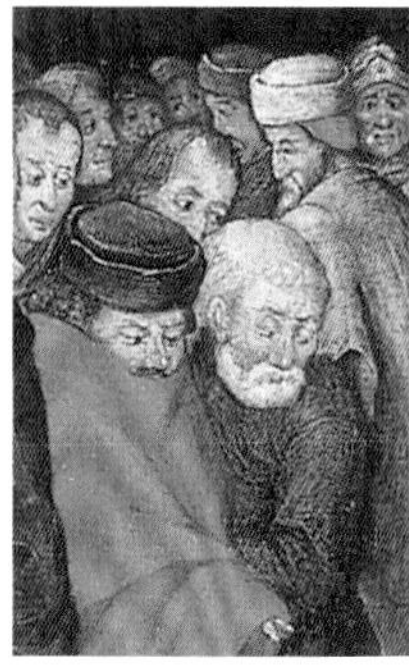

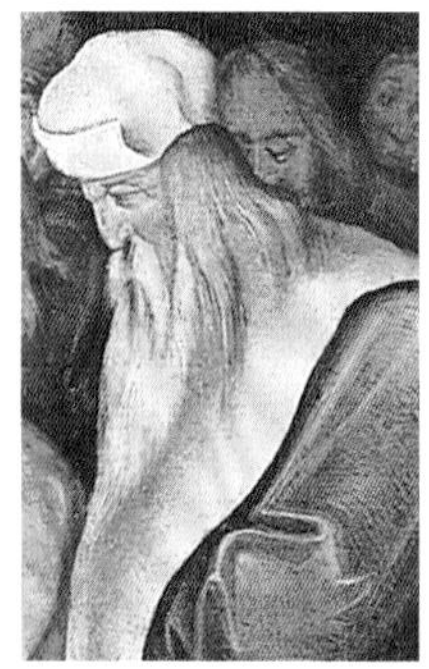

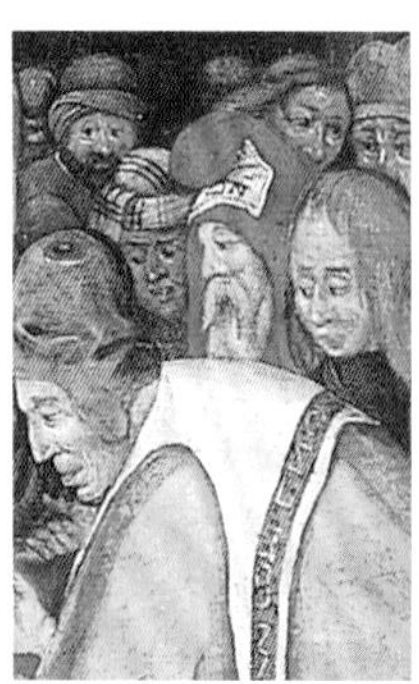

the banks of a pool and the light is diffused through the air's vapour.

Yet the images of mountain valleys, repressed memories in the depths of his consciousness, returned to obsess Bruegel. We are, after all, nothing more than the sum of our memories and the indelible impressions that we have felt at one time or another. Surely Bruegel spent many hours, years after his travels, in intense

Christ and the Woman Taken in Adultery

Pieter Brueghel the Younger, c. 1600
Oil on wood, 28.1 x 40.6 cm
The Philadelphia Museum of Art, Philadelphia

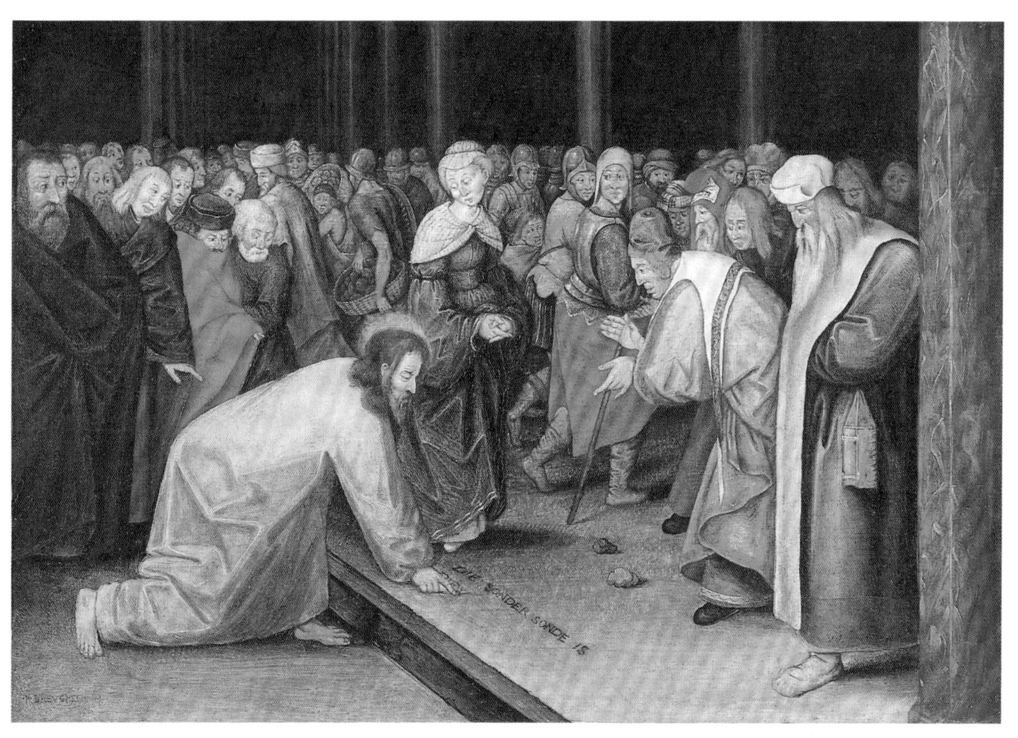
DIE SONDER SONDE IS

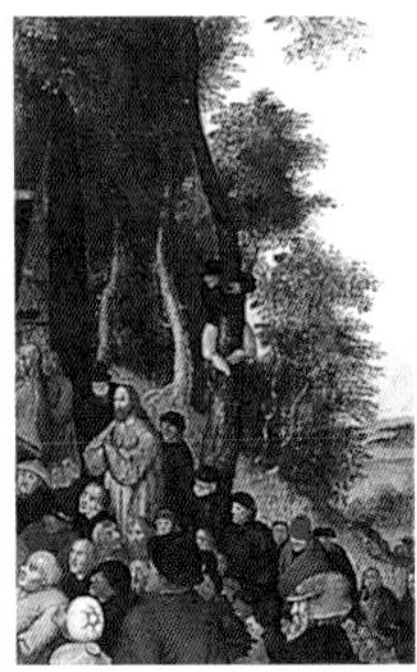

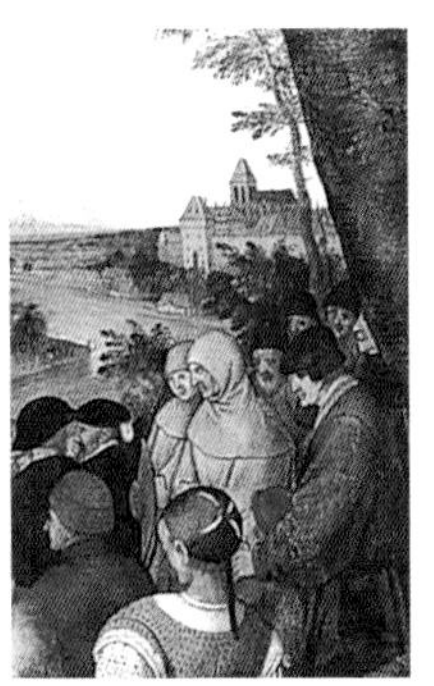

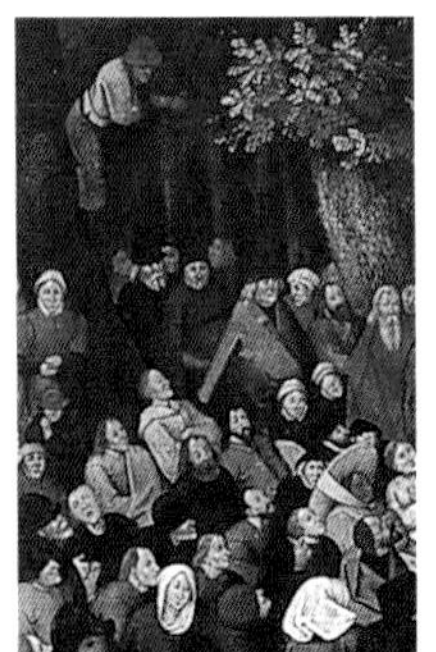

contemplation of the sunlit peaks he had seen. These deeply stirring images were clearly a part of him, and they reappeared at a time when his mature genius sought nourishment in all the sources of sensitivity. He created, this time in paint, imaginary landscapes of an intense reality. The beauty, which had slowly accumulated inside the artist during his solitary contemplation of so many moving scenes, is captured in

The Sermon of Saint John the Baptist

Pieter Brueghel the Younger, 1601
Oil on wood panel, 111 x 175 cm
Rheinisches Landesmuseum, Bonn

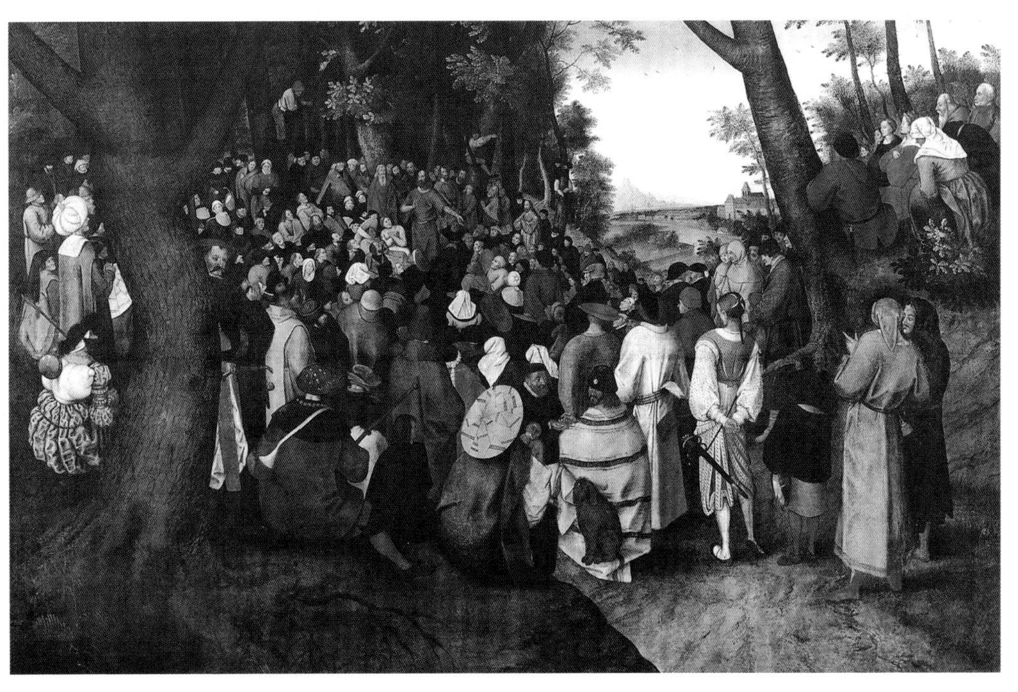

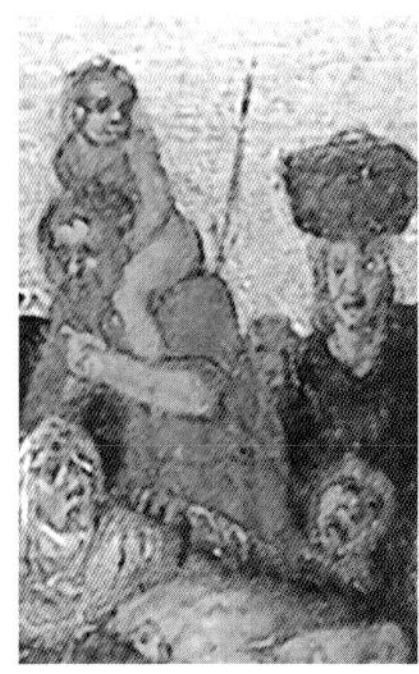

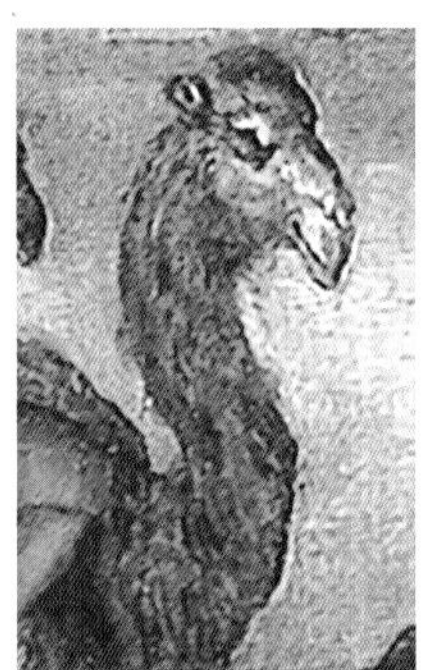

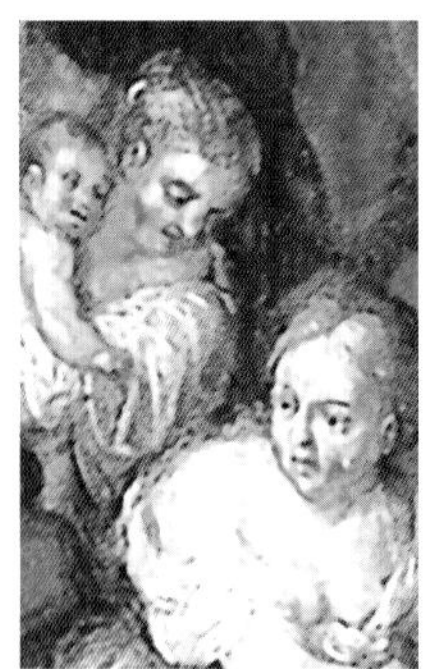

the admirable series of masterpieces created during his final period of creation.

Several works where the landscape appears as an accessory for the unfolding of events should be cited from the outset. None is more grandiose than the setting of *The Battle of the Israelites and the Philistines,* which hangs in the Kunsthistoriches Museum in Vienna. In a wild ravine, two armies drive into one another in an

The Flood with Noah's Ark

Jan Brueghel the Elder, 1601
Oil on copper, 26.5 x 36 cm
Gift of Betty and David M. Koetser
Kunsthaus Zürich, Zurich

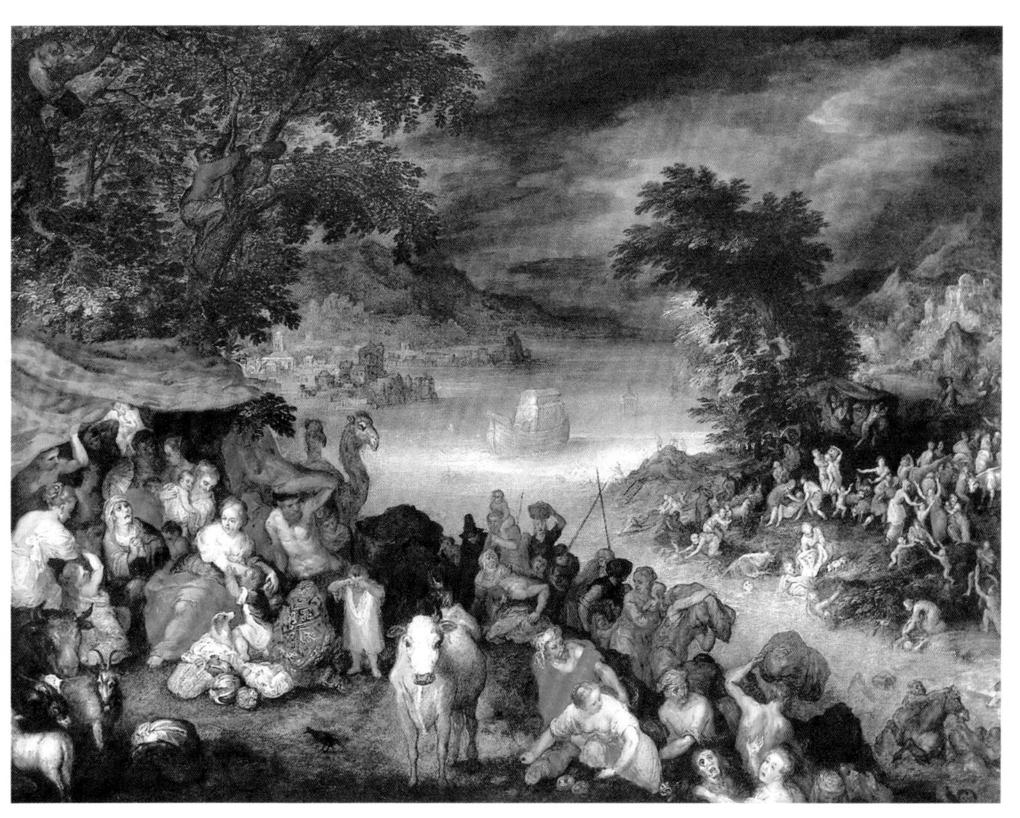

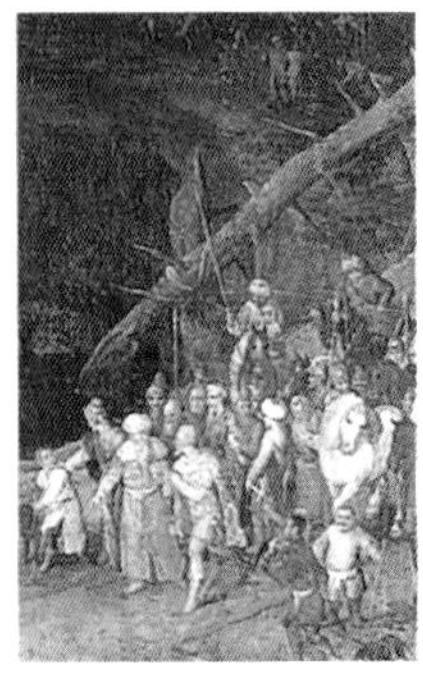

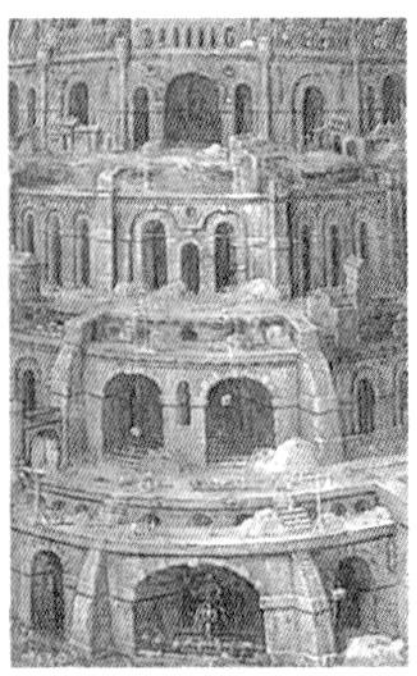

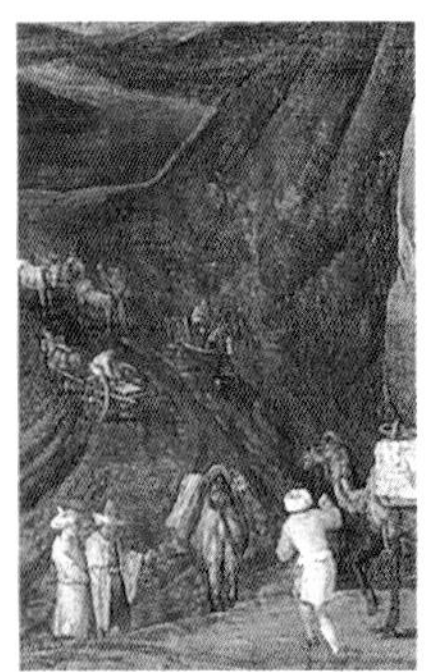

infinite swarm of ironclad knights, bristling with spears and creating the impression of a thick forest. Near the centre of the foreground rises a promontory, and to the right, jagged rocks veiled by sombre pine trees frame the perspective of an opulent city on the banks of a river. It is a powerful study of harmony and balance.

Another example of the same genre, *Christ Carrying the Cross*, also in Vienna, has a tragic and desolate

The Tower of Babel

Jan Brueghel the Elder and Tobias Verhaecht, 1602-1610
Oil on wood, 172 x 225 cm
Koninklijk Museum voor Schone Kunsten, Antwerp

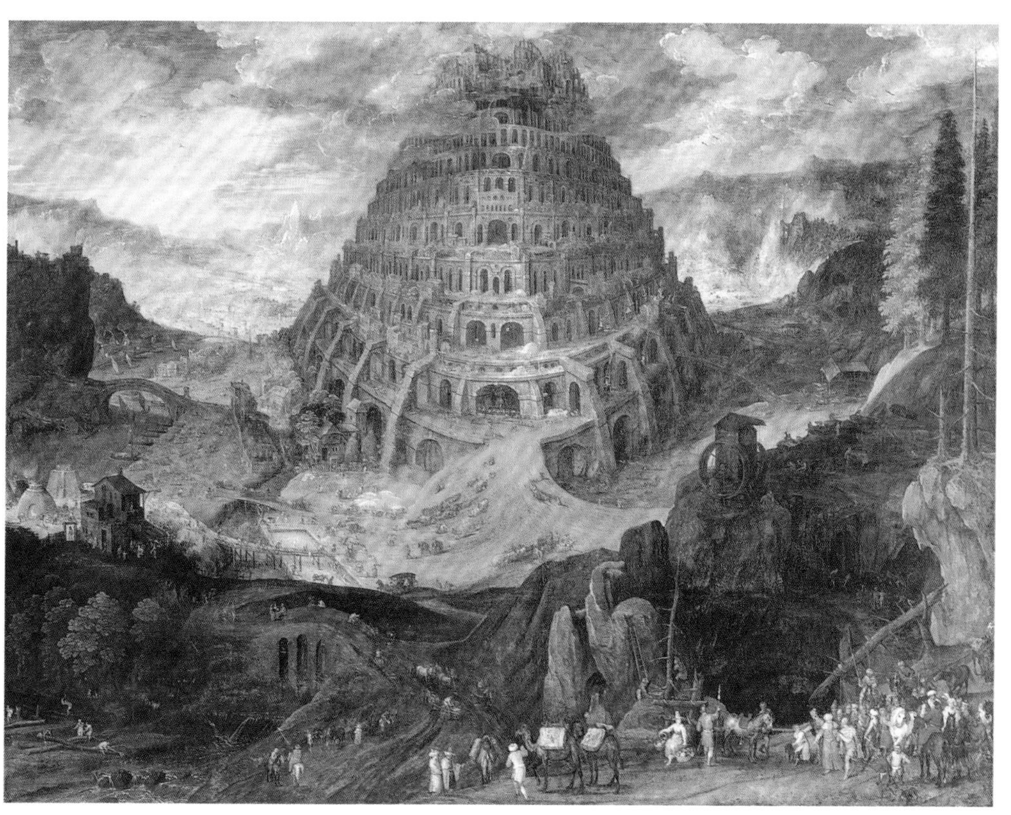

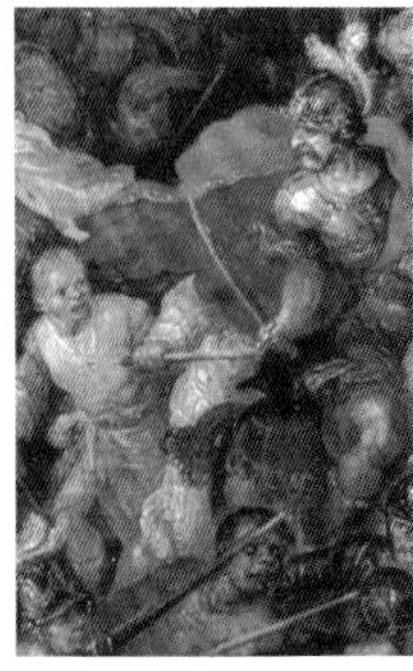

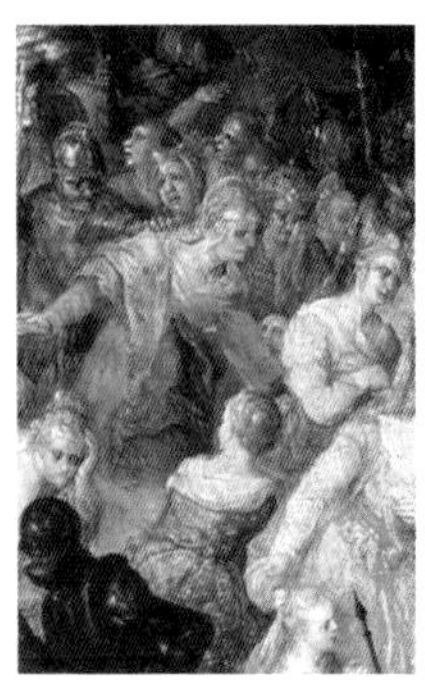

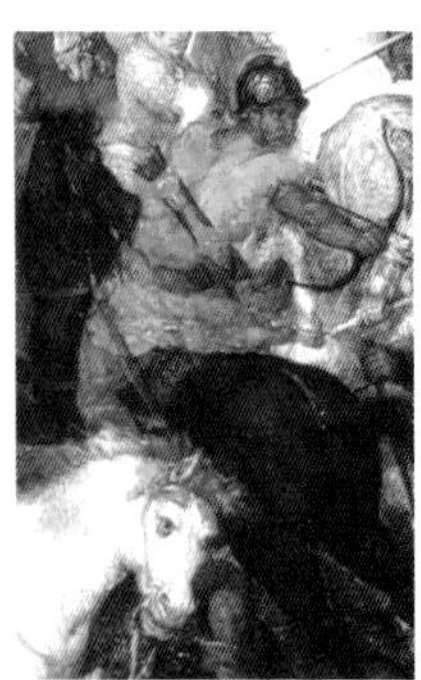

background. An immense horizon unfolds beneath a colourful sky interrupted only by a ravine cutting through its centre, from which rises the sharp needle of a rock formation. As they near the mountains, the rolling plains begin to feature brusque eruptions of rock. *The Tower of Babel* from 1563, again in the collection in Vienna, portrays an impressive ruin where the painter seems to have piled up several Coliseums,

The Battle of Issus

Jan Brueghel the Elder, 1602
Oil on wood, 80 x 136 cm
Musée du Louvre, Paris

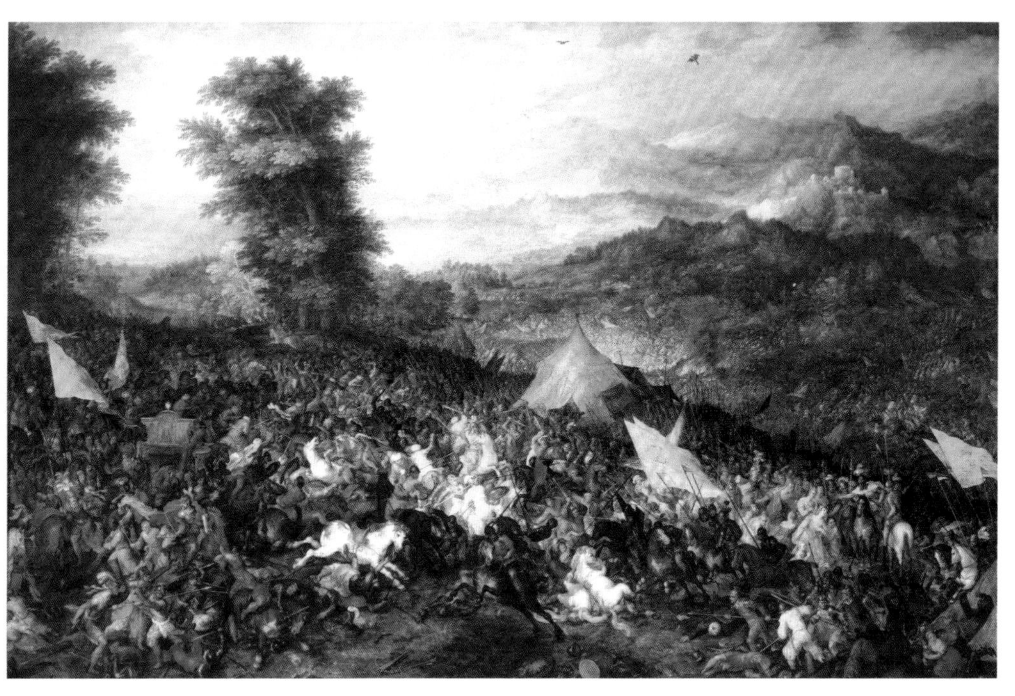

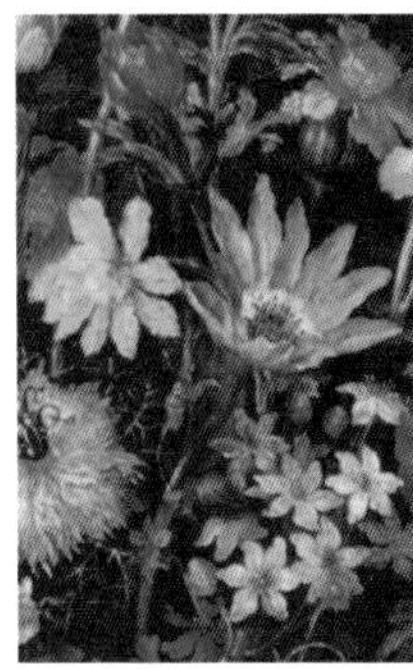

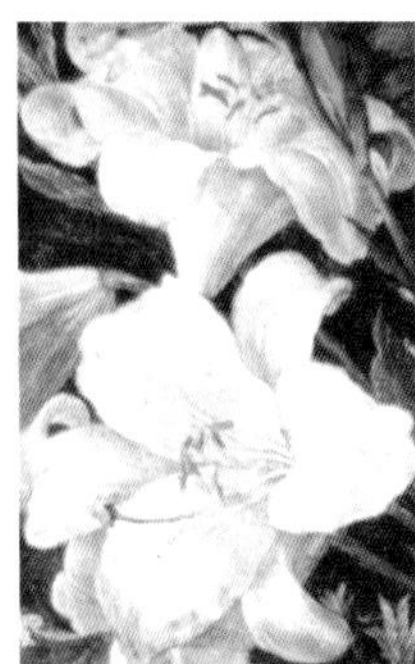

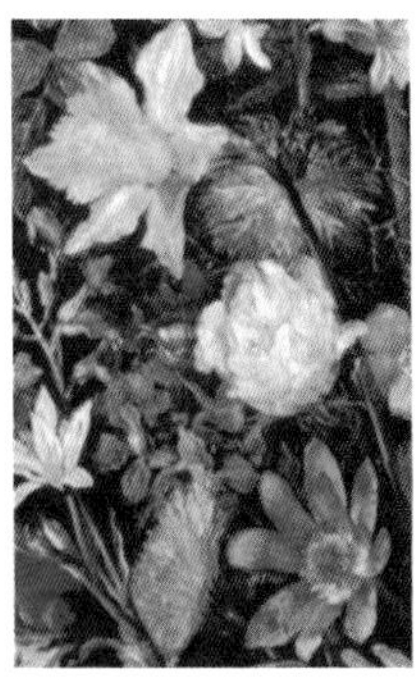

one on top of another, rising above the panorama of a plain where the roofs of a town crowd against each other like a flock of sheep, to be interrupted by rivers and forests at the horizon.

These paintings lead us to a group of works where the subject is reduced to a pretext for the portrayal of its setting. The first of this type is the winter landscape known as *The Gloomy Day*. This work creates a poignant

Bouquet

Jan Brueghel the Elder, 1603
Oil on wood, 125 x 96 cm
Alte Pinakothek, Munich

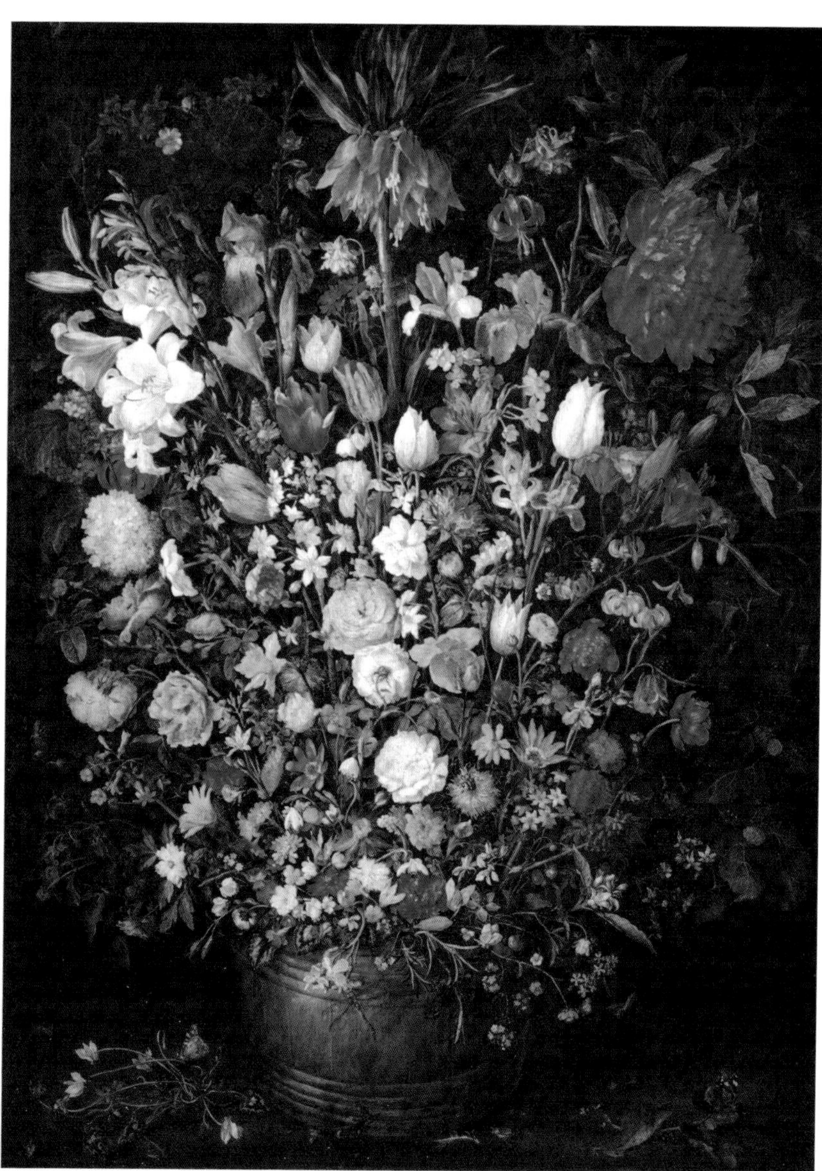

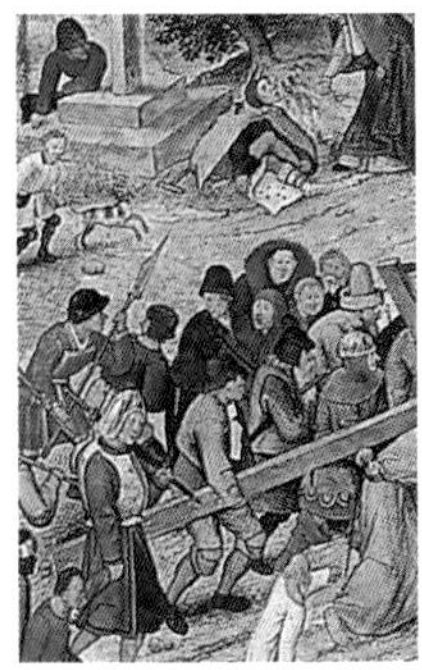

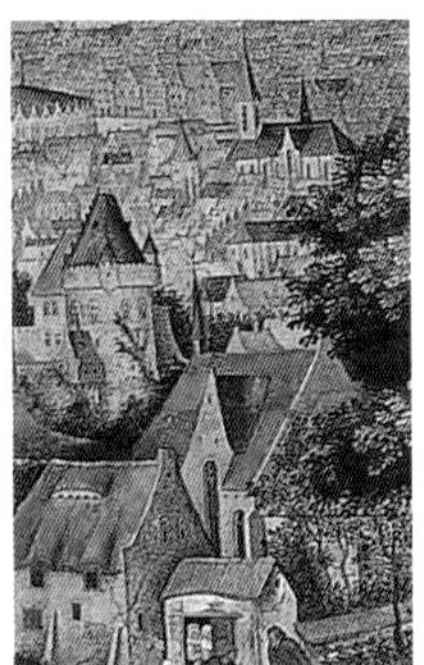

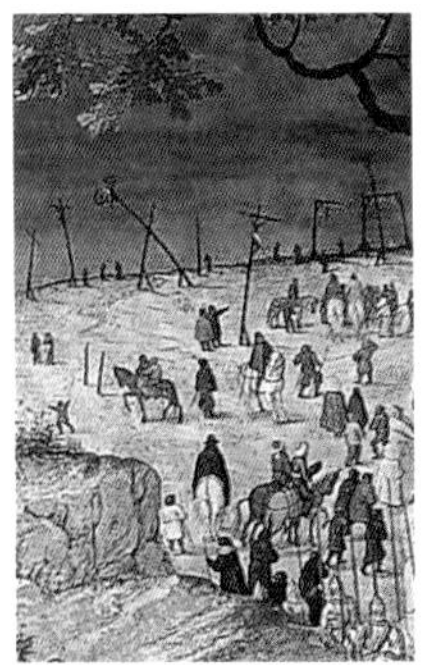

impression. A great burst of light streaks through the tormented sky and is reflected in a tumultuous river, between the two rises a range of mountains lit by their snowy peaks. In the foreground at the left, a cluster of farms and houses carpets the area around the bell tower of a church, and to the right, the edge of a forest can be seen. The trunks of the bare trees, thin and

Christ Carrying the Cross

Pieter Brueghel the Younger, 1603
Oil on wood, 116 x 162 cm
Koninklijk Museum voor Schone Kunsten, Antwerp

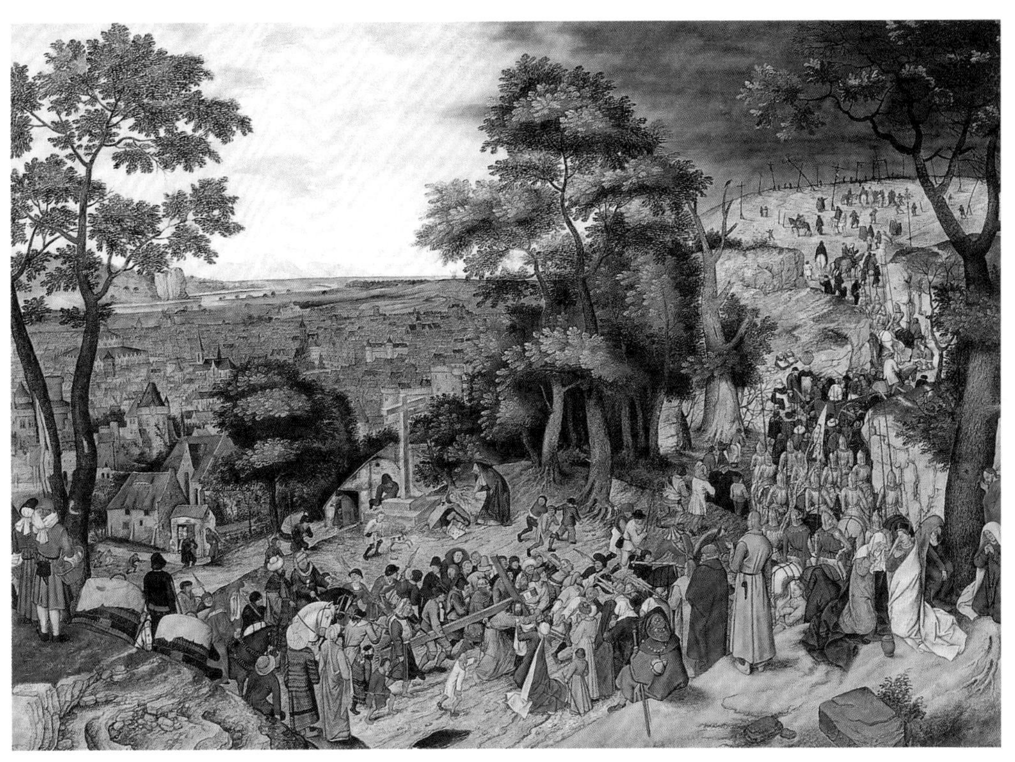

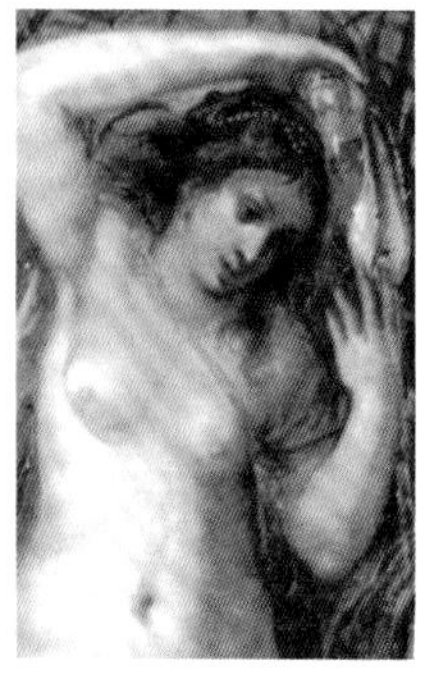

flexible, create a sort of curtain through which the horizon can be seen in the distance. The bold contrast of shadow and light, the knowing gradation between the planes, and the admirable harmony of yellows, tans, and browns qualify this work as a masterpiece. It exudes an ardent melancholy, a strange quality at once gentle and powerful, that touches and penetrates the viewer.

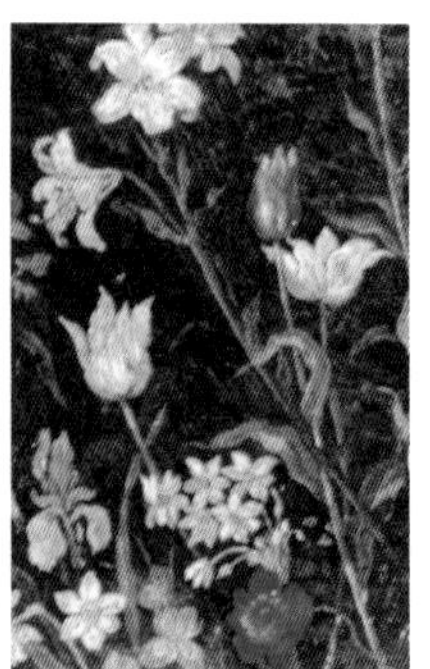

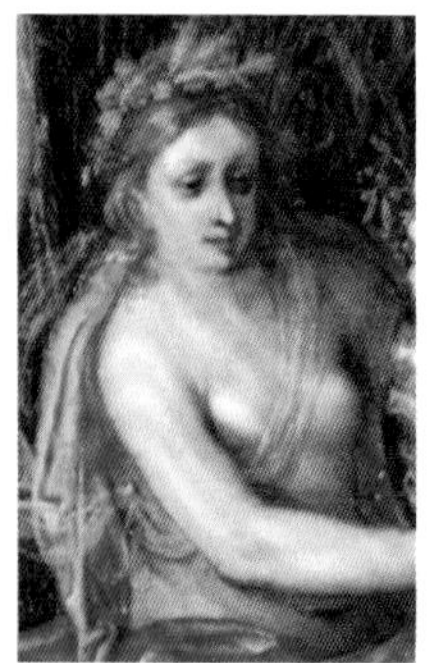

Ceres and the Four Elements

Jan Brueghel the Elder and Hendrick Van Balen, 1604
Oil on copper, 42 x 71 cm
Kunsthistorisches Museum, Vienna

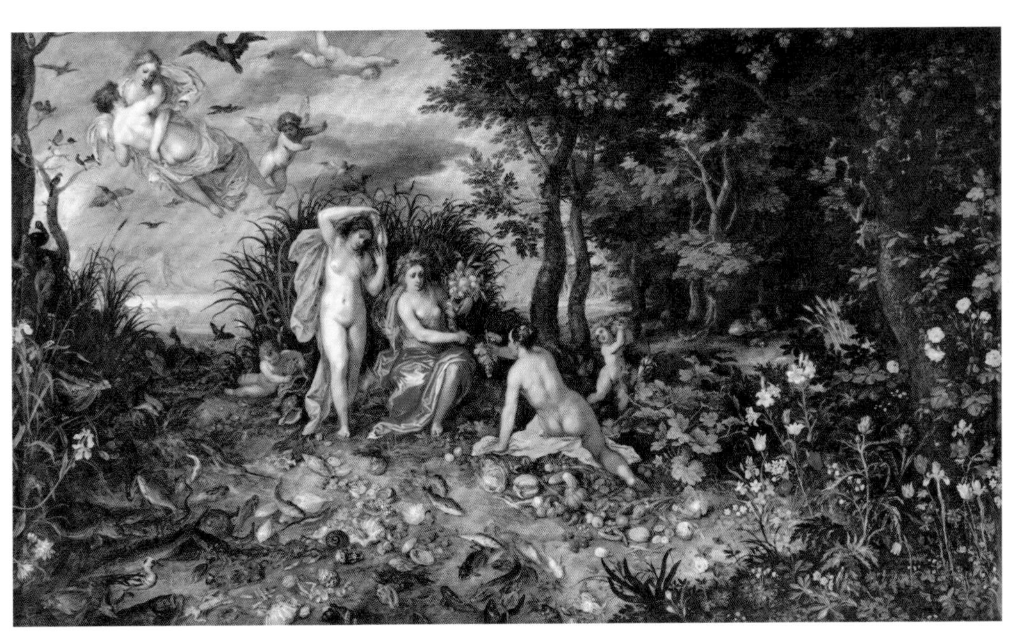

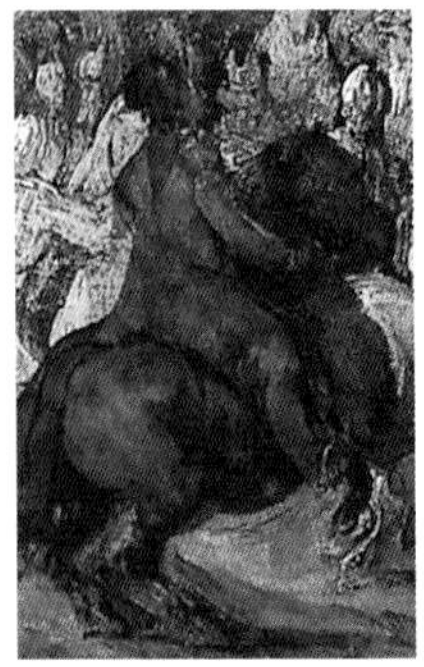

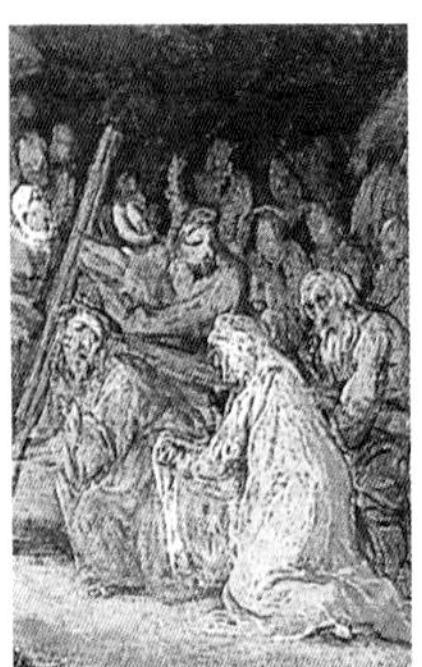

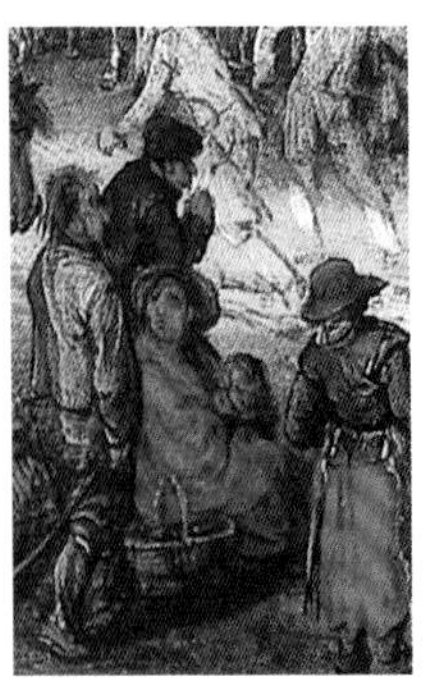

The Return of the Herd is an autumn landscape. The cattle, driven by their keepers' prods, pass along the side of the foreground from right to left. A man on horseback and three other figures on foot follow in their steps. It is difficult to decide which is more admirable: the sober and vigorous lines of the herders or the harried and attractive ensemble of their flock. A river flows in the opposite direction of the cattle, on the other side of

Christ Carrying the Cross

Jan Brueghel the Elder, c. 1606
Oil on copper, 13 x 18 cm
Gift of Betty and David M. Koetser,
Kunsthaus Zürich, Zurich

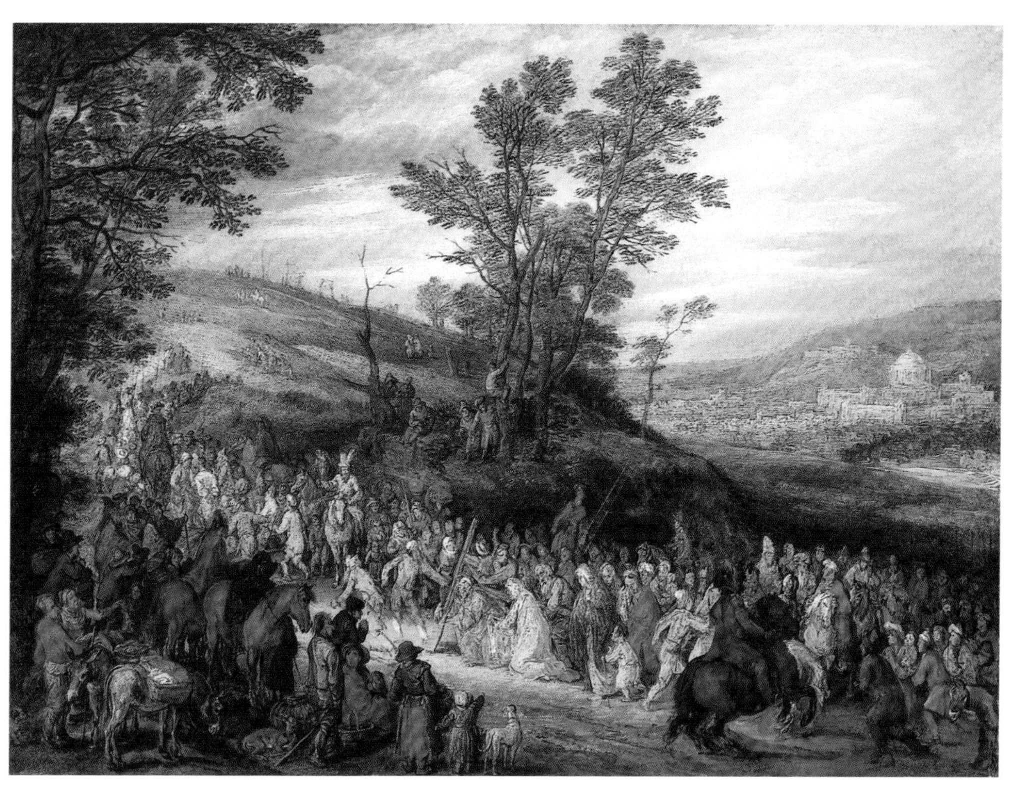

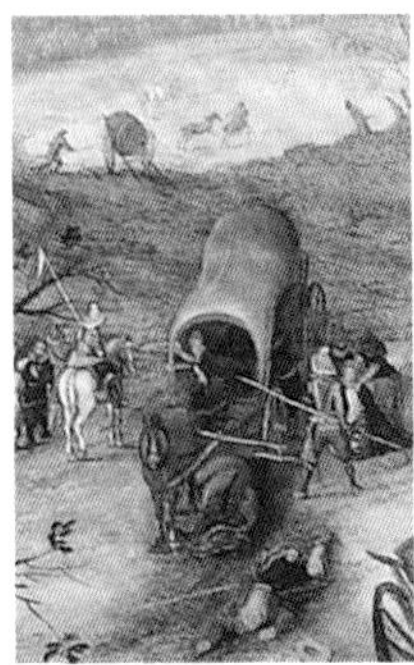

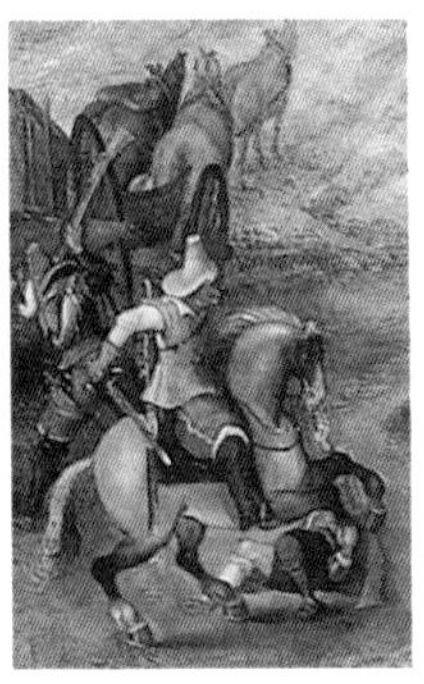

which can be seen abrupt rock formations. A very pale and energetic light passes through the rust-coloured clouds, funnelling and graduating into infinitely nuanced halftones. The summary and unbalanced composition of this work gives the impression of a more immediate reality. It seems to have sprung from the painter's imagination unrefined which makes it appear even more realistic.

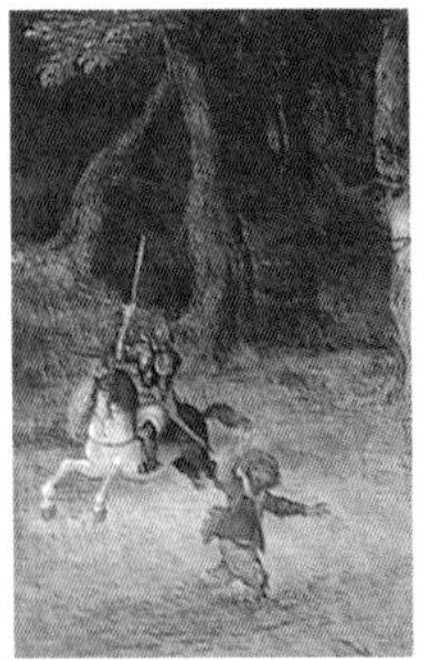

The Ambush

Jan Brueghel the Elder and Sebastian Vrancx, c. 1607
Oil on wood, 44 x 80 cm
Koninklijk Museum voor Schone Kunsten, Antwerp

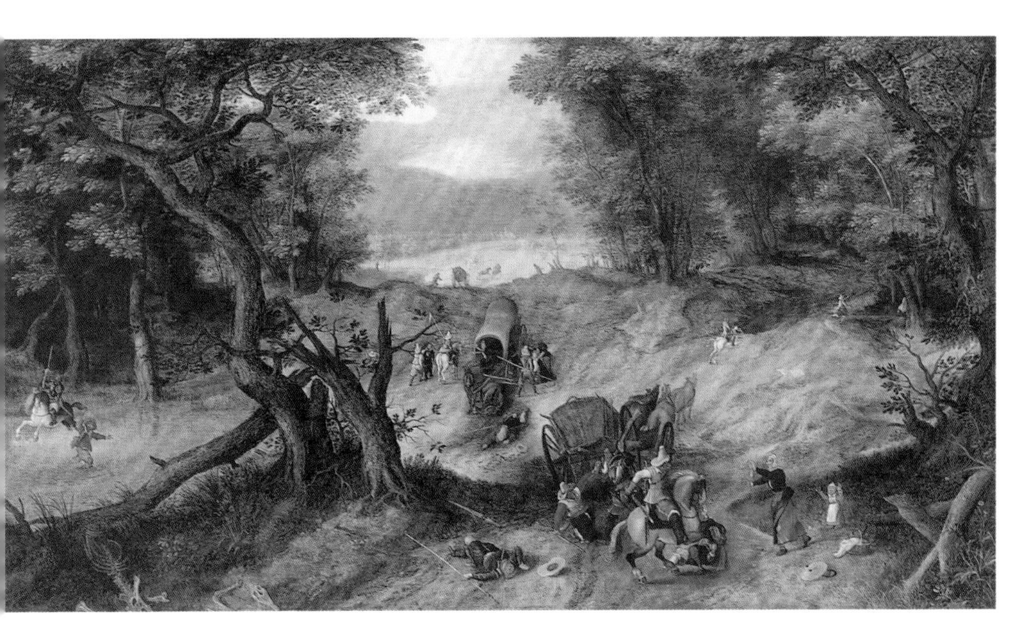

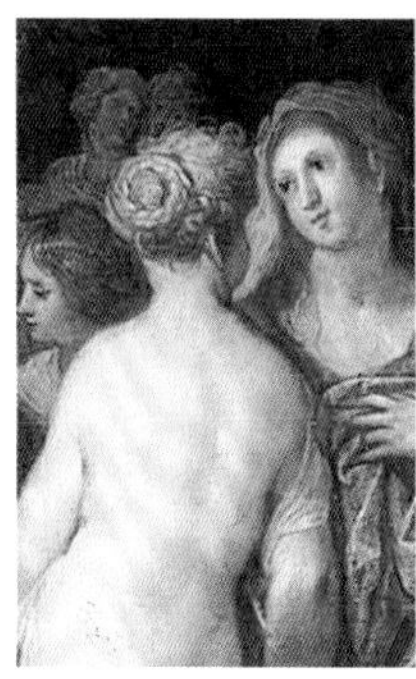

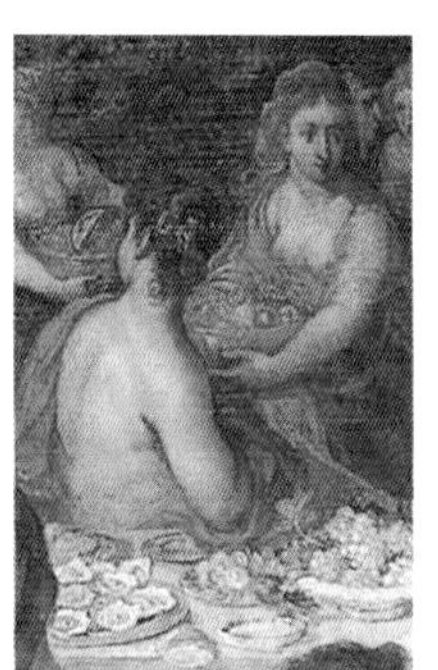

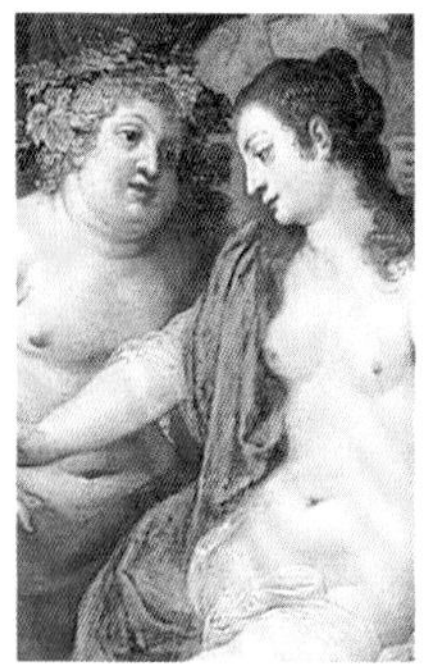

Increasingly, Bruegel abandoned the works that embrace vast stretches of countryside and cram several views into a single gigantic panorama, thus accumulating and juxtaposing places and scenery. Instead, he began to restrict himself to scenes that could be captured in a single glance, concentrating the viewer's emotion where he once dispersed it with his boundless fantasy.

The Marriage of Bacchus and Ariadne

Jan Brueghel the Elder and Hendrick Van Balen, after 1608
Oil on copper, 36.5 x 51.5 cm
Staatliche Kunstsammlungen,
Gemäldegalerie Alte Meister, Dresden

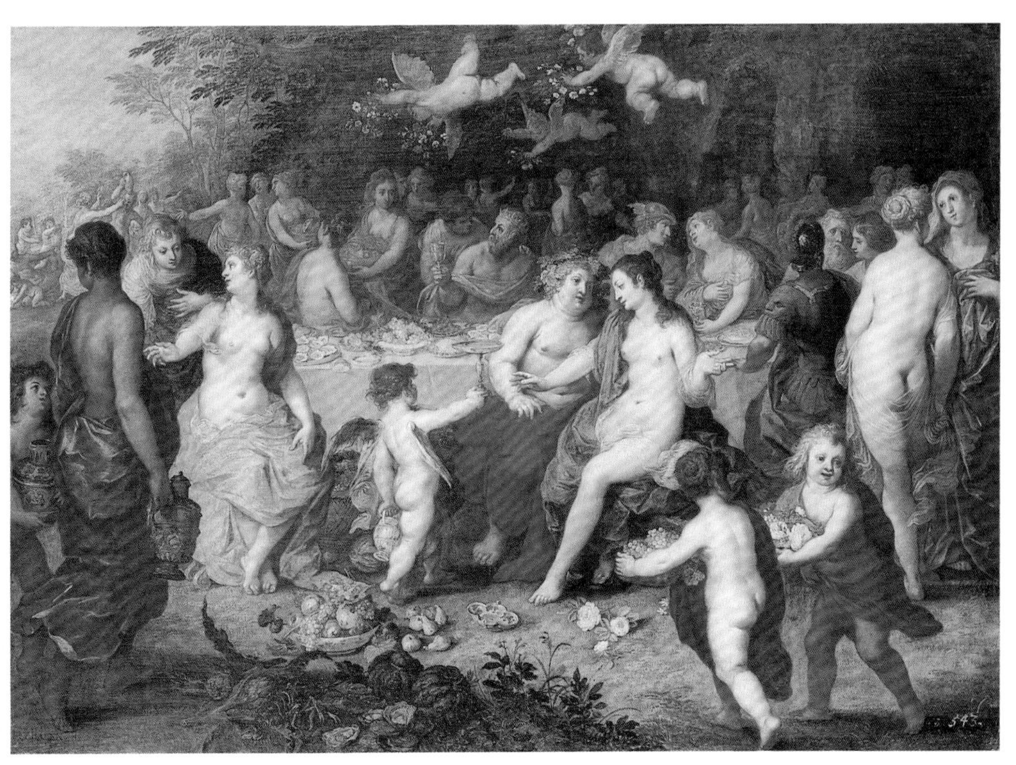

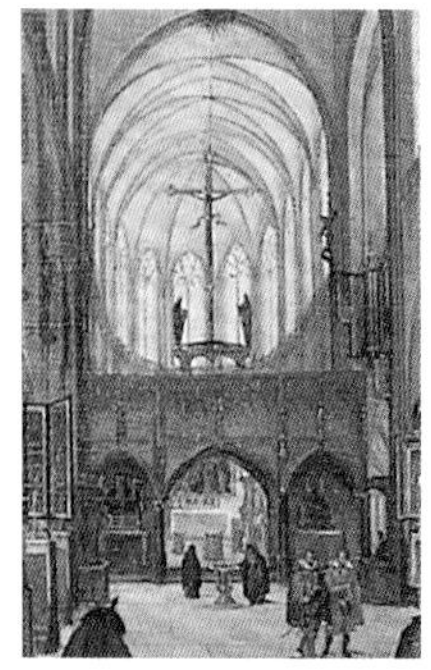

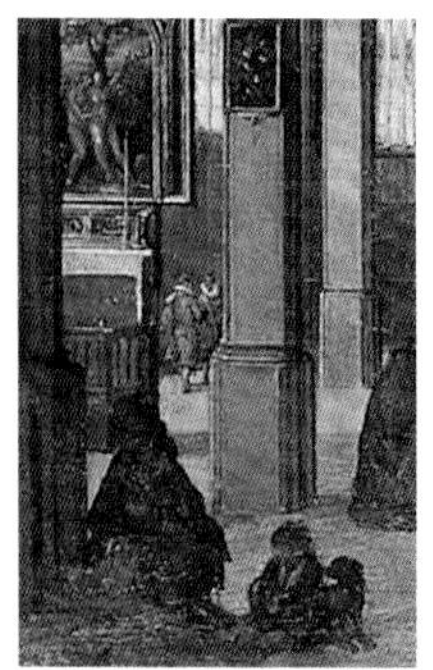

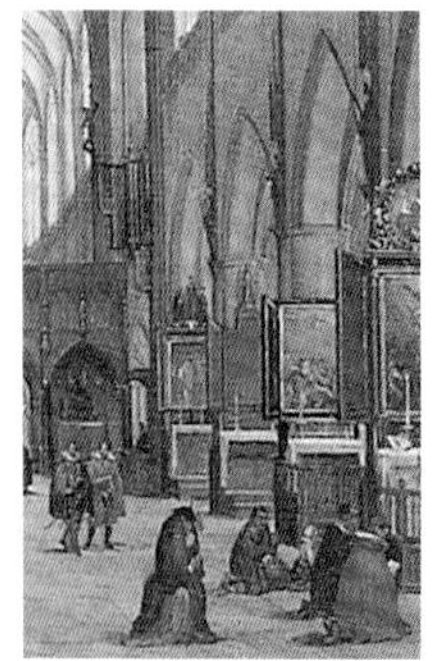

Hunters in the Snow creates a soft symphony of rusts and whites. Several villages are spaced along the right-hand side of the middle ground. Their snow-capped roofs cluster together between the dark lines of hedges and a few groves of trees. In the depths of the valley, two rectangular ponds, like those frequently encountered in the southern Brabant region, spread their sombre and opaque mirrors of ice. On the hillside

Interior of the Antwerp Cathedral

Jan Brueghel the Elder and
Hendrick Van Steenwijck the Younger, c. 1609
Oil on wood, 45.2 x 62.5 cm
Szépmüvészeti Múzeum, Budapest

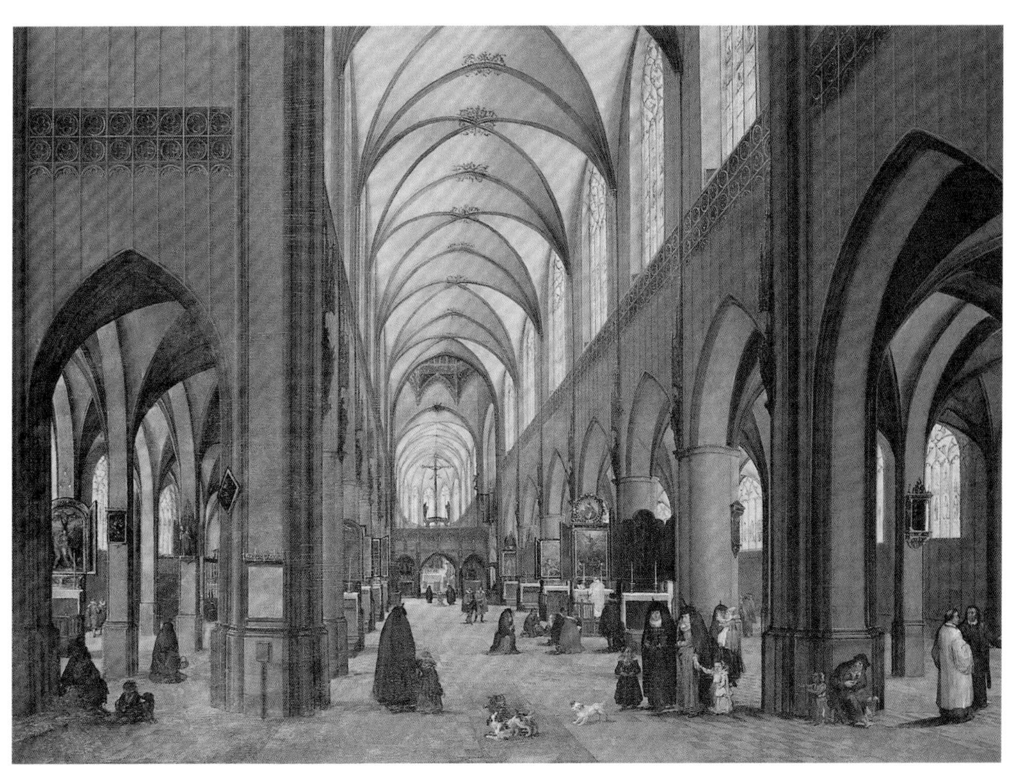

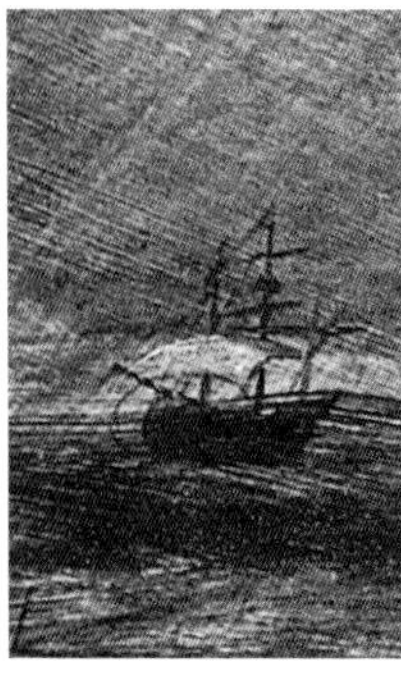

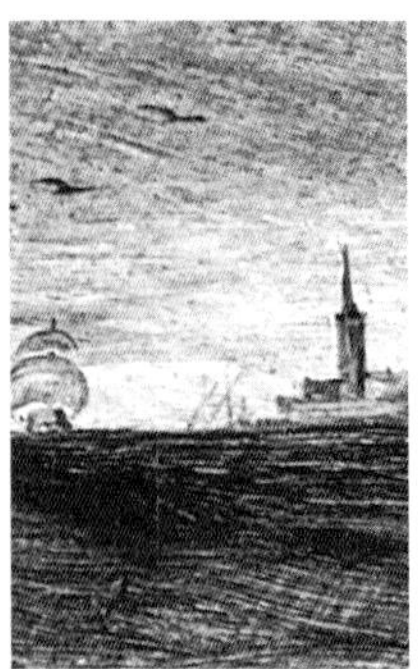

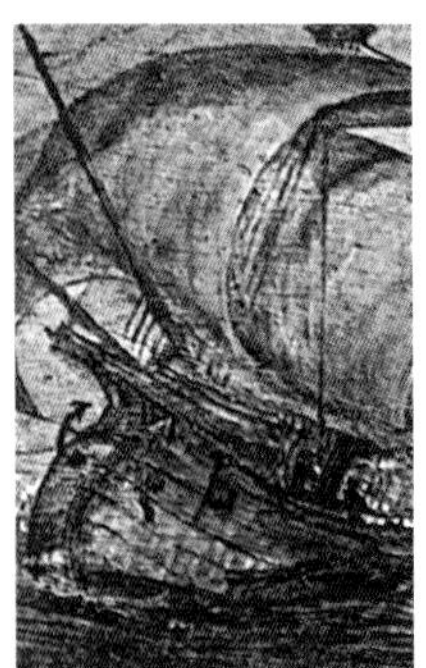

from which the landscape is viewed, three hunters are followed by a pack of greyhounds. Some trees create black bars across the white of the hillside, dispersing the fine hash marks of their branches across the rust-coloured sky. The same accuracy of movement seen in *The Return of the Herd* is found again in this group of hunters with their dogs. The skaters, who move across the ponds in the opposite direction, and the black stains

The Tempest

Pieter Bruegel the Elder (?) or
Joos de Momper the Younger, c. 1610-1615
Oil on wood, 71 x 97 cm
Kunsthistorisches Museum, Vienna

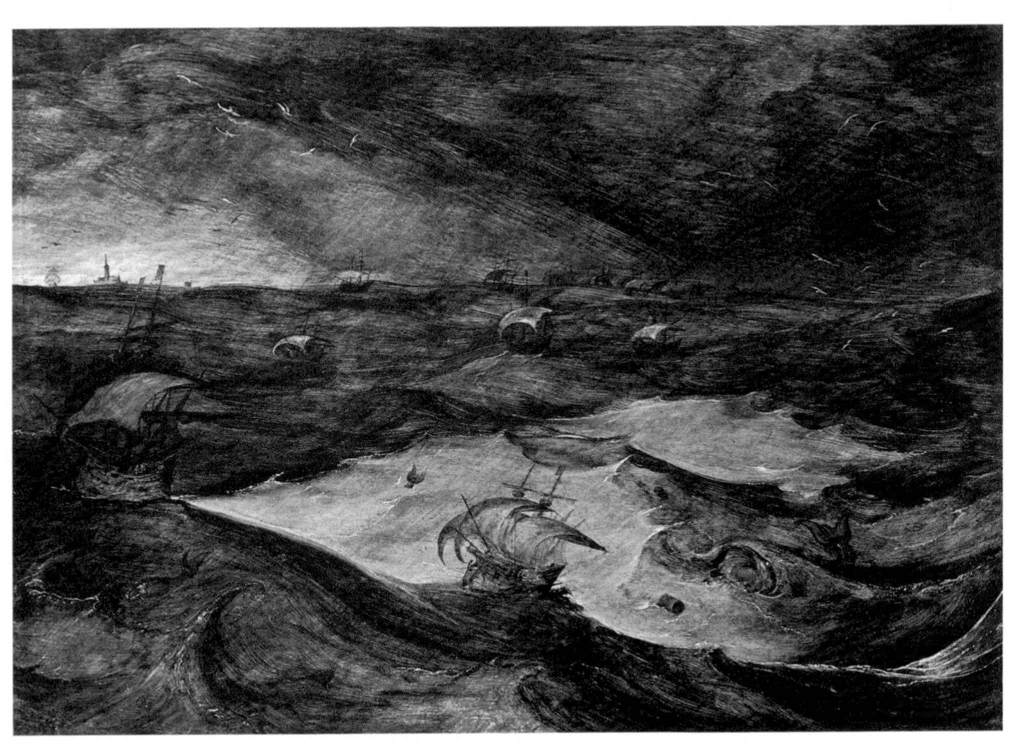

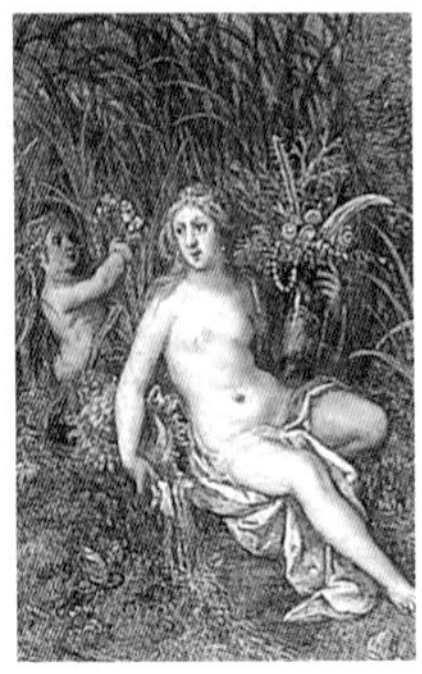
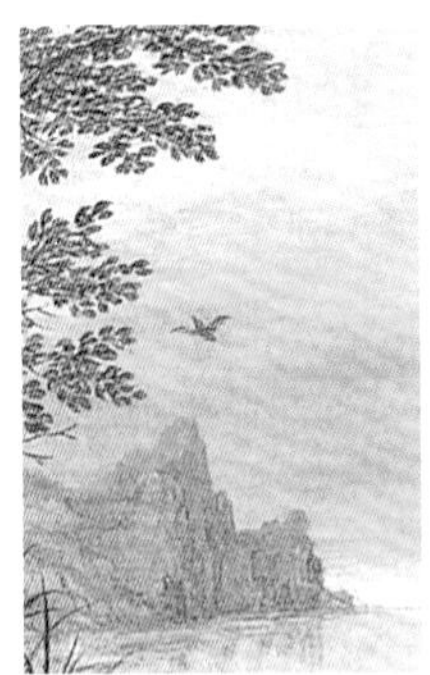
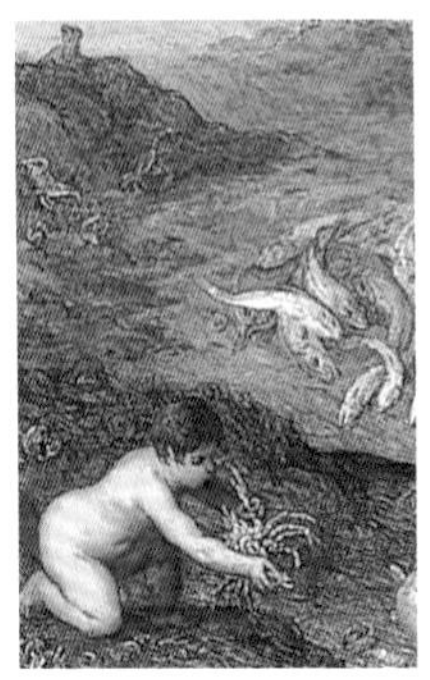

of the crows enliven the solitude of the scene without interrupting its remarkable silence.

In contrast, the painting *Haymaking* is all joy and brightness. A fluid light filters in tones of mauve and blue to the hills of a distant horizon. On the summit to one side thrusts a massive block of rock. A church and a few houses are scattered across a hillside cut by dark vegetation. In the foreground, men and women are

The Allegory of Water

Jan Brueghel the Elder, 1610
Oil on copper, 21.1 x 31.7 cm
Private collection

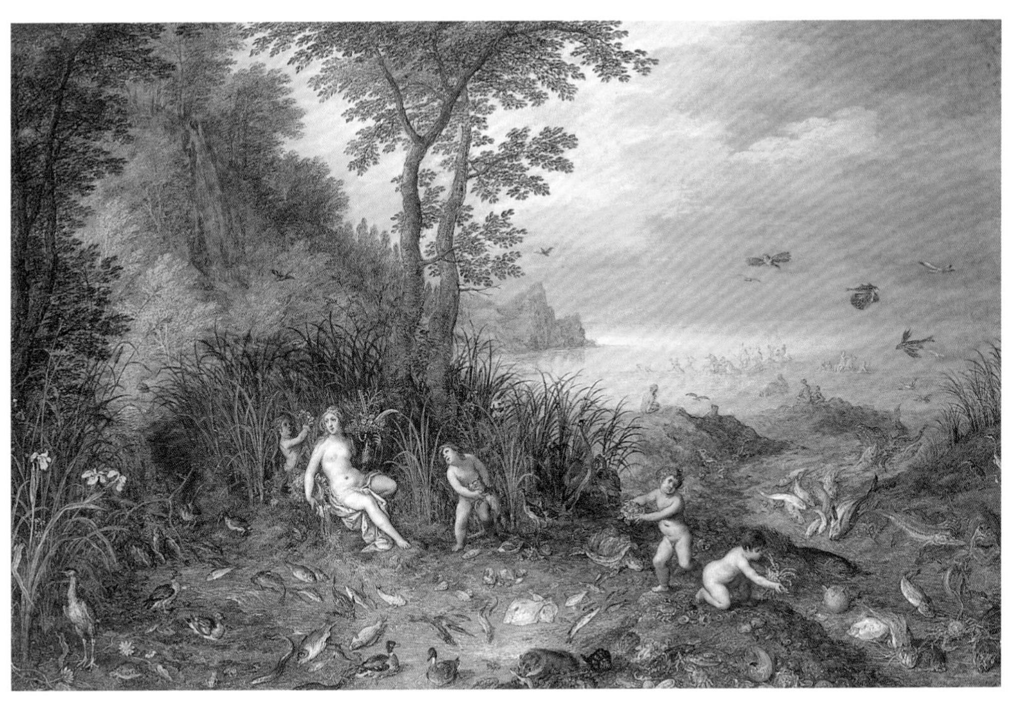

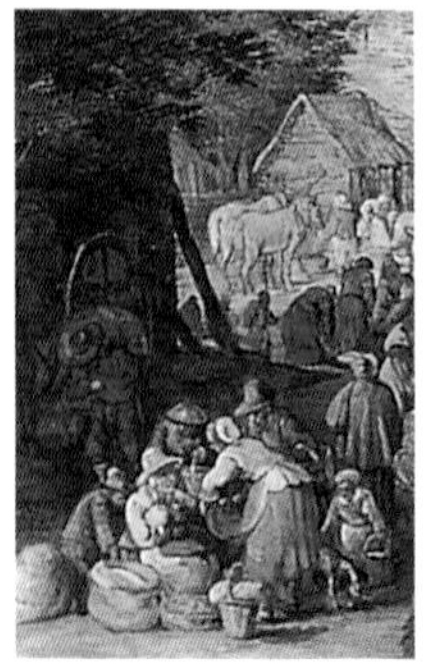

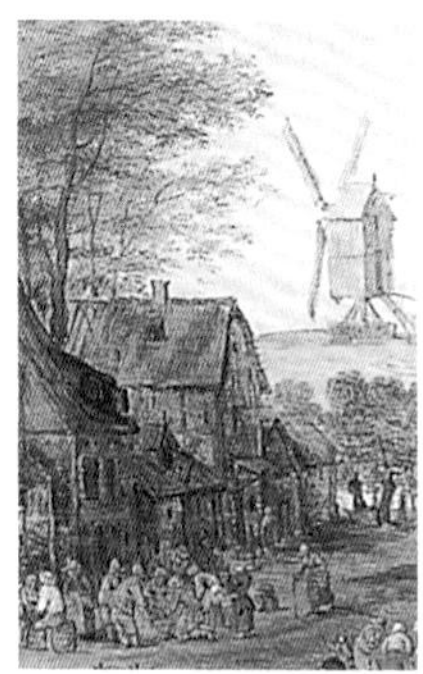

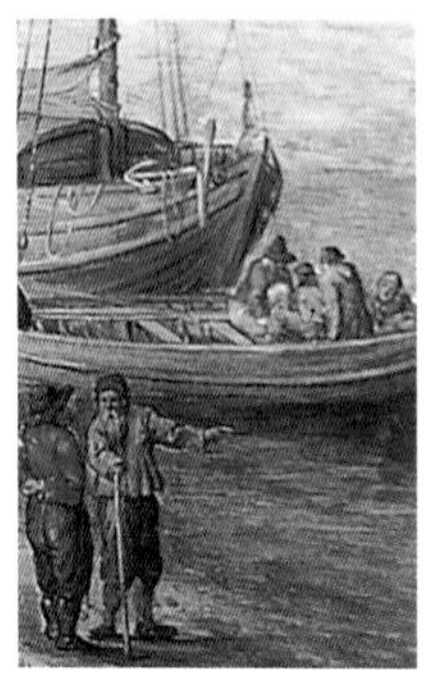

depicted as they gather the cut hay into bundles. A peasant seated in the left-hand corner sharpens his scythe. Three peasant women with rakes on their shoulders descend a path that a group of boys and girls climb, balancing baskets on their heads. The alacrity of the women carrying their rakes and the supple effort of the movements of the basket carriers are translated with extraordinarily assured vigour.

Fishmarket on the Edge of a River

Jan Brueghel the Elder, 1611
Oil on wood, 41.5 x 60.5 cm
Rheinisches Landesmuseum, Bonn

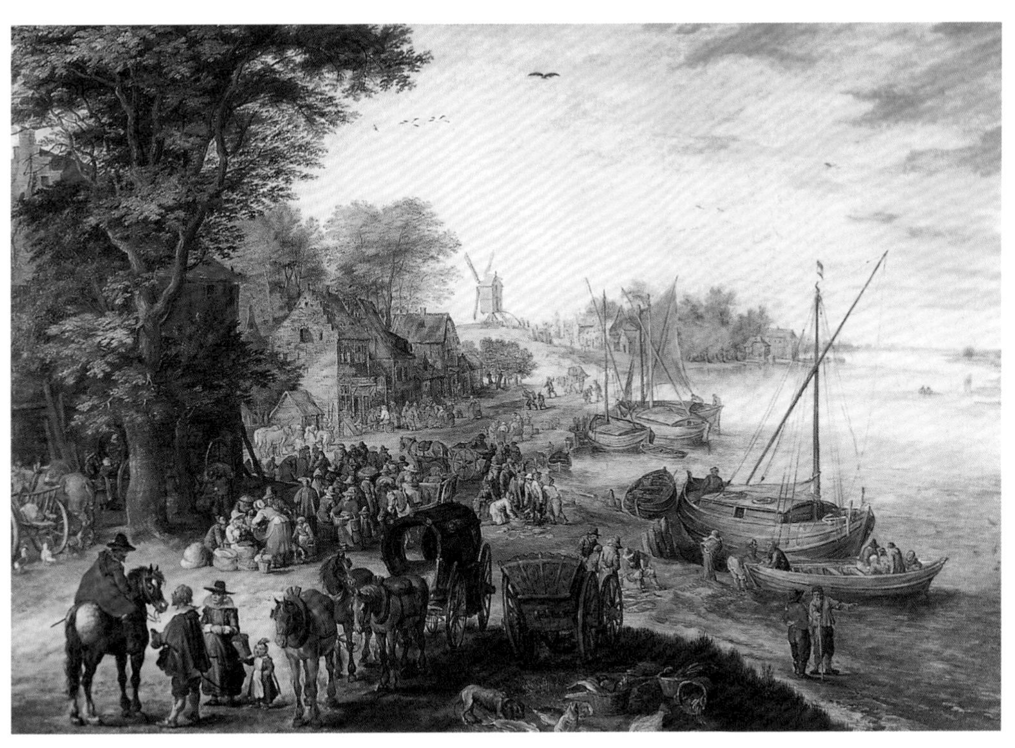

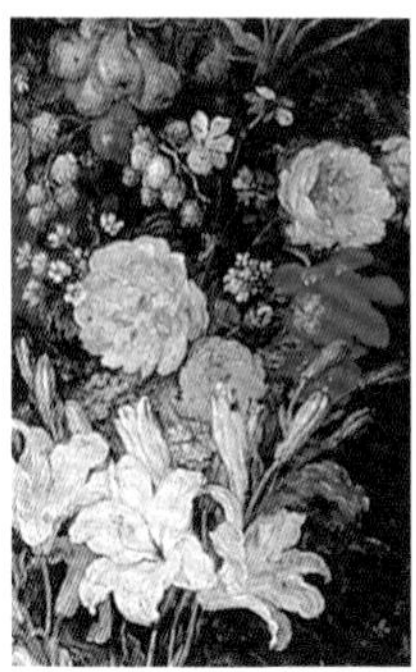

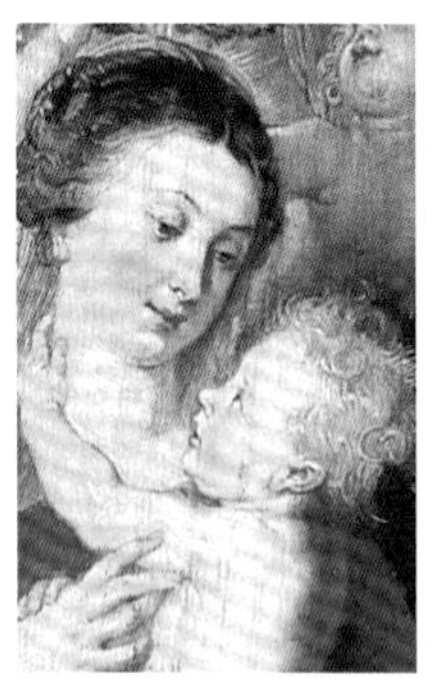

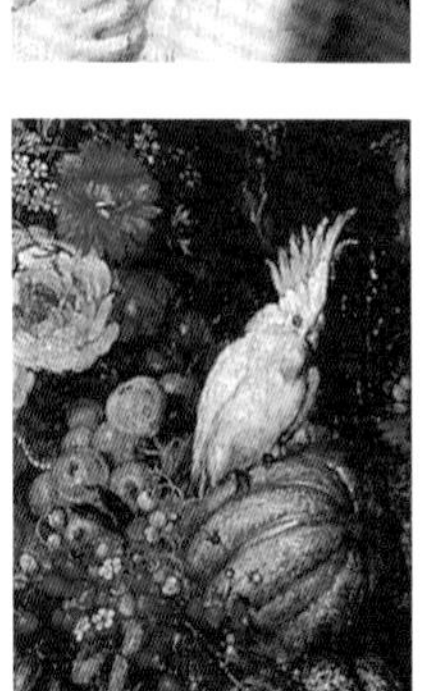

These four works place Bruegel as the first among the landscape painters of his century. The solid qualities of their compositions are allied with a vivid and profound sense of nature and a penetrating emotion. They are a clear measure of his original and sincere genius, and it seems as though he wished to astound us with their dazzling and unexpected glow.

Virgin and Child Surrounded by Flowers and Fruit

Jan Brueghel the Elder
Oil on panel, 79 x 65 cm
Museo del Prado, Madrid

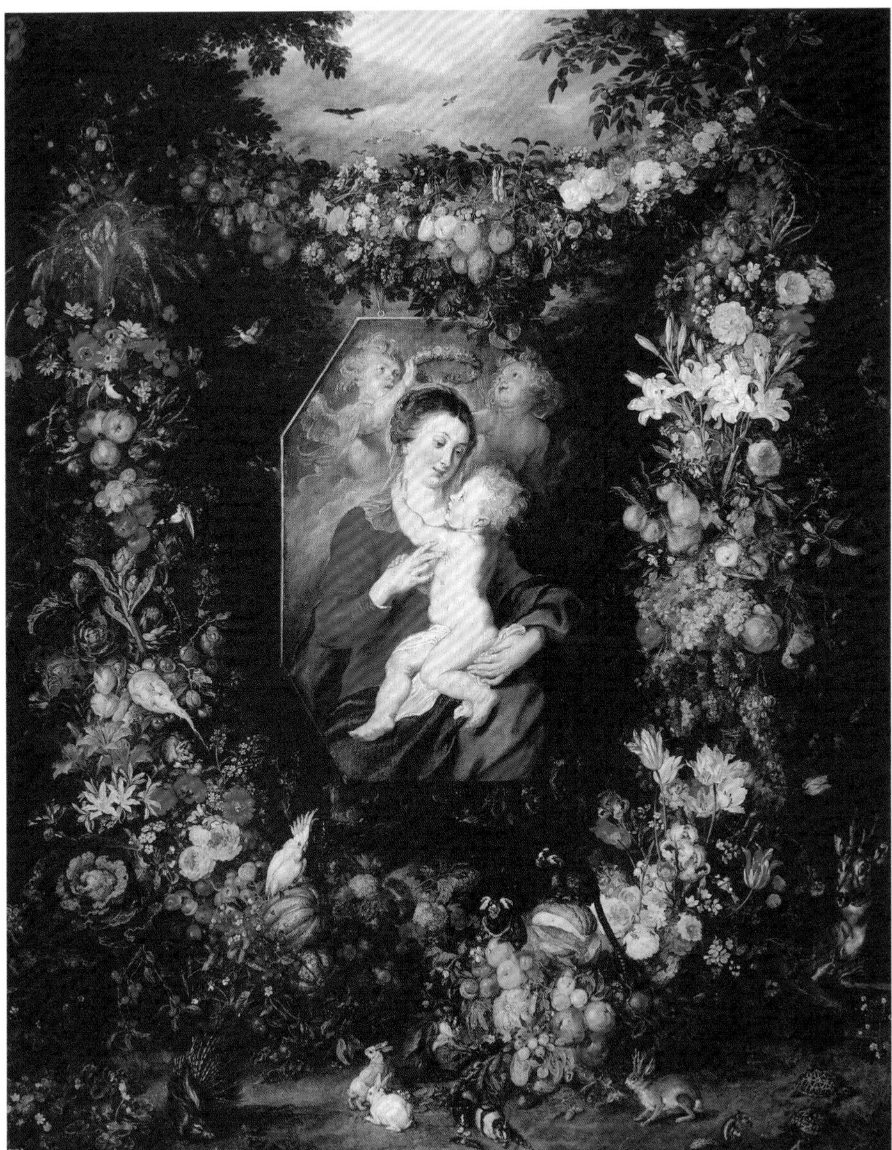

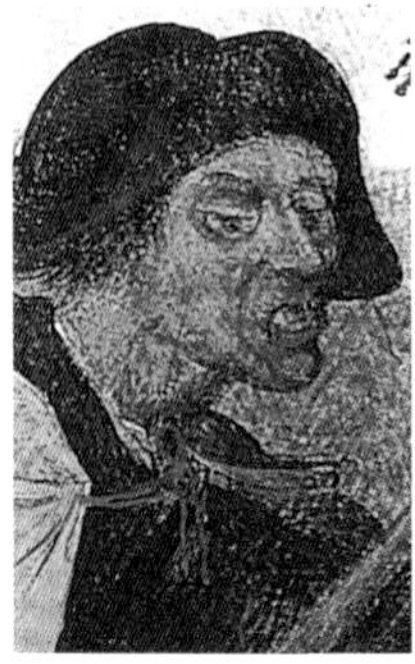

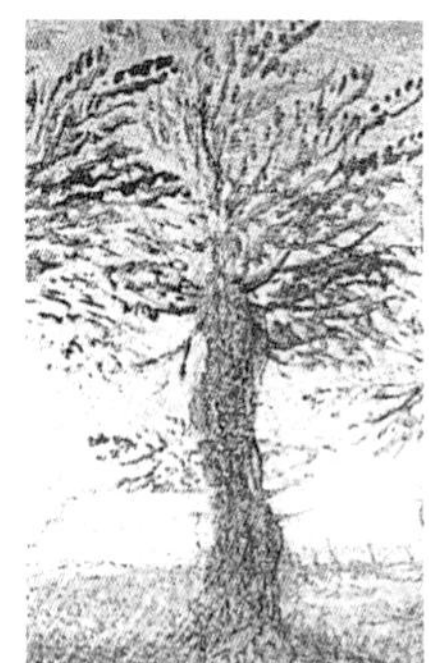

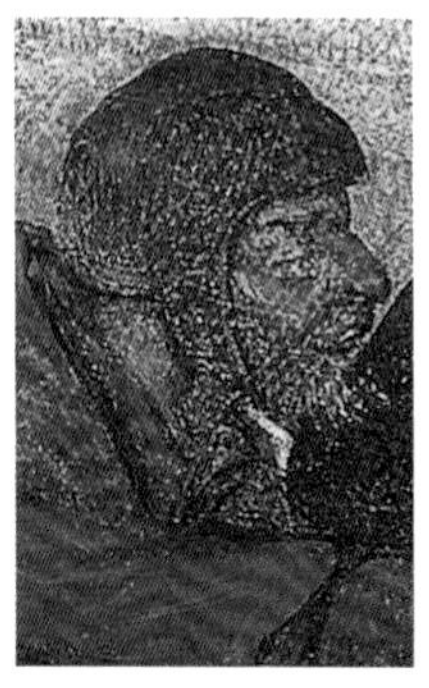

The Conversion of Saint Paul is nothing more than a rock face crossed by a procession of knights and infantry. It would be superfluous to vaunt the life and truth as well as the variety of expressions in this mass, the grandeur of its isolated movements, and the volume of its attitude. In a pile of rocks from which two or three dark pine trees are seen to rise, Bruegel encapsulates a formidable power. Never before was he so sparing and sober

The Parable of the Blind Leading the Blind

Pieter Brueghel the Younger, c. 1616
Oil on wood, diameter: 19.5 cm
Národní Galerie, Prague

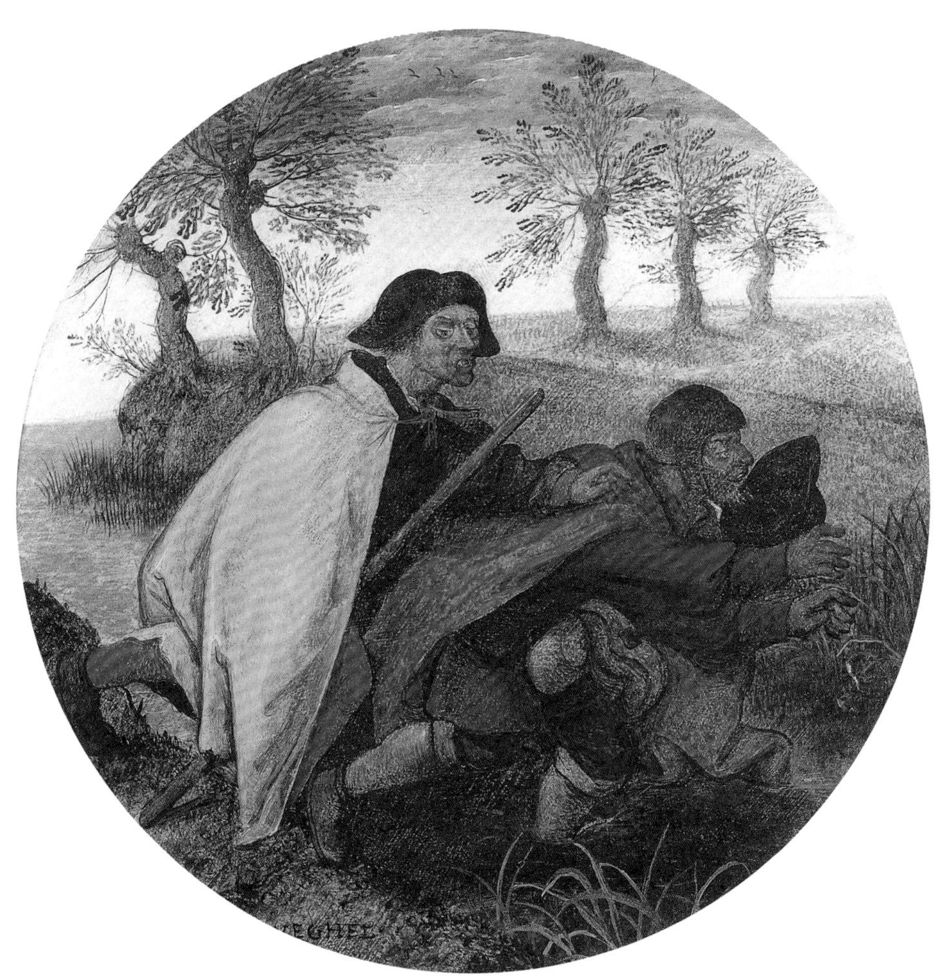

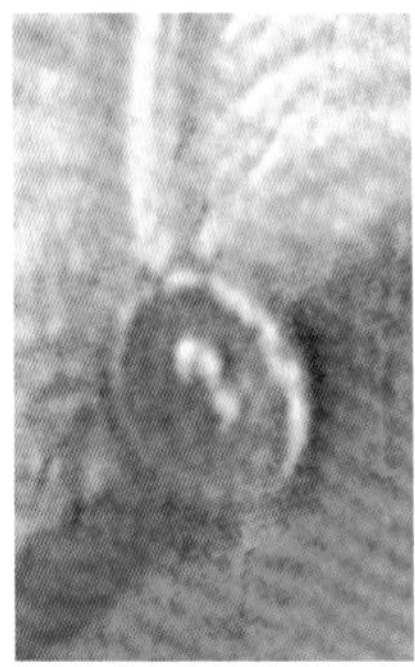

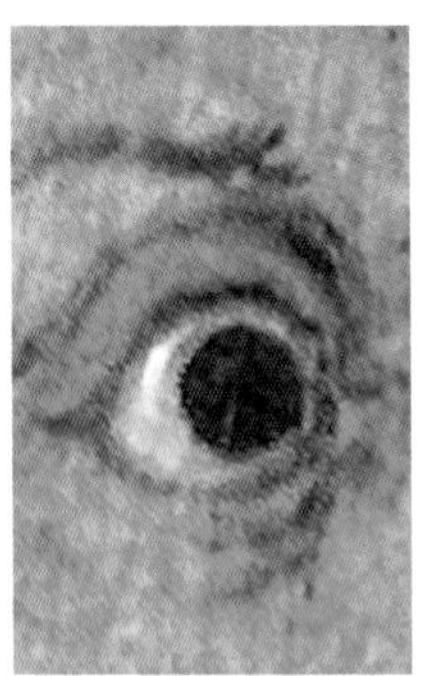

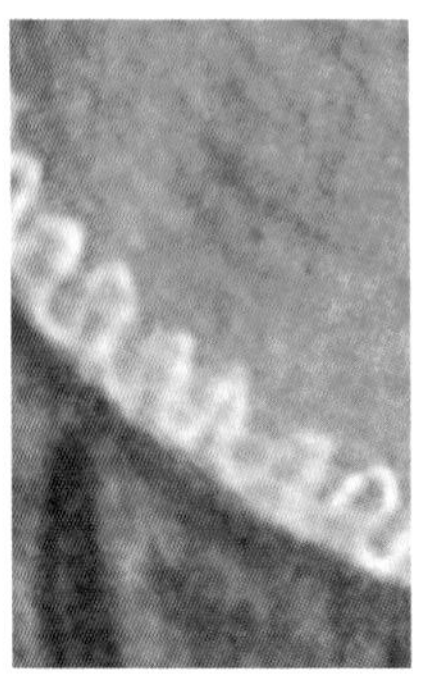

in the details of a work, and this is one of his greatest and most restrained scenes.

In *The Magpie on the Gallows*, Bruegel envelops a distant tree-studded plain crossed by rivers with the luminous mist and fluid atmosphere of a springtime sky. The foreground is a jumble of greenery that has a soft and infinitely delicate quality. A magpie is perched upon a gallows rising from the centre. Just behind it,

Head of a Lansquenet

Pieter Brueghel the Younger, after 1616
Oil on wood, diameter: 32.3 cm
Musée Fabre, Montpellier

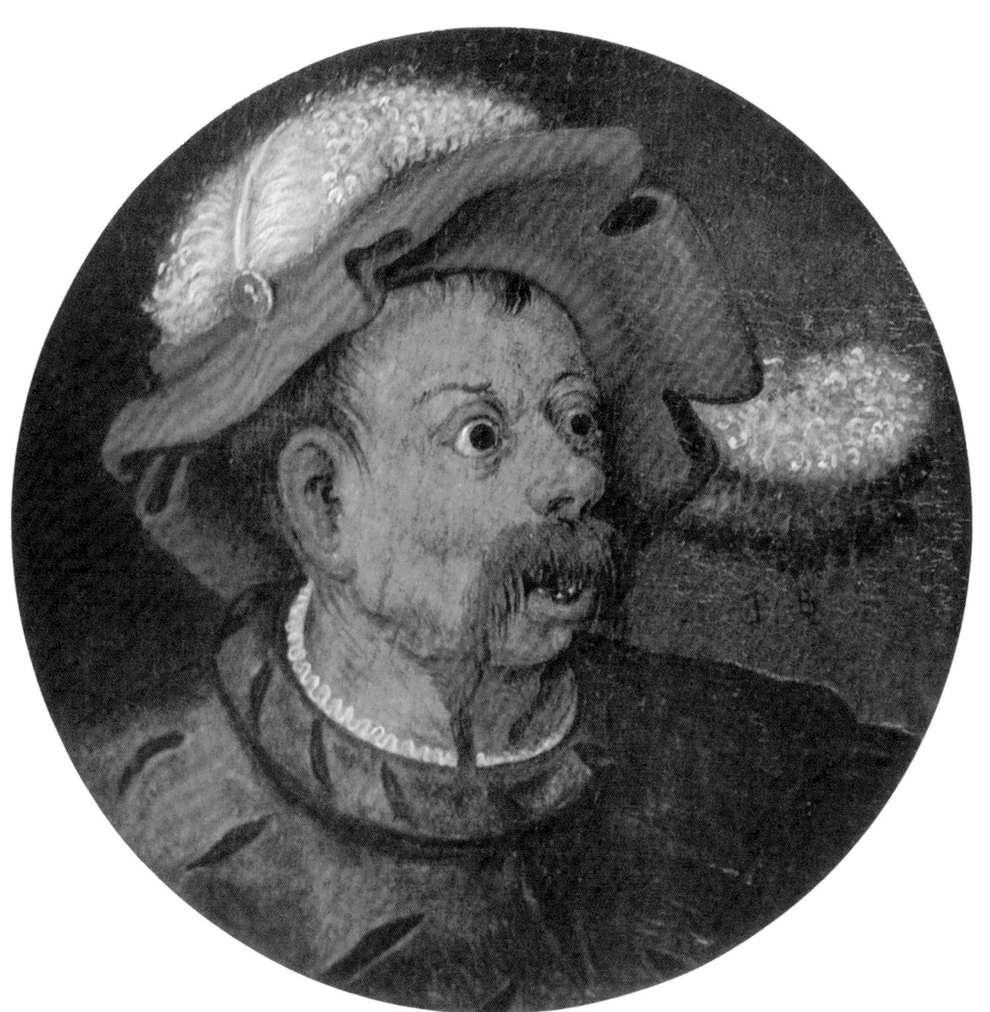

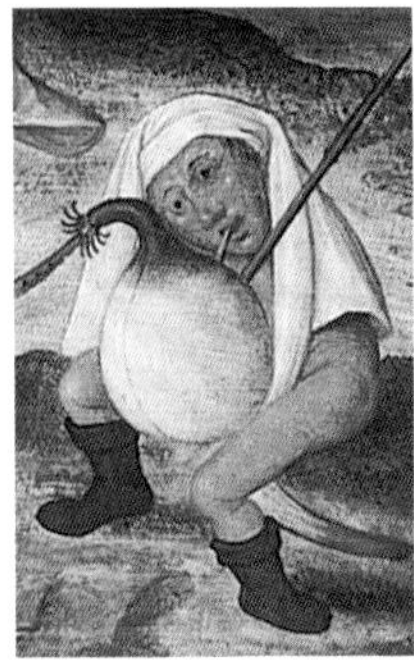

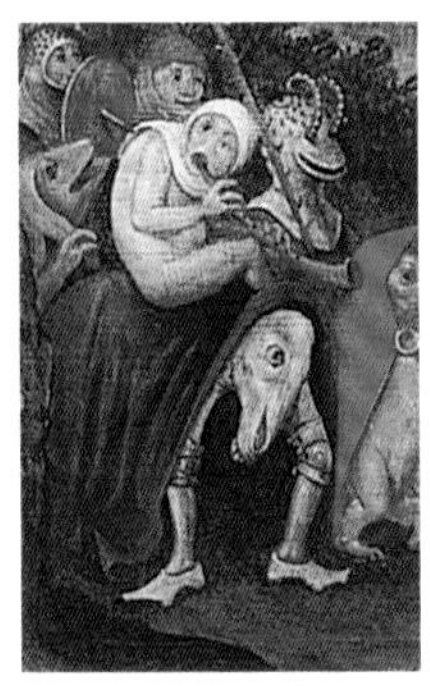

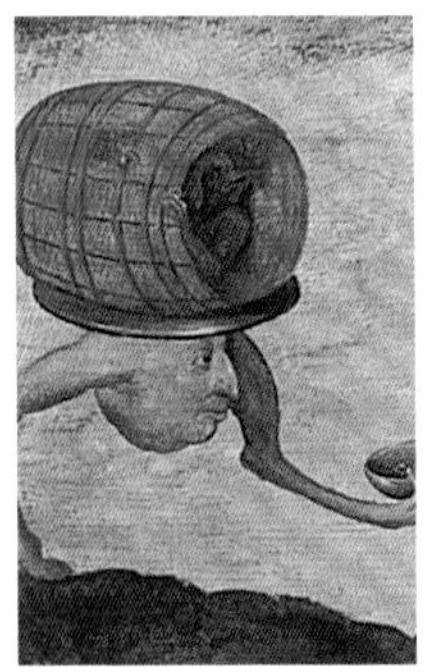

a cross is planted on a mound. Even more than the round trio of interlaced peasants dancing on the grass, the sky bathing the foliage in tender light, and the scene's warm and voluptuous palpitation in general, the triumph of joy and radiant life are proclaimed over everything else. This striking contrast of elements is an optimistic affirmation by Bruegel of the extraordinary life force and tenacious hope that dwelt in the hearts of his people.

The Temptation of Saint Anthony

Pieter Brueghel the Younger or
Jan Brueghel the Younger, after 1616
Oil on wood, 73.5 x 106.5 cm
Copée Collection, Tenneville

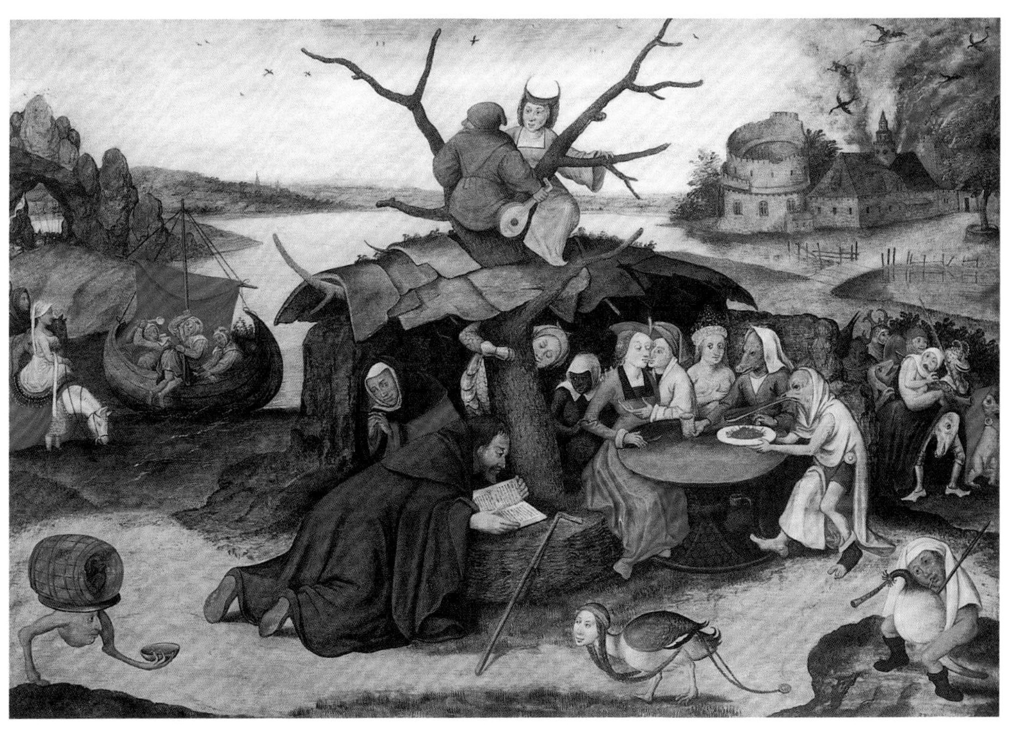

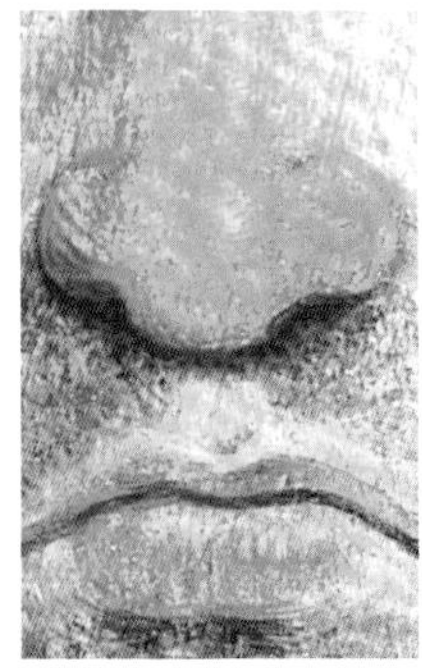

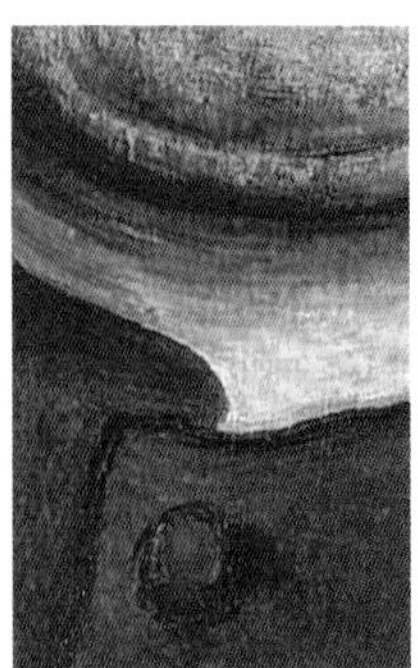

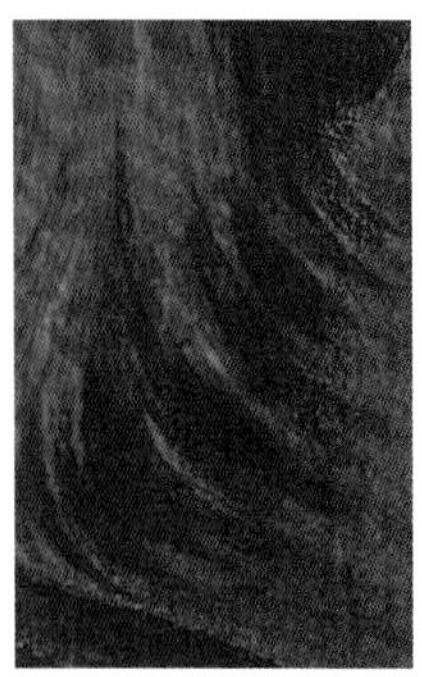

It was in the painting of morals and in immediate observation that Bruegel would find the inspiration for the majority of his works that mark his short but brilliant mature period. The opening of this text described *The Massacre of the Innocents* with its intensely dramatic yet familiar atmosphere.

This painting is clearly a companion piece for *The Numbering at Bethlehem* from 1564. A snow-covered

Peasant's Head

Pieter Brueghel the Younger, after 1616
Oil on wood, 25 x 17.8 cm
Private collection

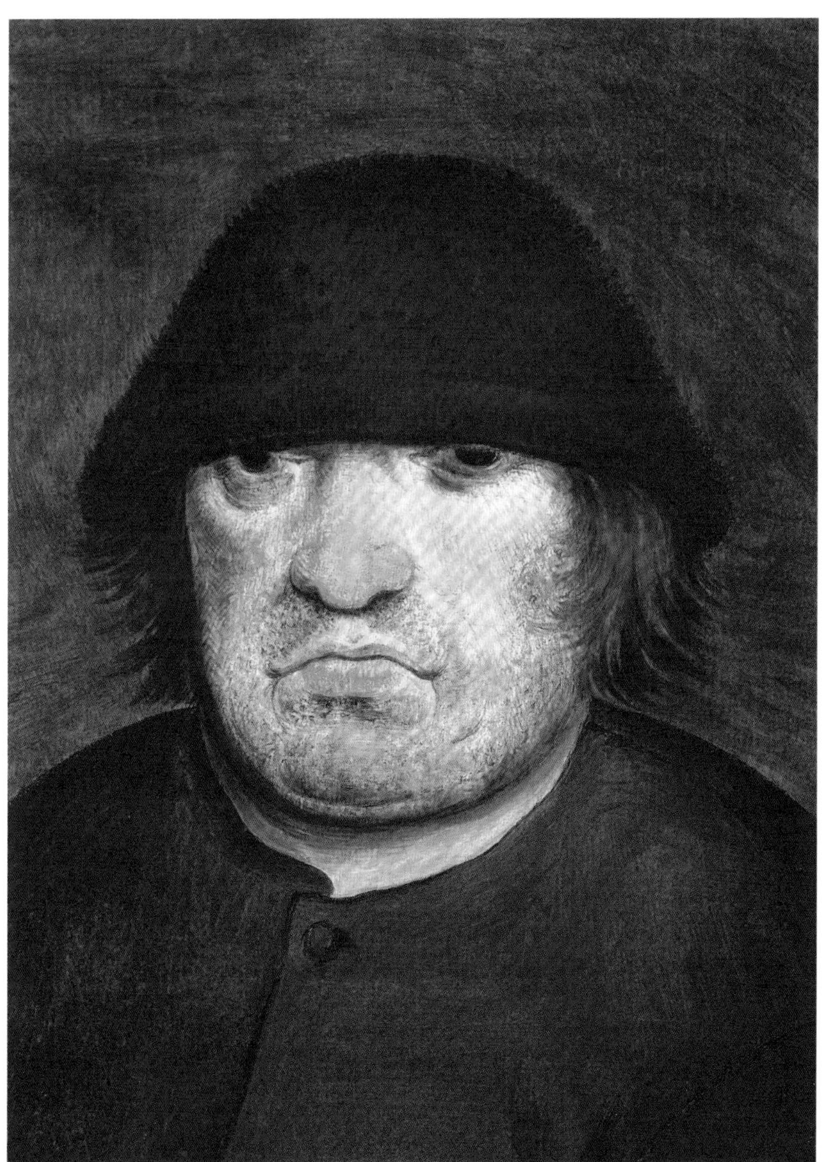

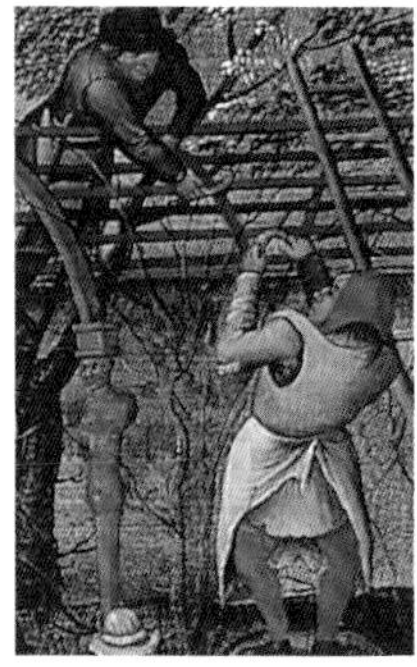

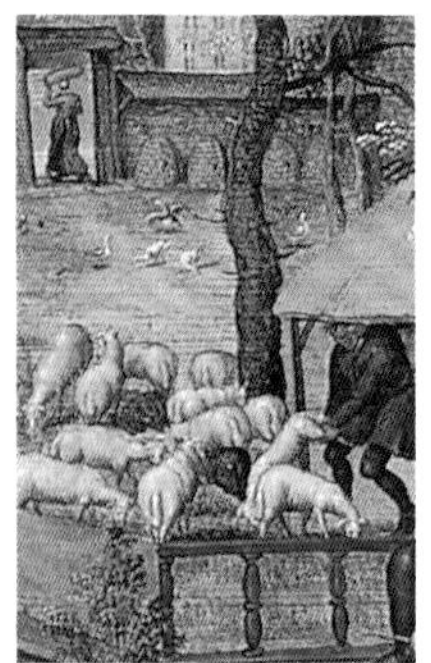

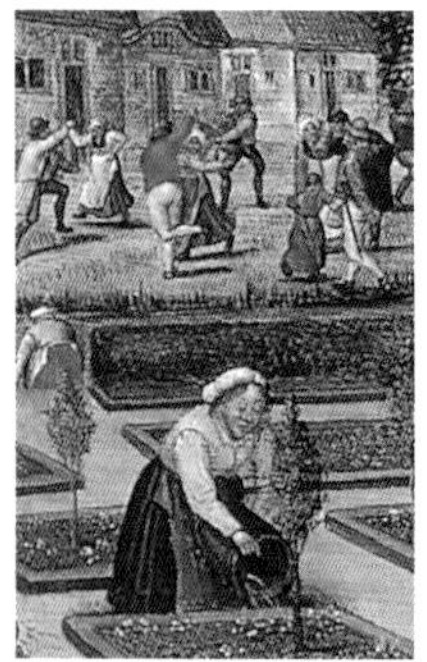

village bustles with good folk occupied with their work and pleasure. The event of a census adds a picturesque element without compromising the image's verism. The king's people probably reacted in just this manner when a particular village was presented with a tax. In the centre of the work, one sees Mary astride a donkey with Joseph and a cow walking at her side, heading towards the house where the scribes have set up their work.

Preparation of the Flowerbeds (Springtime allegory)

Pieter Brueghel the Younger, after 1616
Oil on wood, 43 x 59 cm
Muzeul National de Arta al României, Bucharest

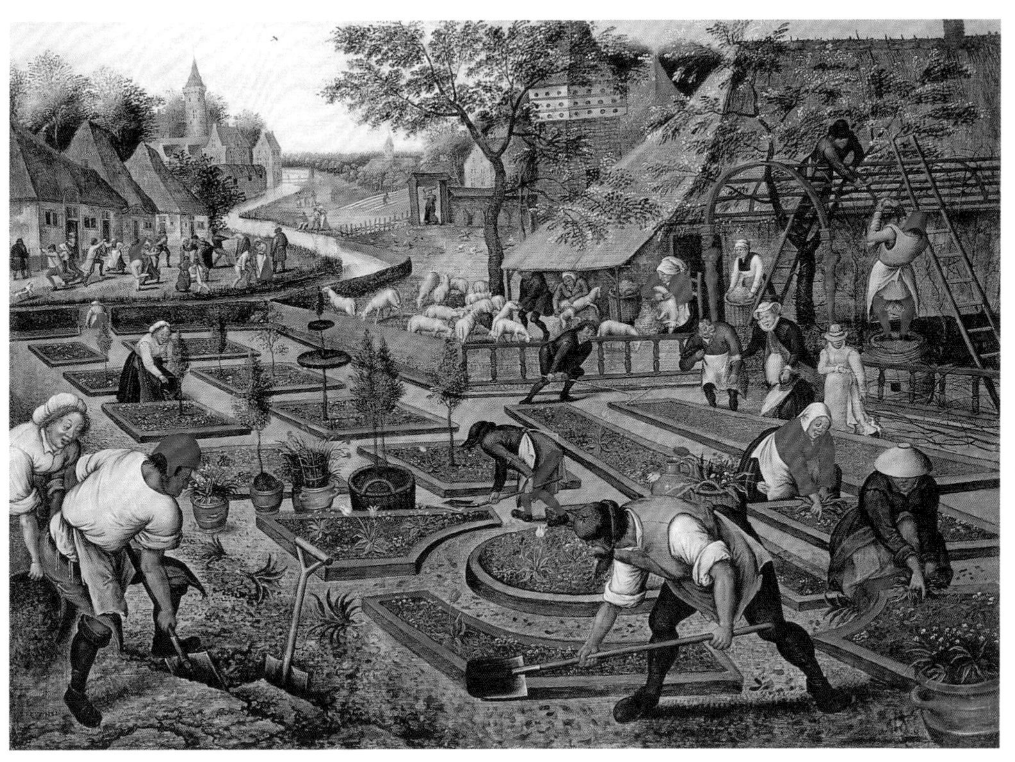

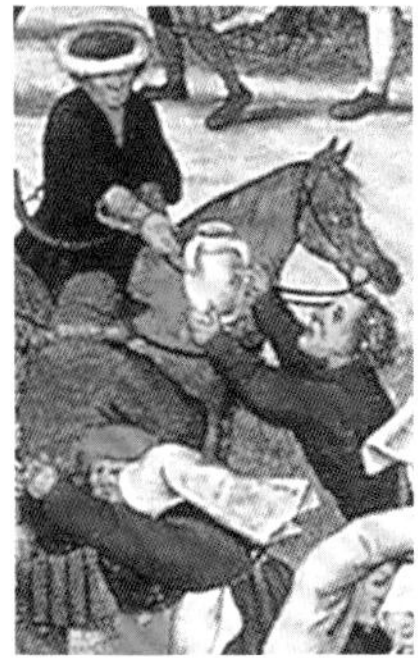

A group of village people have gathered before the scribes, which does not prevent numerous skaters from their revelry upon the pond in the distance or on the corner of the pool at the right. Here, the same accuracy and variety of attitudes as in *Skaters before the Gate of Saint George* can be seen. In the distance, there is a party of hunters with their dog. A peasant woman sweeps away the snow. In the foreground, a peasant bleeds a pig

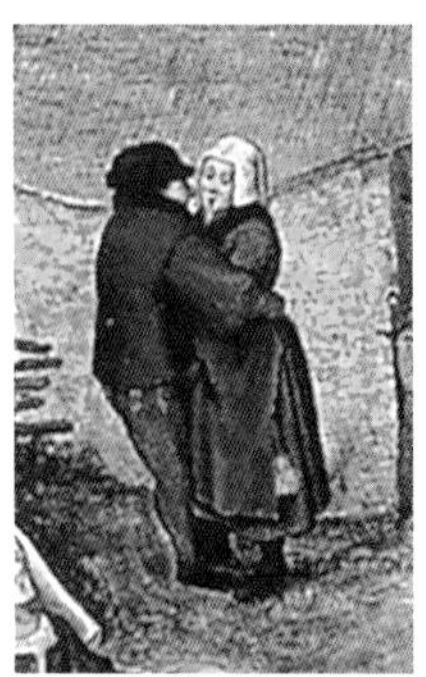

St George's Kermesse

Pieter Brueghel the Younger, after 1616
Alte Galerie des
Steiermärkischen Landesmuseum Joanneum, Graz

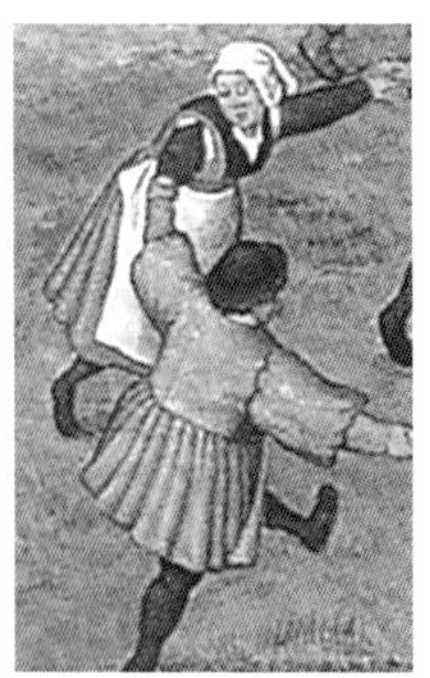

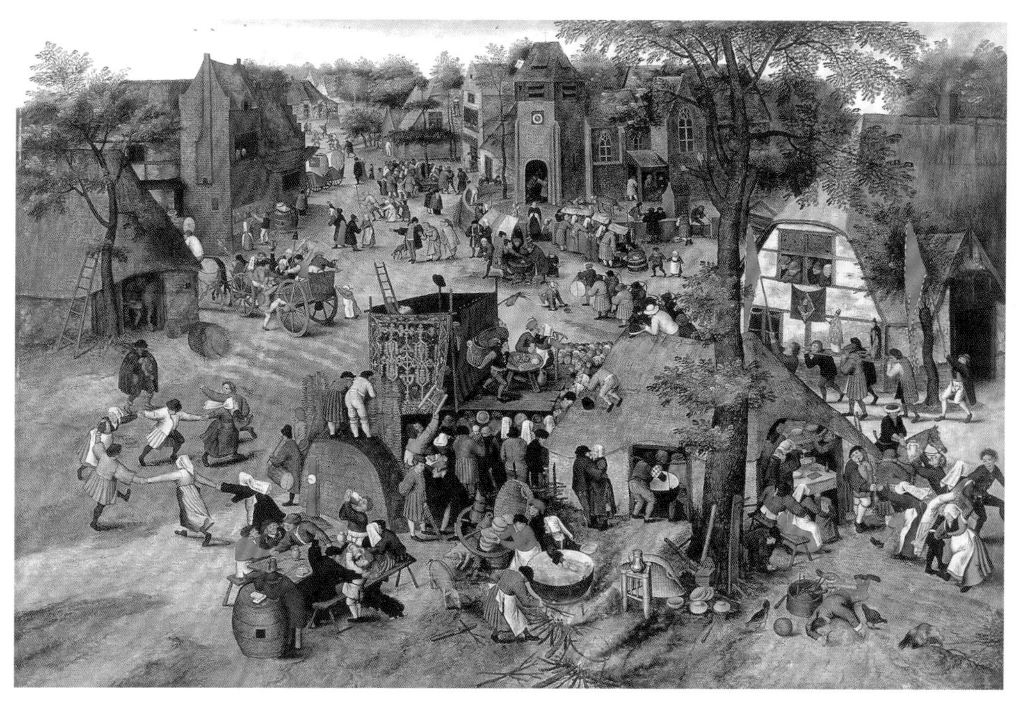

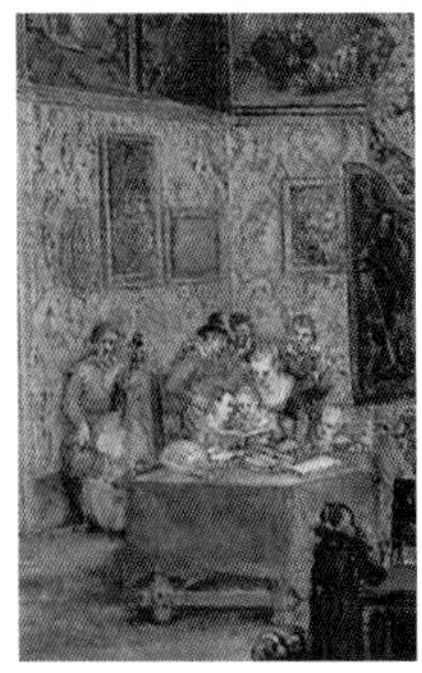

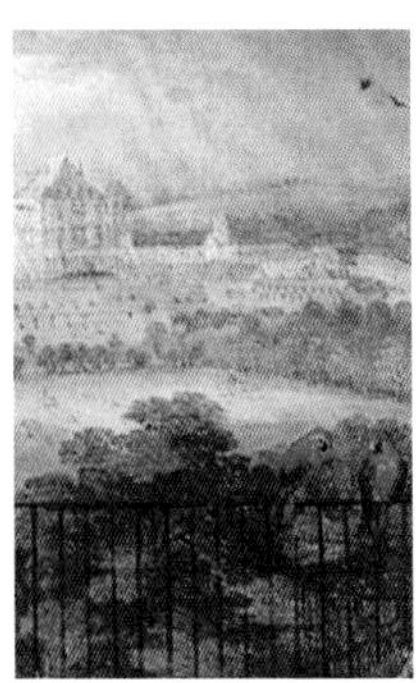

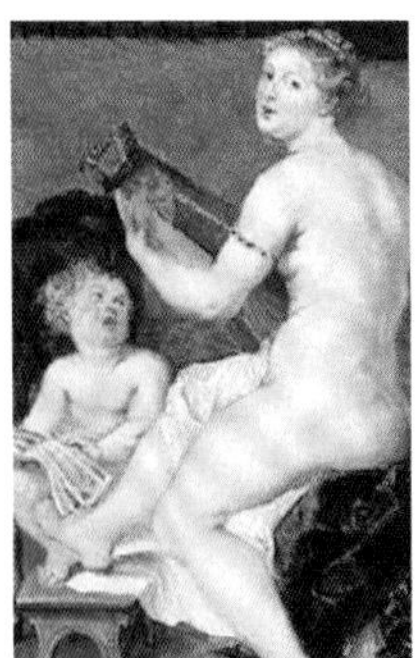

and a housewife catches its blood in a pot as children look on. The village is shrouded under snow and is of a gripping realness, though Bruegel does not overload the scene with details. He clearly reproduced a scene as it was, without any picturesque preconceptions. The group of houses above the pond in the distance are exquisite. The setting sun envelops their delicately nuanced rosy brick walls and their white hoods of snow

The Sense of Hearing

Jan Brueghel the Elder, 1617
Oil on panel, 64 x 109.5 cm
Museo del Prado, Madrid

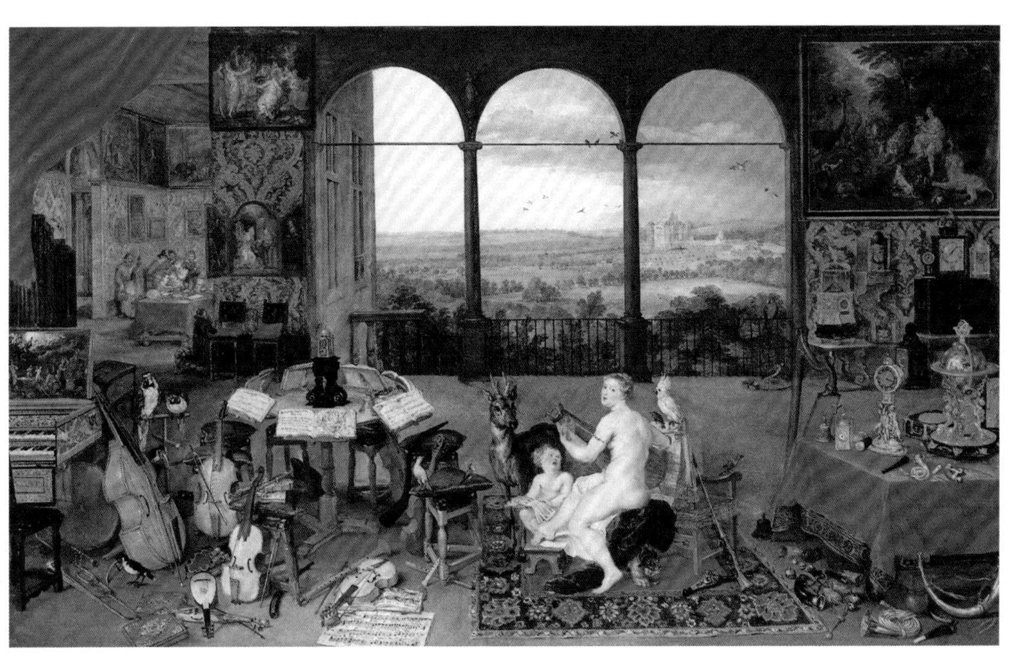

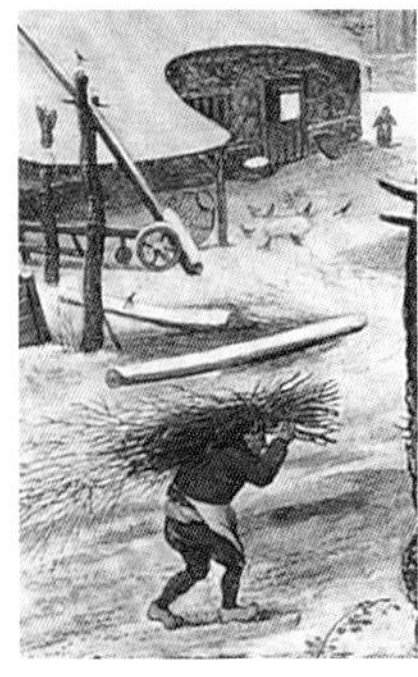

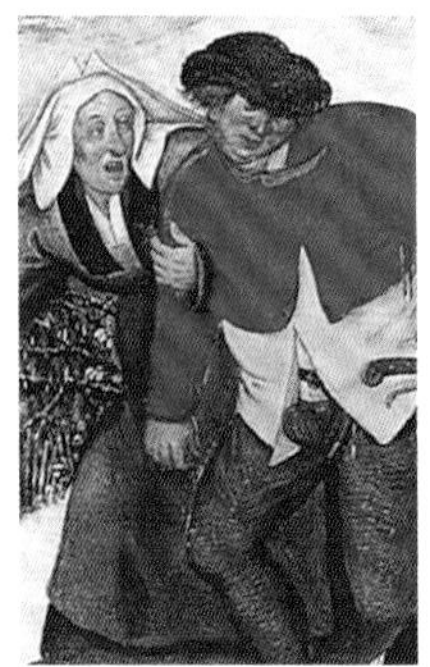

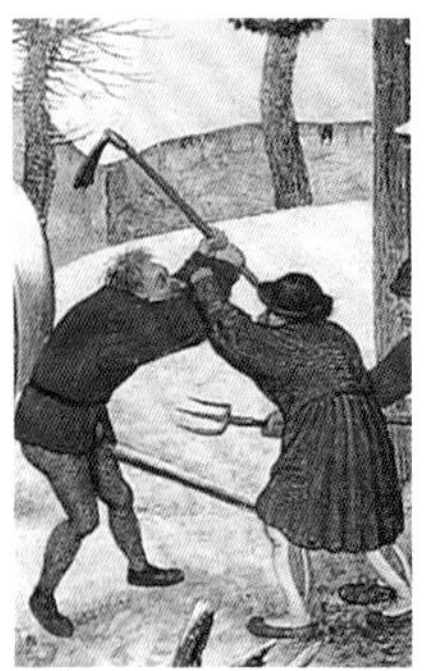

with golden reflections. The dark grey sky reinforces the whiteness of the snow marked by the singular relief of the villagers' tunics and camisoles, painted in blocks of neutral colours, but also browns, reds, and pale blues.

Bruegel did not limit himself to capturing the appearance and gestures of his models. He also strove to render their facial expressions, and his portraits, which are most frequently of peasants, constitute

The Drunk Led Home by his Wife

Pieter Brueghel the Younger, c. 1620
Oil on wood, 41.3 x 64.8 cm
Museum of Fine Arts, Montreal

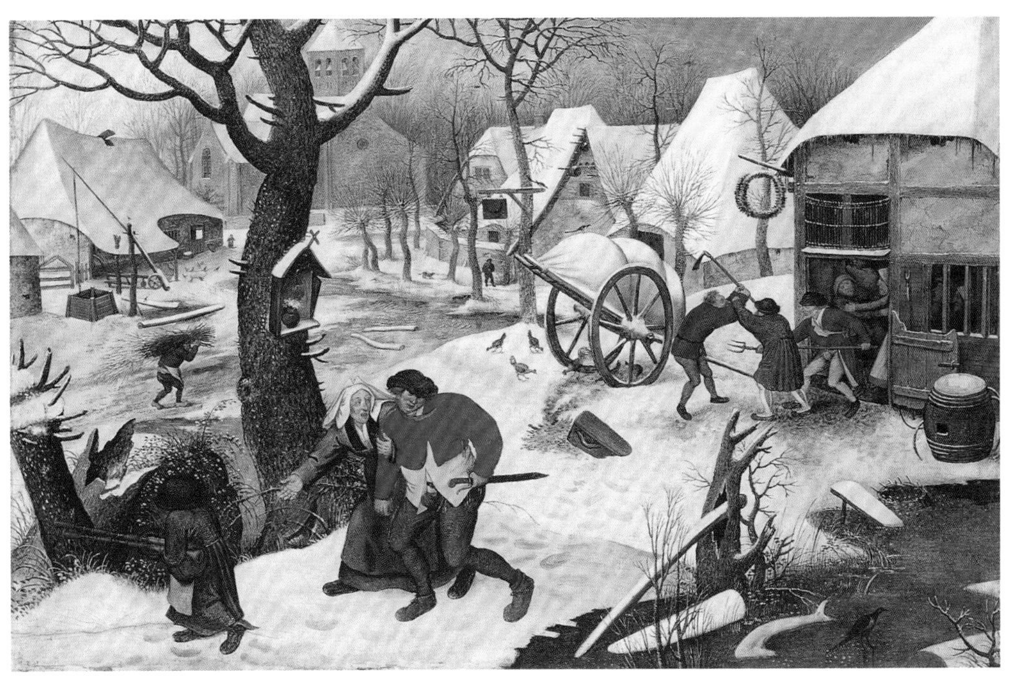

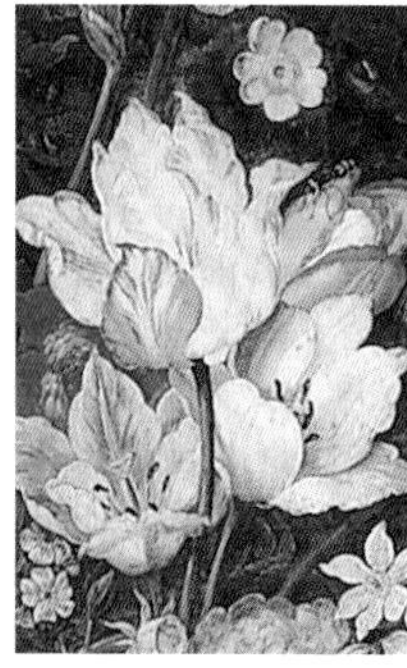

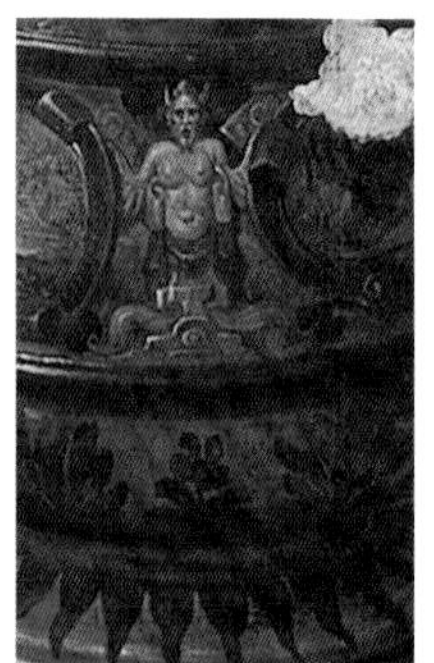

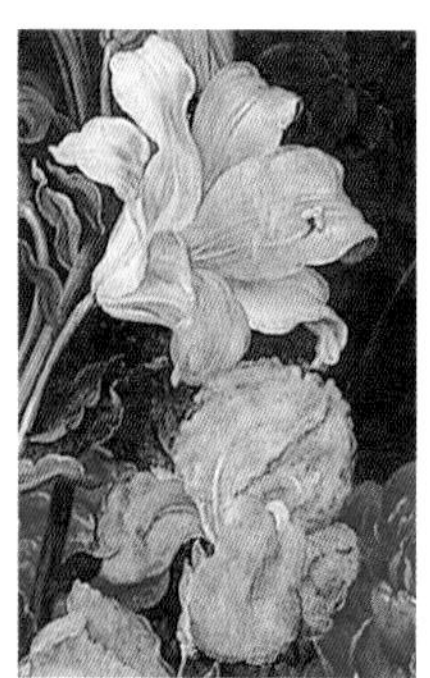

excellent portraits. Each line on their faces hides something, invites us to discover an aspect of the subject's soul, and expresses their personality: shrewdness, stupidity, brutality, and sometimes passing emotions such as joy, fear, and horror.

The profile of his *Portrait of an Old Woman* holds a frightful expression. Her steady gaze and gaping, lipless mouth pulled downwards by a fold revealing

Flowers in a Ceramic Vase

Jan Brueghel the Elder, c. 1620
Oil on wood, 101 x 76 cm
Koninklijk Museum voor Schone Kunsten, Antwerp

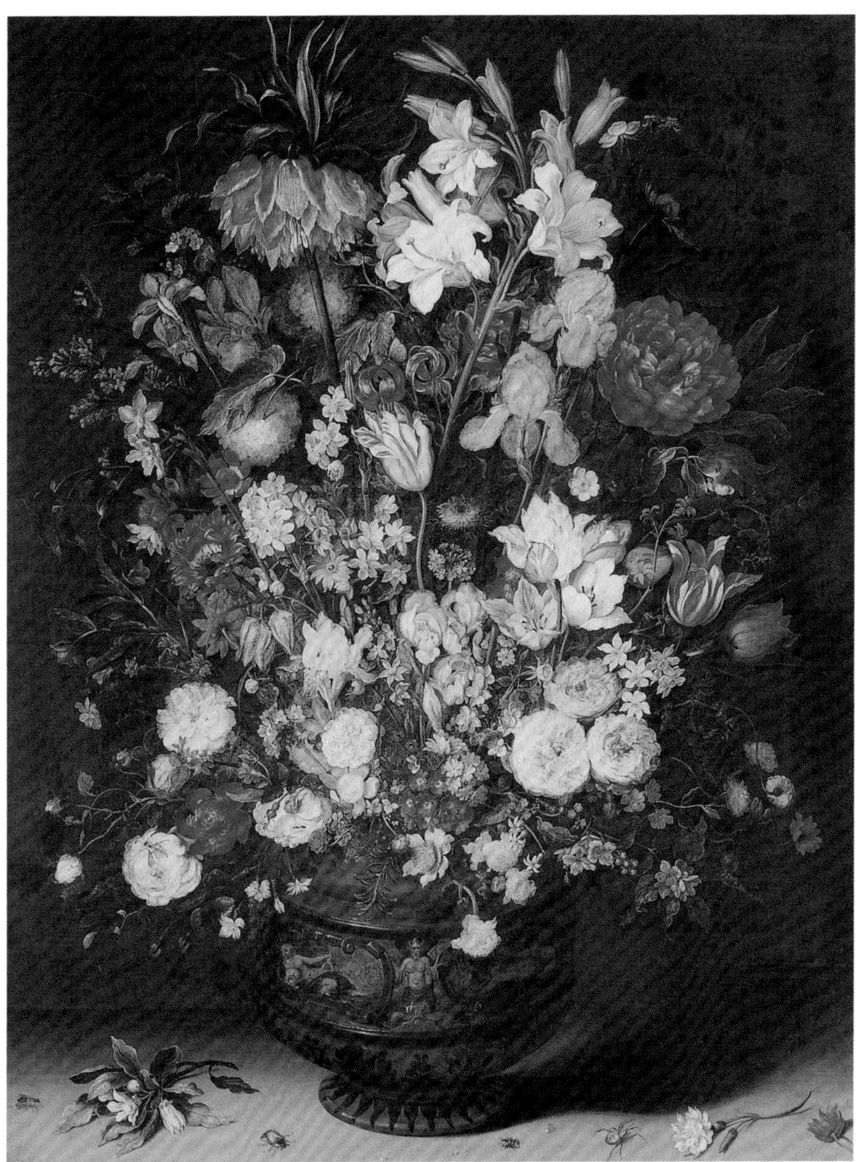

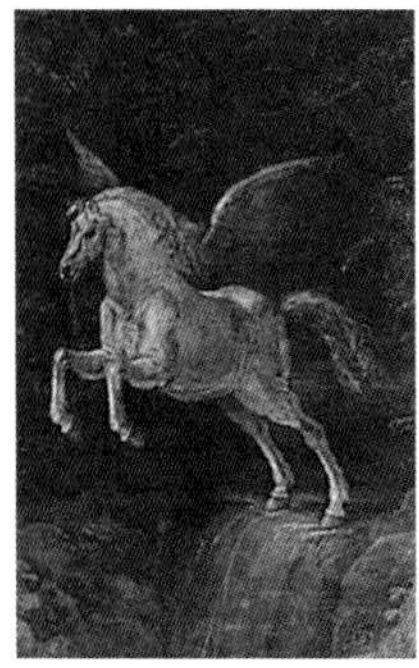

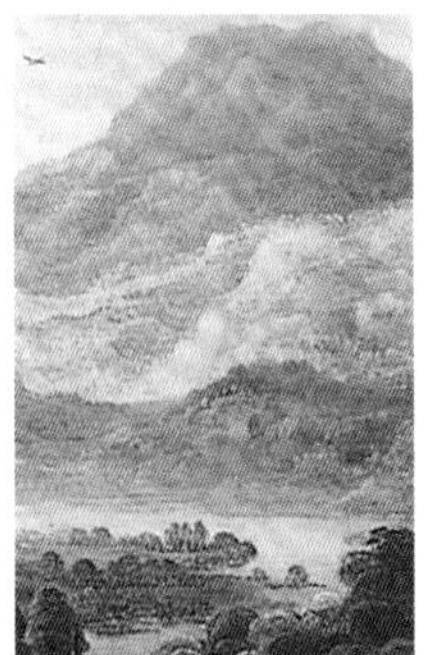

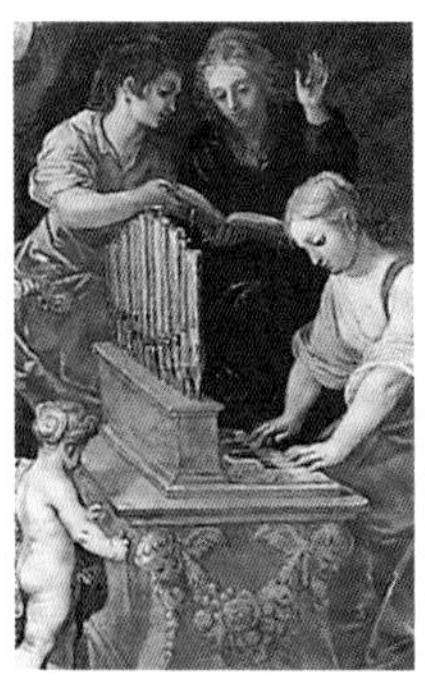

two of her bottom teeth, simultaneously express terror and anger. It is possible that Bruegel used this portrait as a model for his character *Dulle Griet.*

Bruegel seems to have had a predilection for singularly fixed profiles with forward thrusting jaws. Another example can be found in his ferocious *Study for the Battle between the Fat and the Thin.* This is the reason that the *Head of a Lansquenet* in the Musée

Athena Visiting the Muses

Jan Brueghel the Elder or
Jan II Brueghel the Younger,
Joos de Momper the Younger, and
Hendrick Van Balen, c. 1620
Oil on wood, 140 x 199 cm
Koninklijk Museum voor Schone Kunsten, Antwerp

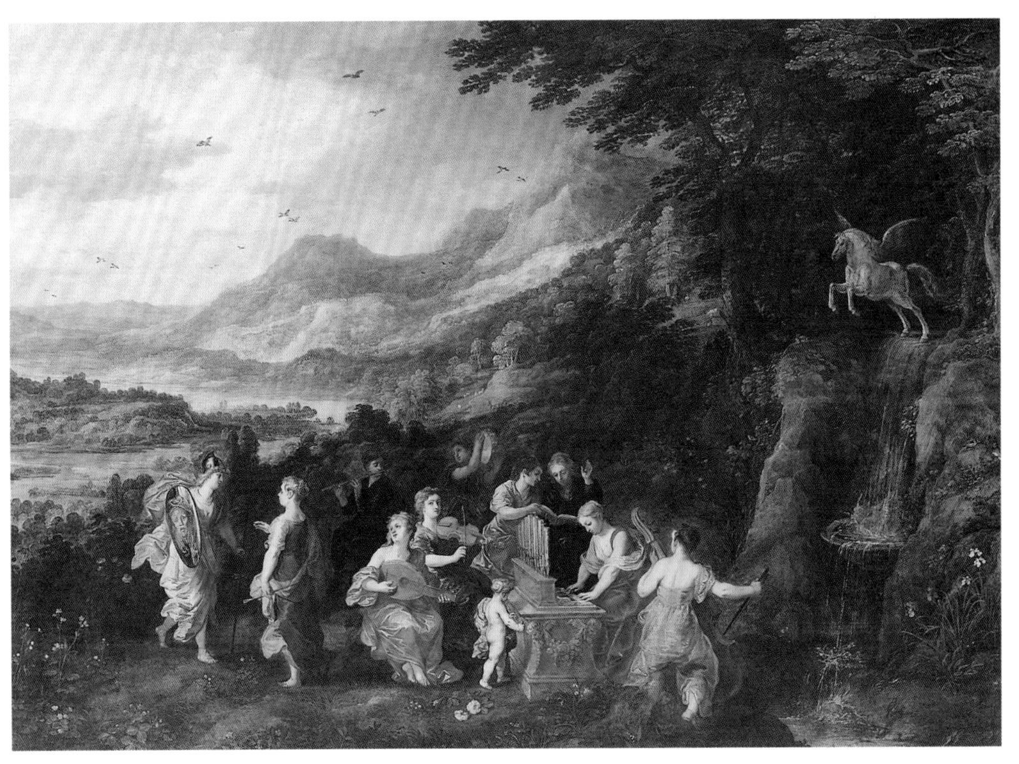

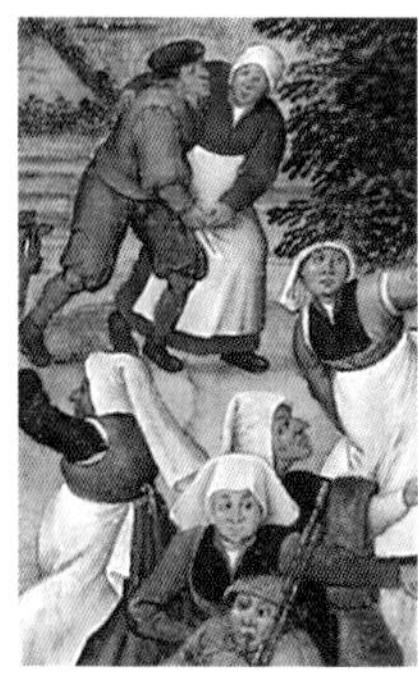

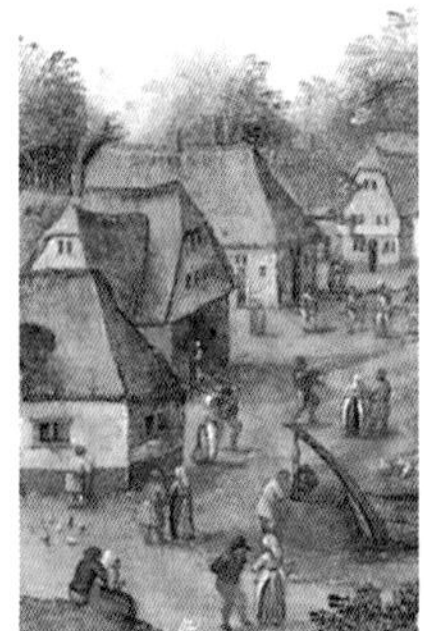

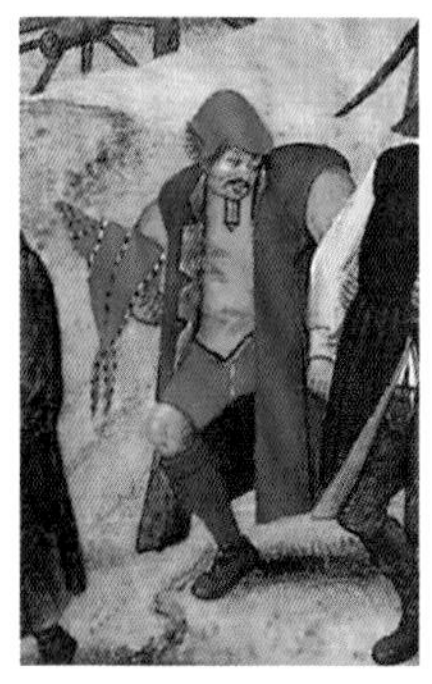

Fabre in Montpellier, with its bestial longing and abject fury, has also been attributed to Bruegel.

In his engravings *The Fair at Saint George* and *The Fair at Hoboken*, he portrays a crowd in a rush of pleasure on the picturesque public squares that were his favourite settings. In his *Wedding Feast* he contents himself with a banquet in a farmhouse. The guests are seated around a long table that occupies the entire

Return of the Fair

Pieter Brueghel the Younger, 1620-1630
Oil on wood, 33 x 57 cm
Private collection

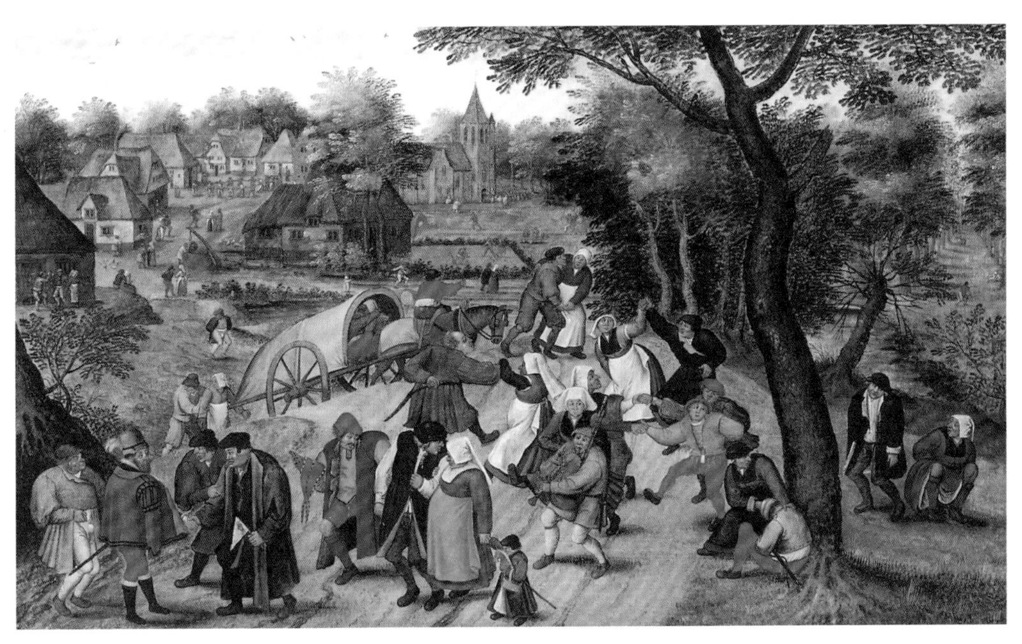

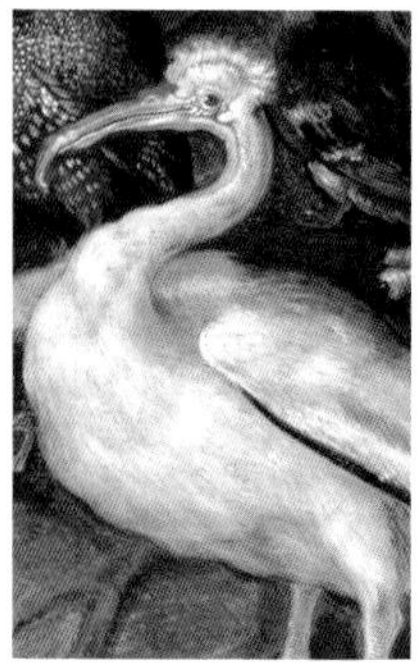

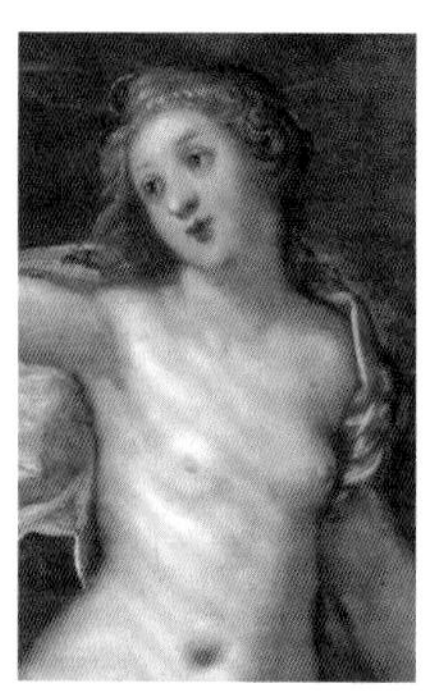

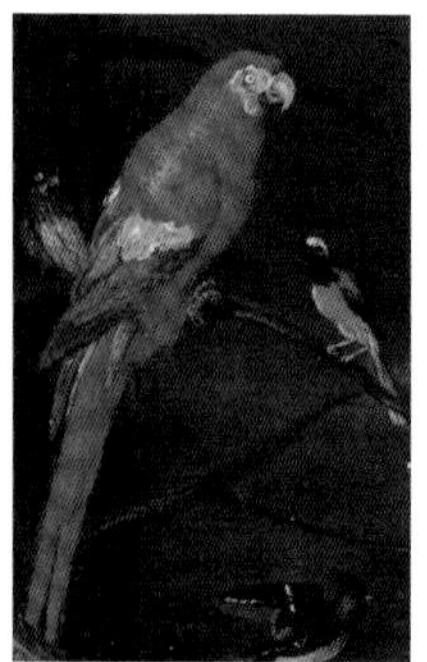

length of the room. In the foreground, two men circulate trays on boards laid across a stretcher. Crocks and jugs decorate the left-hand corner, and a child seated on the ground licks his fingers. Two bagpipers enliven the party and a second table can be seen through an open door in the depths of the scene. A feeling of welcome permeates the scene. The fat girl radiating good health from beneath her dark veil, who welcomes the guest

The Allegory of Air

Jan Brueghel the Elder and
Hendrick Van Balen, 17th century
Oil on copper, 54.5 x 95 cm
Galleria Doria Pamphilj, Rome

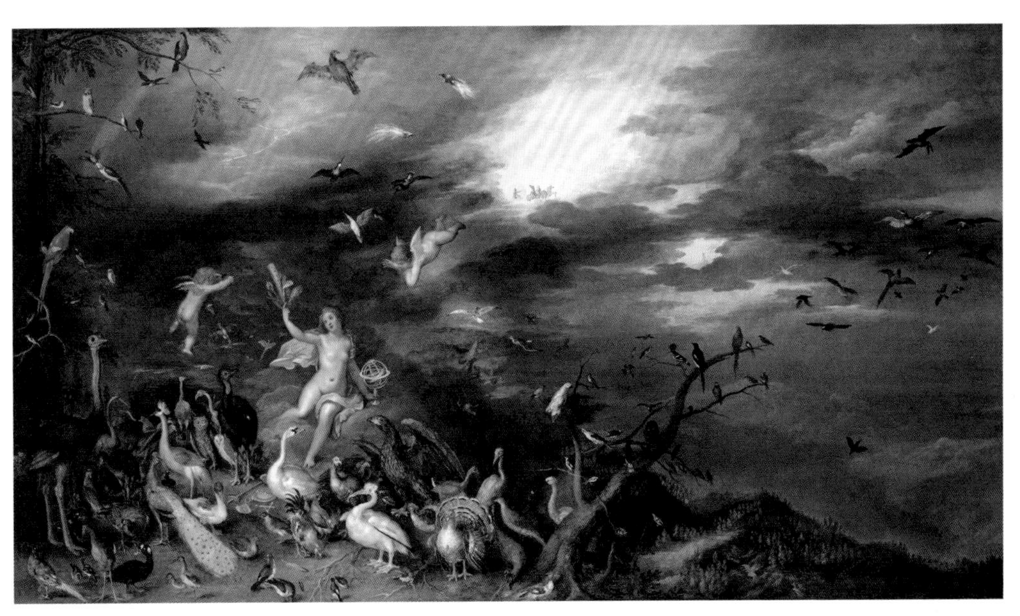

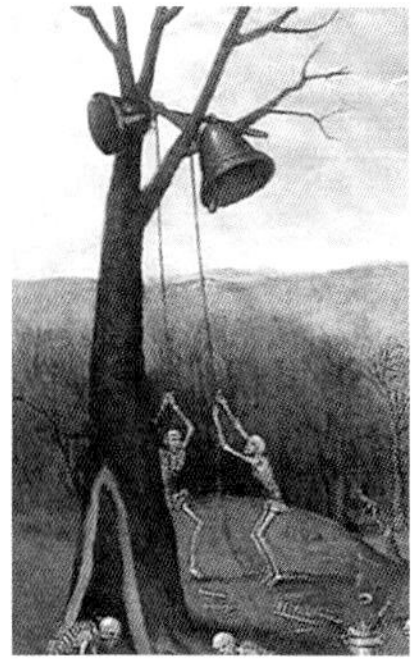

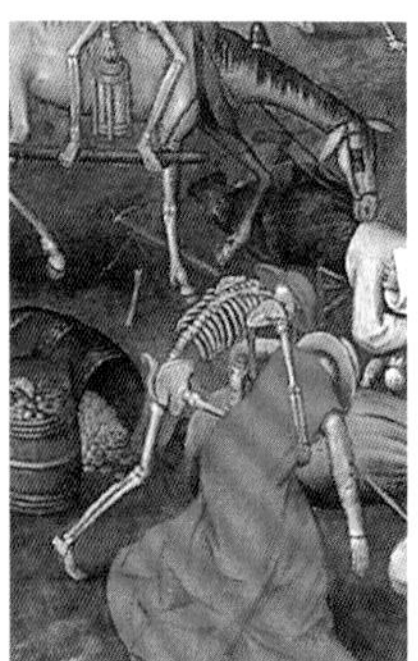

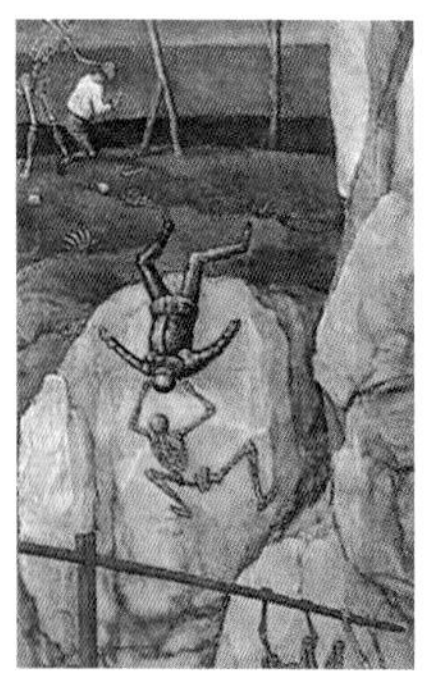

with folded hands and lowered eyes, is clearly not the bride. The pleasure of eating, of methodically gorging oneself and satisfying one's gluttony, is palpable and only aggravated by the periods of deprivation and misery in such troubled times.

In 1569, Bruegel died suddenly at the height of his artistic maturity. He was buried in Notre-Dame de la Chapelle in Brussels. His epitaph reads:

The Triumph of Death

Pieter Brueghel the Younger, 1626
Oil on canvas, 117 x 167 cm
The Mildred Andrews Fund, Cleveland

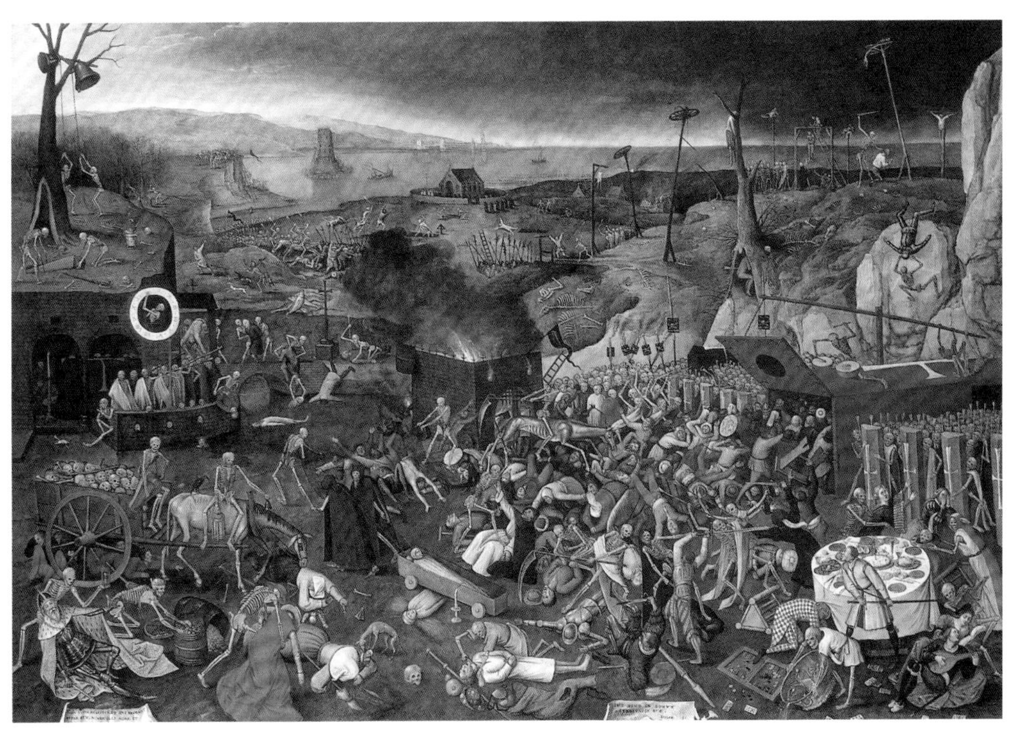

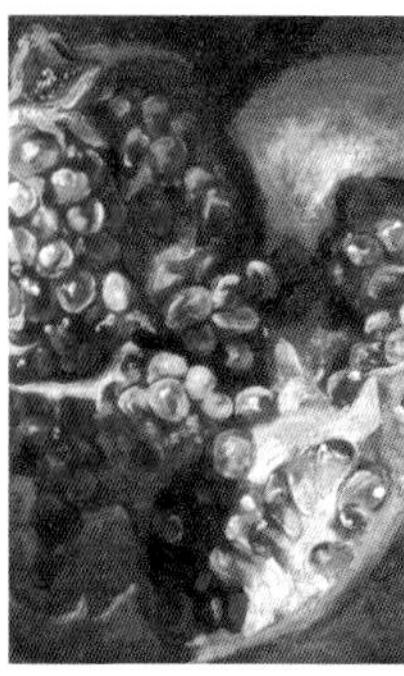

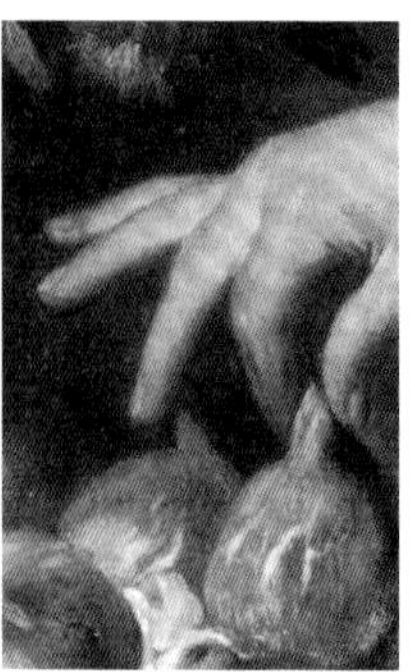

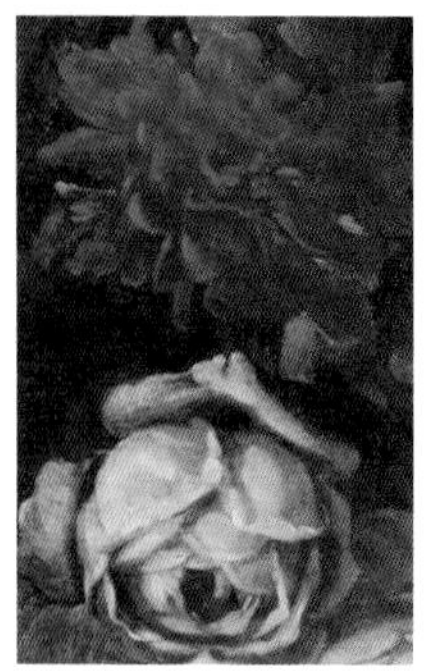

PETRO BREUGELIO

EXACTISSIMAE INDUSTRIAE

ARTIS VENUSTISSIMAE

PICTORI

QUEM IPSA RERUM PARENS NATURA LAUDET

PERITISSIMI ARTIFICES SUSPICIUNT

ÆMULI FRUSTRA IMITANTUR.

Woman Grasping Fruit

Abraham Brueghel, 1669
Oil on canvas, 128 x 149 cm
Musée du Louvre, Paris

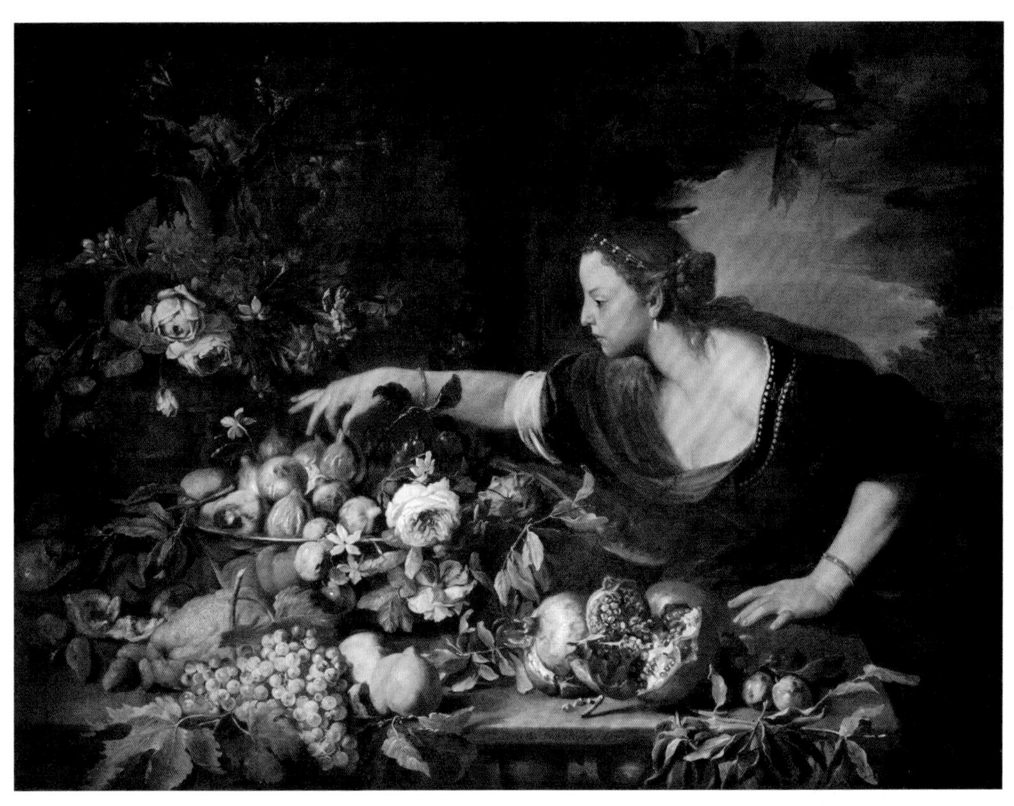

Index

A

The Adoration of the Magi, 1564 93, 95, 97

The Adoration of the Magi, 1595 (?), **Pieter Brueghel the Younger** 175

The Adoration of the Magi, c. 1598-1600, **Jan Brueghel the Elder** 185

The Adoration of the Magi in the Snow, 1567 131

The Alchemist, 1558 19

The Allegory of Air, 17th century,
Jan Brueghel the Elder and Hendrick Van Balen 243

The Allegory of Water, 1610, **Jan Brueghel the Elder** 215

The Ambush, c. 1607, **Jan Brueghel the Elder and Sebastian Vrancx** 207

The Ass in the School, 1556 13

Athena Visiting the Muses, c. 1620,
Jan Brueghel the Elder or Jan II Brueghel the Younger,
Joos de Momper the Younger, and Hendrick Van Balen 239

B

Battle between the Israelites and the Philistines, 1562 73

The Battle of Issus, 1602, **Jan Brueghel the Elder** 197

The Battle of the Amazons, c. 1597-1599,
Jan Brueghel the Elder and Peter Paul Rubens 181
The Beekeepers, 1568 145
The Beggars, 1568 147
Big Fishes Eat Little Fishes, 1556 11
Bouquet, 1603, **Jan Brueghel the Elder** 199

C

The Calumny of Apelles, 1565 111
The Census at Bethlehem, 1566 121, 123
Ceres and the Four Elements, 1604,
Jan Brueghel the Elder and Hendrick Van Balen 203
Charity, from the series *Seven Virtues*, 1559 27
Children's Games, 1560 43, 45, 47
Christ and the Woman Taken in Adultery, 1565 103
Christ and the Woman Taken in Adultery,
c. 1600, **Pieter Brueghel the Younger** 189
Christ Carrying the Cross, 1564 89, 91
Christ Carrying the Cross, 1603, **Pieter Brueghel the Younger** 201
Christ Carrying the Cross, c. 1606, **Jan Brueghel the Elder** 205
Christ's Descent into Limbo, 1561 53
The Conversion of Saint Paul, 1567 133

D

The Dormition of the Virgin, c. 1564 87

The Drunk Led Home by his Wife, c. 1620, **Pieter Brueghel the Younger** 235

Dulle Griet or *Mad Meg*, 1562 67, 69, 71

E

Elck or *Everyman*, 1558 17

F

The Fair at Hoboken, 1559 35

The Fall of Icarus, c. 1555-1560 9

The Fall of the Rebel Angels, 1562 75

The Fight between Carnival and Lent, 1559 37, 39, 41

Fishmarket on the Edge of a River, 1611, **Jan Brueghel the Elder** 217

The Flight into Egypt, 1563 79

The Flood with Noah's Ark, 1601, **Jan Brueghel the Elder** 193

Flowers in a Ceramic Vase, c. 1620, **Jan Brueghel the Elder** 237

G

The Garden of Paradise with the Embarkment of the Animals into Noah's Ark, 1596, **Jan Brueghel the Elder** 179

The Good Shepherd, **Pieter Brueghel the Younger** 157

H

The Harvesters (August), 1565 113

Haymaking (July), 1565 105

Head of a Lansquenet, after 1616, **Pieter Brueghel the Younger** 223

The Hunters in the Snow (January), 1565 107

I

Interior of the Antwerp Cathedral, c. 1609,
Jan Brueghel the Elder and Hendrick Van Steenwijck the Younger 211

J

Juno in the Underworld, c. 1598, **Jan Brueghel the Elder** 187

L

The Land of Cockaigne, 1566 129

Landscape with Diana and Actaeon, c. 1591, **Jan Brueghel the Elder** 171

The Last Judgement, 1558 21

M

Magdalena Poenitens, c. 1553-1556,
Joannes and Lucas van Doetecum (after Pieter Bruegel the Elder) 4

The Magpie on the Gallows, 1568 149

The Marriage of Bacchus and Ariadne, after 1608,
Jan Brueghel the Elder and Hendrick Van Balen 209
The Massacre of the Innocents,
late 16th century, **Pieter Bruegel the Elder** (copy after) 163, 165, 167
The Massacre of the Innocents,
late 16th century, **Pieter Brueghel the Younger** 169
The Misanthrope, 1568 151

N

Naval Battle in the Gulf of Naples, c. 1562 65
Netherlandish Proverbs, 1559 29, 31, 33

P

The Painter and the Collector, c. 1565 99
The Parable of the Blind Leading the Blind, 1568 155
The Parable of the Blind Leading the Blind,
c. 1616, **Pieter Brueghel the Younger** 221
The Peasant and the Birdnester, 1568 153
The Peasant Dance, c. 1568 135
Peasant Wedding, c. 1568 137, 139, 141
Peasant's Head, after 1616, **Pieter Brueghel the Younger** 227
Portrait of an Old Woman, c. 1564 85

Preparation of the Flowerbeds (Springtime allegory),
after 1616, **Pieter Brueghel the Younger** 229
Pride from the series *Seven Deadly Sins*, 1557 15

R

The Rabbit Hunt, 1560 49
The Resurrection, c. 1562 55
Return of the Fair, 1620-1630, **Pieter Brueghel the Younger** 241
The Return of the Herd (November), 1565 115, 117
River Landscape with Resting Hikers, 1594, **Jan Brueghel the Elder** 173

S

Sailing Vessels, 1560-1565 51
The Sense of Hearing, 1617, **Jan Brueghel the Elder** 233
The Sermon of Saint John the Baptist, 1566 125, 127
The Sermon of Saint John the Baptist, 1601, **Pieter Brueghel the Younger** 191
Skaters Before the Gate of Saint George, 1558-1559 25
Solicitudo Rustica, c. 1575-1600 159
Springtime, 1565 109
St George's Kermesse, after 1616, **Pieter Brueghel the Younger** 231
Storm at Sea with Shipwrecks, c. 1595-1596, **Jan Brueghel the Elder** 177
Summer, 1568 143

T

The Tempest, c. 1610-1615,
Pieter Bruegel the Elder and Joos de Momper the Younger 213

The Temptation of Saint Anthony, after 1616,
Pieter Brueghel the Younger or Jan Brueghel the Younger 225

The Tower of Babel, 1563 81, 83

The Tower of Babel, c. 1565 101

The Tower of Babel, 1602-1610,
Jan Brueghel the Elder and Tobias Verhaecht 195

The Triumph of Death, c. 1562 57, 59, 61, 63

The Triumph of Death, 1626, **Pieter Brueghel the Younger** 245

Twelve Flemish Proverbs, 1558 23

Two Chained Monkeys, 1562 77

U, V

The Unfaithful Shepherd, c. 1575-1600 161

Virgin and Child Surrounded by Flowers and Fruit, **Jan Brueghel the Elder** 219

W

The Wedding Dance, c. 1566 119

The Wedding Dance, c. 1597, **Jan Brueghel the Elder** 183

Woman Grasping Fruit, 1669, **Abraham Brueghel** 247